Information and Legislative Organization

Michigan Studies in Political Analysis

Michigan Studies in Political Analysis promotes the development and dissemination of innovative scholarship in the field of methodology in political science and the social sciences in general. Methodology is defined to include statistical methods, mathematical modeling, measurement, research design, and other topics related to the conduct and development of analytical work. The series includes works that develop a new model or method applicable to social sciences, as well as those that, through innovative combination and presentation of current analytical tools, substantially extend the use of these tools by other researchers.

GENERAL EDITORS: John E. Jackson and Christopher H. Achen

Information and Legislative Organization

Keith Krehbiel, 1955-

THE UNIVERSITY OF MICHIGAN PRESS

Ann Arbor

First paperback edition 1992
Copyright © by the University of Michigan 1991
All rights reserved
Published in the United States of America by
The University of Michigan Press
Manufactured in the United States of America

2001   2000   1999   7   6   5

Library of Congress Cataloging-in-Publication Data

Krehbiel, Keith, 1955–
        Information and legislative organization / Keith Krehbiel.
            p.   cm. — (Michigan studies in political analysis)
        Includes bibliographical references and index.
        ISBN 0-472-09460-2 (cloth : alk.) — ISBN 0-472-06460-6 (paper : alk.)
        1. United States. Congress. 2. Policy sciences. 3. Uncertainty.
        I. Title. II. Series.
        JK1061.K74 1991
        328.73′076—dc20   90-49668
                                                              CIP

To the Krehbiel majority—Amy, Sara, and Emily

Preface

The process of legislative research is stimulating not only because of the intrinsic interest of legislative politics but also because of the healthy heterogeneity within the legislative research community. We include politicians, anecdotists, soakers-and-pokers, number crunchers, and proposition provers. We are variously trained as political scientists, journalists, economists, sociologists, and anthropologists. We address an impressive spectrum of issues, ranging from why a certain legislator did a certain thing on a certain day to what is the generic role of legislatures in political systems.

To typecast people or their work is invariably risky. However, risk taking is useful if not essential in expressing the motivation for and nature of this study. A large fraction of legislative research can be placed into one of two categories: empirical and theoretical. (By "theory" I shall mean formal, positive theory.) Granted, as with many so-called typologies in political science, this classification scheme is not a pure typology, which is to say its categories are not mutually exclusive and exhaustive. The work of empirical legislative scholars is not always atheoretical, and the work of formal theorists (at least occasionally) has a stylized fact or two interspersed among assumptions, propositions, and proofs. Still, it is not inaccurate to say that while theoretical research and empirical research have coexisted more-or-less peacefully for some time now, few large-scale projects have subjected positive theories to systematic empirical tests. As such, a rather sizable gulf separates existing literatures.

While theory types and empirical types have managed to coexist throughout the history of legislative studies, several disagreements have arisen among theory types in the past few years. Within the larger political science community, these disagreements are probably not well known, not viewed as particularly important, or both. If so, then I would hasten to add that this state of ignorance or indifference is principally *our* fault. (As a gesture of equity in typecasting, I yield, for the time being, to the typecasts of others. More often than not—and invariably to my discomfort—political scientists cast me as a theory type.) Disagreements within formal-theoretical research may have gone unnoticed for any of several reasons. Perhaps we have selected unrealistic problems on which to work, such as the global cyclicity of majority rule. Perhaps much of our work is not readily accessible to readers who are not mathematically inclined. Perhaps we simply do not know very much about real politics. Disagreements within formal-theoretical research may be viewed as unimportant for essentially the same reasons. If we select uninteresting problems on which to work, fail to make our work accessible, and do not know much about politics, then why should anyone care if we happen to disagree among ourselves?

This book tries to redress these crimes or misdemeanors by addressing a set of substantive issues that empirical scholars have long regarded as important, namely: *How are legislatures organized and why?* It summarizes, in a nonmathematical and accessible manner, two classes of formal theory that claim to answer questions about legislative organization. It then subjects the predictions of formal theories to a diverse set of empirical tests, thereby moving a step or two toward finding out whether formal theorists can offer some insights into real politics. Figuratively, the objective is to build a bridge across the gulf that currently separates the two, often detached types of research identified above.

When I first contemplated and later began this project, several friends and colleagues discouraged me. "You aren't likely to make many friends by emphasizing differences among formal theorists." "You aren't likely to convince many empirical scholars that formal theorists have much to offer." "Hmm. So you enjoy being shot at from both directions?" And so on. In spite of what my friends and colleagues may sometimes think, I put a lot of stock into their advice. Consequently, I took their prognostications seriously for some time. The key piece of advice came relatively late in the project after I had recounted these admonitions and reservations to Richard Fenno, the quintessential friend and colleague. While he seemed to agree with many of the gloomy forecasts, he also managed to cast a more constructive light upon them: "Yes, you *will* be pulled and poked from both sides—and you know what side I'll be pulling from—but that's *good!*" Not knowing for certain the answer to the question—Good for whom?—I nevertheless decided to proceed.

Much to my gratitude and to the book's benefit, a good deal of pulling and poking (and some shooting) came at the prepublication stage. Portions of the work were presented in seminars at Harvard, Princeton, Stanford, UCLA, and Yale. Participants in these were all very helpful. The most exhaustive (and exhausting) seminar experiences occurred during a week-long stay in Rochester, New York, where I presented the first complete draft of the manuscript. The depth, consistency, quantity, and precision of criticisms from this group of graduate students and faculty were phenomenal. Subsequent drafts owe much to David Austen-Smith, Jeff Banks, Larry Bartels, Randy Calvert, Dick Fenno, Bill Riker, Larry Rothenberg, Harold Stanley, and John Wilkerson.

Drafts of chapters were circulated broadly so that I would have opportunities to correct instances of unfairness, misrepresentation, incompleteness, and inaccuracy. On all relevant dimensions—including response rates, quickness and quality of responses, and degree of support for the project—collegiality was exceptional. I received comprehensive and insightful correspondence from Doug Arnold, Stan Bach, Joe Cooper, Mo Fiorina, Rick Hall, John Hibbing, Nelson Polsby, and Steve Smith. My Stanford colleagues were similarly supportive. First I thank Dave Baron for attracting me to the Graduate School of Business and for being an unfailingly generous and encouraging colleague in ways that reach well beyond this project. Likewise, countless conversations with David Brady, John Ferejohn, Terry Moe, Doug Rivers, and Barry Weingast have improved this work significantly, as have classes and conversations with Ph.D. students, among whom Tim Groseclose deserves special thanks. I also appreciate financial support from the Graduate School of Business (including grants from the Bass Foundation and John M. Olin Foundation) and from the Hoover Institution (where I began this project as a National Fellow in 1988–89).

With superlatives running short, my final acknowledgment is to Tom Gilligan. As will soon become obvious, he was instrumental in initiating the theoretical perspective on legislative organization that is advanced here. What is less obvious, but no less important, is that his comments and criticisms have influenced this project on almost a daily basis. As much credit is his as he wishes to claim.

Contents

CHAPTER 1

Introduction

Not enough study has been given to the methods of our legislatures with a view to discovering the principles which have underlain their unfolding history, and the lines along which they may and probably will yet develop.

—Lauros G. McConachie (1898, 37)

It is hard—indeed for the contemporary observer impossible—to shake the conviction that the House's institutional structure does matter greatly in the production of political outcomes.

—Nelson W. Polsby (1968, 165)

The history of the U.S. Congress is one of conflict growing out of article 1 section 5 of the U.S. Constitution, which states that "each House may determine the rules of its proceedings." How can the representative assembly in one of the most durable constitutional governments have spent over two centuries embroiled in disputes related to this seemingly innocuous constitutional provision? Simple. For over two centuries, members of the U.S. Congress, like the "contemporary observer" to whom Polsby refers, have been unable to shake the conviction that battles about rules, procedures, institutional arrangements, or *legislative organization* are in fact battles about public policy and who determines it. Thus, for good reason, students of the U.S. Congress such as McConachie have toiled among legislative procedural ruins in attempts to discover general "principles" of legislative organization.

The history of the study of the U.S. Congress is one of describing the legislature's organizational features and hypothesizing about their causes and consequences. Radically different approaches have been taken in addressing these issues over the last two centuries, with more effort given to description and prescription than to articulation of causes and consequences. However, with rare exception, students of the Congress and of other representative assemblies agree with Polsby's premise that structural features of legislatures "matter greatly in the production of political outcomes" and in the viability of the political system.

> Most people who study politics . . . agree that for a political system to
> be viable, for it to succeed in performing tasks of authoritative resource
> allocation, problem solving, conflict settlement, and so on, in behalf of a
> population of any substantial size, it must be institutionalized. That is to
> say, organizations must be created and sustained that are specialized to
> political activity. (Polsby 1968, 144)

As developed and studied in this book, *legislative organization* refers to
the allocation of resources and assignment of parliamentary rights to individual legislators or groups of legislators. The concept of legislative organization
includes rights to propose legislation, rights to amend legislation proposed by
others, and rights to employ staff to help study and draft legislation and
amendments. The importance of how legislators choose to organize themselves—or equivalently, the importance of their collective decisions regarding
the allocation of resources and assignment of parliamentary rights—is evident
at both micro- and macrolevels of analysis.

At the microlevel, forms of legislative organization bear directly on the
performance of individual legislators within the legislature. Simply put, resources and parliamentary rights are necessary conditions for success in the
legislative arena. Without resources—such as time, money, and staff
support—a legislator cannot study and learn about the content and consequences of legislative policies. Resources, therefore, are instrumental for the
development of policy expertise. Similarly, without parliamentary rights—
such as the rights to propose legislation, to debate the content and consequences of legislation, to propose amendments, and to negotiate compromises—a legislator cannot make noteworthy contributions to the legislative
product. Parliamentary rights, therefore, are instrumental for the effective
expression of policy expertise.

At the macrolevel, forms of legislative organization bear directly on the
performance of the legislature within the political system. On what policy
objectives can a legislature collectively agree? What collective actions, such
as the passage of legislation, are taken that specify means to agreed upon
ends? Once legislation is implemented, how effectively does it meet its objectives? Finally, how important is the legislature in the political system? It is
implicit in many prior works—and explicit in this book—that the way a
legislature is organized largely determines the answers to these questions.
That is, the allocation of resources and the assignment of parliamentary rights
to individual legislators or to groups of legislators shape each of the following: the collective expression of policy objectives, the level of expertise that is
embodied in legislation that seeks to meet legislative objectives, the effectiveness with which legislation is implemented, and, ultimately, the importance of
the legislature in the governmental process.

Two Perspectives on Legislative Organization

The scholarly literature on legislative organization is large and diverse, but its theoretical underpinnings fall fairly neatly into two classes. The intellectual foundations and specifics of *distributive* and *informational* perspectives on legislative organization are reviewed in detail in chapters 2 and 3, respectively. For present purposes, a brief overview of these perspectives provides a backdrop for clarifying the scope and methods of this study.[1]

The Distributive Perspective

Issues of distribution in politics pertain to who gets what and at whose expense. Theories of distribution—particularly formal ones—tend to be individualistic in focus. The distributive perspective on legislative organization depicts a legislature as a collective choice body whose principal task is to allocate policy benefits.[2] Legislators compete with one another over scarce goods, and voting is the chief means by which benefits are authoritatively allocated. Because legislators are subject to periodic elections and electoral constituencies are geographic in the United States, the "electoral connection" implies that any given member of Congress has strong incentives to seek benefits of special interest to his or her constituents (Mayhew 1974; Fiorina 1977). Because geographic constituencies differ in terms of their voters' preferences, economic characteristics, and other policy-relevant attributes, legislators' electorally induced preferences differ as well. So, too, does the intensity with which legislators pursue the various policies. In the vernacular of economic models, the quintessential feature of democratic legislatures is the opportunity for utility-maximizing legislators to capture *gains from trade*.

The challenge of legislative organization within the distributive framework is to capture gains from trade reliably and predictably. For an institution that relies on majority-rule voting, however, this is difficult—presumably more difficult, for instance, than it would be through contractual or market mechanisms (Weingast and Marshall 1988). Incentives of low-benefit individuals to defect from cooperative logrolling arrangements are omnipresent and strong. The solution to this problem is institutional: a set of rules and precedents that facilitates gains from trade by assigning parliamentary rights in accordance with the intensity—and, in practice, the extremity—of legislators' preferences. When the policy-making process is played out in such an

---

1. Each school of thought is an amalgam of theoretical and empirical research, and differences exist within—as well as across—the two schools. However, since intragroup similarities vastly outnumber intragroup differences, I adopt the convention of referring to *the* distributive perspective and *the* informational perspective.

2. Costs are allocated, too, but tend not to be emphasized (see chap. 2).

organizational arrangement, each legislator in effect offers concessions on policies of lesser importance to his or her constituents while reaping disproportionate benefits on the issue of special importance to his or her constituents. In other words, intentional asymmetries in the assignment of parliamentary rights correspond with intended biases in the provision of policy benefits.

The implicit standard of performance of a legislative organization according to the distributive perspective is the degree to which benefits are conferred to members who value them most. More concretely, an effective legislative organization is one in which high-demanders for governmental services fare well.

Although the distributive perspective on legislative politics has been developed most explicitly in works of formal theory, neither its intellectual origins nor its scholarly acceptance is confined to formal theorists. Many of the best and brightest empirical scholars embrace much of this distributive perspective, too. For instance, in the introduction of Brady's (1988) exceptionally comprehensive empirical account of congressional policy-making, legislative politics is characterized as follows:[3]

> An important policy consequence of localized elections is that an intense representation of local interests pervades the House across a broad range of issues. Representatives choose committees that will increase their reelection chances (Eulau 1985; Bullock 1972; and Fenno 1973). Members from agriculture districts serve on the relevant committees and subcommittees; members from other types of districts serve on committees and subcommittees relevant to their constituencies. Thus committees and policy outputs are dominated by local interests. This phenomenon has been called policy-making or control by "little government," "the iron triangles" of interest-group liberalism, pork-barrel politics, and policy reciprocity (Lowi 1979; McConnell 1966; Redford 1966; and Davidson 1981). The name matters little; what counts is that localized interests are recognized as congealed within the structure of the House's policy-making process. Forming majorities capable of enacting major policy changes against a backdrop of institutionally localized interests is a difficult task at best, impossible at worst. (Brady 1988, 7)

The Informational Perspective

Although distributive theories occasionally refer to gains from *specialization* in addition to gains from *trade,* the fact of the matter is that explicit formulations of these theories do not accommodate notions of specialization or policy

---

3. References within the quotation are Brady's.

expertise. Students of the historical development of democratic legislatures would surely regard this as a serious limitation. Long before national or state governments became involved in the wholesale distribution of geographically targeted benefits, legislatures struggled with the problem of obtaining independent sources of information and expertise.[4] Only by extricating themselves from dependence upon information from the executive branch were legislative bodies able to play distinctive and effective deliberative roles within separation-of-powers systems (Maass 1983).

While many historical arguments have normative or functionalist underpinnings, a more recent line of research is exclusively positive and more explicit about not only the collective benefits of policy expertise but also the strategic use of information by individuals or committees.[5] Informational theories, like distributive theories, are individualistic in their axiomatic foundations, but informational theories uniquely embrace the notion of policy expertise as a potential collective good. If obtained and shared, individuals' policy expertise redounds to the whole, that is, to *all* legislators. As in the distributive perspective, informational theories view legislatures as arenas of individual distributive conflict. But unlike the distributive perspective, informational theories also view legislatures as organizations that may reap collective benefits from specialization.

The challenge of legislative organization within the informational framework is thus distinctly different from capturing gains from trade for the distributive benefit of high-demand minorities. Rather, it is to capture gains from specialization while minimizing the degree to which enacted policies deviate from majority-preferred outcomes.[6] As in the distributive perspective, the solution is institutional. However, the focus in informational approaches is on choosing rules and procedures that provide incentives for individuals to develop policy expertise and to share policy-relevant information with fellow legislators, including legislators with competing distributive interests. Thus, legislative organization in the informational perspective consists of a set of rules and procedures that allocate resources and assign parliamentary rights to legislators who can be expected to use resources efficiently and to exercise rights consistent with both individual and collective goals. Legislators who can become specialists at relatively low cost are provided with resources to gather information about the relationship between policies and their conse-

---

4. See, for example, Cooper 1970 and 1988; Harlow 1917; Luce 1922; MacNeil 1963; and Winslow 1931.

5. See Austen-Smith 1990a and 1990b; Austen-Smith and Riker 1987 and 1990; Banks 1989, 1990, and 1991; Gilligan 1989; and Gilligan and Krehbiel 1987, 1989a, 1989b, and 1990.

6. While "majority-preferred outcomes" cannot be defined generally in a multidimensional choice space, the informational theories in question posit a unidimensional choice space (see chap. 3).

quences. Legislators whose preferences are closely aligned with median preferences in the legislature are granted special parliamentary rights. This not only provides incentives for specialization but also minimizes the degree to which specialists can use information strategically to reap individual distributive benefits.

The implicit standard of performance of an effective legislative organization according to the informational perspective is also significantly different from that within the distributive perspective. An informationally efficient legislative organization is one in which collective benefits are reaped from individuals' policy-specific expertise and in which distributive benefits—rather than accruing disproportionately to high-demanders—are carefully kept in check by legislative majorities.

Objectives and Approaches

The ultimate objective of this book is to answer the following question. Are the major principles of legislative organization exclusively or predominantly distributive, or are they first and foremost informational? The immediate objective is to determine how best to find an answer.

Intuition is one obvious approach. Indeed, upon first consideration, each view of legislative organization seems perfectly intuitive. Do legislators feel the tugs of constituency and respond to them by pursuing policies that confer concentrated benefits to their constituencies? Of course. Do they adopt and abide by rules and procedures that facilitate these goals? They certainly try. Does a legislature as a collective entity have an innate need for policy expertise, and do legislators as individuals have innate (or constituency-induced) policy interests? Surely. Do legislative institutions such as the committee system try to capitalize on this alignment of collective needs and individual (or constituency) interests? So it would seem.

Indisputably, these empirical questions follow from the two perspectives on legislative organization. Similarly, the answers to the questions are sufficiently intuitive that they, too, seem indisputable. Perhaps, then, the objective of this book should be summarily dismissed as posing a false dichotomy between two theoretical perspectives, in which case more exciting empirical questions can be addressed more directly, unencumbered by theory. Although it has to be taken on faith for the time being, to walk uncritically along this path of intuition is to risk getting lost. Nearly everyone agrees that logical incompatibilities should be avoided in social sciences. Yet, logical incompatibilities arise when the theoretical foundations and empirical implications of the two perspectives on legislative organization are carefully spelled out and compared. Indeed, in several key instances it is essentially impossible to subscribe simultaneously (and with logical consistency) to both of the classes of theory in question. In turn, this suggests that understanding legislative organization requires a *joint* theoretical and empirical approach. Theoretical analysis is needed to identify clearly a set of hypotheses about legislative organization, to expose the logical foundations of such hypotheses, and to compare and contrast hypotheses that are derived from alternative theoretical frameworks. Empirical analysis is needed to refute or corroborate theories. In the present case, empirical analysis is especially important since different theories often yield different predictions. Thus, while a reliance on intuition is perhaps an obvious approach to the study of legislative organization, it is not a satisfactory approach.

Distributive and informational theories of legislative organization have distinctly different empirical implications at each of two observable levels of legislative choice: the *policies* enacted by legislatures, and the *institutions* developed and employed by legislatures (alternatively, organizational forms, rules, procedures, or legislative organization). Both of these seem to be promising candidates for observation. However, in light of existing theory, data, and empirical techniques, the institutional focus clearly dominates the policy focus in terms of its likelihood of yielding a clear answer to the focal question about distributive and informational foundations of legislative organization. To see why, I will discuss the policy focus and its associated ambiguities before adopting the institutional approach.

Limitations of a Policy Focus

One way to test theories of legislative organization is to observe legislative policies. The informational perspective adheres to the principle of chamber control over its allocation of resources and assignment of parliamentary rights and, thus, implies that final policies will not depart widely from those espoused by moderate legislators. In contrast, distributive views are better characterized as the parent chamber delegating parliamentary rights to intensely interested high-demand minorities that then engage in logrolling. As a result, policies will depart widely from those espoused by moderate legislators.

If it were possible, on a comprehensive issue-by-issue basis, to derive comparable estimates of legislators' individual policy positions and the legislature's collective policy choices, then a focus on policies might shed light on the focal question about legislative organization. If policy choices tended to comport with moderate voters' preferences, then we would question the distributive perspective. If they were significantly biased in the direction of high-demanders, then we would question the informational perspective. The necessary conditions for such a comprehensive study are very stringent, however. The requisite econometric techniques exist, but they in turn require a set of roll call votes with properties that, in practice, are not often met.[7] Implementation of the techniques that focus on policies is further complicated if the legislative provisions subject to roll call votes do not have precisely defined attributes (such as dollars) or are multidimensional (for example, involve large and complex substitute amendments).

If the necessary conditions for systematic empirical studies are not likely to be met over a representative range of policy domains, then we are left with little more than a mixture of intuitions, anecdotes, and, in the best case, policy-specific studies from which to assess the theories of interest. And even though intuitions, anecdotes, and policy-specific studies can be surveyed as if they were a representative sample of comparable observations, the results are mixed and thus not definitive in terms of the ultimate research objective. Granted, the weight of intuitions and anecdotes tends to favor the distributive perspective. We are told repeatedly that committees largely call the shots in the legislative process,[8] and it often seems as if committees are stacked. For example, we observe a preponderance of prodefense legislators on armed services committees, a preponderance of rural members on agriculture committees, a preponderance of westerners on the interior committees, and so on. More to the point, we observe a great deal of defense spending (perhaps more than a majority would like), impressive quantities of agricultural subsidies (perhaps more than a majority would like), and nontrivial expenditures by the Bureau of Reclamation (perhaps more than a majority would like). Observations such as these are not definitive, however, insofar as median preferred levels of governmental support for defense, agricultural, or public works projects have not been estimated.[9] Moreover, studies that have circumvented this problem by calculating the requisite estimates of preferences seem, if anything, to be inconsistent with the distributive perspective. For example, two studies have found that high-demand committee members in the Senate were unsuccessful in passing a minimum wage bill whose level exceeded that preferred by the Senate's median voter.[10]

As if this casual weighing of intuitions and evidence were not ambiguous enough, the outlook for a policy-based study of legislative organization becomes even dimmer when contemplating the feasibility of more comprehensive applications of the aforementioned estimation techniques. On more complicated policy issues—such as environmental policy, health care, and

---

7. For a simple application of one such technique, details on more complex applications, and a discussion of the trade-offs, see Krehbiel and Rivers 1988.

8. See Fenno 1966 and 1973; Goodwin 1970; Manley 1970; McConachie 1898; Price 1972; Shepsle 1978; Smith and Deering 1984; and Wilson 1885.

9. See Bartels 1990 for an important exception in defense policy, albeit with a substantive focus on constituency influence.

10. See Krehbiel and Rivers 1988; and Wilkerson 1989.

taxation—the main dimensions of conflict are nebulous, and this further confounds the estimation of preferences. Finally, even if all of these obstacles were overcome, inferential difficulties with respect to the two theoretical perspectives would remain. For example, systematic evidence of policies that cater to high-demanders would be necessary for support of the distributive perspective on legislative organization. However, if the behavior surrounding policy-making and the institutional arrangements in which it occurs happen not to be consistent with the assumptions and predictions of distributive theories, evidence of high-demand outcomes would not be sufficient for convincing support. In short, an exclusive focus on *policy outcomes* is neither the most direct nor the most feasible approach to identifying the principles of legislative organization.

A closely related and somewhat more promising approach to testing theories of legislative organization is to observe *policy-making behavior* to infer whether it is motivated primarily by distributive or informational concerns. From a distributive vantage point, we would expect to see concerted and successful attempts by high-demand legislators to engage in logrolling. A distributively effective legislative organization has rules to ensure that deals struck in early stages of the legislative process cannot be undone in later stages. Thus, we would expect to see legislators choose and abide by such rules in the course of distributive policy-making. From an informational vantage point, in contrast, policy-making behavior should be directed less toward logrolling than to the acquisition of policy expertise. High-demand legislators may exist, and, indeed, they may like logrolling. However, since an informationally effective legislative organization is one that uses rules to encourage specialization rather than to facilitate gains from trade, logrolling efforts should be minimally successful. Moreover, rules and procedures should tend to thwart such efforts rather than facilitate them.

To illustrate the limitations of an empirical approach that focuses on policy-making behavior, we perform a three-step exercise. First, we choose a policy domain that has historical importance in U.S. politics and that, accordingly, has received frequent and intense scrutiny by political scientists. The issue is agriculture. Second, we note that in terms of the two perspectives on legislative organization, this choice clearly favors the distributive perspective. Agricultural policy is among the most distributive of all policies, perhaps topped only by rivers and harbors legislation (which has been on the wane in the last two decades) or defense contracting (whose geographic incidence is more widespread than it first seems, due to subcontracting). Third, we survey several studies of agriculture policy-making to see whether the evidence points decisively in the distributive direction with respect to key issues of legislative organization. The logic of the exercise is simple. If an empirical focus on policy-making behavior is a promising way to validate theoretical perspectives on legislative organization, we should, at a minimum, be able to find unambiguous evidence in this thoroughly studied policy domain. Specifically, we would like to answer the following questions definitively.

- Do agricultural high-demanders seek and receive assignments to agriculture committees and subcommittees?
- Are committee and subcommittee members *not* interested in specialization?
- Are logrolling attempts common, successful, and attributable to distributively motivated choices of legislative procedures?

Composition of Agriculture Committees
On first pass—and certainly as folklore would have it—the issue of composition of the Senate and House Agriculture Committees and their subcommittees is no issue at all. The House committee is stacked with representatives from rural districts, and the Senate committee is stacked with senators from farm belt states.[11] "It is a fact of farm politics that lawmakers come to personify the crops grown in their home states."[12] Furthermore, agriculture subcommittees are organized on a commodity-specific basis, and "usually a member is assigned to at least one commodity subcommittee of his choice" (Jones 1969, 157).

Of the three questions raised, the one pertaining to committee composition has the clearest answer. Yet, even this issue is less cut-and-dried than the first pass indicates. Members of the agriculture committees may be high-demanders, but they are high-demanders with some important qualifications. While members tend to gravitate to commodity-specific and constituency-consistent subcommittees, case after case suggests that, when push comes to shove, a legislator's support for subsidies is confined to his or her own special commodity. Committee members' demand may be high, but it is not wide. Thus, for example, Jones (1962) chronicles battle after battle that erupted in full committee after commodity-specific subcommittees reported their proposals. Similarly, Weber (1989) and a series of feature stories on agriculture policy-making emphasize other important issues that split members within the ostensibly homogeneous high-demand agriculture committees. Intracommittee conflict has erupted over issues that pit big-farm versus small-farm interests, agribusiness versus family farmers, agricultural versus environmental interests, and market versus nonmarket approaches to production problems. Other rifts have arisen surrounding trade restrictions, the nature and quantity of agriculture research, and rural electricity and power issues.[13]

---

11. See, for example, Ferejohn 1986; Jones 1962 and 1969; Ripley 1969; and Weber 1989.

12. *Congressional Quarterly,* August 12, 1989, 2117.

13. See *Congressional Quarterly,* January 26, 1985, 135–40; July 27, 1985, 1471–72; August 17, 1985, 1637–40; September 21, 1985, 1985; November 8, 1986, 2822; and August

Specialization in Agriculture Committees

Casual observation of the composition of agriculture committees suggests that at least some agriculture politics are, indeed, distributive politics. But perhaps the high-demand nature of committee members' preferences serve informational goals by enabling agriculture committees to capitalize on high-demanders' greater willingness to study commodity-specific problems.

Agricultural issues are indeed complex issues, and case studies and news features occasionally stress the role of expertise in the policy successes of committee members. Based on his study of Congressman Richard Nolan (D.–Minn.), Weber, for example, writes that "judgments about good public policy and what the individual can do to realize policy objectives involve complex calculations about the relationships between means and ends" (1989, 87). Similarly, a story about the experiences of a uniquely low-demand Senate Agriculture Committee Chairman (Patrick Leahy, D.–Vt.) stresses his "close working relationship with the ranking Republican, Richard G. Lugar of Indiana. Lugar immerses himself in the details of agriculture policy, and Leahy has rarely acted on any legislation without Lugar's support for the product. Sometimes the chairman has had to rely on Lugar's expertise."[14] However, while expertise sometimes plays a role in agricultural policy-making (as evidenced by Lugar), it is not a given (as evidenced by Leahy). Jones further stresses the limits of expertise when attributing the failure of the omnibus agriculture bill of 1958 to its being "such a large and complicated piece of legislation," provisions of which were regarded as "drafted hurriedly" and as "unrealistic solutions" to the difficult problems at hand (1962, 333 and 340).

In short, the evidence cuts both ways. Specialization surely plays some role in agricultural policy-making, and agriculture committees probably organize, in part, to provide incentives for their members to specialize. However, the pursuit of distributive benefits surely plays a role in agricultural policy-making, too, and almost no one disputes that commodity-based subcommittees are organized attempts to facilitate gains from trade.

Logrolling in Agriculture Committees

Case studies on agricultural policy-making leave little doubt about whether logrolling attempts are common. They are. However, the willingness to engage in logrolling is one thing, while the ability to secure gains from trade is quite another. With regard to capturing gains from trade and the role procedures play in these attempts, the evidence is again mixed.

In a historical study that spans parts of four decades, Ferejohn (1986) discusses the intricacies of two forms of logrolling: the classical, cross-

---

12, 1989, 2116–20; *National Journal,* November 11, 1985, 2535–39. Studies of the agricultural interest group environment affirm many of these divisions. See, for example, Salisbury, Heinz, Laumann, and Nelson 1987.

14. *Congressional Quarterly,* August 12, 1989, 2118.

commodity logroll (via subcommittees), plus the broader cross-issue logroll between agricultural and food stamps programs.[15] His thesis—to make a long and complex story short and simple—is that there was both a will and a way for high-demand legislators to capture gains from trade. Specifically, a minority coalition favoring agriculture and a minority coalition favoring food stamps not only desired to form a majority but also found institutional means to strike a mutually desirable deal. The key institutional innovations, according to Ferejohn, were to initiate the food stamps program within the Agriculture Committee's jurisdiction and to exploit restrictive procedures throughout the process to keep the deal from falling apart. These distributively effective procedures include standing committees' gatekeeping power, restrictive rules on the floor, conference committees, and restrictive procedures governing consideration of conference reports.[16] Overall, this evidence suggests that gains-from-trade behavior not only is prevalent but also is facilitated by the structural features stressed in distributive perspectives on legislative organization.

Not all of the evidence is consistent with the distributive perspective, however. Weber's case study includes examples of subcommittee disputes spilling over to committee stage and committee disputes spilling over to the floor stage. Ferejohn's study includes examples of floor disputes spilling into and out of the conference committee stage. Finally, Jones's studies provide thorough accounts of the policy-making process in 1958 as one in which the House Agriculture Committee informally agreed to use an "omnibus procedure" in which ten commodity-specific subcommittees would write their own proposals, after which the full committee would assemble them, title-by-title, into one large bill. In theory, the execution of this plan should have been no different from the execution of the larger logroll that Ferejohn studied. In practice, however, the plan faltered at almost every juncture. Some subcommittees had trouble reaching agreement, notwithstanding their common high-demand, commodity-specific interests. For example, on the Cotton Subcommittee, different members backed plans supported by different interest groups, while some members sat back quietly "and were satisfied to wait and vote against the final bill" (Jones 1962, 335). A dispute arose in the Dairy Subcom-

---

15. His study focuses more on the cross-issue logroll than the antecedent cross-commodity logroll. See also Ripley 1969.

16. Some reservations pertaining to preferences and procedure can be raised about Ferejohn's argument. The most important of these is that evidence of a pro-food-stamps *majority* can be found as early as 1958, when the entrepreneur in the logrolling saga, Mrs. Leonor Sullivan (D.–Mo.), succeeded in bringing up a food-stamps-only bill under suspension of the rules, effectively circumventing the Rules Committee (an alleged gatekeeper). The bill received less than the requisite two-thirds vote but more than a majority. If one interprets this vote as a truthful expression of House preferences, then the alleged logroll was not between two otherwise helpless *minorities* but rather an agreement between a minority composed of proagriculture members and a

mittee that pitted eastern against midwestern dairy farmers, and, to make matters worse, both of these blocs were threatened by "the general attitude among committee members that dairy interests have always been favored" (Jones 1962, 338). Decision making in the full committee was contentious. As members of the full committee looked ahead, they became convinced that portions of the bill "would be removed on the House floor" (Jones 1962, 343). In fact, even this dismal forecast proved overly optimistic. First, the rule providing for consideration of the agriculture omnibus bill was defeated in the House, with committee members divided in the vote to bring their bill to the floor. Next, the Senate passed its farm bill and sent it to the House, after which the House Agriculture Committee amended the Senate's bill and brought it to the floor under suspension of the rules.[17] The House again rejected the bill. Finally, the committee stripped additional proagriculture provisions (wheat and dairy) from the bill and finally succeeded in passing it under suspension (Jones 1969, 162).

This multicase survey of agriculture policy-making is not intended to resolve any issues. On the contrary, it is meant to suggest that the key issues of legislative organization probably cannot be resolved by observing policy-making behavior alone or by relying solely on case-study techniques. Even in the best-case scenario—that of a carefully studied domain of policy-making in which we would expect, a priori, to find clear and convincing evidence of procedurally enhanced gains from trade among high-demand minorities—the evidence is murky. Self-selection? Probably. Homogeneous, high-demand committees? High-demand, yes; homogeneous, no. A desire to engage in logrolling? Certainly. Successful logrolls? Sometimes. Choice of procedures to secure logrolls? Perhaps, but of questionable effectiveness. Moreover, even if the evidence on agriculture policy-making were uniform and unambiguous, it remains doubtful that the agricultural policy domain is representative of what legislators do, how policy-making unfolds, or the laws legislatures pass. Indeed, some scholars have emphasized the peculiarities of the agricultural policy process (Jones 1962; Weber 1989). Thus, while case-specific observations of policy-making behavior and policy outcomes may shape our intuitions about legislative organization, they are just as likely to bias our perceptions.

---

steadily growing *majority* composed of food stamps advocates. Then, the unsolved puzzle is why food stamps advocates bothered to coalesce with proagriculture forces. Indeed, as time went on (and as Ferejohn documents) the existence of the food stamps majority was less and less in question, and food stamps supporters, predictably, were more and more inclined to go it alone with respect to agriculture enthusiasts.

17. Suspension of the rules is a procedure in which, via two-thirds majority vote, the House may pass a bill. The procedure is restrictive in the sense that separate amendments are not allowed. See Bach 1984 and 1990 for excellent discussions of this procedure and Cooper 1990 for data on its contemporary use.

In either instance, this empirical focus cannot resolve outstanding issues about legislative organization.

An Institutional Focus

Ultimately, to understand legislative organization is to understand *legislative institutions,* that is, rules and precedents that act as binding constraints on legislators' behavior.[18] As will become evident below, the predictions of distributive and informational theories of legislative organization are least ambiguous and most direct in terms of institutions. This fact—which is reinforced by the aforementioned problems that accompany the observation of policies and behavior—suggests that the most promising empirical approach is an institutional approach. In particular, the primary empirical focuses in this book are on standing committees and their formation, rules governing the amendment of legislation in the parent chamber, and rules and precedents governing the resolution of interchamber differences in legislation. In studying these, two questions will arise repeatedly. How and why did these legislative institutions arise? How and why are these legislative institutions employed?

Many of the institutional details that arise in the course of the study are susceptible to the figurative charge of missing the forest for the trees (or, perhaps in some instances, leaves). One response to this charge is that leaves or trees are intrinsically more interesting than forests, but this is a matter of taste rather than truth. The better response is that the alleged narrowness of the institutional approach is consistent with a straightforward methodological premise. In testing theories about complex human interactions in complex settings, clarity of inference is facilitated by focusing on more immediately observable implications of theories. Of the two levels of observation at which theories of legislative organization have implications—policies and institu-

---

18. This definition of legislative institutions may appear simply to redefine the difficult question as: What are rules and precedents? Follow-up questions of this sort can lead to an infinite regress and thus probably cannot be preempted. I will nevertheless take one additional step and offer a working definition of rules and precedents that is adequate for present purposes. Rules and precedents are codified practices that are broadly perceived as binding constraints on behavior. The chief limitation of this definition is embodied in the question: Suppose legislators choose to change the rules; then were such (ostensible) rules indeed binding constraints on behavior? My possibly puzzling answer is yes, provided that no higher rules were violated when changing the lower rules. (Thus, for example, when in the revolt against Cannon, the Speaker was stripped of his parliamentary right to make committee assignments, that parliamentary right clearly *was* a rule: it was codified, it was practiced, and it was constraining up until the time at which the rule was changed, in accordance with the House's rules for changing its rules.) The choice to include precedents in the definition of institutions has a similar defense. Precedents have a constraining effect on the Speaker's rulings. And, even though such rulings can be overturned (as was the case in the Cannon revolt), codified practices govern such overturning, too. See Bach 1987 for an insightful discussion of these challenging issues.

tions—the institutional implications are clearly the most immediate. Thus, only after we have collected and assessed systematic empirical evidence about these can we be confident that our understanding of legislative behavior and policy is based on a solid theoretical foundation.

Finally, it bears repeating why a solid theoretical foundation is essential as we work toward a cumulative and more comprehensive understanding of legislative institutions, behavior, and policy. In the absence of an explicit and empirically corroborated theory, we run a strong risk of being unjustifiably receptive to combinations of detached arguments that—while intuitive—are unnecessarily ambiguous, logically incompatible, or both.

Two Postulates of Legislative Organization

To reap the benefits of a joint theoretical-empirical approach, the remainder of this study seeks to conform with orthodox tenets of positive social science. Postulates are empirically motivated. Theoretical assumptions are explicit and precise. Theoretical results follow logically from the assumptions. Empirical predictions are extracted from theoretical results. And empirical predictions are refutable. That is, key concepts can be measured, measures are amenable to data analysis, and data analysis makes it possible to support or refute the theories in question. The review of distributive and informational theories in chapters 2 and 3 makes frequent reference to two postulates of legislative organization: majoritarianism and uncertainty.[19]

Majoritarianism

As organizations of collective decision making, legislatures operate continuously and interactively in two domains of choice: *procedure* and *policy.*

---

19. Most of the theories claim to be positive, and all of the formal theories adopt (at least implicitly) a third postulate: utility maximization. Although a case can be made that utility maximization should be added to the list of postulates of legislative organization, I elected not to include it for two reasons. First, it has become an orthodox assumption of positive models of legislative behavior, and I do not wish to refight old battles about whether legislators are or are not utility maximizers. The reader will see soon enough that there is no shortage of substantive differences between theories of legislative politics that employ identical utility maximization axioms. Most of the disputes highlighted in this study are substantive rather than methodological and thus can be resolved with evidence rather than methodological discourse. By comparison, disputes about utility maximization are uninteresting precisely because they probably cannot be resolved via evidence and are unlikely to be resolved via methodological discourse. (Analogously, in Euclidean geometry one is unlikely to demonstrate convincingly—either via theoretical discourse or observation—that points have no area, lines have no width, etc.) Second, the utility maximization axiom is obviously not unique to the subject of legislative organization or, for that matter, to politics. This is not to deny the central role the axiom plays in the theories under review. It is only to delineate the objectives of the study.

THE MAJORITARIAN POSTULATE. *Objects of legislative choice in both the procedural and policy domains must be chosen by a majority of the legislature.*

The Majoritarian Postulate has one obvious and one subtle component. The obvious component pertains to the *policy domain* of legislative choice. Policies cannot be enacted except with the consent of more than half of the legislature's members. This is not only an incontrovertible empirical feature of general parliamentary law but also a conventional assumption in formal theories of legislative decision making. The subtle component pertains to the *procedural domain* of legislative choice. Procedures or, more generally, organizational forms cannot be adopted except with the consent of more than half of the legislature's members. While this component cannot be regarded as an incontrovertible empirical feature, it nevertheless follows straightforwardly from majoritarianism in general parliamentary law combined with article 1 section 5 of the U.S. Constitution. If majoritarianism and the constitutionally stipulated endogeneity of procedural arrangements are taken literally, then the conclusion of Henry Cabot Lodge, for example, is inescapable: "No set of rules can shift the responsibility which lies in the majority" (Mc-Conachie 1898, 86). That is, majorities determine policy choice and procedural choice, and no choice of the latter can undermine the fundamental principle of majoritarianism in democratic, collective choice institutions.

Is the Majoritarian Postulate sensible? Since reasonable people disagree on this issue, it is worthwhile to raise some disagreements immediately to clarify the role of the postulate in the analysis. Consider four instances of legislative organization in the House of Representatives and their corresponding majoritarian and nonmajoritarian interpretations.[20]

Committee Assignments
In the U.S. House, individual members seek preferred committee assignments by making formal requests and by lobbying leaders, including state or regional representatives, whips, the majority or minority leader, the Speaker, and a select few party members who draw up committee slates. After these slates are drawn up, they are packaged and presented to the House. To become final, slates must be approved by a parent-chamber majority.[21]

---

20. Although most of the analysis in this book focuses on the U.S. House, which is often regarded as more of a majoritarian body than the Senate, chap. 7 conjectures that the principles of legislative organization identified and supported by the theoretical and empirical analyses are general properties of Western democratic legislatures.

21. Clause 6(a)(1) of rule 10 of the House says: "The standing committees specified in clause 1 shall be elected by the House at the commencement of each Congress, from nominations submitted by the respective party caucuses." The Senate has a similar rule.

The majoritarian interpretation of the committee assignment process rests on the simple fact that regardless of who proposes slates, a chamber majority must approve them. Nonmajoritarian interpretations are more common, however. Invariably (if implicitly), they rest on the claim that final votes on committee slates are pro forma. If this final majoritarian stage is truly trivial, then the key decisions are made in prior stages. The extent of nonmajoritarianism depends on who are regarded as the key decision makers. More often than not the process of committee assignments is characterized as one of self-selection.[22] This view can take several forms, all of which are clearly nonmajoritarian. A pure interpretation of self-selection would be that every legislator is a dictator with respect to his or her committee seat(s). The more common interpretation is that leaders are sufficiently accommodating with respect to fulfilling legislators' requests that de facto self-selection occurs within bounds of seat availability. But even in this interpretation, committee assignment decisions are regarded as centralized, intraparty, leadership affairs. In other words, the process is not majoritarian in terms of the Majoritarian Postulate.

The Discharge Procedure
Since 1910, the House has had a procedure whereby a bare majority (currently, 218 members) can sign a petition to make it possible to discharge a standing committee from consideration of a piece of legislation. If a subsequent discharge motion receives a majority of votes, then any member who signed the petition can make another motion to bring the bill before the House. To pass, this motion, too, requires the support of a parent-chamber majority.[23]

The majoritarian interpretation of the discharge procedure rests on the simple fact that both the initiation and the implementation of the discharge process requires a chamber majority. Nonmajoritarian interpretations are more common, however. Just as floor votes are dismissed as pro forma in the context of committee assignments, the discharge procedure is dismissed as inconsequential in terms of standing committees' rights to pigeonhole legislation. Invariably (if implicitly) this interpretation rests on the claim that the procedure is cumbersome. Evidence cited for this interpretation is its rare use. The corresponding inference is that standing committees have de facto gatekeeping powers that, in turn, are inimical to the Majoritarian Postulate.

The Rules Committee
The House Committee on Rules may write a resolution to bring a bill to the floor immediately or at any specified time. Thereby, the bill may avoid what,

22. See chap. 4 for a more comprehensive review and analysis.
23. Clause 5 of rule 13 provides for "a Calendar of Motions to Discharge Committees." Clause 4 of rule 27 describes the procedure in detail.

under normal circumstances, would be a long or interminable wait on one of the House's Calendars. Such a resolution (also known as a "special order" or "rule") is presented to the House. To take effect, it requires the support of a parent-chamber majority.

The majoritarian interpretation of the Rules Committee and special orders rests on the simple fact that all special orders require majority approval in the parent chamber. Nonmajoritarian interpretations are more common, however. In former Congresses, nonmajoritarian interpretations of the Rules Committee rested on instances of alleged obstructionism, the classic case being Chairman Howard Smith and civil rights (Jones 1968; Cummings and Peabody 1969).[24] In the contemporary Congress, the Rules Committee is widely regarded as a party and partisan organ or, alternatively, as an "arm of the leadership" (Oppenheimer 1977). Those who prefer nonmajoritarian interpretations do not dispute the need for special orders to command majority support on the floor. Rather, they tend to discount the significance of this requirement, using a variety of arguments. For example, Democrats may not be cohesive on many issues, but at least majority party leaders can usually round up the requisite votes for "procedural," if not "substantive," motions. Furthermore, as an arm of the leadership, the Rules Committee can extract promises from committees on behalf of the majority party rather than the House. It can also credibly threaten not to write favorable rules or, perhaps more powerfully still, refuse to write a rule at all. If valid, these arguments are surely difficult to reconcile with the Majoritarian Postulate.

Designation of Conferees

The Speaker of the House is formally empowered to designate conferees to represent the House in conference committees. The Speaker's designated list of conferees cannot be challenged. However, the motion to go to conference requires the support of a parent-chamber majority.[25]

The majoritarian interpretation of conferee selection rests on the simple fact that the motion to go to conference requires the consent of a majority.[26] Nonmajoritarian interpretations are more common, however. They tend to

---

24. Contrary to the implications of most works on the "autocratic" powers of the Rules Committee, the committee can be discharged. Of course, this fact does not resolve the present interpretive disagreement. It simply diverts attention back to the second example of majoritarian ambiguity—the discharge procedure.

25. Clause 6(f) of rule 10 says: "The Speaker shall appoint all select and conference committees which shall be ordered by the House from time to time. In appointing members to conference committees the Speaker shall appoint no less than a majority of members who generally supported the House position as determined by the Speaker. The Speaker shall name Members who are primarily responsible for the legislation and shall, to the fullest extent feasible, include the principal proponents of the major provision of the bill as it passed the House."

26. Unanimous consent is common in practice, but unanimity is not necessary.

dismiss the majority requirement and focus on the more centralized decision, in this case the Speaker's drawing up the list of conferees, usually in consultation with the chairman of the standing committee.[27] If the Speaker's behavior is, indeed, unaffected by other majoritarian choices—such as his election by the House, amendment activity on the legislation in question, instructions to conferees, or the vote on the motion to send the legislation to conference— then this interpretation, too, contradicts the Majoritarian Postulate.

For each of these four examples, different interpretations stem from different perceptions regarding the significance of what might be called remote majoritarian choices. Majoritarian interpretations regard these choices as significant in spite of their remoteness. Nonmajoritarian interpretations regard them as insignificant because of their remoteness. For committee assignments, the remote majoritarian choice is the House's vote on party-proposed slates. For discharge, the remote majoritarian choices include the 218 or more signatures on the discharge petition, the vote on the motion to discharge, and the vote to bring the bill before the House. For votes on special orders, the remote majoritarian choices are the House's votes on appointment of Rules Committee members and on bill-specific special orders. For conferee appointments, the remote majoritarian choices are votes on motions to go to conference and on the selection of the Speaker, who is assigned the parliamentary right to appoint conferees.

All of these aspects of legislative organization can be traced to majoritarian collective choices *in principle*. What is not known is the degree to which aspects of legislative organization conform to majoritarian principles *in practice*. Generally, does the existence of these remote majoritarian choices condition legislators' behavior at the various stages of legislative organization? Specifically, are ostensibly oligarchical party leaders cognizant of, and constrained by, the forthcoming floor vote when making committee assignments? Are putatively partisan Rules Committee members cognizant of, and constrained by, the forthcoming floor vote when writing special orders? Is the seemingly dictatorial Speaker cognizant of, and constrained by, his past and future elections as Speaker when selecting slates of conferees? These are empirical questions and, as such, no useful purpose is served by further inspection of evidence-free arguments about various interpretations. A more promising approach is positive. Informational theories posit that legislatures are majoritarian in the manner reflected by the Majoritarian Postulate. This study will proceed to juxtapose and test the empirical implications of informational theories with those of other theories that are less reliant upon the Majoritarian Postulate.

---

27. See, for example, Nagler 1989; Shepsle and Weingast 1987a and 1987b; and Smith 1989.

Uncertainty

The Majoritarian Postulate of legislative organization sharply distinguishes between (yet applies to each of) two domains of legislative choice: procedure and policy. The second postulate makes a similarly fundamental distinction between *policies,* which are objects of legislative choice, and *outcomes,* which are consequences of enacted policies and are not objects of legislative choice.

> THE UNCERTAINTY POSTULATE. *Legislators are often uncertain about the relationship between policies and their outcomes.*

Like the Majoritarian Postulate, the Uncertainty Postulate has an obvious component. The quantity and quality of information available to legislators is such that legislators must choose policies whose consequences they cannot fully and perfectly anticipate. Unlike the Majoritarian Postulate, the Uncertainty Postulate has no subtle component that may render it suspect. Its truth seems indisputable.

Overview

What remains in dispute—and what this book seeks to resolve—is whether the explicit incorporation of the Majoritarian and Uncertainty Postulates into theories of legislative organization is significant. Since postulates (or axioms) are not directly testable in positive theories, we need standards for assessing their practical significance. These are readily available. First, do theories that embody the Majoritarian and Uncertainty Postulates yield empirical expectations that differ substantively from theories in which either or both of these postulates are contradicted? Second, are the expectations of theories that conform with the postulates borne out in systematic data? These issues guide us through the next five chapters, which are organized as follows.

As noted above, the preponderance of formal theory of legislatures has been in the tradition of distributive politics and thus focuses on who receives benefits from legislative policy choices and at whose expense. The most prevalent question about legislative organization in this research is: How can legislative institutions be designed so that legislators capture gains from trade? To date, most distributive theories are not consistent with the Uncertainty Postulate and are consistent with the Majoritarian Postulate only at the level of policy choice. Key features and examples of these theories are presented in chapter 2. Three predictions about legislative organization emerge from a representative collection of works. These pertain to the composition of committees, the rules used to consider specific bills, and the willingness and ability of a legislature to commit credibly to the use of such procedures.

Also noted above, a new class of theory of legislatures is in the tradition of games with incomplete information. The legislative versions of these informational theories subscribe more closely to the Majoritarian and Uncertainty Postulates of legislative organization. Majoritarianism governs both policy and procedural choice. Uncertainty is formally characterized as incomplete information about the relationship between policies and their ultimate consequences. Reviewed and illustrated in chapter 3, informational theories also yield predictions that pertain to the composition of committees, rules used to consider specific bills, and the willingness and ability of a legislature to commit credibly to its institutional arrangements. In most instances, the predictions of informational and distributive theories are different. Thus, the combined sets of predictions from chapters 2 and 3 provide a useful theoretical foundation for the empirical analysis that spans chapters 4–6.

When making the transition from theoretical to empirical chapters, it is important to remember that even though the two classes of theories yield different predictions with respect to legislative organization, they could in principle be merged.[28] Perhaps no more than a few readers will be inclined to contemplate—much less develop—a hybrid gains-from-trade/informational theory. Remaining readers can rest assured, however, that their relative lack of theoretical ambition poses no handicap to understanding the thesis of the study, provided that the following issues are kept in mind. First, there is nothing inherently nonmajoritarian about distributive-theoretic approaches. It just so happens that, historically, distributive theories have been less concerned with majoritarianism in the domain of procedural choice than have been informational theories. Second and similarly, information-theoretic approaches are not inherently limited in their applicability to legislative environments characterized by policy uncertainty. In fact, when such uncertainty diminishes to zero within an informational theory, a perfect-information distributive theory results.[29] Finally, the reason this study tends to stress differences in theoretical approaches is not because the approaches are entirely different from one another. Rather, by highlighting differences we are able to learn more clearly which exogenous features of the legislative environment are and are not capable of explaining variation in legislative institutions and their use. Surely no class of theory will explain all variation while the other

---

28. If this were to be done satisfactorily, however (which is to say, in a formal, explicit, and general way), the theoretical task would be Herculean for reasons that will become increasingly clear as the complexity of existing theories unfolds.

29. It is a simple one relative to most exclusively distributive theories. Nonetheless, it can be used to derive predictions.

explains none, and likewise no theory is likely to be all right while the other is all wrong.[30] The more realistic aim is to see which existing theories can explain some variation and to gain insights about why. With these issues in mind, the three empirical chapters address three stages of the legislative game.

Chapter 4 is a study of the pregame phase of legislative politics: the formation of standing committees. By focusing on the historical development of the committee system, contemporary committee assignment procedures and behavior, and the composition of standing committees, I assess the evidence for the theoretical expectation that the existence of committees and sustenance of committee-centered organizational arrangements have more to do with informational than distributive concerns.

Chapter 5 is a study of the midgame phase of legislative politics: the choice and uses of procedures governing consideration of committees' legislation. Relevant predictions here pertain to when and why "rules" (special orders in the House) constrain noncommittee members' amendment rights. This analysis also illuminates the informational determinants of legislative organization.

Chapter 6 is a study of the endgame phase of legislative politics: the choice of procedures for resolving bicameral differences in legislation. Its empirical analysis parallels that in chapter 4. The historical development of conference committees and alternative institutional arrangements, as well as the contemporary use of such procedures, suggests that these are institutions of majority control rather than devices for furthering distributive objectives of standing committees.

Overall, the theoretical arguments and empirical tests support the following thesis, whose specific components and more general implications are drawn out in chapter 7. Distributional concerns—whether in the classical sense of who gets what, when, and how, or in the contemporary sense of how legislators capture gains from trade—are undeniably a part of legislative politics. However, current distributive theories mischaracterize the key components of legislative politics in theoretically and empirically significant ways. In contrast, informational concerns—in the sense of how politicians can be provided with incentives to study public problems and formulate public policy—are at the heart of legislative organization. By implication, the uncertainties confronted by members of a majoritarian, collective choice body cannot be ignored when seeking a deeper and more accurate understanding of legislative politics.

---

30. Neither are the two classes of theories studied here nested in the sense that one predicts everything the other predicts, plus more.

CHAPTER 2

Distributive Theories of Legislative Organization

Senator Gravel:[1] *When _____ (a powerful senior Senator) has a project in here that he wants, that project carries an extra weight. It is a lot more than _____ (a very junior Senator's) project. If anyone in this Congress or in the media of this country is immature enough to think that this is not the case, then they shouldn't be, they are not mature enough to serve, in this Congress. So from my point of view, there is no reason why we shouldn't see those names so we know who is involved.*

Senator Buckley: So we know how to distribute the pork.

Senator Gravel: Not necessarily. To understand what we are doing politically, because it does offer political consequences. I think that is part of the maturity of being a political person.

—S.Rept. 93–615, 138

Congress is terrible, unbelievably bad, at logrolling and porkbarreling.

—Arthur Maass (1983, 69)

Distributive issues—whether economic, political, or ethical—always involve two questions. The first question is as explicit in distributive theories as it has been in modern political science literature at least since Lasswell (1936): Who gets what? The second question varies in explicitness: At whose expense? An intuitive overview of these themes is captured in a simple example.

EXAMPLE: Two money-lovers on a stroll simultaneously spot a dollar on the sidewalk. Both want the dollar and thus pick it up together. Each realizes

---

1. Chairman of the Water Resources Subcommittee of the Senate Committee on Public Works during a markup in which Buckley, a freshman, argued against the Senate practice of publishing names of senators alongside their proposed water projects. (Gravel's statement is edited, changing only the grammar.)

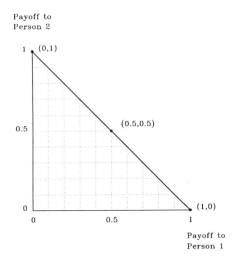

Fig. 2.1. Two-person divide-the-dollar example

that he or she lacks exclusive claim to the dollar, so the question of how to divide it arises. If they come to a mutual agreement, they have up to 100 cents to gain. Otherwise, neither gets anything.

The payoff space for this example is shown in figure 2.1. Three facets of the example are central to distributive theories of politics. First, it is a *collective choice* situation, since players must reach a decision (or fail to reach a decision) together. Second, there are *prospects for gains* from a collective agreement, since any number of attainable agreements would make both players better off, while failure to agree (e.g., by jointly grabbing the dollar, ripping, and destroying it) results in foregone benefits and zero payoffs. But third, in spite of the prospects for gains from collective choice, there is some *inescapable conflict* over who gains how much and at the other's expense. Indeed, conditional on a collective choice that exhausts the dollar—represented by the diagonal line in figure 2.1—interests are diametrically opposed. Along the maximum joint-payoff frontier, the game is zero-sum: any move that benefits one person necessarily comes at the direct expense of the other.

When focusing on legislative politics, distributive theories are remarkably similar to this simple divide-the-dollar example. Indeed they invariably capture some, and often all, of these features. Given some space of feasible outcomes, such as the gridded triangle in figure 2.1, legislators are assumed to have payoff functions that diminish with policy distance from legislators' ideal points on relevant dimensions. For instance, person 1's ideal point is (1,0);

person 2's is (0,1); and each person's payoff declines as a function of deviations from his or her ideal point.[2]

What are the origins of ideal points or legislators' preferences? Almost always, theories assume that the origins are electoral. Mayhew (1974, 1–9), for example, bases his arguments on the explicit assumption that members of Congress are single-minded seekers of reelection. Similarly, but with greater formality, Fiorina (1974, chap. 2) posits that legislators maximize electoral support, Shepsle and Weingast (1981a and 1984a) employ the assumption that legislators maximize net district benefits, and Cox and McCubbins (1989) assume that legislators maximize their probability of reelection. These assumptions, in turn, enable derivation of electorally induced preferences over a legislative policy space.

A wide range of empirical implications has been derived from distributive theories. These pertain to legislative organization (the origins and consequences of the committee system, leadership, parties, and rules and procedures), legislative behavior (constituency service, committee work, roll call voting, and legislative oversight), and legislative policy (the ultimate distributive properties of legislation itself, i.e., who gets what and at whose expense?). Of these, the policy implications of distributive theories have tended to attract the most attention. The single policy implication to which distributive theorists subscribe, at least implicitly, is that most politics is "clientilistic" in the sense of Wilson (1980, 369), and that most legislation is "particularistic" in the sense of Mayhew (1974, 53–55) or "distributive" in the sense of Lowi (1964, 690). In other words, legislation generally confers concentrated benefits to constituents (or districts) while broadly dispersing costs.[3] One key consequence of these distributive tendencies is the oversupply (in terms of economic efficiency) of policy benefits. Two leading distributive theorists summarize as follows:

> The transformation of economic costs into political benefits implies that the politically optimal scale [of policy outputs] is systematically larger

---

2. Different distributive theories make different assumptions about whether one legislator bears costs when others receive benefits. Although it seems most reasonable to assume that the distribution of benefits (e.g., dams, bridges) to one legislator costs others (e.g., through taxation), this is not always represented formally. If not, then the statement about monotonically declining utility with policy distance requires qualification. For instance, in figure 2.1, the relevant policy for person 1 is the horizontal axis; for person 2 the vertical axis.

3. Mayhew and Lowi sometimes question the cognizance of cost-bearers with regard to their burdens. For example, Lowi writes that distributive policies "are policies in which the indulged and the deprived, the loser and the recipient, need never come into direct confrontation. Indeed, in many instances of distributive policy, the deprived cannot as a class be identified,

than its economic counterpart. Expenditure policies are therefore biased so as to be larger than the economically efficient scale. The very label "pork barrel," deriving from the first major congressional expenditure program in the nineteenth century, the improvement of rivers and harbors, connotes economically unwarranted projects. This same tendency to overspend is present to some extent in all expenditure programs. (Shepsle and Weingast 1984b, 356)

Though subordinate in the above quotation, rivers and harbors legislation has played prominently in motivating, and serving as an empirical referent for, formal theories of distributive politics. Occasionally this is a source of suspicion. Arnold, for example, notes that "most of what we know about how Congress makes project decisions concerns the selection of water projects. The literature in this area is extensive, considering that less than one percent of the federal budget goes to water projects" (1981, 530). However, the contrast between the prevalence of rivers-and-harbors based models and the relative paucity of rivers and harbors legislation should not be overdrawn.[4] The key point is that distributive theories consistently presume that legislators' preferences are geographically based and therefore that legislative decision making provides opportunities for *gains from trade*. This concept is the single most salient theme in distributive theories and thus will be a recurrent theme in both the theoretical and empirical portions of this book.

In the policy game in a legislature like the U.S. Congress or a state legislature, to take a prominent example, there is an attitude of live and let live. Each legislative agent seeks to obtain benefits for his constituency and, even in failure, he can claim credit for having fought the good fight. Each agent behaves essentially this way and expects all others to behave similarly. Although there are some exceptions, the *general rule* does not impose sanctions on those who seek to place the distributive and regulatory powers of the state in the service of their constituents. *That's the system.* (Shepsle 1986a, 69; italics added)

Historical Overview

Beginning in the late 1970s, literature on legislative politics began to expand from informal descriptions to formal theories. Under the banner of New

---

because the most influential among them can be accommodated by further disaggregation of the stakes" (1964, 690), implying that the losers exist but are somehow anonymous.

4. For example, Arnold's statement ignores Shepsle and Weingast's claim that general-benefit legislation carries district-specific benefits, e.g., defense contracting.

Institutionalism,[5] research of positive political theorists exhibited a growing interest in identifying the institutional underpinnings of "the system" described above. The potential value of these efforts is enormous. Increasing explicitness about the rational foundations of legislative behavior can yield increasingly sharp predictions about legislative organization. Predictions, in turn, may be amenable to empirical tests. Empirical tests have been somewhat slow in coming, and it is precisely this lag that motivates chapters 4–6 of this book. To guide the empirical analysis, however, a more detailed theoretical overview is needed.

Many early formal theories admirably sought a more complete characterization of actual institutions and of strategic behavior within institutionally rich settings. Its primary stimulus was a body of literature that was neither descriptive nor institutional and whose abstract decision makers were utterly nonstrategic: namely, the theoretical research on the instability, thus unpredictability, of the majority preference relation.[6] Historically, formal theorists have taken theoretical results seriously that give conditions under which majority-rule outcomes may lie anywhere in an n-dimensional policy space. (Other catchphrases in this literature include "chaos theorems," "anything-can-happen results," and "generic instability of majority voting.") For example, a recent contribution begins:

> Even in the wake of the structure induced equilibrium revolution, the literature on the positive theory of legislatures remains under the spell of McKelvey and his colleagues. While proponents of the new approach have shown that under specialized assumptions, legislative rules lead to stability, floor behavior for most legislation in Congress is typically governed by an open rule, seemingly putting us back in the world of cycling and the absence of equilibrium. Because of the lack of restrictions under the open rule presumed by most models, this view appears to imply that anything can happen on the floor. (Weingast 1989a, 795)

In 1981, Gordon Tullock wrote a provocative essay that challenged the empirical relevance of chaos results by raising the question: "Why so much stability?" A spate of publications followed, most of which embraced the philosophical underpinnings of the New Institutionalism.[7] Now the chaos-

---

5. Other fields, such as international political economy, have different conceptions of what this term means. The definition used here is that literature falling within the structure-induced equilibrium tradition. See Shepsle 1986a, 1986b, and 1989 for reviews, and Grofman 1989 for a defense of a relatively narrow definition.

6. See, for example, Arrow 1951; McKelvey 1976; Plott 1967; and Schofield 1978.

7. The list for *Public Choice* alone includes Benson 1983; Dobra 1983; Enelow 1986; Hill 1985; Hoenack 1983; Koford 1982; McCubbins and Schwartz 1985; Niemi 1983; Ostrom 1986; Shepsle 1986b; Shepsle and Weingast 1981b; and Tullock 1981.

stability dialogue is over a decade old, and the position of New Institutionalists has itself exhibited admirable stability. In various ways, shapes, and
forms, the preponderance of this literature suggests that rules, procedures,
institutional arrangements, organizational forms, etc., constrain the outcomes
attainable under majority rule. In other words, institutions are theoretical
solutions to the chaos problem.[8]

This argument is plausible enough at a theoretical level, particularly if
one begins—as most formal theorists do—with the presumption that theoretical results on chaos pose problems worth solving. Along the path from theoretical discourse to empirical implications, however, some scientifically
sticky issues emerge.

The first of two related problems is a subtle reversion to functionalism.
The history of thought on the causes of institutional arrangements can be
summarized as follows. As of 1976, when the spell of McKelvey and his
colleagues was cast, formal models of collective choice suggested that majority rule was inherently unstable. However, observed outcomes from majoritarian collective choice bodies are stable. Formal theorists therefore asked
what modeling adjustments could be made to yield stable outcomes and came
up with an answer: incorporate institutions.[9] The ensuing research shared the
theme that institutions constrain outcomes or, alternatively, that structures
induce equilibria. Functionalism creeps in when this standard argument is
taken one step farther. Aldrich, for example, writes:

> I take the basic theoretical thrust of the new institutionalism to be a
> search for coherence in a general institutional setting, a simple majority
> rule setting, where there is no guarantee that there is any. I take it even
> further by believing that politicians themselves are aware of the possibil-
> ity of incoherence, even chaos, under undifferentiated simple majority
> rule. I take it, that is, that politicians created such institutional devices as

---

8. Two exceptions to this generalization and a key definitional issue should be noted.
Niemi's 1983 argument is unique in that it is more preference based than institution based, while
Ordeshook and Schwartz 1987 attempt to resurrect the "anything-can-happen" result in an institutional context. In New Institutionalism studies more broadly, "institution" is rarely defined
explicitly, and sometimes it is explicitly undefined (Shepsle 1986a, 66). As a theoretical matter,
however, what New Institutionalists call institutions are always *binding constraints on behavior*
in the (more-or-less) formal choice setting under analysis. For example, a "rule" that bans
proposals to a committee's bill on the floor is an "institution" or "structure" because it constrains
behavior.

9. Shepsle (1979) popularized this answer. A more complete intellectual history, however,
would show that Kramer's (1972) paper on "Sophisticated Voting over Multidimensional Choice
Spaces" contains solution concepts and results very much like Shepsle's, even though Kramer did
not employ institutionalist language, and his analysis, unlike Shepsle's, presumed sophisticated
behavior.

political parties, committees, and rules of order to impose some coherence, sensing—perhaps even knowing—of the chaos that can ensue in their absence. (1988, 26)

Similarly, Ferejohn's account of agricultural policy-making concludes: "The endemic instability of logrolls induced members to invent institutions that embody and stabilize agreements" (1986, 252).

That institutions arise because they induce stability is intuitive. However, its functionalism is ironic in light of the intellectual history of legislative studies more broadly. Most formal theorists are self-proclaimed positivists whose relatively rigorous deductive methods were to have been improvements over the more inductive methods of behavioralists. Likewise, the methods of behavioralists were to have improved upon those of functionalists whose methods had come to be regarded as unscientific.

While functionalism can be found in some of this research it is not a universal trait, and when it surfaces it tends to be inconspicuous. In contrast, formal theorists of legislatures have been consistently and conspicuously infatuated with the chaos problem. Since the aim of this book is primarily empirical, it is not necessary to enter into deep theoretical discussions about chaos here. It is only necessary to ask whether the problem is empirically significant and, if so, whether formal theories can hope to resolve it. I have two responses. The first response borders on "inside baseball" and—to be frank—is inconsequential for the remainder of the chapter. The second response comes to the essential point.

First, regardless of whether or not the abstract property of global cycling has widespread empirical manifestations, New Institutionalism approaches seem to be questionable theoretical tools for yielding testable insights about legislative organization. On one hand, if cycling is more of a theoretical puzzle than an empirical problem, then this research program is clearly more of a theoretical than empirical enterprise. On the other hand, even if cycling is a genuine empirical problem, then existing New Institutionalism theories seem hard pressed to solve the problem in a logically complete and consistent way if the Majoritarian Postulate is operable at the level of procedural choice as well as policy choice. The reasoning here is simply an adaptation of Riker's (1980) inheritability argument. If legislators cannot agree on stable policies, how can they be expected to agree on stable institutional forms (procedures) that are implicitly associated with those very policies on which they cannot agree?

Second, although issues such as these have been debated a lot, they are not likely to be resolved convincingly by the kind of abstract discourse in much of the theoretical literature and in the previous paragraph. However, they might be resolved by extracting predictions from the relevant theories and subjecting them to evidence. If so, then it suffices only to touch on chaos issues en route to empirical implications. In this spirit, the remainder of the chapter steers toward empirical implications and away from the chaos problem whenever possible. The consistent objective throughout this chapter and the remainder of the book is to take distributive theories seriously as sources of empirical predictions, even though their formal arguments may at times seem questionable.

Three Distributive Views of Legislative Organization

The term *distributive* can be used in two slightly different but not incompatible ways. The first and relatively narrow meaning is simply *pork barrel politics*. Distributive politics in this sense involves policies that confer concentrated benefits to a few but disperse the unavoidable costs of such policies to many. Often these policies have geographically concentrated effects as well, as in the case of rivers and harbors projects. The second, and somewhat broader, meaning of distributive politics concerns policies that determine *who gets what, and at whose expense.* Rather than the concentration versus dispersion of costs and benefits, the two central features in this conception are scarcity and conflict. Political benefits are not in infinite supply, and political actors have competing preferences. The process of collective choice under these conditions is, therefore, inescapably a process of distribution. With only so much to go around—i.e., to distribute—it soon becomes inevitable that whenever someone gains, someone else loses.[10] In short, by either definition, the concept (like the theories to be discussed) lacks a common-good component.[11]

A comprehensive review of distributive theories is a painstaking undertaking and, for present purposes, an unnecessary one. All that is necessary is to review in moderate detail a representative sample of research that has distributive origins to see how theorists have chosen to work with and depart from early types of distributive theory. Three such works are discussed below. First is an essay by the founding father of the New Institutionalism, Kenneth

---

10. The reason for the qualification ("it soon becomes inevitable") is that it is theoretically possible to characterize situations in which everyone can be made better off by a policy change (specifically, and by definition, in the case of an initial, non-Pareto policy). But this is a mild qualification for two reasons. First, such policies seem quite unnatural. Second, if and when they exist, and given conflict of interest, actors will agree only that a move is desirable; they will not agree on what move is desirable. Thus, in reaching their collective decision, distributive issues (in the broader sense of the term) inevitably set in.

11. Notice that this broader conception subsumes other types in others' typologies. For example, Lowi's "redistributive" and "regulatory" politics are distributive in this sense of the

Shepsle. Second is an article by Barry Weingast and William Marshall that builds jointly on New Institutionalism research and concepts from economic research on industrial organization. Third is a pair of papers—one by David Baron and John Ferejohn, the other by Baron—that break more sharply from the formal techniques of New Institutionalism but are nonetheless distributive. Confining attention to these works serves several purposes. It provides an overview of formal theorists' thinking about legislative organization. It illustrates different ways in which distributive theories have sought to cope with functionalistic tendencies and chaos problems. It points to some emerging disagreements, in spite of the common distributive base from which these (and other) scholars work. It sharpens the focus on legislative organization not only as a crucial determinant of policy choice but, eventually, as a phenomenon requiring a causal explanation itself. And, most important, it affords an opportunity to highlight empirical implications that can be compared, contrasted, and tested.

The New Institutionalism Perspective

As the New Institutionalism movement enters its second decade, one strategy for summarizing the insights and contributions of the movement is to review some recent work by Kenneth Shepsle. Since his pathbreaking study in 1979, Shepsle has been a prolific proponent of formal theory as a means for understanding legislative politics, and his contributions include several review essays (1986a, 1986b, and 1989). Of these, the study that is representative of the work as a whole, yet most explicit about institutions as possible objects of choice (i.e., as endogenous), is the 1986 essay "Institutional Equilibrium and Equilibrium Institutions."

The essay begins with a discussion of the chaos "crisis in formal political theory" and a claim that "the crisis has not yet passed, but surely it is passing as formal theorists devise and discover new ways to reason about the problem of voting instability" (Shepsle 1986a, 51). Thereafter, the essay is divided into two parts. The first part, "Institutional Equilibrium," chronicles the development of New Institutionalism studies in the structure-induced equilibrium (SIE) tradition. The second part, "Equilibrium Institutions," contains several new ideas about the evolution or choice of legislative institutions. I will briefly sketch the institutional-equilibrium argument[12] and focus on the equilibrium-institutions arguments, of which the latter are more closely related to this book.

---

term. So are Wilson's "majoritarian" and "interest-group" politics. What, then, is ruled out? The prospect of passing policies that make everyone better off. I elaborate in chapter 3.

12. Several reviews exist elsewhere (Shepsle 1986a and 1986b; Krehbiel 1987a and 1988).

Institutional Equilibrium

The theoretical issues under the rubric "institutional equilibrium" are precisely those summarized above. What binding constraints on behavior ("institutions") can be incorporated formally into spatial models to generate stable outcomes ("structure-induced equilibria")? In legislative settings, the answers invariably center on committees and rules. Shepsle summarizes what he showed in his earlier work: that if a policy space is divided and delegated to subsets of legislators (committees), and if those members are given special rights, such as "gatekeeping powers" or "closed rules," then final decisions by the full legislature will not be chaotic. The inference is that such forms of legislative organization account for the stability of outcomes, which is the essence of "institutional equilibrium."

Equilibrium Institutions

Shepsle is clearly aware of, and on occasion seems to subscribe to, the Majoritarian Postulate as it relates to procedural choice. For instance, in a more recent but very similar work he writes:

> The research program spawned by this idea [SIEs], however, leaves an important unfinished aspect. Institutional arrangements are taken as exogenous. With this approach we don't know *why* the collectivity goes about its business in some particular way. The structure-induced equilibrium approach elaborates the temporally subsequent effects of structure and procedure while ignoring temporally prior causes. It is my view that one cannot understand or explain institutions, however, without first explicating their effects. So it is quite proper to examine effects first. But the rational choice of institutions remains a challenge. (Shepsle 1989, 137–38)

The issue addressed in the second part of the 1986 essay is whether we can reason in parallel fashion about *policy choice* on the one hand and *institutional (procedural) choice* on the other. Shepsle's contention is that we cannot.

Again, the motivation for the discussion is the chaos problem: more specifically, Riker's argument that the generic instability of policy choice ought eventually to back into (or be "inherited" by) the institutional choice process, making that process unstable as well. Shepsle responds by attempting "to drive a wedge between choice of policy and choice of institutional arrangements, suggesting that the latter is not an instance of the former" (Shepsle 1986a, 69).

Surprisingly, the key ingredient in Shepsle's hypothesized wedge is uncertainty.[13] The argument is that efforts to change rules are risky, and such

---

13. This is surprising for two reasons. First, there are few explicitly SIE models that are not perfect information models (see, however, Denzau and Mackay 1983). Second, elsewhere Shep-

risks serve to buffer institutional choice from the presumably inherent in-
stabilities of policy choice. The supporting datum is from the U.S. House.

> Could turn-of-the-century progressive legislator George Norris anticipate
> no sanctions if he tried but failed to reduce the powers of Speaker Joseph
> Cannon? I hardly think so. It is risky to try to change institutional
> arrangements in a manner adverse to the interests of those currently in
> control. Failure has its consequences so that anyone initiating such at-
> tempts at change must weigh the expected benefits of success against the
> certainty of sanctions if he fails. In short, even though some legislative
> majority might prefer arrangement p to the existing arrangement q,
> efforts to promote p will be damped by the risks of failure. These risks
> would seem not to play nearly so prominent a role in the politics of
> ordinary policy. (Shepsle 1986a, 69–70)

The logic resembles the adage: a bird in the hand is worth two in the
bush. Legislators may not be happy with their existing institution's equilibrium (that is, the outcome associated with the existing organizational form
or, figuratively, the bird-in-hand). But given their incomplete information
about alternative institutions' equilibria (the birds-in-bush), they are inclined
to hold on to what they have.

Implications
This thesis about the stickiness of institutions has interesting implications for
the future of theoretical research in which the chaos problem looms large. In
one respect the notion of a chaos buffer between policy choice and institutional choice nullifies the significance of Shepsle's problem of "equilibrium
institutions" or, equivalently, Riker's problem of "inheritability." If, as argued, chaos does not back into the domain of institutional choice, then theorizing about legislative politics as a process in which institutions are given
(i.e., exogenous) is acceptable after all. One needs only to characterize the
institutions that exist and then to theorize—not to worry about institutions as
objects of choice. This is essentially what New Institutionalism research has
done historically. However, this approach plainly contradicts the procedural
portion of the Majoritarian Postulate, since in this approach institutions are
not treated as objects of majoritarian choice.

In terms of the Uncertainty Postulate, the implications of Shepsle's hypothesized wedge between policy choice and institutional choice are mixed.
On one hand the argument rests on uncertainty. On the other hand the argument implicitly presumes that legislators, through SIE reasoning, know with
certainty the equilibrium outcome of their current institutional arrangement.

sle (with Weingast) has questioned the significance of incomplete information models and warned
of their "extremely delicate, fragile, and specialized" results (Shepsle and Weingast 1987b, 939).

This is tantamount to perfect information in the domain of policy choice and, therefore, contrary to the Uncertainty Postulate as stated in chapter 1.

Finally, while Shepsle does not present any explicit predictions about legislative organization, he regularly and approvingly refers to the research of Weingast and Marshall, who do provide explicit predictions and to whose work I turn momentarily. In transition, it should be stressed that Shepsle's perspective on legislative organization (or "equilibrium institutions") is overtly distributive.

> Legislators . . . have differential concerns. Some care principally about one bundle of policy dimensions while others are mostly concerned about some different bundle. These differences in salience suggest the possibility of gains from trade, each group trading off influence in one area in exchange for disproportionate influence in the other. (Shepsle 1986a, 73)

An Industrial Organization Perspective

Weingast and Marshall's "The Industrial Organization of Congress" (1988) makes a significant step toward studying legislative organization as a phenomenon worth explaining in its own right and thus fits squarely within the topic of this book. It also provides a clearly distributive perspective on legislative organization and thus fits squarely within the topic of this chapter.

Objective and Assumptions
Weingast and Marshall's objective is "to explain the pattern of institutions within the legislature that facilitates decision making" (1988, 133). The assumptions and informal style of argumentation are in the tradition of Mayhew, whose well-worn quotation is used to introduce the article.

> The organization of Congress meets remarkably well the electoral needs of its members. To put it another way, if a group of planners sat down and tried to design a pair of American national assemblies with the goal of serving members' electoral needs year in and year out, they would be hard pressed to improve on what exists. (Mayhew 1974, 81)

Weingast and Marshall seek to elaborate on both the characteristics and causes of this finely tuned institution. Their argument begins with three assumptions:

- Congressmen represent the "politically relevant" portion of their constituencies.
- Parties do not constrain legislators' behavior.
- Legislation requires a majority of votes for passage.

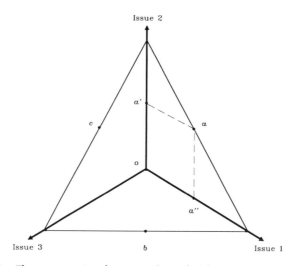

Fig. 2.2. Three-person (or three-committee) legislature with pork barrel preferences

The main consequence of these is a set of policy objectives of legislators that interchangeably can be called *particularistic, pork barrel,* or *distributive preferences.* Characterization of legislators' preferences is central to all distributive theories, and therefore requires special attention and illustration.

The key to Weingast and Marshall's distributive characterization of legislative decision making is their first assumption, and especially its qualifying clause: "politically relevant." Essentially, the electoral connection makes it inevitable that some constituents care more about some issues than do other constituents. Thus, intensely interested constituents have relatively large incentives to vote for, make campaign contributions to, and lobby in attempts to influence, their congressmen. This, in Weingast and Marshall's terms, is exactly what makes these constituents "politically relevant" to their re-election-seeking legislator. In turn, the goals or preferences that are induced on the legislator by the electoral connection are to pursue the interests of these intense, highly participatory, high-demand, special-interest groups.[14]

Translation of this verbal argument into conventional spatial preferences is straightforward and illustrates clearly the main institutional design problem that Weingast and Marshall address. In very much the manner of the two-person divide-the-dollar example given above, figure 2.2 shows pork barrel preferences in three dimensions for three legislators. Constituencies differ, so different constituencies have different "politically relevant" groups who pursue different interests. In the simplest three-dimensional case of figure 2.2,

---

14. On explicit derivation of induced preferences of this sort, see Shepsle and Weingast 1981a and 1984a.

the three legislators represent three significantly different constituencies and are high-demanders on three different dimensions of the policy space.

The essential feature of pork barrel preferences is not that legislators care about one and only one dimension of the policy space, as in this pure example.[15] Rather, it is that, given majority voting, any configuration of pork barrel preferences has the property that there are no natural majorities for any individual policy. In other words, "Legislators pursue their reelection goals by attempting to provide benefits to their constituents (assumption 1). Acting alone, they cannot succeed (assumption 3)" (Weingast and Marshall 1988, 137). Figure 2.2 illustrates the argument. Acting in isolation, legislators 1 and 2 would oppose a high-demand proposal by legislator 3 on policy 3. Legislators 2 and 3 would oppose a high-demand proposal by legislator 1 on policy 1. And so on.

Finally, an implicit but necessary assumption in Weingast and Marshall's theory is that legislators would very much like to logroll. For example, by assumption legislators 1 and 2 prefer a legislative outcome in which each gets something (e.g., point *a*) to one in which neither gets anything (the origin, *o*, of the space). Likewise for legislators 1 and 3 and point *b*, legislators 2 and 3 and point *c*, and legislators 1, 2, and 3 and "universalistic" outcomes in which all three are recipients of particularistic policies.

In total, the assumptions about preferences are in perfect accord with the overview of distributive theory given above. They guarantee the existence of opportunities for gains from trade in legislative settings.

The Enforcement Problem

Weingast and Marshall's creative fusion of pork barrel preferences with industrial organization economics makes it natural to think of a legislature as a market-like organization in which—although votes are not explicitly bought and sold with money—trades nevertheless occur through policy barter. Indeed, the concept of trading is so central to this theory that Weingast and Marshall use the terms *policy* and *bargain* interchangeably.[16] This brings us within one short step of their focal problem in legislative settings. Gains from trade cannot be obtained because of a ubiquitous "enforcement problem." Logrolls are desired by legislators, given their pork barrel preferences. However, if and when proposed, a package of particularistic policies can always be picked apart by low-demand majorities. In other words, incentives to renege on policy bargains are omnipresent.

---

15. This strict assumption could be relaxed, for instance, by allowing ideal points to be pulled away from the axes somewhat.

16. For example, "The types of policies (i.e., legislative bargains) that emerge from this theory parallel those predicted by the vote-trading models . . ." (Weingast and Marshall 1988, 134).

Inadequate Solutions

Of course, incentives to renege on agreements occur in many economic settings as well (although in most economic settings reneging does not entail a majority vote). Thus, one might speculate that either a market arrangement or some contractual arrangements might suffice as remedies for the gains-from-trade problem. Weingast and Marshall dispute this. They do not explicitly incorporate any of the obstacles to contractual solutions to the gains-from-trade problem (e.g., transaction costs, moral hazard, asymmetric information, or unforeseen contingencies), but they do discuss the economic literature on contracting and the theory of the firm. Reviewed briefly in a legislative context, these standard industrial organization problems are asserted to be legislatively insurmountable. Similarly, Weingast and Marshall discuss but do not formally analyze the role of reputations or repeated play in achieving gains from trade. However, they conclude that reputations through repeated play cannot solve the basic gains-from-trade problem.

The Proposed Solution

If not markets, contracts, or reputations, then what is an effective way for a legislature to capture gains from trade? Weingast and Marshall's reasoning treads a unique, industrial organization path, but their destination looks a great deal like most New Institutionalism theories. In particular, the solution is "an idealized legislative committee system" with three components that Weingast and Marshall call a *jurisdictional system,* a *seniority system,* and a *bidding mechanism* for committee seats.

The jurisdictional system includes several assumptions that are common in earlier formal theories. Each committee is given exclusive rights over a policy area. (In spatial models, a jurisdiction is defined as a dimension or set of dimensions in a multidimensional policy space). A committee has a "monopoly right to bring alternatives to the status quo up for a vote before the legislature." Thus, if a majority on a committee chooses not to propose a change, then the legislature has no recourse: the policy persists. In this respect a committee not only has a unique jurisdiction, it also has absolute gatekeeping powers within that jurisdiction.

The seniority system is characterized as "a property rights system over committee seats" in which a member cannot be forced off a committee against his will, cannot sell or trade his committee slot, and cannot be denied the chairmanship if he accumulates the committee's maximum continuous service.

The bidding mechanism for filling vacant committee seats is not explicitly defined but, in effect, means that over an extended period committee assignments are governed by "self-selection" (Weingast and Marshall 1988, 145–46).

Enforcement Properties

Weingast and Marshall's "committee system" is then assessed in terms of its ability to solve the gains-from-trade problem. Given some bargain,[17] the incentives to renege persist: such incentives are inherent properties of pork barrel preferences. However, due to the assignment of parliamentary rights in the committee system, the opportunities to act on such incentives do not exist.

For instance, reconsider figure 2.2. Suppose legislators 1, 2, and 3 are now high-demand committees in Weingast and Marshall's committee system. Suppose further that in the past a trade had been arranged in which committees 1 and 2 agreed to capture the gains from the simple-majority logrolling outcome *a*. Does a majoritarian incentive to nullify this deal cease to exist upon the passage of *a*? No.[18] Committees 2 and 3, for example, would like to change the policy to point *a'*. Committees 1 and 3 would like to change the policy to point *a''*. However, the relevant question is not about behavioral incentives (preferences) but rather behavioral opportunities (institutions). Specifically, does the assignment of parliamentary rights provide an opportunity for reneging? It does not. Committee 1, as a gatekeeper, can block any and all changes in its jurisdiction (the center-to-southeast axis). Committee 2, as a gatekeeper, can block any and all changes in its jurisdiction (the vertical axis).

In summary, the distinctly institutional solution to the gains-from-trade problem is to assign parliamentary rights selectively to committees which, because a "bidding mechanism" determines their composition, are high-demanders on behalf of their politically relevant constituencies.

Propositions

The industrial organization theory yields three propositions about legislative organization. Weingast and Marshall state these explicitly and explore them briefly using mostly secondary sources.[19]

- "The assignment process operates as a self-selection mechanism.
- Committees are not representative of the entire legislature but are composed of 'preference outliers,' or those who value the position most highly.

---

17. Weingast and Marshall are much more explicit about the issue of enforcing trades once arranged than about reaching the initial agreements. In this respect, the theory is probably best viewed as one that focuses more on the maintenance of particularistic policies than on their initiation.

18. The example presumes that nonrecipients of a policy bear some costs for the policy, e.g., tax revenues needed to implement it, negative externalities, etc.

19. Reservations may be expressed regarding whether these propositions can be derived from the three stated assumptions. However, in keeping with my previously stated objective, the predictions will be taken seriously and carried through the empirical chapters.

- Most centrally, committee members receive the disproportionate share of the benefits from programs within their jurisdiction" (Weingast and Marshall 1988, 148–49).

Summary

As a theory of legislative organization, "The Industrial Organization of Congress" has four features worth underscoring for purposes of this book.

First, its premise is unquestionably distributive: legislators seek to capture gains from trade, and the legislative organization reflects this objective. Both as a practical matter and under the assumptions of the theory, this gains-from-trade pursuit is one in which the relevant performance criterion is the degree to which policy outcomes are particularistic—catering, of course, to high-demanders. That is, a rationally designed legislature is one that facilitates the choice of policies that confer concentrated benefits to constituents while spreading costs broadly. "Who gets what?" is the primary question; "At whose expense?" is tertiary; and final policy outcomes—in apparent contrast to Weingast and Marshall's assumption 3 and the Majoritarian Postulate—are not majoritarian. That is, policy by policy (spatially, dimension by dimension) a majority always exists that would like to reduce the level of particularistic benefits.

Second, due to Weingast and Marshall's subtle shift in characterization of the legislative design problem as one of adopting institutions to solve an enforcement problem (rather than a chaos problem), their distributive theory addresses issues of legislative organization more directly than earlier theories in the distributive tradition.[20]

Third, functionalism does enter into the thesis implicitly. Broadly construed, Weingast and Marshall's argument is of this form. A gains-from-trade problem exists. Markets cannot solve it. Reputations cannot solve it. Institutions can solve it. Thus, institutions exist in order to capture gains from trade.

But finally, neither the functionalism nor chaos undertones are overly distracting because Weingast and Marshall offer three important and refutable propositions.[21] If further empirical analysis is supportive of the predictions, we surely should view this perceptive and influential theory as offering a viable, distributive explanation for observed forms of legislative organization.

---

20. The enforcement problem and majority-rule instability are still closely related, however. In the spatial setting, for example, Weingast and Marshall's enforcement problem clearly exists because logrolling policies are (potentially) unstable under institution-free majority rule. (I say "potentially" with the benefit of hindsight captured from Baron and Ferejohn 1989a, to be summarized below.)

21. A fourth proposition pertaining to the use of rules is contained in the text but not listed with the three. It is discussed below and tested in chap. 5.

Game-Theoretic Perspectives

Shepsle's reflections on "equilibrium institutions" remained consistently close to his conception of New Institutionalism and attempted a head-on attack of the chaos problem. Weingast and Marshall began from a somewhat different distributive perspective, reached an essentially New Institutionalist solution to the gains-from-trade problem, but flirted a bit with chaos and functionalism along the way. In the final pair of distributive theories to be reviewed, Baron and Ferejohn break more sharply from prior distributive theories by formally analyzing fully specified games of bargaining in legislatures. This discussion focuses on the predictions of some recent game theories, highlighting their implications for the choice of rules governing the amendment process in legislative settings.[22]

Positive-Sum Legislative Bargaining

Baron and Ferejohn's article "Bargaining in Legislatures" (1989a) is an excellent example of comparative institutional analysis. In the spirit of the New Institutionalism, the presumption is that institutions bear on policy choice and thus have potentially important implications for legislative organization. The n-person legislature that is analyzed is one of quintessential distributive politics. The legislature is assigned the task of dividing a dollar via simple majority-rule voting. As in the introductory example in this chapter, players are in complete disagreement with regard to how the dollar is to be divided. But while each player wants to maximize his or her shares, players are indifferent about changes in other players' shares, holding their own share constant. That is, the question "At whose expense?" does not arise.

Players are assumed to know each other's preferences and the rules of the game. Thus, the theory is one of complete information in terms of preferences and rules. However, uncertainty plays a role in the theory in the form of a "random recognition rule." In particular, when players commence decision making, they do not know who will be called upon to offer a proposal. Formally, a proposal is simply a statement of how much of the dollar will be distributed to each player.

The game may be played over extended periods or "sessions," and legislators may be "impatient" in the sense of preferring a fixed portion of the dollar in the current session to an identical portion in a later session. An equilibrium strategy configuration in the bargaining game is a complete prescription for all legislators of which motion to make upon recognition and how to vote when any possible motion is put to a vote. The equilibrium concept requires that at every stage that may be reached in the course of play,

---

22. The first part of the discussion is an abbreviated and nontechnical version of that found in Krehbiel 1988.

it is in the interest of each legislator to adopt the specified strategy. Thus, the theory is noncooperative.

A "closed rule" is defined as a game form in which a randomly recognized player offers a proposal that is promptly (i.e., without amendment) voted up or down by the legislature. If a majority votes yes, the game ends and payoffs are awarded. Otherwise, the session ends, the dollar shrinks to reflect legislators' impatience, and a new session begins. Theoretically, this process may be repeated infinitely.

A "simple open rule" allows an unlimited number of proposals to be considered. First a player is recognized to make a proposal. Then another player is recognized who either amends the original proposal or moves the previous question, bringing the initial proposal to a vote. If a proposal passes, the game ends. Otherwise, the dollar shrinks and the game continues into the next session.

Equilibria are identified for open and closed rules, and several interesting comparisons follow. The key empirical insights can be extracted from two parallel sets of findings for the two rules. The closed rule equilibrium has these properties:

- The legislature always comes to an agreement in the first session, so all of the gains from exchange are captured.
- The proposer reaps highly disproportionate benefits.
- The number of recipients of positive benefits is a bare majority or minimal winning coalition.

The open rule equilibrium has these properties:

- The legislature may not reach a decision in the first session, so it may not capture all gains from exchange.
- The proposer receives disproportionate benefits, though less than he or she would receive under the closed rule.
- Numbers of recipients of positive benefits may exceed a bare majority, but for most parameters values fall substantially short of a universalistic coalition.[23]

Thus, comparative analysis of open and closed rules reveals that expected payoffs under closed rules are greater than those for open rules in this distributive setting. The implication for a legislature's choice of rules is that closed rules (or, more realistically, restrictive rules) will be selected on distributive legislation.

---

23. The parameters in this case are the discount rate and the size of the legislature.

Distributive Efficiency of Legislative Bargaining

In "Majoritarian Incentives, Pork Barrel Programs, and Procedural Control," Baron (1990) sharpens the focus on choice of rules for distributive policy-making. Baron's model adopts all the basic features of Baron and Ferejohn's divide-the-dollar model with the chief exception that legislators' utility is defined over taxes (costs) as well as policy benefits. The empirical justification is obvious: pork barrel programs must be funded, and taxation imposes electoral costs, just as distributive policies confer electoral benefits. Baron also avoids several questionable assumptions of other pork barrel theories. First, no presumption is made that aggregate benefits exceed aggregate costs (an assumption that ironically rules out the prospect of classical, i.e., inefficient, pork barrel projects).[24] Second, no ad hoc distinction is made between political and economic costs and benefits.[25] Third, the characterization of preferences does not presume an illusion in the electorate about costs and benefits associated with policies. Finally, unless stated otherwise (as in the closed rule analysis), the model does not impose procedural restrictions on legislators.[26] The significance of these alterations in assumptions is apparent in Baron's distinctly different results.

First, equilibria are identified in which coalition sizes are rarely larger than minimal winning and always smaller than universalistic.[27] Second, distributively inefficient programs—that is, a set of pork barrel projects whose aggregate costs exceed their aggregate benefits—can indeed be passed by a majority without a presumption that political costs and benefits are different from economic ones, or that the electorate suffers from fiscal illusion, or that restrictive procedures institutionalize inefficiency. Third, Baron identifies a distributive rationale for open rules, in contrast to the New Institutionalism theories that posit procedural restrictions and in contrast to Baron and Ferejohn's model. In particular, relative to the use of closed rules to consider a committee's distributive legislation, open rules not only restrain committee power (here, disproportionate distributive benefits to the proposer) but may also limit the inefficiency of the pork barrel.

Predictions of Distributive Theories

Most of the discussion thus far has been conducted at an abstract level. While theoretical issues are important, to become consumed by them would be

---

24. Cf. Shepsle and Weingast 1981a; Weingast 1979; and Weingast, Shepsle, and Johnsen 1981.

25. Cf. Shepsle and Weingast 1981a; and Weingast, Shepsle, and Johnsen 1981.

26. Cf. Fiorina 1981; and Krehbiel 1989.

27. This result is similar to Baron and Ferejohn's (1989a) but different from all prior distributive theories.

contrary to the broader purpose of the book, which is to rely on data to resolve theoretical disputes. Needed, then, is a concise set of concrete predictions. The list that follows, while not exhaustive, is broadly representative of the empirical implications from extant distributive theories.

Committee Selection and Composition

> PREDICTION 1: FORMATION OF COMMITTEES. *To facilitate gains from trade, committee assignments will be governed by self-selection, and committees will be composed of homogeneous high demanders or preference outliers.*

In many instances this is an assumption in distributive theories, but Weingast and Marshall's industrial organization perspective provides a rationale for, if not prediction of, self-selection and preference outliers. In either case, these are necessary conditions for the substantive policy implications that most distributive theories stress. Weingast and Marshall's third proposition, for example, is that "committee members receive the disproportionate share of the benefits from programs within their jurisdiction" (1988, 149). This is inextricably related to their first and second propositions concerning self-selection and outliers, respectively. Similarly, Shepsle and Weingast (1987a) propose a theory of "committee power" in which standing committees obtain distributive benefits in excess of what noncommittee members prefer. This could not happen unless committee preferences diverged from floor preferences in the manner assumed in Shepsle and Weingast's theory and implied by Weingast and Marshall's. Therefore, although this implication is a prediction about the early stages of the legislative process, its truth is essential in the derivation of the policy implications commonly associated with distributive theories.

Rules

Differences within the class of distributive theories are greatest with respect to parliamentary rights granted to committees and the rules governing amendments to their bills on the floor. Therefore, this set of predictions is theory-specific.

> PREDICTION 2A: PROCEDURAL RIGHTS GENERALLY. *To enforce gains from trade, standing committees—particularly those whose jurisdictions include highly particularistic policies—will be granted favored procedural status throughout the process.*

PREDICTION 2B: RESTRICTIVE RULES. *To hasten agreement, closed rules will be used on highly distributive legislation.*

PREDICTION 2C: UNRESTRICTIVE RULES. *To minimize distributive inefficiency, open rules will be used on distributive legislation.*

The first implication is invariably an assumption in New Institutionalism models, although the forms of procedural protection exogenously given to committees are increasingly diverse. To date, these include gatekeeping powers,[28] closed rules,[29] modified rules,[30] ex post vetoes in conference,[31] and a guaranteed (i.e., commitment to) up or down vote on conference reports.[32] While these are assumptions in many theories, Weingast and Marshall provide a distributive rationale for this kind of arrangement, too. Restrictive procedures are seen as devices for sealing bargains where reputations, for instance, are insufficient. To the degree that incentives to renege on deals are greatest in distributive arenas, the hypothesized connection between rules and distributive legislation follows.

The second prediction follows clearly from Baron and Ferejohn's article. Because the equilibrium under the closed rule has the property that a decision is always reached in the first period, legislators never incur costs from delay, as is sometimes the case under the open rule.

The third prediction follows from Baron's model in which costs of pork barrel programs are borne by all legislators. In this model the closed rule has the undesirable property of allowing a wider range of inefficient pork barrel projects to pass than could be supported as equilibria under an open rule.

Commitment

PREDICTION 3: PROCEDURAL COMMITMENT. *To reliably capture gains from trade, legislatures will commit to institutional arrangements that confer benefits to distributive high demanders.*

The term *commitment* has a special meaning in formal theories and is especially important in the context of theories of legislative organization in which procedures are determined endogenously. A legislature is assumed to commit

---

28. See Denzau and Mackay 1983; Krehbiel 1985; and Shepsle and Weingast 1981b.

29. See Denzau and Mackay 1983; and Weingast and Moran 1983.

30. See Gilligan and Krehbiel 1988. See also Weingast 1989a for an analysis of a variety of rules under the rubric of "the open rule." In Weingast's theory, committee members have amendment rights not available to noncommittee members, so in this regard the rules may be more aptly regarded as modified.

31. See Shepsle and Weingast 1987a.

32. See Shepsle and Weingast 1987a.

to an institutional arrangement (such as Weingast and Marshall's "committee system" or Baron and Ferejohn's "closed rule") if legislators are formally denied an opportunity to change the arrangement subsequent to its adoption and irrespective of intervening behavior. For example, commitment to a closed rule for consideration of a committee's bill means that no matter how extreme the committee's proposal, legislators may not amend it; they may only vote it up or down. Procedural commitment is a general feature of distributive theories. As with committee composition, the theoretical status of institutional features is not the same in all theories. In New Institutionalism theories, commitment exists by virtue of the fact that institutions are exogenous. In Weingast and Marshall's industrial organization theory, however, commitment to their "committee system" is more aptly viewed as a result or derivation from their assumptions. Finally, in Baron and Ferejohn's and Baron's research, comparable analysis of open and closed rules yields straightforward derivation of ex ante procedural preferences of legislators. Because these, in turn, are readily amenable to predictions about choice of rules, the analytic step from these models to one in which rules are endogenous is a short one. Nonetheless, when this step is taken, the implicit presumption is that a rule once chosen cannot be rescinded or substituted later in the process depending on the initial proposal.

Procedural commitment, then, is a universal feature of extant distributive theories. Also universal is the rationale for commitment in such theories: to secure gains from trade.

Summary

Table 2.1 provides a summary of the distributive theories reviewed in this chapter. Columns on the table correspond with the three types of distributive theory on which the chapter has focused: New Institutionalism, industrial organization (with some New Institutionalism features), and game theories. Rows list areas in which the theories either make key assumptions or have observable implications. An (A) or (I) denotes whether the entry is an assumption or implication, respectively, in the given theory. Finally, the theories are evaluated in terms of their conformity with the Majoritarian and Uncertainty Postulates of legislative organization as introduced in chapter 1.

New Institutionalism

As indicated above, New Institutionalism theories te to assume much of what the industrial organization theory derives, such as homogeneous high-demanders on committees and strong forms of delegation of parliamentary rights to committees. Another way of stating this tendency is simply to note that New Institutionalists—in spite of their interest in the origins as well as consequences of institutions—invariably characterize rules, procedures, committee systems, etc., as being outside the domain of legislative choice. Some analysis of the comparative consequences of amendment rules has been conducted, but few predictions have emerged about bill-specific procedural choice. Be that as it may, the theories do have interesting policy implications, the most salient of which is that committees, when composed of homogeneous high demanders and granted special procedural rights, reap disproportionate particularistic benefits. The operable phrase here is "committee power," and in the context of the theories under consideration, this is a wholly distributive phenomenon. Who wins? Committees. At whose expense? The larger legislature's.

New Institutionalism theories are only partially consistent with the Majoritarian Postulate and are inconsistent with the Uncertainty Postulate. Elaboration in reverse order is most intuitive. Almost all New Institutionalism theories assume complete information; moreover, deviations from this norm put committees in informationally disadvantageous positions by positing that the committee knows less about the consequences of policy or the nature of chamber preferences than do noncommittee members (Denzau and Mackay 1983). Similarly, almost all New Institutionalism theories posit an institu-

TABLE 2.1.   Summary of Assumptions and Implications of Distributive Theories

	New Institutionalism	Industrial Organization	Game Theory
Committees			
Assignments	Self-selection (A)	Self-selection (I)	—
Composition	Homogeneous high demanders (A)	Homogeneous high demanders (I)	Homogeneous high demanders (A)
Procedures			
Committee rights	Strong delegation (A)	Strong delegation (I)	Mixed (A)
Amendment rules	Mixed (A)	Restrictive (A,I)	Baron and Ferejohn: Closed (I) Baron: Open (I)
Commitment	Yes (A)	Yes (A)	Yes (A)
Outcomes			
Committee power	Yes (I)	Yes (I)	Constrained (I)
Coalitions	—	Universalistic (I)	Majoritarian (I)
Postulates			
Majoritarian			
Policy choice	Yes	Yes	Yes
Procedural choice	No	Partial	Yes*
Uncertainty	No	No	No

*Can be interpreted as such, with commitment.

tional arrangement and set of rules governing amendments rather than allowing such features to arise endogenously. When the assumed form of exogenous institutional arrangement includes the normal set of procedural rights granted to committees (always some of the following: gatekeeping powers, restrictive amendment rules, an ex post veto, or restrictive postconference procedures), the models' explicit majoritarian assumption regarding policy choice is somewhat misleading. Obviously it covers only policy choice—not procedural choice. Less obviously, this limited coverage of the Majoritarian Postulate leads to a form of policy antimajoritarianism. If institutions constrain behavior, and the constraints are biased in favor of committees, then the inability of the legislature to change institutions that yield nonmajoritarian policies is tantamount to the legislative majorities being unable to effect policy choices to their liking.

Industrial Organization

The close cousin of New Institutionalism models—Weingast and Marshall's industrial organization approach—departs from its forerunners in two promising ways. It allows some institutional features to arise endogenously, and it provides a wider range of empirical implications. Most of the institutional implications of the theory are consistent with what formerly had been assumptions. Parliamentary rights are delegated to high-demand committees. Most of the policy implications are compatible with, and more explicit than, the implications of prior theories. Policy is overwhelmingly distributive, outcomes are nonmajoritarian dimension-by-dimension, and coalitions of beneficiaries are "universalistic" (Weingast 1979). Everyone's high-demand preferences are satisfied to some degree, notwithstanding issue-by-issue majority opposition.

While uncertainty sometimes enters Weingast and Marshall's discussion and their theory points toward procedures as endogenous phenomena, the Uncertainty Postulate plays no formal role in the theory and the Majoritarian Postulate is confined to the domain of policy choice. The theory tells how a collection of minority, high-demand legislators can reap gains from trade from a "committee system." But the theory does not expressly grant the power to any majority to change the system.

Distributive Game Theories

Finally, the game-theoretic approach to distributive politics carries over relatively little from prior distributive models except, of course, the premise that the central issue in legislative organization is how to capture gains from trade. When given committee interpretations, the theories presume some degree of deviation in chamber-committee preferences, but they make relatively weak assumptions about committee rights. For instance, committees do not have gatekeeping powers in the New Institutionalism sense although they are given the right to make the first proposal. The two game-theoretic models also provide clear (but different) predictions about bill-specific rules, and their policy implications are considerably different from prior distributive models. Some gains from trade are reaped in equilibrium, but outcomes are not universalistic.[33] The identifiable consequences of procedures include not only gains from trade but also (in Baron's model) providing a lower bound on the inefficiency of distributive bargaining. Thus, Baron's model predicts that unrestrictive procedures will be used on economically inefficient, particularistic bills.

The status of the game theories in terms of the postulates is somewhat better than that of the industrial organization theory. With only one exception to date (Baron and Ferejohn 1988), game-theoretic distributive models are of the complete information variety. However, they are amenable to interpretation as if they provided for endogenous institutional choice with procedural commitment. In this sense, these models also more closely conform to the Majoritarian Postulate at the levels of policy and procedural choice.[34]

Two Cases of Distributive Politics

The purpose of the previous discussion was to develop clearly but non-technically the empirical predictions of distributive theories. I now conclude with two cases that move rather abruptly from the pristine world of formal theory to the murky world of congressional politics. The cases illustrate several concrete legislative analogs to the abstract theoretical components discussed above, including the distributive motivations for legislative behavior, how distributive desires are manifested in the composition and behavior of standing committees and subcommittees, and how the House and Senate use and fight about procedures. At many junctures, the cases raise questions about distributive depictions of the legislative process. However, it is crucial always to read these and other cases presented in the book in the proper vein. They are not intended as support or refutation of the theories in question; they are only offered as illustrations that the components of the theories have real-world counterparts. In all instances, assessments of the

---

33. Technically, they may be, but only under highly unrealistic parameter values: a combination of a very low number of legislators and a very high discount rate.

34. Additionally, Baron and Ferejohn's game-theoretic models can be interpreted as raising serious doubts about the severity of the chaos problem even at the theoretical level. In the context of prior theoretical research, the bargaining models presume radical divergence in preferences and thus would seem a priori to be the most problematical in terms of the cycles posing problems of institutional design. Yet, even under an open rule—which, in New Institutionalism vernacular, is a relatively "institution-free" setting—equilibria are identified. Likewise, the functionalistic fallacy that "institutions create stability, therefore institutions exist to create stability" is no longer relevant.

predictions of theories should rest not on cases but rather on more systematic empirical analysis.

Case 1: Buck(ley)ing Universalism

Distributive theorists, especially of the formal genre, instinctively object to the use of the term *norm* when users casually presume that a norm somehow explains a pattern of behavior or type of legislative outcome.[35] The reasoning underlying such objections is that a norm is a phenomenon in need of a theoretical explanation. The interesting question, then, is: Why, or under what conditions, is it rational for individuals to conform to a norm? In this same spirit, distributive theories are often claimed to be consistent with—or to "support" as equilibrium phenomena—congressional norms such as reciprocity (Fiorina 1981), deference (Shepsle and Weingast 1987a), or universalism (Weingast 1979).

The case of Senator James Buckley and his crusade against the widespread distribution of pork barrel projects is often cited as support for universalistic distributive tendencies in Congress and, more specifically, as evidence of the effectiveness of kinds of punishment strategies that make universalism a norm in the equilibrium sense. Two questions can be addressed by examining this case.

- Was Buckley punished for his alleged attempts to violate a distributive norm?
- If so, was the punishment effective?

To date, the modal answers have been resounding yesses. The academic origin of the story seems to be in a footnote in which Mayhew writes that Buckley "tried to delete forty-four public works projects at the *committee* stage in the Senate. The members voted down *all his amendments except* the ones cutting out projects in New York; these latter they adopted" (1974, 91–92; italics added). Cited is an article by Richard Reeves in *New York* magazine. In this passage, Reeves indeed implies (and Mayhew infers) that the only projects to be stripped were New York's: "[Buckley] spent even more time in a quixotically courageous fight to eliminate 'pork barrel' from public works legislation—until his peeved colleagues reacted by eliminating New York's pork: $14 million to clean up New York harbor, and an unspecified amount to correct beach erosion on Long Island from Fire Island to Montauk" (Reeves 1974, 78). This account—and especially its undocumented assertion about

---

35. See, for example, Shepsle and Weingast 1987a on the norm of deference to committees.

"peeved colleagues"—is probably primarily responsible for the popularity of the case among distributive theorists.

Whatever the origins of the celebrated case, some heretofore overlooked facts in it are consistent with an interpretation that differs significantly from that which has become common. Specifically, a more complete account illustrates how universalism may be difficult to sustain as an equilibrium in real legislative settings, because the punishment strategies on which it rests are either not played or, if played, are ineffective in deterring the deviant behavior at which they are targeted.

Punishment

Senator Buckley was a member of the Water Resource Subcommittee of the Senate Public Works Committee. During Senate consideration of the 1973 Rivers and Harbors Bill (S. 2798) in the subcommittee, Buckley sought to eliminate forty-four projects totaling $109 million of the $1.2 billion bill. First Buckley attempted to strip these projects en bloc. The subcommittee, however, preferred section-by-section consideration of the bill as the sections would be affected by Buckley's proposal. Because of the way the bill was written, the subcommittee's procedural choice was tantamount to project-by-project consideration. When the subcommittee finished its work, nine of Buckley's amendments had been agreed to. Included in these were two projects from Buckley's home state, New York.

Congressional documents contain little evidence for the interpretation that the subcommittee was punishing Buckley for violating a norm of universalism, however, and more than a little evidence contradicts this interpretation. First, Buckley himself offered the proposals to strip the New York projects. Second, he was mainly pleased with the subcommittee's decision to strip the New York projects.[36] Third, seven other projects were stripped, too, presumably on their cost-benefit merits. Had this been an instance of hardball distributive politics rather than a case-by-case consideration of merits, the subcommittee easily and more expeditiously could have voted down Buckley's original bundle of forty-four stripping amendments and followed up with a single New York stripping amendment. Instead, it was the subcommittee rather than Buckley that insisted on a section-by-section review, and the comprehensiveness of its proceedings was the source of considerable pride when the bill reached the floor. Finally, Buckley's subcommittee successes included more than the nine stripping amendments. He also persuaded the subcommittee to combine many of the individual demonstration projects into a single demonstration program. Through mandatory information sharing, his

---

36. More specifically, he stated that his colleagues did the right thing but for the wrong reason. The New York projects were stripped to conform with the practice of meeting the wishes of the Senator in whose state the projects are to reside (*Congressional Record*, January 21, 1974, S 82).

amendment resulted in an estimated savings of $61 million over five years.[37] Overall, the evidence for punishment of Buckley by fellow Senators is meager. If anything, Senators came to appreciate Buckley's committee work.

Deterrence

Distributive theories presume not only that deviators from norms will be punished but also that such punishment will be effective in bringing about compliance with an equilibrium strategy (here, the norm of universalism).[38] If the facts cited thus far do not materially undermine the punishment interpretation of the subcommittee's actions, then is the remainder of the legislative history consistent with the notion of deterrence implicit in universalistic distributive theories? The facts speak directly to this question.

Buckley resumed his antipork crusade in the full committee. His general strategy was to object to any project or section in the legislation that was inconsistent with regular authorization practices or did not have a national policy rationale. For example, he opposed road construction by the Army Corps of Engineers because it was outside the Corps' responsibility under contemporary law. Most of his amendments failed in the full committee, so perhaps this, too, might be construed as punishment (albeit punishment of a less-targeted nature, since no additional New York projects were cut). If so, did he throw in the towel after the Public Works Committee finished its work? Buckley's statement in the committee's report forecasts the answer: "I propose to re-offer one or more of the above amendments when the bill comes to the Senate floor."[39]

Buckley made good on his promise by continuing his fight on the floor. Occasionally joined by Senator William Proxmire (D.–Wis.), he was ineffective in terms of amendments.[40] On the other hand, the bill included changes in the authorization process that made it fiscally responsible relative to prior similar measures.[41] Finally, although Buckley and five other Senators opposed the bill, it passed and was sent to conference. In the conference com-

---

37. Many of these projects had to do with streambank erosion, a subject about which the subcommittee agreed more information was needed prior to funding widely distributed individual projects (S.Rept. 93–615, 139).

38. More precisely, in game-theoretic terms, it is the expected effectiveness of punishment strategies that keep the prospective deviator from deviating in the first place. Thus, in the case under consideration, we are "off the equilibrium path" since Buckley has violated the norm (i.e., equilibrium strategy). The issue is whether the deterrent seems to be corrective with respect to deviating strategies.

39. S.Rept. 93–615, 140.

40. For example, his amendment to strip ten projects from the bill received only nine votes (*Congressional Record*, January 21, 1974, S 95).

41. See, for example, *Congressional Record*, January 21, 1974, S 72, regarding the new process whereby projects could be deauthorized and, more broadly, *Congressional Quarterly*, January 26, 1974, 152–53.

mittee, to which Buckley was not appointed, New York's projects were restored. (They had been included in the House's bill.) Nonetheless, Buckley spoke against and voted against the conference report. Thus, at every subsequent stage of the legislative process the putative punishment in subcommittee had little, if any, deterrent effect.[42]

Implications

The following implications contrast the discussion of distributive theories generally and thus should be entertained as I move to systematic analysis. First, committees—even classical pork barrel committees—may not be composed of homogeneous high-demanders. Second, bill-specific choice of procedures may have as much to do with discerning the merits of programs as with maximizing the distribution of particularistic benefits. Third, the absence of commitment to restrictive procedures for pork barrel programs may be legislatively useful, if not intentional.

Case 2: 1989 Supplemental Appropriations

Civics books often tell how a typical bill becomes a law but fail to note that a typical bill is an elusive animal. H.R. 2072, Dire Emergency Supplemental Appropriations and Transfers, Urgent Supplementals, and Correcting Enrollment Errors Act of 1989, was not a typical bill and should not be regarded as such. Nonetheless, it, too, is a useful vehicle for raising and illustrating some issues at the heart of legislative politics and, more specifically, at the heart of distributive theories of legislative organization. Roughly paralleling the concluding list for the Buckley case, the three distributive predictions, and the data analysis in chapters 4–6, the case of supplemental appropriations contains illustrations of each of the following issues:

- Are committees composed of homogeneous high-demanders?
- Are conference committees procedurally advantaged high-demanders that acquire disproportionate distributive benefits?
- Can and does the House commit to the use of restrictive procedures to facilitate gains from trade? at the floor stage? at the postconference stage?

---

42. One might argue that the ultimate punishment came in 1976 when Buckley lost his seat to Daniel Patrick Moynihan. This is not only well beyond the scope of the relevant formal models but also doubtful. New York was in the Democratic camp in 1976, voting for Carter over Ford by 52 percent to 48 percent. Moynihan is a relatively conservative Democrat (a "neoliberal") by New York standards, yet he captured only a slightly greater vote share than Carter, winning (54 percent to 45 percent). Furthermore, Buckley's original election was, arguably, a three-candidate fluke of sorts, in which he captured only 39 percent of the vote, so it is hardly as if Moynihan's victory was a stunning upset.

Presidential Context

The presidential torch was passed from Ronald Reagan to George Bush in uncertain budgetary times. The Reagan Revolution, begun eight years hence, wound down about as steadily as federal deficits were cranked up. Throughout Reagan's two terms, the Congress engaged in a seemingly endless string of budgetary innovations with mixed success and mixed evaluations. In the early 1980s, the budgetary rage of Boll Weevils and Republicans was "reconciliation"—an initially arcane but eventually significant statutory provision whereby a congressional budget resolution instructs authorizing and appropriating committees to report legislation that reduces expenditures, increases revenues, or alters entitlement programs.[43] But Republican successes in cutting taxes in 1981, Democratic midterm gains in 1982, and a recession in 1981–82 undercut the effectiveness of reconciliation as a budget-balancing device. Soaring deficits and searing debates followed.

The next major innovation came in 1985 when Congress passed the Gramm-Rudman-Hollings antideficit act. Gramm-Rudman, as the bill came to be called, had as checkered a history as reconciliation.[44] First, the Supreme Court declared the bill unconstitutional. Next, the bill was constitutionally reconstructed. Finally, budgetary innovations resumed, ranging from shameless circumvention techniques to increasing presidential intervention. Precipitated by the 1987 stock market crash, Reagan set the precedent of executive intervention by instigating a "budget summit." A series of bipartisan negotiations prior to the start of the congressional budget cycle culminated in an "agreement" whose status and content were matters of constant dispute. Some legislators regarded it as binding; some regarded it as merely suggestive; some regarded it as unconstitutional; some regarded it as garbage. But few disputed the significance of the event.

Scarcely had the bright-eyed Bush and Quayle administration begun its work in 1989 when the expected (if not inevitable) occurred. Agencies, consultants, and economists alike all agreed qualitatively if not quantitatively that federal spending was on a collision course with Gramm-Rudman. The new president, who had campaigned long and hard on the twin themes of "A Kinder, Gentler Nation" and "No New Taxes," decided to follow his predecessor's lead and begin negotiations with congressional leaders to address possibilities for achieving his goals. After weeks of frustrating talks, leaders "declared victory and went home" with little other than a broad agreement to cut $28 billion from the fiscal 1990 budget.[45]

---

43. These were the practical, but not necessary, consequences of the use of reconciliation. It is theoretically possible that reconciliation could be used, say, to increase outlays and reduce revenues (Schick 1981).

44. The name of the third author of the act was its first, and possibly most permanent, victim of economizing.

45. *Congressional Quarterly*, April 15, 1989, 804.

The agreement for fiscal 1990 posed one set of problems.[46] A more immediate problem was how to get through fiscal 1989 without triggering the not-
so-kind, not-so-gentle Gramm-Rudman sequestration procedure. Although the
press reported almost nothing about the implications of the summit for fiscal
1989, it soon became evident that the new president wanted to live by the old
rules for supplemental spending. The 1987 postcrash summit called for supplemental appropriations only under "dire emergencies," and Bush chose to
include only a few items under this rubric. He proposed that Congress pass a
supplemental appropriations bill totaling $2.2 billion. Its main components
were $854 million for veterans, $892 million for guaranteed student loans, and
$423 million for foster care.[47] Additionally and crucially, he stipulated that any
additional spending in other areas was to be offset by savings.

Congressional Action
House Appropriations Subcommittees. From the outset, members of the House
and Senate Appropriations Committees treated the president's request for
veterans as an irresistible vehicle for spending above and beyond the president's
wishes. The House took the lead in marking up Bush's proposal. In a matter of
two days in early April, the subcommittees of the House Appropriations
Committee had more than doubled the president's $2.2 billion request, report-
ing measures to the full committee that totaled $4.6 billion. Some of the
proposed supplements to the supplemental were classical particularistic provisions, such as $599.7 million to cover the previous summer's firefighting
expenses in the West, $250 million for Japanese-American reparations, and
$126.6 million for Trade Adjustment Assistance to workers harmed by imports.
Other, general interest provisions were politically attractive in light of public
opinion; for example, widespread anxiety about the nation's drug problem
prompted the Subcommittee on Commerce, State, and Justice to add $725
million without any corresponding savings. In spite of the Bush administration's interest in the drug issue,[48] OMB Director Richard Darman, upon
learning of the subcommittee's actions, promptly issued a veto threat, dubbing
the congressional plan a "clear violation" of the budget agreement. As the bill
moved into the full Appropriations Committee, Darman began negotiating with
the ranking Republican on the committee, Silvio Conte (R.–Mass.), to pare
back the bill's "extraneous" provisions.[49] In short, the subcommittees seemed
to be precisely what distributive theories say they are: high demanders of
particularistic policies.

46. Senator James Exon (D.–Nebr.) said, "If anybody thinks Rosemary's baby was ugly,
they should take a look at this newly hatched agreement" (*Congressional Quarterly*, April 22,
1989, 881).

47. H.Doc. 101–40.

48. In September, the drug issue was the sole focus of Bush's first nationwide presidential
address.

49. *Congressional Quarterly*, April 27, 1989, 883–84.

House Appropriations Committee. The administration's efforts to amend the bill were unsuccessful even though, from Darman's perspective, Conte's proposed amendment represented much more give than take. It allowed increased funding for antidrug programs, kept the added firefighting funds, provided for $1.2 billion for veterans (cf. Bush's original request of $892 million), and limited the size of offsetting cuts for these expenditures. Still, the amendment was defeated 18 to 28 on a straight party vote. When the full committee had completed its work, the proposed total had increased to $4.74 billion. Cross-party heterogeneity of preferences within the full committee had emerged, but the committee's high-demand overtones remained strong.

Rules Committee. In late April, the Rules Committee held hearings to determine the conditions under which the supplemental appropriations bill would come to the floor. Representative Quillen (R.–Tenn.) proposed that the bill not go to the House at all until the Appropriations Committee made further cuts. The Rules Committee's compromise was to propose a rule that provided for consideration of two amendments: one offered by Majority Leader Thomas Foley (D.–Wash.), and the other by the Appropriations Committee's ranking Republican, Silvio Conte (R.–Mass.). Each of these amendments would make across-the-board cuts in other appropriations not covered in the supplemental to compensate for outlays in the supplemental. Conte's amendment would cut only domestic appropriations, however.[50] Was the Rules Committee trying to facilitate gains from trade? It is not clear.

House Floor 1. The rule was accepted by the House, and H.R. 2702 came to the floor. In his introductory remarks, House Appropriations Committee Chairman Jamie Whitten (D.–Miss.) stressed the Senate's historical pattern of adding special provisions to supplemental appropriations bills and suggested that it was important that the House do some of the same so that it would have negotiating strength in conference. But Conte regretfully broke with the chairman. Calling the bill "Christmas in April," Conte repeated the administration's argument that the supplemental was a violation of the budget summit agreement of 1987. At the conclusion of general debate, Conte asked and received unanimous consent that the bill be "open to amendment at any point."[51] Later, in a no-lose ploy to place the onus of painful cuts solely on Foley or to embarrass Foley's party with a loss, Conte chose not to offer his amendment. So the first major proposal was Foley's amendment to offset the discretionary portion of the bill with a 0.57 percent cut in all defense, foreign aid, and domestic programs, thereby reducing the level of spending authority and outlays $2.4 billion and $1.4 billion, respectively. With the support of a coalition of Republicans and ninety-two defecting Democrats of all stripes, Foley's amendment was defeated. The bill was promptly withdrawn and sent

---

50. *Congressional Record,* April 26, 1989, H 1376.
51. *Congressional Record,* April 26, 1989, H 1384–1408.

back to Appropriations for what Speaker Wright called "certain corrective surgery."[52] By defeating the Foley amendment, the high-demand committee seemed momentarily to have gotten what it wanted. However, the bill did not coast to final passage.

House Floor 2. Three weeks later, the Appropriations Committee came back to the floor with its bill pared back by approximately $1 billion. Chairman Whitten sought unanimous consent to bring up the bill, stating that if consent were given the House would be able also to consider an amendment that would strip the antidrug money, which Republicans had been calling "veto bait." Representative Frenzel (R.–Minn.) objected to Whitten's request on the grounds that the House should consider a "clean supplemental," that is, a bill with only the provisions requested by Bush. So the bill went back to committee again.[53]

A Clean Bill. A day later, Frenzel and other Republicans were granted their wish for a pork-free, fiscally responsible bill. An entirely new measure, H.R. 2402, provided for veterans funding only, was passed by voice vote, and was sent to the Senate. The Senate was unwilling to forego the opportunity to use veterans funding as a vehicle for other pet projects but unable to kill the highly popular measure outright. Its crafty compromise was to pass H.R. 2402 with an amendment that provided the veterans' funds only through June 15. The Senate then declared itself in recess, and sent the amended bill back to the House. This strategy ensured that if the House were to concur with the Senate amendment and pass the bill, another veterans' vehicle (a "must-pass" bill) would be waiting and ready to haul pork after congressmen returned from their Memorial Day recess. Thus, stripping attempts continued.[54]

House Floor 3. The House did not accept the Senate's version of the veterans-only bill but rather resumed consideration of the original and much larger supplemental, H.R. 2072, in late May. Succumbing to the House's pressure for the committee to pare back the bill still further, Whitten brought the bill back to the floor for the third time. The rule under which the bill was considered this time (H.Res. 160) had several special features.

- It permitted consideration of an amendment by Whitten to reduce the antidrug money and other committee add-ons.
- It gave Conte the right to propose an amendment to strip all except the veterans' provision from the bill.
- It allowed AuCoin (D.–Oreg.) to propose a funding scheme whereby SDI funds would be reduced to offset the costs of the antidrug provisions.

---

52. *Congressional Record*, April 26, 1989, H 1421.
53. *Congressional Record*, May 17, 1989, H 1999–2001.
54. *Congressional Quarterly*, May 10, 1989, 1179.

- It allowed for remerging the previously passed H.R. 2402 with the supplemental under consideration.

The rule was controversial, to say the least. Minority Leader Bob Michel (R.–Ill.) called it a "two-headed malodorous swamp animal which the Rules Committee deposited on the floor." Barney Frank (D.–Mass.) and Gerald Solomon (R.–N.Y.) sparred over whom was being "gagged" by the rule and why. And Robert Walker (R.–Pa.) epitomized the milquetoast faction with this less-than-ringing endorsement: "I wanted to rise and praise, in the bipartisan spirit, the creativity in this rule." But the rule passed, so H.R. 2072 was once again before the House.[55]

Whitten's amendment to reduce his own committee's add-ons passed. The AuCoin amendment failed. Conte again elected not to offer his amendment; however, he sought the substantive equivalent by offering a motion to recommit with instructions to strip all but the veterans' provisions. Apparently more-or-less content with the reductions that had been made, the House voted against the motion to recommit, passed the Whitten-amended bill, and sent the bill to the Senate.[56]

Senate. The Senate wasted no time putting its own distributive stamp on the bill. The Appropriations Committee immediately axed all $822 million of the House's antidrug spending and then fought off all attempts to restore it in committee and on the floor. However, consistent with House members' pork barrel prognostications, the committee did not resist the temptation to add special projects, including $75 million for a radio telescope in West Virginia, a $3.2 million grant to California for reinstating a state Occupational Safety and Health Administration, $1.6 million for the Urban Education Foundation in Philadelphia, $200,000 for a grant to the University of South Carolina, and others. By June 7, the bill had passed through the Senate with some additional pork added on the floor. Then the Senate formally requested a conference.[57]

House Floor 4. In agreeing to the Senate's request for a conference, the House unanimously voted to instruct its conferees "not to meet with the managers on the part of the Senate on other issues until resolution of supplemental funding for Department of Veterans' Affairs Medical Care." Conte proposed the motion to instruct, after which he gave an impassioned plea to conferees to reduce the amount of particularistic spending. "Veterans are being held hostage . . . to the other body's pet projects:

- Hostage to $75 million for a radio telescope in West Virginia. [Byrd, Chairman, Senate Appropriations Committee (SAC)]

55. *Congressional Record*, May 24, 1989, H 2105–8.
56. *Congressional Record*, May 24, 1989, H 2104–32.
57. *Congressional Quarterly*, June 3, 1989, 1309–13.

- Hostage to a $1 million community gym for the Navy in landlocked West Virginia. [Byrd, Chairman, SAC]
- Hostage to a $250,000 warning system for chemical plants in West Virginia. [Byrd, Chairman, SAC]
- Hostage to $900,000 more for Logan County Airport in West Virginia. [Byrd, Chairman, SAC]
- Hostage to $250,000 drought information center at Kansas State University. [Dole, Senate Minority Leader]
- Hostage to a $400,000 Yellowstone fire research project at the University of Wyoming. [Simpson, Minority Whip]
- Hostage to a provision urging that the Department of Agriculture buy more apples.
- Hostage to $130 million increased authorization for the Bonneville lock project. [Garn, SAC member]
- Hostage to $200,000 for University of South Carolina to study drug abuse. [Hollings, SAC member]
- Hostage to $1.6 million for job training in Philadelphia. [Specter, SAC member]
- Hostage to $500,000 for Mill Creek Lake, OH.
- Hostage to $3 million for toxicological research in Jefferson, AR. [Bumpers, SAC member]
- Hostage to Shinnecock Inlet, NY. [D'Amato, SAC member]
- Hostage to the Dubuque City Island Bridge [Harkin and Grassley, SAC members]
- Hostage to $50 million in army winter clothing manufactured in 10 states.
- And on and on."[58]

Conference 1. Conferees conformed with the House's instructions to reach an agreement on the veterans' portions of the bill. Their success with regard to fiscal restraint on particularistic expenditures was an item of continuing dispute, though. The committee issued a report in true disagreement on the antidrug provisions.[59] This meant that the fate of the bill could not be determined by a single up or down vote in the House and Senate.

---

58. *Congressional Record,* June 13, 1989, H 2492–96 (bracketed comments added). Conte's allegations are sound but somewhat misleading insofar as all of the Senate-added provisions had at least some support from respective state delegations in the House.

59. Often Appropriations measures are reported from conference in technical disagreement, which means that conferees actually agreed, but for procedural reasons (such as exceeding their scope or incorporating legislative language) they deemed it necessary to give the parent chambers the opportunity to consider separately those portions of the bill to which objection may be heard. See Bach 1984 for an excellent discussion.

House Floor 5. For a variety of reasons, it was necessary to go to the Rules Committee for a special order governing consideration of the conference report.[60] The rule, H.Res. 180, provided for several votes: first on the portion of the report in agreement (Bush's original three requests, plus myriad Senate and House add-ons), next on the antidrug provisions (included only in the House's version), and finally on two relatively minor provisions. The rule passed on a voice vote, somewhat to the surprise of many Democrats who expected Conte to mount a fierce fight against the rule in an attempt to defeat the report. The ensuing debate on the report was predictably contentious. Led by Conte, who reiterated his regrets about his split with Whitten, Republicans and some southern Democrats complained about the "pure pork" that survived. At the conclusion of debate, Conte offered a motion to recommit the bill to conference, but the motion was rejected. Then the portion of the report in agreement was put to a vote. Having widely but inconspicuously circulated a list of pork barrel recipients to members, Republicans attracted the votes of 36 southern Democrats and 16 nonsouthern Democrats to defeat the report outright, 201 to 218. Thus, the provisions in disagreement never came to a vote. Immediately, Whitten made a unanimous consent request for a new conference. Within minutes, the request was granted and a slate of conferees was appointed.[61]

Conference 2. By the next day, a new conference report had been produced. The amount of antidrug money had been reduced from $822 million to $75 million. The significance of the latter figure (aside from its representing a 91 percent reduction) is that it exactly and purposely equaled the sum of reductions in chairmen-supported particularistic projects that the conferees had cut out of the bill. Cutting funding for West Virginia's (Byrd's) radio telescope appropriation in half freed $37.5 million, while Whitten's consent to reduce farm operating loans from $70 million to $32.5 million freed another $37.5 million.[62]

Senate Floor 2 and House Floor 6. The Senate passed the new report on June 22. The bill came to the House for the sixth time on June 23. Conte finally endorsed it, saying "What we have done here is resolve all the problems that were in the bill when it came to the floor [on June 21]." The House agreed to the report, 318 to 6, that day. On June 30, President Bush signed the bill into law.[63]

---

60. An additional sticking point was an attempt by VA and HUD conferees to exceed budget limits through accounting procedures. Robert Traxler (D.–Mich.) testified before the Rules Committee for a waiver. But Budget Chairman Panetta (D.–Calif.) testified against the waiver and won the day: the Rules Committee chose not to include the requested waiver.

61. *Congressional Record,* June 21, 1989, H 2999–3041.

62. *Congressional Quarterly,* June 24, 1989, 1523–25.

63. *Congressional Quarterly,* June 24, 1989, 1523–25.

Summary. The case illustrates each of the following (and more). First, standing committees may be high demanders, but their heterogeneity may undermine the effectiveness of their high-demand efforts. In this case, committees were monitored every step of the way, sometimes even by their own members. Second, logrolling desires are strong within and across committees. However, they, too, were monitored every step of the way. Third, conferees have some unique parliamentary rights. However, such rights can be taken away about as easily as they are granted. Fourth, collective choices about procedures are common. In this case, they were grounds for policy-relevant battles every step of the way.

Conclusion

Neither the cases of distributive politics nor the review of distributive theories in this chapter is intended to prove anything. However, the cases are suggestive with respect to the theories. The legislative history of the 1973 Rivers and Harbors Bill indicates that when attention is directed to individual behavior in specific instances of distributive politics, the kinds of punishment strategies needed to support universalistic equilibria may be impractical. Likewise, the case of 1989 supplemental appropriations indicates that, although legislators may like logrolling, it is difficult for them to devise procedures that enable them to commit either to logrolls or to restrictive procedures that facilitate logrolling. Contrary to the assumptions or implications of earlier distributive theories but more in line with recent game-theoretic distributive theories, gains from trade are difficult to capture in any universalistic sense. Bargains can and do come unraveled even in a highly institutionalized legislature, and the two cases illustrate the practical difficulties of designing a legislature exclusively around distributive politics.

Notwithstanding these potential pitfalls, efforts to theorize about the distributive aspects of legislative choice have many of the markings of good, normal science. Development of the field has exhibited increasing explicitness in three areas: assumptions, derivation of results, and extraction of empirical implications. Moreover, in some instances the predictions of distributive models differ, thus creating the possibility of empirical tests that discriminate between theories. Before beginning the empirical tests, I will review a body of theoretical research that owes much to the distributive theories reviewed above.

CHAPTER 3

Informational Theories of Legislative Organization

Knowledge will forever govern ignorance, and a people who mean to be their own governors must arm themselves with the power that knowledge gives them. A popular government without popular information or the means of acquiring it is but a prologue to farce, or tragedy, or perhaps both.

—President James Madison[1]

Everywhere, political decisions depend on their effectiveness on the correctness with which the relevant reactions to them have been predicted.

—Karl Deutsch (1963, 159)

Distributive theories have done so much to set the stage for political scientists' perceptions of the U.S. Congress that a contemporary rendering of Madison's admonition would declare the prologue over but hasten to note that the legislative show goes on. Moreover, today's cast of congressional characters reflects Madison's worst dreams. Actors do not play informational roles in distributive theories. They are too busy pursuing parochial constituency interests. According to the distributive script, today's congressmen indeed act out a "farce, or tragedy, or perhaps both."

To be cynical about the contemporary Congress is as easy as to be critical of formal theories of congressional politics. All that is required is a few factual tidbits that reflect badly on the institution or that cannot be reconciled with existing theory. Making fun of the Congress is like shooting fish in a barrel. Taking jabs at formal theories is, if anything, easier.

To be constructive about the shortcomings of Congress and congressional scholarship is more difficult, however. For congressmen, the irresistibly tempting response to criticism of their institution has been to "run for Congress by running against it" (Fenno 1975). For congressional scholars, the similarly tempting response is more aptly described as "hit and run": to raise criticisms and then to move on to easier research questions.

---

1. As quoted by Sen. Mark O. Hatfield (1967, 20).

This chapter resists the hit-and-run temptation with a constructive attempt to improve upon distributive theories. The objectives are to retain the most promising elements of existing theory, to introduce and defend some alternative assumptions, to summarize a series of new theories that are amenable to empirical analysis, and to try to explain phenomena that are anomalies with respect to distributive theories. Informational and distributive theories are similar in two respects. Both characterize politics as a game of conflict over who gets what at whose expense, and both assume that conflicts are resolved by rational or goal-oriented actors. However, informational and distributive theories are different in two other respects that pertain directly to the postulates of legislative organization articulated in chapter 1. Majoritarianism is more far-reaching in informational than in distributive theories. Uncertainty about the relationship between policies and their consequences is absent in distributive theories but crucial in informational theories.[2] By the end of this chapter, we will be able to identify clearly the differences in empirical expectations that are indirectly attributable to these theoretical postulates. First, it is useful to provide some empirical motivation for uncertainty as it is represented in informational theories.

Other things being equal, legislators would rather select policies whose consequences are known in advance than policies whose consequences are uncertain. Under conditions of relative certainty, legislators can plan and make the most of credit-claiming. (Alternatively, if collective choices happen to be less in line with individual preferences, dissatisfied legislators can plan and implement blame-avoidance strategies to minimize losses.) Under conditions of relative uncertainty, however, surprise and the prospect of embarrassment lurk beneath any policy choice. Implicit in this risk-aversion assumption about legislators as individuals is a more commonly articulated view about the legislature as a collective entity. A well-designed legislature is a producer, consumer, and repository for policy expertise, where "expertise" is the reduction of uncertainty associated with legislative policies. To illustrate the existence of uncertainty and the coincident need for expertise, only a copy of a newspaper on an average weekday is needed.

EXAMPLE: In the summer of 1989 while *Batman* was breaking movie theater box office records, the look-alike B-2 "Stealth" bomber seemed to be setting records for airtime on the nightly news. However, in Congress, legisla-

---

2. The different embodiments of majoritarianism in distributive and informational theories are not fundamental differences in the theoretical approaches, since distributive theories could, in principle, expand the reach of majoritarianism to include procedural choice as well as policy choice. The fact of the matter is that they rarely have done this. In contrast, differences between theoretical approaches in terms of uncertainty are fundamental. It is simply not possible to accommodate uncertainty, as defined in chap. 1, without having an informational theory.

tors were having an inordinately difficult time deciding on a level of authorization for not only the B-2 program, which the Pentagon priced at $70 billion, but also the perennial administration request for the Strategic Defense Initiative, also known as SDI or *Star Wars* (the box office hit of a decade earlier). It was not because congressmen had qualms about providing for the national defense—particularly not the conservative members of the House and Senate Armed Services Committees. Rather, it was because of the extreme difficulty of discerning how funding for programs such as Stealth and Star Wars would eventually translate into a hopelessly amorphous but nonetheless desirable outcome: national defense. Statements by individuals during the House debate on SDI reflect this collective uncertainty about the relationship between policies (authorization levels) and outcomes (levels of national defense).

> Mr. Kyl: A lot of my colleagues have just said that they are just not sure whether it [SDI] will work. Mr. Chairman, the point here is to provide a funding level sufficient to find out the answer to that question. My amendment would have done that. The gentleman [Mr. Bennett] will argue that his amendment will do it. I do not think it will. But I think all of us understand that the Boxer-Dellums amendment will not even begin to get close to providing those funds necessary to conduct the tests to find out whether SDI will work so that we can make an informed judgment. (*Congressional Record,* July 25, 1989, H 4207–08)

> Mrs. Boxer: . . . Star Wars is the "Would-you-believe, never-mind"[3] system of the military budget, and now the gentleman from Arizona [Mr. Kyl] in his debate, I think, brought some more of a sense of humor to this debate when he says that America spends almost as much on panty hose as it does on Star Wars. I cannot help but bring a sense of humor to that analogy. . . . My colleagues, take it from me, panty hose is affordable. Star Wars is not. Panty hose has a clear function. Star Wars does not. Panty hose has a mission that does not change every day. The Star Wars mission has changed from a protective shield to military installation defense to accidental launch protection to brilliant pebbles to terrorist deterrence. Let us face it, Star Wars has changed more times than Imelda Marcos has changed her shoes. (*Congressional Record,* July 25, 1989, H 4207)

EXAMPLE: In the 1980s the federal government (with at least the implicit endorsement of Congress) adopted a series of measures bearing on the operation of the Department of Housing and Urban Development. Several of these

---

3. References to television's Don Adams in "Get Smart" and the late Gilda Radner as Emily Latella in "Saturday Night Live."

provided for a transfer of its critical functions away from HUD and into the private sector. The eventual consequences of these policies were astounding to almost everyone: administrators, interest groups, and congressmen representing the full spectrum of housing preferences. Unexpected consequences arose from the following programs, and more.

- "Full-service property manager program. Instituted in 1986 as a more efficient approach to managing H.U.D.-controlled properties by contracting out to private companies. An audit found 'significant adverse conditions which impact on the health and safety of tenants.'
- "Co-insurance. A mortgage insurance program introduced in 1983, in which private lenders assume about 20 percent of the risk of insuring mortgages. The Government assumes responsibility for the remaining 80 percent. But private lenders oversee most of the underwriting, credit checks, and appraisals. Losses in the program are estimated at $1 billion.
- "Private escrow agents. H.U.D. sales of foreclosed houses are handled by private escrow agents instead of staff lawyers with H.U.D. as previously. Losses are estimated at $20 million to $100 million."[4]

The costs of inadequate expertise were twofold. Obviously, the government wasted a lot of money. Less obviously, congressmen were embarrassed by the whole ordeal.

The common feature of examples such as these is that legislators often do not know the effects of policies under consideration. Congressmen would like to have been able to forecast the provision of housing services as a consequence of privatization of HUD procedures, and they grappled in earnest with the implications of a range of proposals for national defense. But informed decision making was elusive.

An adequate explanation of how legislators seek informed decisions in the face of uncertainties such as these is currently beyond the scope of most formal theories, because such theories do not accommodate three potentially important features of legislative politics. First, acquiring policy expertise is costly. Second, such expertise would be potentially beneficial to all legislators if it were acquired. Third, the potential benefits of policy expertise will be realized only if institutional arrangements are such that some legislators have strong incentives to specialize and to share their expertise with their fellow legislators.

The premise that legislators often do not know the precise consequences of

---

4. See *New York Times*, July 31, 1989, and September 28, 1989. By September, 1989, new information indicated that the situation was worse still.

the policies they enact is evident not only in newspapers but also in the empirical research on Congress. Every study on legislative staff acknowledges it,[5] as do case studies,[6] the vast majority of studies on committees,[7] and much of the literature on the waxing and waning of legislatures vis-à-vis executives.[8] Until recently, however, it has proven difficult to analyze these self-evident empirical truths in a theoretically tractable way. In a path-breaking work, Austen-Smith and Riker (1987) brought a powerful set of theoretical tools from economics to bear on collective choice settings. They studied the "coherence" of a committee choice process in which committee members possessed private or asymmetric information about the consequences associated with various policy proposals. Their analysis suggested that opportunities for strategic use of information are so extensive that, except under the most extreme circumstances, the collective wisdom of the committee—that is, full, precise, and truthful aggregation of private information—could not work its way into the collective choice.[9] In this respect, a collective choice process in the presence of asymmetric information is fundamentally "incoherent."

At approximately the same time, Tom Gilligan and I began work on some similar theoretical problems with similar theoretical tools but with slightly different substantive interests. Like Austen-Smith and Riker, we wanted formally to characterize uncertainty, asymmetry, and strategic use of information in collective choice processes. But, in contrast to Austen-Smith and Riker's focus on decision making within a single committee, our substantive interests rested more broadly on sequential committee-legislature decision making. Among the issues analyzed were conditions under which a committee can exercise power in the distributive theoretical tradition, conditions under which a committee can be informative, effects of amendment rules on the informativeness and power of committees, conditions under which committees devote resources to specialize, and how a legislature can be optimally designed in the face of the tensions and trade-offs between "distributional" and "informational" aspects of collective choice.

Obtaining theoretical insights about these substantive concerns required some extensive technical analysis, which is reported in detail in four articles (Gilligan and Krehbiel 1987, 1989a, 1989b, and 1990). Since the primary

5. See Balutis 1977; Buchanan, Eulau, Ferguson, and Wahlke 1970; Davis 1975; Hammond 1984; Huckshorn 1965; Malbin 1980; Manley 1968; Ornstein 1975b; Patterson 1970; Porter 1974; Sabatier and Whiteman 1985; Schick 1976; Schneier 1970; Scicchitano 1981; Uslaner and Weber 1977; Webber 1984; and Wissel, O'Connor, and King 1976.

6. Asbell 1978; Bailey 1950; Bauer, Poole, and Dexter 1963; Bendiner 1964; Jones 1975; Reid 1980; and Whalen and Whalen 1985.

7. Fenno 1966 and 1973; Goodwin 1970; McConachie 1898; Morrow 1969; Price 1972; Smith and Deering 1984; Wilson 1885.

8. Burns 1949; Galloway 1946; Huntington 1969; MacNeil 1963; and Sundquist 1981.

9. See also Austen-Smith 1990a and 1990b; and Austen-Smith and Riker 1990.

objective in this book is to test existing theory—not to teach or develop new theory—a nontechnical approach is taken here. First, the key concepts in informational theories are reviewed with frequent references to earlier empirical research that motivated the theory. Second, the role of sequence in the games is clarified by graphing and tracing through a composite game. Third, the major principles derived from legislative signaling games are concisely stated and copiously illustrated. Fourth, these principles are translated into more concrete predictions that are conducive to hypothesis testing in chapters 4–6. Finally, the main theoretical arguments and empirical implications of chapters 1–3 are recapitulated.

Key Concepts in Informational Theories

Formal notation can become quite cumbersome in games with incomplete information. Here it will be relegated to a few footnotes and otherwise confined to a single abbreviation. Let LSG stand for *legislative signaling game.* The objective of this section is to give a moderately detailed overview of LSGs with reference to their key concepts. While the concepts are perhaps new and odd, their substantive motivation is old and common.[10]

Incomplete Information, Policies, and Outcomes

Incomplete information is the distinctive feature of informational theories that enables formal analysis of otherwise theoretically intractable conceptions of specialization, deliberation, and debate. The key distinction is between policies and outcomes. *Policies* are the objects of legislative choice.[11] *Outcomes* are the effects of policies upon their enactment and implementation.[12] Legislators in games with incomplete information are fundamentally outcome-oriented and thus concerned with posturing and policies only insofar as they are means to ends. Legislators are assumed to be utility maximizers (as in distributive theories), but their utility is determined by outcomes—not by policies.[13] That is, passage of a given policy has no bearing on a legislator's utility apart from the outcome associated with that policy. The exclusively

---

10. Appendix A summarizes the concepts discussed in this section and serves at least one of three purposes. It maps out what this section covers, it is a brief refresher course for readers who have already covered this material and prefer to skip to the section on principles of legislative signaling, and it is a reference guide that may be useful later in the book if some of these concepts fade from memory.

11. Synonyms for policies include proposals, bills, legislation, and laws.

12. Consequence is sometimes used synonymously with outcome.

13. Utility functions are quadratic in the outcome space. The substantive implication of this assumption is that legislators are risk-averse. A legislator always prefers (*a*) an outcome with certainty to (*b*) a lottery whose expected outcome is that which he could have with certainty.

outcome-oriented actors in information-theoretic models therefore are quite different from Mayhew's strategic actors. Mayhew writes, for example:

> It may occur to the reader that the earlier discussion of policy making could have been set up as a collective goods problem. That is, on matters like regulatory policy members could have been portrayed as seekers of effects unable to achieve them because of the difficulty of generating collective action. *But to argue this way would have been a mistake. The notion of members as seekers of effects needs a razor taken to it; the electoral payment is for positions, not effects.* (1974, 146 n. 153; italics added)

While Mayhew's claim is strong, it should be noted that he makes it in the context of a discussion about the importance of legislators who perform "institutional maintenance" roles. Informational theories move rational choice theories in precisely this direction. They are formal characterizations of how self-interested, outcome-oriented legislators provide incentives for individuals to be institutional maintainers where, here, institutional maintenance refers to rationally specializing and rationally sharing the fruits of specialization.

In distributive theories, policies and outcomes are one and the same. A legislator's utility is defined over a space and, upon collective choice of a point in that space, payoffs are awarded in accordance with her utility function. In this sense, what she sees (a policy) is exactly what she gets (an outcome). In informational theories, however, legislators are initially uncertain about the relationship between policies (which they see and choose directly) and outcomes (which they can only forecast as a function of the policy under consideration and a random variable). Because a legislator's utility is defined over outcomes, not policies, the collective choice of a policy (what she sees) may or may not be clearly indicative of the legislator's utility (what she gets). The outcome (consequence of the implemented policy) coincides with a legislator's expectations only to the extent that she has precise information about how a policy is transformed into a final outcome or, alternatively, how a law is implemented and its consequences are felt.

Empirical research on information seeking in legislatures often distinguishes between two types of information—*political* and *policy*—where political information refers to what outcomes various political actors want and policy information (sometimes called *technical information*) refers to what policies result in desired outcomes. Although this conceptual distinction is common,[14] empirical studies tend to find that legislators do not make it (Feller

---

14. For specifics, see Arnold 1990; Truman 1957, 334; Webber 1984; and many of the sources cited in n. 5.

et al. 1975; Sabatier and Whiteman 1985). In any event, informational models effectively subsume these concepts. Incomplete "policy information" is explicitly characterized by assuming that legislators are uncertain about the relationship between policies and outcomes.[15] Incomplete "political information" could also be analyzed in this framework by stipulating that political uncertainty pertains to preferences over policies. That is, legislators may be uncertain about what policies other legislators want. Which characterization is more intuitive or appropriate is a matter of taste and evidence, respectively. But it bears emphasizing that each form of uncertainty rests on the distinction between policies and outcomes. Policies are means. Outcomes are ends. Thus, for example, Luce implicitly adopts this distinction when writing that "In the making of a law, two things are to be done: the principle or purpose [end] is to be agreed upon; and the way of accomplishing it [means] is to be determined" (1922, 87). LSGs take the first of Luce's "things" as fixed: legislators are assumed to know what "principle or purpose" (outcome, end) they desire. In contrast, "the way of accomplishing it" (the policy or means to the end) is unknown unless legislators devote resources or effort to specialization.

Asymmetric Information, Specialization, and Expertise

Asymmetric information refers to a condition in which some legislators have better knowledge than others about the relationship between policies and outcomes. Precision of expectations about this relationship is roughly what empirical scholars mean by *specialization* or *expertise*. In most legislatures, expertise is universally needed but not uniformly distributed. So the normal situation is that:

> Outside of the areas in which he himself has special knowledge or interest, the legislator needs sources of information which can combine, in one neat package, an evaluation of a program's significance, popularity, and relationship to other negotiable issues. (Schneier 1970, 18)

LSGs provide committees with opportunities to specialize (i.e., to acquire asymmetric information) to meet these needs. Specialization, while necessary, is not a sufficient condition for informed legislative decision making because committee specialization inevitably creates opportunities for strategic use of information. Given a complete and formal description of a choice setting—including legislators with different preferences and information, rules of procedure, the sequence of actions to be taken, and incomplete

---

15. Formally, $x = p + \omega$, where x is the outcome in R^1, p is a policy in R^1, and ω is a random variable whose precise value is unknown but whose distribution is known.

information about the relationship between policies and outcomes—it may be rational for committee specialists not to make public their private knowledge about the policy-outcome relationship.[16] In such instances, reduction of policy uncertainty for the collective benefit of legislators becomes a turkey shoot. If actual or "realized" outcomes happen to correspond precisely with the legislature's expectations, the policy (bullet) only serendipitously achieves the desired outcome (hits the target). On the other hand, outcomes or consequences of policies may be unanticipated due to the absence of specialization or the unwillingness of specialists to divulge their private information. Thus,

> A chairman is sometimes also criticized on the grounds that, in the words of one congressman: "Often he is trying to squirrel away information. He doesn't even want some of the committee members to be well informed, much less the average member of Congress." (Clapp 1963, 256)

Complaints of this sort are not uncommon. LSGs can be used to discern when and why "squirreling away information" occurs.

Players, Signals, Inferences, and Beliefs

Generically, the *players* in incomplete information games are categorized as senders and receivers. In LSGs, the sender is the committee; the receiver is the legislature. All LSGs analyzed thus far contain either two or three players. The "committee" refers to the player or players who have a right to offer the first proposal(s), and the "legislature" is a shorthand reference to the legislature's median voter. Additional details on moves and their order are provided in the next section.

When the committee (as sender) is a specialist (asymmetrically informed) and proposes a bill (takes an action), the legislature (as receiver) tries to ascertain what the committee knows that the legislature does not know. In this way, the action of the committee contains an implicit message or *signal* about its private information. The legislature observes the committee's bill and uses this observation as the basis for making an *inference* about the committee's private information. Stated in other ways, the receiver tries to decipher, unjam, unpack, or take the noise out of the committee's signal.

---

16. Signaling games are sometimes alleged to show that players with private information can get what they want by lying. To make a long story short, the allegation is itself a lie with respect to the signaling games in question. Any ostensible attempt to lie by the committee is detected by the rational legislature and compensated for in its behavior (rules permitting). Committees, therefore, typically do not get what they want. A more accurate and less surreptitious way to characterize their behavior is as concealing private information. Sometimes this is called *pooling*.

The product of the legislature's inference, based on the committee's bill, is a new or updated set of *beliefs* about the relationship between policies and outcomes.[17] These updated beliefs then form the basis for the legislature's final expected utility maximizing policy choice, that is, the policy that, in accordance with the rules and consistent with the legislature's beliefs, yields an expected outcome at, or as near as possible to, the legislature's ideal point.

Signaling models are relatively new to political science, but the behavior they characterize has been described for decades in a variety of ways. For example, in a superb multistate study of legislative specialization, Buchanan et al. elaborate on the differing roles of the committee specialists and noncommittee nonspecialists.

> The expert describes the consequences of proposed actions, Dahl (1950) says. He "interprets reality" and formulates the alternative ways a decision might influence the course of events, given this reality. The nonexpert decision maker, on the other hand, tends to see alternatives in the light of values—his own or his constituents'. Foreseeing, with the expert's help, the consequences of some policy these values suggest, he is able to clarify his preferences and choose between the relevant alternatives. (1970, 638)

Roll call voting studies on cue taking also capture many of the elements of information transmission.[18] Their premise, consistent with that of LSGs, is that legislators need information about the policy choices they must confront but may not understand. Therefore, legislators devise strategies to cope with uncertainty. Taking cues from other, relatively informed legislators is conceptually the same as receiving signals. The chief exception is that game-theoretic characterizations of sending messages and receiving signals tend to be more explicit about the strategic aspects of information transmission.

Legislative Equilibrium

The main analytic objective in LSGs is to identify and interpret equilibria. A legislative equilibrium differs from equilibria in most distributive models in a manner that parallels the distinction between New Institutionalism and game-theoretic distributive models. In distributive models in the New Institutional-

---

17. In Gilligan and Krehbiel 1987 and 1990, all players have common beliefs about the random nature of this relationship at the start of the game. In Gilligan and Krehbiel 1989a and 1989b, it is assumed that the committee has specialized before the game begins.

18. See, for example, Cherryholmes and Shapiro 1969; Kingdon 1973; and Matthews and Stimson 1975.

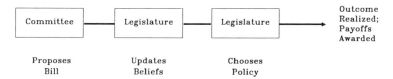

Fig. 3.1. Simple legislative signaling game

ism tradition, an equilibrium is characterized as a stable outcome, given some assumptions about procedure and behavior. An equilibrium in an LSG is defined explicitly in terms of behavior and beliefs of players rather than in terms of the stability of the outcomes associated with such behavior and beliefs.[19] Consider the simple LSG illustrated in figure 3.1. Assume that the committee has private and perfect knowledge about the outcomes associated with policies (i.e., the committee is a policy specialist), but the legislature knows only that a given bill yields outcomes distributed over a specified range. The following sequence of strategic actions takes place. The committee proposes a bill. The legislature updates its beliefs. The legislature chooses a policy (perhaps, but not necessarily, the bill). Finally, the outcome is realized as a function of the legislature's policy choice, and payoffs are awarded to the two players—the committee and the legislature—as a function of the closeness of the realized outcome to their most preferred outcomes.

Equilibria in LSGs all have the property that at each stage of the game, each player responds optimally to every other player, given current beliefs. Applying this general property to the game in figure 3.1, a *legislative equilibrium* is a bill choice by a committee, a set of beliefs by the legislature, and a policy choice by the legislature, such that actions of the players are expected utility maximizing, and the beliefs of the legislature are realized in equilibrium. Realization of beliefs means that the legislature's inference about the committee's information is not disproved by, say, a realized outcome outside the anticipated range as given by the legislature's updated beliefs.

Explicit and concrete examples of legislative equilibria of this kind probably do not exist in the empirical literature. However, the equilibrium concept is closely related to the dominant themes of deliberation and discussion in

---

19. The equilibrium concepts used in LSGs are variations of sequential equilibria. The concept of a sequential equilibrium was first developed by economists—implicitly in works by Akerlof (1970) and Spence (1974) and explicitly in works by Kreps and Wilson (1982a and 1982b), Milgrom and Roberts (1982a and 1982b), and others. The concept is similar to that used by Baron and Ferejohn (1989a and 1989b) and Baron (1990). The main difference is that, due to incomplete information, beliefs (and their updating) are incorporated into definitions of sequential equilibria.

Arthur Maass's insightful book, *Congress and the Common Good*. Maass begins by asserting that

> the duty of governmental institutions is to promote the articulation by groups and individuals of their preferences for the political community. . . . Instead of conducting a political process that simply aggregates and reconciles narrow group or individual interests, government conducts a process of deliberation and discussion that results in decisions that are based on broader community interests, and it designs and implements programs in accordance with these decisions. (Maass 1983, 5)

Taken out of context, such passages are open to a wide range of interpretations. But later in his critique of existing legislative theory, Maass identifies as key pitfalls of leading theories their inability or unwillingness to incorporate information acquisition, deliberation, and discussion. Characterizing the governmental process generally as "a continuous process of discussion . . . where the broad standards are agreed on" (7), Maass stresses that the legislative process plays an informational role above and beyond that which is feasible in other stages.

> The legislative process takes over from the electoral stage and translates into rules of law the general ideas endorsed by the electorate. The legislators—both the president and Congress—by means of special techniques for discussion and decision, including the capacity to use effectively more information than the electorate can use, accomplish something which their constituents are incapable of accomplishing. (7)

Maass sees "pma" models and "utility maximization" models[20] as fundamentally incapable of reflecting his conception of the "common good" and concludes that "a new theory of the role of legislative committees is needed" (39).

Informational theories are sympathetic to this view with two important qualifications. The first qualification is that Maass's conception of the "common good" has two components. One pertains to discerning what is in the public interest à la Rousseau. The other pertains to determining how the governmental process works to achieve that interest. Informational theories are silent with respect to the first component. However, the reduction of uncertainty about the relationship between policies and outcomes is perfectly

---

20. By "pma" (partisan mutual adjustment) models, Maass means pluralism. By "utility maximization" models, he means positive political theory models as of 1983, i.e., those that focused mainly or exclusively on distributive politics.

compatible with the second component.[21] The second qualification is that some elements of Maass's theory are normative rather than positive—that is, discussions of what ought to be rather than what is. Informational theories are careful not to take for granted that meaningful deliberation and discussion occur (or, equivalently, that uncertainty is reduced via specialization and information sharing). They only characterize choice processes in a manner such that the political game has a common-good component that, by definition, political actors all value. Thereafter, two sets of questions—analytical and empirical—are raised. Analytically, what are the conditions under which legislative equilibria possess a Maass-like property of deliberation and discussion or an information-theoretic reduction of uncertainty through specialization and information transmission? Empirically, are legislatures in fact designed such that these theoretical conditions are met?

Using the concept of a legislative equilibrium, any number of organizational arrangements can be analyzed to determine whether normative ideals are attainable in the presence of legislators who are assumed to use information strategically. Regardless of the specific arrangement under consideration, the resulting equilibrium has two kinds of properties of interest: informational and distributional.[22] Both of these highlight the role of committees in the legislative process.

Informational Efficiency

Due to legislators' risk-aversion and the characterization of incomplete information as uncertainty about the outcomes associated with policies, informational theories have a positive-sum component in addition to the standard conflict of interest (or zero-sum) component of distributive theories. Regardless of where the realized outcome lies, all legislators benefit from the reduction

---

21. In parallel fashion, informational theories capture the second, but only the second, of two components of Fenno's (1973) conception of "good public policy." The first of these is the pursuit by individuals of their ideological objectives. The second is the acquisition of expertise so that legislation meets those objectives. While the conceptual similarities between Maass's "common good" and Fenno's "good public policy" are apparent, the mode of analysis of these two scholars is quite different. Broadly, Fenno sees "good public policy" as one of several possible individual goals, while Maass sees the "common good" as a normatively desirable outcome of collective decision making.

22. The terms *distributive* and *distributional* are nearly synonymous but used somewhat differently. Distributive is used here mainly as an adjective for models or theories to stress their substantive motivation in literature on distributive politics. Distributional is used mainly in the context of informational theories. While it pertains to the who-gets-what component of informational theories, such theories do not capture the concentrated-benefits, dispersed-costs feature as explicitly as distributive theories.

of uncertainty about the relationship between policies and outcomes. That is, relative to situations in which specialization is either (*a*) absent or (*b*) present but concealed by the committee, everyone benefits from knowing a priori what outcome will emerge from an agreed upon policy.

In LSGs, the *informational efficiency* associated with an equilibrium refers to the amount of reduction of uncertainty in the course of the choice process, independent of the distributional (who-gets-what) characteristics of the realized outcome. More concretely, the analytic issues include: conditions under which a committee specializes, and the degree to which, if it specializes, its private information becomes available to the legislature in the course of equilibrium behavior. Committees are said to be *informative* to the degree that they not only specialize but also make their expertise available to the legislature. Defined as such, informational efficiency can be regarded as capturing an essential (positive) portion of Fenno's "good public policy" goal or Maass's notion of meaningful deliberation and discussion. An organizational design that fosters informative committees is an institutional means to policy ends via the reduction of uncertainty.

While it may seem obvious that a rational legislature will always appoint a committee, provide it with resources, adopt rules to encourage specialization, and force the committee to share its expertise, this is often impossible. Resources to defray a committee's cost of specialization may be limited.[23] The policy in question may be hopelessly complex, so that the legislature is better off allocating its resources elsewhere.[24] Legislators' preferences may be too divergent from one another for legislators to come to an informed agreement.[25] Or, even if the prospect for agreement on informationally efficient choices is present, the incentives for strategic use of information may be too great for the committee to share its expertise.[26] Formal analysis identifies precise limitations on, yet also ways of enhancing, the informative role of committees in the legislative process. Again, while some of the theoretical tools and language are new, most of the ideas are not.

Long ago a framework for distributing the work-load—the committee system—evolved. It permits specialization, but it creates as well as

23. See sources cited in n. 5.

24. Buchanan et al. (1970), for example, identified cross-state variation in legislative specialization and attributed it to state-specific policy problems and more or less efficient allocation of legislative resources to meet those problems.

25. Fenno (1966) notes years in which the House Appropriations Committee is unable to "come out united" in favor of its bill.

26. Kingdon (1973), for instance, relays anecdotes of members' distrust of Armed Services Committee members' statements because the latter are regarded as "biased." See also Clapp 1963.

solves problems: how may committees be kept flexible enough to deal with changing conditions, on what basis are chairmen to be selected, on what criteria are committee decisions to be made, when is the house to ratify them? In response to the need of members for more guidance than the committee system provides, an informal system of expertise appears to have been developed alongside, and overlapping, it. Trusted members who are believed to have superior knowledge of certain subjects achieve recognition as specialists. They guarantee to their fellows the feasibility of certain proposals, challenge others. They process and digest raw facts and communicate them in the form of "do" or "don't" recommendations—recommendations expressed in the authorship of bills, by questions in hearing, by stands taken in caucus, by remarks made at lunch. The experts appear, to some extent at least, responsible to their fellows for exercising restraint in their espousal of personal interest. Thus they help others distinguish "reality" or "technical knowledge" from "values," "preferences," or "political knowledge" in areas unfamiliar to them. In recompense for their efforts they are given the confidence of their fellows—their bills go through, they shape policy—they have power. (Buchanan et al. 1970, 650)

The conception of the "power" of legislative committees as described in this passage is quite different from that which emerges from standard, perfect-information spatial models of legislative politics. Introduction of the distributive counterparts to the concepts of informational efficiency and informative committees leads to a clarification of these different conceptions of committee power.

Distributional Losses

Assessment of the distributional property associated with an equilibrium uses the legislature's median voter's ideal point as a baseline. To the degree that expected outcomes in the equilibrium deviate from this point, the legislature is said to incur a *distributional loss*. This focus, of course, is not unique to informational models. As discussed in chapter 2, the issue of who gets what and at whose expense is the primary focus of distributive models.[27] Whenever

---

27. The reason distributional losses are identified expectationally rather than with certainty stems from the fact that the legislative equilibrium may be informationally inefficient. That is, expertise may not be obtained because it is not worthwhile for the committee to specialize. Or, expertise may not be incorporated into the legislature's final policy choice because it is disadvantageous to the committee to divulge its private information. In these instances, distributional effects are identified by asking where, given equilibrium behavior and beliefs, realized outcomes will lie on average.

a distributional loss is incurred by the legislature, a comparable distributional gain is reaped by the committee.

Committee Power

Two fundamentally different conceptions of the power of committees correspond to the informational and distributional properties of legislative equilibria.

Distributive committee power refers to behavior that results in committee gains at the expense of a majority. In instances of distributive committee power, a committee exercises its parliamentary rights to get a majority to do what is not in the majority's interest with respect to a single issue.[28] Examples include Shepsle and Weingast's (1987a) model in which a committee with an "ex post veto" can initiate (and maintain) policies that move (keep) the status quo toward its ideal point and away from the ideal points of a chamber majority, and Weingast and Marshall's (1988) industrial organization theory in which stable policies have the property that policies resulting from high-demand cross-committee logrolls are sustained in spite of their policy-by-policy nonmajoritarian status.[29]

Informational committee power, in contrast, refers to behavior that re-sults in gains to committee and noncommittee members alike. In instances of informational committee power, a committee credibly transmits private infor-mation to get a majority to do what is in the majority's interest. Informational committee power is perfectly analogous with Neustadt's (1960) notion of presidential power as the "power to persuade." A president gets what he wants not by commanding others to act contrary to their interests (which, were it to occur, would be analogous to distributive committee power). Rather, his power comes from persuading others that, contrary to their prepersuasion beliefs, what he wants *is* in their interest. Maass has a similar argument about the power of executive's legislative liaisons and concludes that committee power in Congress, too, is informational as defined here (1983, chap. 3). Polsby's description of House committees is also mainly informational (1968, 166), as are Kingdon's (1973) and Fenno's (1966 and 1973). Luce's descrip-tion of parliamentary committee power is informational as well (1922, 88). Finally, in a similar vein but broader context, so is Deutsch's: "If many studies of politics have stressed *power,* or enforcement, it should now be added that information precedes compulsion" (1963, 151).

---

28. Notice that even in a multidimensional spatial setting, a "majority's interest" is always well-defined over single, unidimensional issues. When references are made to nonmajoritarian outcomes, the baseline is always the median voter's ideal point on a unidimensional space.

29. Elsewhere I have subdivided this conception of distributive committee power into positive and negative committee power, depending on whether the committee may move or merely maintain policies toward or near its ideal point, respectively (Krehbiel 1988). This distinction will not be employed here.

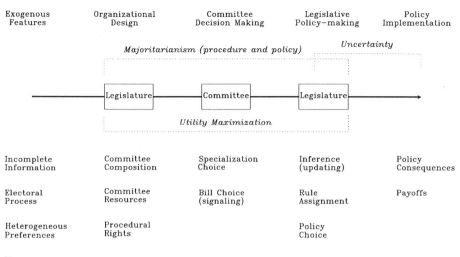

Fig. 3.2. Composite sketch of legislative signaling games and postulates of legislative organization

Structure of the Models

Figure 3.2 is a composite representation of four legislative signaling games that share basic assumptions. While a precise and comprehensive understanding of LSGs requires consulting and working through the original, more mathematical works, this section provides an adequate working overview by tracing through the five columns of the figure, emphasizing empirical referents for the components of the models and the overarching postulates of legislative organization that distinguish informational from distributive theories.

Exogenous Features

Several characteristics are taken as fixed or exogenous. The chief of these, incomplete information, was discussed above. Additionally, the models are motivated by some standard conceptions of the electoral process. Legislators obtain their jobs from an electorate. Voters in the electorate are diverse in terms of their basic values, needs, and wants. Although LSGs do not model the electoral process explicitly, the implicit presumption is that diversity in the electorate translates into diversity in the legislature in two ways that LSGs do model explicitly. First, legislators are presumed to have heterogeneous preferences. Second, they are presumed to have diverse skills.

Heterogeneity of preferences in LSGs is much the same as in distributive models. As noted above, legislators are assumed to have spatial preferences, and different legislators possess different ideal points in the outcome space. Thus, distributional conflict exists in informational games just as in distributive models.

Diversity of skills, however, is another feature that distinguishes informational from purely distributive models. Legislators are elected from constituencies with conflicting distributive interests, and distributive models accommodate this diversity nicely. But legislators themselves are also diverse in terms of their substantive policy interests. The use of the word *interest* in this context is somewhat unconventional. It bears no necessary relationship to preferences (as in: What interests will the legislator pursue?), but rather pertains to what issues the legislator finds interesting. When attempting to organize informative committees, a legislature as institutional designer exploits the fact that this skill-based interest may affect the quality and quantity of work a legislator will do.

Organizational Design

The conception of a well-designed legislature as one that taps the diverse skills of its legislators has been discussed extensively in empirical and organization theory literature.[30] A recurring theme in this book is that LSGs can offer uniquely precise and distinctively different insights into issues of organizational design. To begin to identify these, we move to the organizational design stage in figure 3.2 and note some distinguishing features of LSGs vis-à-vis organization theories of legislatures and more recent distributive theories.

Differences between organization theory and informational theories pertain mostly to the explicitness with which predictions about legislative organization are derived and the relative ease of observability of phenomena about which LSGs offer predictions. I generally regard these as differences more of style and technique than of substance and, therefore, will forego an extended discussion of them.[31]

Differences between distributive theories and informational theories pertain mostly to the status of institutional arrangements in the legislative process. Each class of models usually assumes that a committee system exists, and this assumption is clearly consistent with the empirical tradition of congressional scholarship. "The familiar legislative device which facilitates specialized consideration of substantive matters, and thus counteracts the accepted principle of generalization is, of course, the standing committee" (Buchanan et al. 1970, 737). Hereafter, LSGs uniquely allow several institu-

---

30. See, for example, Bryce 1905; Cooper 1988; Davis 1975; Harlow 1917; Maass 1983; McConachie 1898; Porter 1974; and Winslow 1931.

31. See Gilligan and Krehbiel 1990 for a more detailed comparison of organization theory with a game-theoretic model of institutional maintenance.

tional features to arise endogenously as products of an explicit choice process. While diverging from theories of the New Institutionalism school, informational theories cling to more traditional views of the committee system. Consider, for example, the "informal agreement" described by Buchanan et al. immediately following the excerpt quoted above:

> But even committees are denied the formal authority that might accompany their specialized responsibility. They remain in theory representative of the whole house; their purpose is ostensibly economy of attention; their decisions are revocable by a bare majority. It is by tradition and informal agreement that their authority is in fact recognized, and their decisions are occasionally overridden. (Buchanan et al. 1970, 737)

What, then, are some of the informal agreements (i.e., endogenous choices about legislative organization) that have been regarded as historically important and that can be studied both theoretically and empirically?

First, the composition of committees can be important in the legislative design process. Several related questions have been addressed by informational theories. Should a committee be composed of members who are homogeneous in their support for certain measures, along the lines of Thomas Jefferson's advice: "Don't put the baby to a nurse that careth not for it"?[32] Or should they be heterogeneous to foster a legalistic sort of adversarial process from which a "just" or "good" proposal emerges? Should committees be representative of the parent body so they are more likely to serve as faithful agents of the legislature? Or should they be composed of preference outliers who, in the spirit of distributive theories, propose policies whose likely consequences diverge from those preferred by relatively disinterested or uninformed members of the legislature?

A second set of issues pertains to resources and parliamentary rights that the parent chamber grants or denies committees to facilitate or impede their specialization efforts. Resources include office space, staff, and investigative authority. Parliamentary rights include committee members' agenda setting or proposing powers, and protection from nonmembers' amendments on the floor.

Committee Decision Making

Given a conception of an optimal legislative organization as one that exploits institutional endogeneity to meet a combination of distributional and informational objectives, informational theories proceed by allowing committees to

---

32. In spite of this often quoted phrase, Jefferson can hardly be regarded as an advocate of granting extensive parliamentary rights to committees. Indeed, the historical context in which he uttered it was one of great reluctance to turn matters over to standing committees.

do more than act as distributive, division-of-labor devices. Along the lines most persuasively argued by Cooper (1970) and clearly embraced by Fenno (1966 and 1973), Manley (1970), Maass (1983), and others, another role of committees of equal or greater historical importance is informational. Committees are also specialization-of-labor devices.

The subservient nature of committees in informational theories cannot be overemphasized. Committees are exclusively instruments of the legislature that perform for the legislature.[33] Committee composition is determined by the legislature; it is not governed by self-selection, as commonly presumed in distributive approaches. Rules governing the consideration of committee bills are chosen by the legislature; there is no presumption of "closed rules," "ex post vetoes," or "gatekeeping powers."[34] And committee resources are not to be taken for granted by distribution-sensitive legislators; they are to be granted by the information-sensitive legislature. Of course, all of these potential features of organizational design may be realized within the theory, and whether they are realized has a bearing on committee decision making. But a key difference between informational and distributive theories is that committee types, rules, and resources arise from within informational models because of the constitutional provision that the legislature determines the rules of its proceedings.

As a function of the resources and parliamentary rights that committees receive in the organizational design stage and of expectations regarding the policy-making stage, the committee makes two choices. First, it decides whether to expend its resources (if any) to specialize. Second, it chooses a bill to propose to the full legislative body. Because actors in LSGs are sophisticated in the sense of making current choices on the basis of the expectations regarding future behavior, these choices depend crucially upon what the legislature will do in the policy-making stage.

Legislative Policy-Making

At the legislative policy-making (or floor) stage, the legislature does three things. First, based on its observations of committee decision making—specifically, the committee's specialization and bill choices—the legislature

---

33. On committees as agents of the legislature, see Buchanan et al. 1970, 637 and 646; Clapp 1963, 250; Cooper 1988, 307; Maass 1983, 32 and 39; McConachie 1898, 117–18; and Winslow 1931, 184 and 561.

34. See, for example (respectively), Weingast and Moran 1983; Shepsle and Weingast 1987a; Denzau and Mackay 1983; and Krehbiel 1985 and juxtapose their assumptions with the general discussion in Clapp 1963, chap. 6. Clapp, for instance, responds to allegations of committees' pigeonholing and delaying tactics with these seemingly ageless words: "But it [gatekeeping, etc.] is much more limited than it used to be, although the political scientists haven't completely caught up with that fact" (1963, 254).

makes an inference about the committee's private information (if any). In other words, as summarized above, the legislature updates its beliefs about the relationship between policies and outcomes. Second, it makes a rule assignment for the committee's bill.[35] The most common rules analyzed are open rules, which permit amendments by the legislature, and closed rules, which allow the legislature only to accept the committee's bill outright or reject it in favor of a status quo policy (whose consequences are also uncertain in the absence of information transmission). Third, it makes an expected utility maximizing policy choice in accordance with the rule.

Policy Implementation

After the legislature makes its policy choice, the strategic stages of the game are complete. All that remains is determination of policy consequences. Substantively, this can be interpreted as implementation of the legislature's policy. Conceptually, implementation is the mapping of the legislature's policy choice from the policy space (in which legislative choice occurs) to the outcome space (over which legislators' utility is defined). Given a realized outcome, payoffs are awarded and the game ends.

Five Principles of Legislative Signaling

Detailed discussions and formal proofs of the equilibria in legislative signaling models can be found in the works cited previously. The immediate objective is to expose intuition rather than to exhibit technique. This is achieved by stating five principles that are representative of the formal derivations from LSGs and by illustrating these principles with a variety of cases: hypothetical and real, apolitical and political. (All of the principles are ceteris paribus statements.)

Composition of Committees: Preference Outliers

> THE OUTLIER PRINCIPLE. *The more extreme are the preferences of a committee specialist relative to preferences of a nonspecialist in the legislature, the less informative is the committee.*

The Outlier Principle is the most robust property of legislative signaling models. It holds for homogeneous and heterogeneous committees, under open, modified, and closed rules, and with or without procedural commitment. The central intuition is that when specialists' and nonspecialists' policy

---

35. In Gilligan and Krehbiel 1987, the legislature was assumed to commit to a rule prior to the committee's specialization decision. The sequence was changed and a comparable game analyzed in Gilligan and Krehbiel 1989b.

objectives are similar, specialists will have greater incentives to reveal clearly their private information.

Case: Car Buying

Suppose you are interested in purchasing a car but you have neither the money to buy a new car nor the automotive expertise to assess accurately the quality of used cars. You are given the choice of buying one of two used cars that, to the best of your knowledge—which is not good—appear to be of absolutely identical quality. That is, they are the same model, have the same mileage, the same number of dents and scratches, and the same estimated air pressure in the tires (which, like all ignorant consumers, you kicked).

- Car *A* is for sale by KK's Auto-Mart, whose salesman, KK, tells you: "This is a great car. You'll be very happy with it."
- Car *B* is for sale by your father, a retired used car salesman who lives two blocks from you, has no second car, and thus can be expected occasionally to borrow the car you buy. He tells you: "This is a great car. You'll be very happy with it."

Which car do you buy?

With the exception of the sellers' interests, everything in the case is intended to be equal. This is not to deny that ample opportunity exists for injection of extraneous facts that lead to a wiseacre answer of "car *A*." That's the wrong answer, though, for a straightforward reason. When other things truly are equal, an uninformed buyer (generically, the receiver of a signal) is inclined to believe (view as truthful, impute precise meaning to, perceive as informative, etc.) statements of others who are not only informed but also have compatible interests. In this example, it is not the buyer's trust of his father that makes car *B* the wise choice. The example is purposely silent on matters of trust. It is that the seller of car *B* occasionally needs reliable transportation and thus has interests that are aligned with the ignorant but conveniently located buyer. If the car really were a lemon, the father would prefer to sell it to a different buyer and have his son take a gamble with KK.

Case: The Soviet Threat

Turning from cars to communists, consider executive-legislative relations on defense policy in the early 1980s and assume the following. The Pentagon has an informational advantage vis-à-vis the Congress with respect to the seriousness of the Soviet threat. Both the Defense Department and the Congress (unitary actors for purposes of the example) want to provide for an adequate national defense. But the Pentagon is a budget maximizer à la Niskanen

(1971), while the Congress wants to trim the fat in the Pentagon to meet as many of its domestic demands as possible. Secretary Weinberger (erstwhile "Cap the Knife" but reincarnated in the Reagan years as "Cap the Ladle") testifies before Congress. He says, in effect: "The Soviet threat is really big. We need lots of money this year." Two questions expose more of the signaling intuition of the Outlier Principle.

- How much information is conveyed by Weinberger's statement?
- What if he had instead said: "It's not so bad now. We can live with a 0 percent real increase this year"?

The answer to the first question is "Not very much." Given Weinberger's extreme prodefense preferences, he is likely to make such a request under a wide range of circumstances: roughly, if the threat were huge, large, medium, or small (anything but *very* small).

The answer to the second question is contained in this reasoning by Congress (as receiver): "If Weinberger says the Soviet threat isn't that bad, then it really must be small. Of all people, Cap would be among the least likely to propose a freeze on defense spending, since it would be very difficult—given his preferences—to appropriate too much."

Extremity of preferences of an informed actor (the sender) does not make information transmission impossible. It does, however, make the signaling noisy or uninformative for many more states of the world (in this case, practically everything except "no Soviet threat") than would be the case with, say, a Carlucci or a Cheney.[36] Consequently, the realized outcome from any given level of expenditures is highly unpredictable, and the uninformed decision maker (here, Congress) reaps only a fraction of the potential benefits from policy expertise.

Case: Cue Taking
John Kingdon's (1973) exceptional interview-intensive study, *Congressmen's Voting Decisions,* contains innumerable references to the importance of expertise in the legislative process and the sources on whom uninformed legislators rely. A small sample follows (italics added).

---

36. Even Cheney—a moderate relative to Weinberger—has not brought fully informative signaling to congressional-legislative defense policy formation, however. In discussions on the Stealth bomber, for example, he gave the following testimony to the Armed Services Committee: "There is a perception abroad in the land [*sic*] that peace is at hand because of the changes in the Soviet Union and that allows us to make changes in our military posture. I think that is not the case" (*New York Times,* July 26, 1989). Although this statement occurred prior to the dramatic events in Eastern Europe in the fall and winter of 1989, similar statements can be found with respect to the size of the resulting "peace dividend."

- "When congressmen name their informants, however, listed among them are nearly always *members of relevant committees.* Of those cases involving informants with expertise, indeed, 98 percent are on the committees." (83–84)
- " 'You find out that you can't possibly know about everything. Your constituents expect you to, but you just can't. So you start to seek out fellow members who are of the *same philosophical bent* as you and who are on the committee that heard the experts and considered the legislation. You rely on them.' " (12)
- "In selecting congressmen upon whom to rely, the first rule appears to be, as one respondent put it, '*Choose those you agree with.*' " (72–73).
- " 'On something like banking and currency, I don't pretend to be acquainted with it, so I just ask _____ or _____. These are *people who think exactly like I do,* and I don't need to be an expert.' " (74)

Kingdon's observation of committee- and preference-based cue taking in the House is apparently quite general. Stevens (1971) also observed it in the House.[37] Ornstein (1975b) observed it in the Senate. Wissel, O'Connor, and King (1976) found indirect evidence of it in eight state legislatures, as did Uslaner and Weber (1977) in a sample of state legislators from all fifty states. Conversely, others have noted the problems associated with reliance on outliers for behavioral cues. McConachie (1898, 118), for example, discusses why extreme conference committees are regarded as unreliable sources of information, while Clapp (1963, 227) and Asher (1974, 72–74) discuss the problems committees face when their subcommittees are composed of outliers.[38]

Composition of Committees: Heterogeneity

THE HETEROGENEITY PRINCIPLE. *Committee specialists from opposite sides of a policy spectrum are collectively more informative than specialists from only one side of the spectrum.*

The Heterogeneity Principle is a close cousin to Fenno's (1966 and 1973) descriptions of the House Appropriations Committee "coming out united" behind its bill. In the language of signaling models, the key concept is confirmatory signaling. The underlying logic is simple. Two informed opinions are better than one, especially when the informants are natural adversaries. In one respect, this is simply an extension of the old saw "Politics makes strange

---

37. Cited in Ornstein 1975b, 175.
38. See also Davidson 1974; and Muir 1982.

bedfellows." But the distinctive twist is informational. The bedfellows in a signaling game are not participants in a conventional two-policy logroll in which *A* gives *B* the policy that *B* wants badly, *B* gives *A* the policy that *A* wants badly, and each incurs relatively small costs on the giving side of the bargain.[39] Rather, they are competing specialists who, in at least some states of the world, can come to agreement on a single policy that makes both of them better off in spite of the presence of distributional conflict.

Case: Loan Defaults

In 1981, the federal government spent $235 million to cover defaulted student loans. By 1989 the rate at which students skipped out on debts under the federal loan program had increased nearly eightfold. As of 1989, thirty-seven cents out of every GSL dollar went to cover unrepaid loans. Any policy change that seeks to reduce defaults is subject to uncertainty with respect to the recovery of funds and prospective students' educational opportunities. A reasonable expectation is that political actors—such as cabinet heads, leaders of interest groups that are directly affected, and committee leaders—are better informed of such consequences than average legislators.

Under the Reagan administration, Education Secretary William Bennett had become concerned with default rates. Bennett's proposal to target all schools with default rates in excess of 20 percent was criticized as extreme and unrealistic by education groups, the Democratic Congress, and eventually Bush's Secretary of Education, Lauro Cavazos. The proposal was, in beltway-speak, born dead.

The responses to Cavazos's proposals, in contrast, were mildly positive. It is not the positiveness per se that is of interest for the Heterogeneity Principle. Rather, it is the information implicit in the statements of informed actors because they come from sources who have divergent (heterogeneous) preferences.

First and obviously, Cavazos endorsed his proposal, just as Bennett had endorsed Bennett's proposal, Weinberger endorsed high defense spending, Oliver North endorsed aid to the Contras, and mothers of America endorse apple pie. But considered jointly, the more informative signals came from congressional and interest group leaders.

- The Chairman of the House Education and Labor Committee's Subcommittee on Postsecondary Education, Pat Williams (D.–Mont.), said, "It is a good first step. On this one I think Cavazos gets an 'A.'"
- The president of the National Association of Trade and Technical

---

39. Spatially this requires a two-dimensional model, and all legislative signaling models to date are one-dimensional.

Schools, Stephen J. Blair, called the proposed rules "thoughtful and reasoned." Even though he regarded them as "tough and will have an adverse effect on a number of students and schools," he added that "we're confident the regulations will help to substantially reduce those defaults among trade and technical schools."[40]

Why are these endorsements informative? Because of the divergent preferences of their sources vis-à-vis a relatively conservative and budget conscious administration. Pat Williams has a record of moderately strong support for federal involvement in education.[41] The National Association of Trade and Technical Schools represents about one-third of the schools that would be hardest hit by the new rules.

The case of student defaults shows how heterogeneous moderates can be informative. The next cases illustrate a hybrid of the Outlier and Heterogeneity Principles: heterogeneity is not a sufficient condition for meaningful signaling when informed actors are extreme preference outliers on opposite ends of a policy spectrum.

Case: Hot Air on Clean Air
In July, 1989, reports began to surface regarding the Bush administration's drafts of legislation to amend the Clean Air Act. Major components of these initiatives included auto emission limits and measures that would require industry to reduce emissions of toxic substances. Consider three signals.

- William Fay, a spokesman for an industry coalition that was actively lobbying at the time, denounced the measure as being much more costly than the administration estimates and as not giving industry the flexibility it needs to reduce pollution.
- David Hawkins, a senior lawyer for the Natural Resources Defense Council and former Assistant Administrator of the EPA for air programs in the Carter administration, denounced the program as a "major retreat from the President's promises."
- William Rosenberg, Assistant Administrator of Bush's EPA, said, "I believe that the negotiations on the language are going very well and that the bill that emerges will follow the letter and spirit of the president's commitments."[42]

---

40. See *New York Times,* June 2, 1989.

41. Barone and Ujifusa, for example, refer to Williams as an "old-fashioned liberal Democrat . . . solid pro-labor, pro-teacher" (1986, 785).

42. See *New York Times,* July 12, 1989.

Six lips moved, but what was their collective message? Specifically, what is the likely consequence of the proposed policy? Everyone made statements that were predictable, given their preferences, but incompatible, given the significant differences in their preferences. As such, the statements collectively convey little information about the consequences of the proposed policy.

Uninformed players cannot discern specialists' private information when they know specialists' preferences, when such preferences are extreme, and when, accordingly, specialists have incentives to transmit nonconfirmatory signals.

Case: Noise in H313

In a chapter entitled "External Controls over Bills Reported by Committees," Arthur Maass presents a case of housing legislation in 1972 that illustrates the role of the Rules Committee (which meets in Capitol Suite H313) as an agent of control on behalf of the House. The events also have a transparent interpretation in terms of the absence of confirmatory signaling by a committee whose principal actors are heterogeneous outliers.

In 1972 the Housing Subcommittee of the House Committee on Banking and Currency reported a bill to the full committee after lengthy hearings. The full committee then held more hearings and considered the bill in executive session over a period of six weeks from late July to mid-September. This long deliberation was due in good part to a conflict within the committee between the full committee chairman, Wright Patman (D.–Tex.) and the chairman of the Housing Subcommittee, William A. Barrett (D.–Pa.). Patman and others offered dozens of amendments in the full committee. Finally the bill was reported three weeks before Congress was to adjourn by a vote of nineteen yes, three no, six voting present. However, twenty-five of the committee's thirty-seven members wrote supplementary views in the committee report.

The committee formally requested a rule. Before the Rules Committee, William B. Widnall (R.–N.J.), ranking Republican on the Housing Subcommittee, said that Patman had made a mockery of the legislative process by his dilatory handling of the bill during full committee sessions. Patman, although he formally requested the rule, said to the Rules Committee: "It's a good bill in many ways. You do what you want." Faced with this intramural squabble, the Rules Committee voted 9 to 5 against a rule. It was protecting the House from incompetent work in the legislative committee. (Maass 1983, 83)

In most of the illustrations of the Outlier and Heterogeneity Principles, it was taken for granted that policy experts existed.[43] Yet, in at least some legislative settings—such as noninstitutionalized organizations or even institutionalized ones that are forced by the electorate to confront exceedingly difficult policy problems—specialists may not exist. Then an informationally efficient legislative organization must address the antecedent issue of how to encourage specialization (the organization design stage in figure 3.2). In two of the four asymmetric-information legislative models cited above, the choice of the committee to specialize is endogenous, that is, explicitly modeled as a strategic choice within the game. The remaining principles extend the focus to a set of endogenous institutional issues that, when studied empirically, can shed additional light on the usefulness of informational theories.

Legislatively Rational Outliers

> THE INFORMATIVE OUTLIERS PRINCIPLE. *Preference outliers* may be *informative relative to nonoutliers if they are able to specialize at lower cost than nonoutliers.*

The strongest form of the Outlier and Heterogeneity Principles—that all committees should be perfect microcosms of the parent chamber—is too strong for most legislative settings. Individuals with extreme preferences cannot realistically be deprived committee seats when members of most legislatures are guaranteed at least one committee seat, and, thus, it would be difficult to keep all outliers off all committees. More relevant than this combinatorial qualification, however, is the implication from the theory of the organization of informative committees that outliers *may* play an informative role.[44] The necessary conditions are that outliers are able to specialize at a lower cost than moderates, and that the legislature's savings in terms of lower resource transfers (e.g., staff) to the committee offset the informational loss from the inferior informativeness of an outlying committee. Granted, this condition is a mouthful. Two examples help to clarify it.

Case: Commissioned Research
Suppose that an academic discipline—say, political science—benefits from precise exposition and dissemination of a narrow field of study that *may* become important in furthering the discipline but whose importance has yet to

---

43. The possible exception was Maass's housing example. I cannot discern from the excerpt whether the committee's signal was noisy due to "incompetent work," as Maass claims, or due to strategically noisy transmission of information by expert committee leaders with divergent preferences.

44. See Gilligan and Krehbiel 1990.

be established. Moreover, the field is presently inaccessible to all but a handful of members of the discipline, and those few happen to be aficionados of the field. If a designated, trustworthy, and representative agent of the discipline, such as the editor of one of its journals or publisher at a reputable press, were empowered to commission someone to study the field and write a comprehensive article or book about it, whom should he or she appoint to perform the task? A continuum of possibilities emerges, but two discrete options illustrate the costs and benefits of rational appointment strategies in the presence of uncertainty.

- Option *A* (Outlier). Assign the task to an aficionado who has done some research in a related area. Although he will be predisposed to present and evaluate the literature favorably, he can be expected to specialize in this area quickly and to need relatively few resources or inducements for his efforts.[45]
- Option *B* (Inlier). Assign the task to a neutral political scientist, even though she has no related professional experience, will have to begin the project from scratch, and will require more compensation than the outlier.

The outlier option may have a disciplinary resource advantage. Given the outlier's predisposition, the editor or publisher might actually entice him to do the requisite tooling up to write a respectable work. Indeed, once suitably equipped, he may even contribute further by improving upon the literature. Meanwhile, the inlier goes about furthering her own field in which she has a comparative advantage.

The inlier option may have a signaling advantage. Since the outlier is, by definition, predisposed to liking research in the field, his review of it is likely to be noisy according to the theory. Under a wide range of conceivable states of privately observed quality, the outlier would report the same thing. Thus, uninformed readers would not know exactly what to believe. The inlier, in contrast, might report more clearly. But she will report more clearly and credibly only if she can be enticed to achieve the requisite level of expertise. Otherwise (and bringing us closer to legislative settings), the following situation emerges. Studies by academics who do not understand their field are not valuable to their discipline, just as committee reports by committee members who do not understand their jurisdictions are not valuable to their legislature.

So herein lies the rub: whether the greater specialization bang-for-the-buck associated with outliers offsets their lesser informativeness—or, alter-

---

45. To be true to the theory, it is important that the appointee not be a specialist upon assignment.

natively, whether the relatively high specialization costs associated with in-liers are justified by their greater informativeness—is ultimately an empirical issue. My intuition is that in legislative settings these necessary conditions for rational outliers are fairly strong, that is, not likely to be met.[46] But I repeat: this is not a theoretical issue, and certainly not a matter to be entrusted to my intuition. It is an issue for the analysis of data to resolve.

Case: The Sonny Side of Outliers

Representative Gillespie V. "Sonny" Montgomery was a decorated combat veteran in both World War II and Korea. In 1980 he retired as a major general in the Mississippi National Guard. A bachelor, he spends most of his time in his House office, which is decorated with model helicopters and jets, an AK-47 assault rifle used by a North Vietnamese soldier, and various awards, including the Hellcat of the Year and the Silver Helmet. Montgomery has served on the Veterans' Affairs Committee since 1969 and has been its chair-man since 1981.

So what?

First, Montgomery's credentials are such that one can well imagine him being a low-cost specialist in the sense of the theory of organizing informative committees. Second, in spite of his generally high level of support for vet-erans' programs, he has a reputation for keeping his committee's legislative requests under control. Representative Wayne Dowdy (D.–Miss.) praises both Montgomery's effort and his sense of the sentiment of the House, saying "He spends so much time in his work he pretty much knows how everything is going to go in his committee and on the floor." Representative Harley Stag-gers (D.–W.Va.) affirms Montgomery's constrained demands, saying that "[he] walks a fine line between doing what he can for vets and being fiscally responsible."[47]

In short, preference outliers, as low-cost specialists, *may* be informa-tionally efficient and legislatively rational.

Bill-Specific Procedures

THE RESTRICTIVE RULES PRINCIPLE. *Restrictive amendment procedures can provide incentives for committees to specialize and to be inform-ative.*

---

46. Clever readers who may regard the existence of this book as inconsistent with this guess are reminded that it was not commissioned. Still, the prospect of noisy signaling should be entertained even here (see chap. 7).

47. See *Congressional Quarterly*, July 1, 1989, 1602.

Throughout the postbehavioral or New Institutionalism years, increasing attention has been given to the procedures used by the House and Senate to consider individual bills. On the House side, these include the Consent Calendar,[48] suspension of the rules,[49] and special orders.[50] In the Senate, they include unanimous consent agreements.[51] Often these procedures are restrictive in terms of time allotted for debate and amendments allowed for consideration. Why do legislators collectively choose to zip their lips and tie their hands?

For comparative purposes, begin by reconsidering the standard, perfect-information, multidimensional model of distributive politics. Legislative choice occurs over a wide range of issues. On any given issue, a majority of decision makers are not deeply concerned about policy outcomes. However, a few people can always be found who care very deeply about the issue. Conceivably, in such settings a legislature collectively would want to constrain itself by passing a rule (or, more broadly, adopting a set of institutions) that grants high-demanders rights to make proposals consistent with high-demand preferences and that denies low- or no-demanders the right to propose amendments. The outcome associated with this institutional arrangement has the property that everyone gets his or her desired high-demand outcome on the issue of greatest concern while getting nothing (except a cumulatively ballooning tax burden or budget deficit) from all other issues of near indifference. The logic here is an institutional variation on Sam Rayburn's often quoted behavioral theme: "If you want to get along, you have to go along." Stated distributionally (and sorely lacking in Mr. Sam's folksy flair): "If you want to get a lot where you want it really badly, you have to give a little over and over and over where you don't much care—except maybe when you add it all up."

Chapter 2 discussed and illustrated the issue of commitment in the context of distributive theory, and here we elaborate on another potential limitation. The distributive view of legislative organization—like the formal models from which it arises—has no place for specialization. In contrast, the informational rationale for restrictive rules rests jointly on distributional and specialization considerations.

The distributional logic in informational theory is straightforward. Given a set of policies whose consequences are unknown, a legislature may benefit from delegating to a committee the task of acquiring expertise about the policy. But specialization requires effort. It is easier to entice people into

---

48. Bach 1988.
49. Bach 1986 and 1990; Gilligan and Krehbiel 1987b.
50. Bach 1981a and 1981b; Bach and Smith 1989.
51. Keith 1977; Krehbiel 1987; and Smith and Flathman 1989.

exerting effort if they have reason to believe a greater payoff awaits them for a job well done. One way of creating such expectations in a legislative setting is to promise a potentially expert committee a restrictive rule. In the end, the committee is made better off because its ability to make a "take-it-or-leave-it" offer effectively guarantees it a distributional commission of sorts.[52]

The informational logic is somewhat less intuitive but no less important. The key attribute of informative committees is that *everyone* in the legislature benefits from revelation of policy expertise, independent of the distributional properties of realized outcomes. The fact that "everyone" includes committee members gives an added boost to this informational rationale for restrictive rules. Committees not only may get the distributional bonus if they specialize; they also share the common good of informational efficiency. Furthermore, for reasons that are more thoroughly described elsewhere, the informational efficiency of restrictive rules almost always exceeds that of unrestrictive rules.[53]

Case: Architectural Contracting

An architect prides himself on his ability to create aesthetically pleasing designs, to develop a keen sense of his clients' functional needs, and to find designs that meet those needs. Indeed, he is so careful and thorough that, by the time he completes a set of plans, he knows better than his client what is in his client's interest. Suppose two prospective clients with identical functional needs and design tastes come to the architect and contract for his services. Each proposes a different contractual arrangement.

- Contract *A*—call it restrictive—stipulates that upon the architect's completion of plans, the client will look at the plans and then decide whether to accept them as-is or reject them. If the client accepts the plans, the architect gets the job and oversees it until completion. No major changes may occur in the interim because the alteration penalties to the client are exorbitant. Thus, the architect's payoff includes not only the contracted price but also artistic satisfaction from having fully and unalterably implemented a functional, yet aesthetic, design.
- Contract *B*—call it unrestrictive—stipulates that upon the architect's

---

52. The perfect-information theory of this type is Romer and Rosenthal's (1978) model in which an agenda setter (representing, for instance, a school board that proposes to an electorate an amount of educational expenditures) extracts "rents" from the median voter. See also Denzau and Mackay 1983 for an analogous legislative model and a decision-theoretic uncertainty extension, and Rosenthal 1989 for an excellent review of "the setter model."

53. The exceptions are if the legislature cannot commit to rule (Gilligan and Krehbiel 1989b) or, trivially, when the committee's and legislature's ideal points are identical. In either of these cases, the two rules are both perfectly informationally efficient.

completion of the plans, the client may change them as he wishes while the work is going on because the client can afford add-on or alteration fees. The architect's payoff therefore includes the agreed upon price, but the aesthetic component of his payoff is vulnerable to the kitschy whims of the client.

Under which contract is the architect likely to exert more effort on behalf of the client? The answer that is consistent with informational theory is contract *A*. Its take-it-or-leave-it feature approximates a closed rule in legislative situations. Just as the restrictive contract encourages effort on the part of the architect, which in turn facilitates good design, a restrictive rule encourages specialization on the part of a committee, which in turn facilitates good public policy.

Case: Tax Legislation (A)
Legislators have a lot to gain from expertise in tax policy. Conversely, they have a lot to lose from bungled tax policy. A recent and painful reminder of the latter is the political catastrophe surrounding catastrophic medical insurance for the elderly.[54]

Given the complexity and importance of tax policy and the history of hard work by revenue committees, it is not surprising that the House Ways and Means Committee has a history of receiving restrictive rules for its legislation (Bach and Smith 1989; Fenno 1973; Manley 1970). The Restrictive Rules Principle suggests why this is not just a historical quirk. Restrictive rules can be forms of either encouraging or paying off the committee for grappling with difficult issues.

But neither is it surprising in light of mishaps such as catastrophic medical insurance that the Ways and Means Committee is not guaranteed closed rules. Rare but occasional use of unrestrictive rules has the desirable property, from the legislature's perspective, of minimizing or eliminating distributional losses while continuing to reap informational gains. Bach and Smith (1989, 166) present data indicating that from the 94th through 99th Congresses, Ways and Means percentages for unrestrictive rules were 30.0 percent, 9.5 percent, 17.9 percent, 0.0 percent, 9.3 percent, and 0.0 percent, respectively.

Commitment to Procedures

THE PROCEDURAL COMMITMENT PRINCIPLE. *Informational efficiency entails distributional losses under procedural commitment, but not under noncommitment.*

---

54. See *Congressional Quarterly,* September 16, 1989, 2397–98.

The case of tax legislation was truncated because its significance extends to the Procedural Commitment Principle, which accentuates the trade-offs between the legislature's informational and distributional goals and therefore helps to synthesize informational and distributive theories.

Case: Tax Legislation (B)
The tax policy coin has two sides, and Ways and Means Chairman Dan Rostenkowski (D.–Ill.) exemplifies them both.

- Side *A* is informational and is embodied in Rostenkowski's reflections on the 1986 Tax Reform Act: "On my tombstone, I want the question, 'Is it good law?'"[55] Granted, the Outlier Principle suggests that Rostenkowski is not the most credible sender of this self-serving message. (The chairman went on to assert that the answer to his question was "yes.") But the informational component of the Restrictive Rules Principle tells us to entertain it nonetheless.
- Side *B* is distributional and identifies some ways in which "good policy" must be obtained. Another news feature on the Ways and Means Chairman begins:

  Representative Dan Rostenkowski is the champion horse-trader in Congress. A few years ago when the monumental tax legislation he was sponsoring was coming unraveled, he called the members of his Ways and Means Committee into his office one by one. For a lawmaker from rural Alabama, the chairman agreed to allow tax exemptions for bonds used to attract businessmen to small towns. For a Texan, he promised that oil companies could write off some drilling costs. For a Long Island Congressman, he promised tax breaks to solid waste treatment plants. He wrote in special provisions for sports stadiums in Cleveland, Miami, Chicago, Memphis, and Northern New Jersey, for a convention center in Miami, and for a parking garage in Charleston, S.C. And so forth and so on until he had 19 members, a majority of the committee, lined up. After that, it was only a matter of time before the overall bill was passed by the House. "Politics," he is fond of saying, "is an imperfect process."[56]

  "Imperfect" because a distributional pricetag is attached to specialization.

Meanwhile, on the Senate side of the Capitol, the Chairman of the Finance Committee, Lloyd Bentsen (D.–Tex.), illustrated the limits of buying votes with distributive benefits. Calling Rostenkowski's decision to consider

---

55. See *New York Times*, February 5, 1989.
56. See *New York Times*, June 16, 1989.

lowering capital gains taxes "bad tax policy," he announced that industry-specific transition rules—a common way of conferring particularistic benefits in the making of tax policy—would no longer be the modus operandi in the Finance Committee.[57]

Distributional concerns sometimes weigh heavily on legislators' minds, and by no means do informational theories overlook distributive demands. Nonetheless, informational theories are fundamentally different from distributive theories in both the assumed and derived roles of pork barrel politics in the legislative process. Pork is not the do-all and end-all of legislative behavior, legislative organization, or legislative policy outcomes. Thus, legislatures will be reluctant to commit to parliamentary arrangements that "institutionalize" gains from trade. Likewise, in informational theories, distributional issues merely form the basis of conflict. To be sure, conflict is a major part of what makes legislative politics fascinating, and distributive policies are sometimes useful currencies with which to pay off hardworking committee members who contribute to informational efficiency in the legislative process. However, informational theories place distributive politics in a different perspective. Pork may be a lubricant for the legislative machine, but it is not the machine's main product.

Predictions

The cases and citations accompanying the five principles of legislative signaling are not intended to serve as definitive evidence regarding informational theories. They are intended only to summarize and illustrate some results from a recent line of theoretical research that is easily related to a long line of empirical research. It should be increasingly clear that the informational departures from distributive theories are nontrivial in terms of empirical implications, and soon I shall turn to systematic empirical analysis that sheds light on competing predictions. To structure that analysis, I first state five predictions that parallel the five principles of LSGs and that are translated into testable hypotheses in chapters 4–6.

Preference Outliers

> PREDICTION 1: OUTLIERS. *Legislative committees will* not, *as a matter of practice, be composed predominantly of high demanders or preference outliers.*

---

57. See *New York Times*, June 13, 1989.

Relative to committees that are microcosms of their parent chamber, preference-outlying committees are informationally inefficient, distributionally nonmajoritarian, or both. They are informationally inefficient because, other things being equal, they are less likely than nonoutliers to specialize and less likely to divulge their private information when they specialize.[58] They are distributionally nonmajoritarian if, to induce them to specialize, the parent chamber must commit to the use of a closed rule for the committees' proposals.[59]

Heterogeneous Committees

> PREDICTION 2: HETEROGENEITY. *Legislative committees* will *be composed of heterogeneous members, that is, legislators whose preferences represent both sides of the policy spectrum.*

Other things being equal, heterogeneous committees enhance informational efficiency without distributional losses. The key concept is *confirmatory signaling.* If a committee is composed of policy specialists whose preferred outcomes bookend the preferred outcome of the legislature's median voter, opportunities for credible transmission of private information are enhanced. Moreover, when heterogeneous committees reach "bipartisan agreements" (Manley 1970), "come out united" (Fenno 1966), or send "confirmatory signals" (Gilligan and Krehbiel 1989a), the advantages from the legislature's perspective are twofold. Obviously, informational efficiency is enhanced. Less obviously, distributional losses are small or nonexistent.[60]

Legislatively Rational Outliers

> PREDICTION 3: EXCEPTIONAL OUTLIERS. *Exceptional cases with respect to the Outlier Prediction will involve members with extreme preferences who can specialize at lower cost than moderates and, therefore, may be comparatively informative in spite of their preference extremity.*

This is a strong, necessary condition that qualifies the Preference-Outlier Prediction. Clearly, not all committees will be perfect microcosms of the

---

58. For the case when other things are not equal, see Prediction 3.

59. The "both" case is an extension from the second observation. When the legislature commits to a closed rule, both informational efficiency and distributional losses are increasing in the divergence of committee-legislature preferences (Gilligan and Krehbiel 1989b).

60. They are nonexistent in the case of open or modified rules, but "small" relative to homogeneous committees in the case of closed rules. See Gilligan and Krehbiel 1989a, table 2.

parent body. But informational theory implies that when preference-outlying committees are appointed, such appointment is attributable to the informational role they play through low-cost specialization.

Bill-Specific Procedures

PREDICTION 4: RESTRICTIVE RULES. *Use of restrictive rules will be positively associated with committee specialization, nonoutlying committees, and heterogeneous committees.*

A rationally designed legislative organization is one that may tie its own hands or delegate special parliamentary rights to its committees, notwithstanding the distributional losses that may ensue. Informational theories tell us why and when restrictive rules are most likely to be used.

The "why" has two parts. First and most intuitively, a legislature's commitment to restrictive rules encourages committee specialization because the prospective specialists (the committee) are ensured a distributional gain at the end of the game. Second and more subtly, restrictive rules are informationally efficient. This result holds under both procedural commitment and noncommitment, albeit for somewhat different reasons. In the commitment case, the informational efficiency of the closed rule stems from the fact that under a relatively wide range of situations, a committee finds it in its interest to share its expertise under restrictive rules. Under open rules, in contrast, a committee has a greater incentive to suppress what it knows, since noncommittee members could and would turn the committee's private information against it by amending the bill. In the noncommitment case—that is, when the committee must propose its bill without the knowledge of the rule under which it will be considered—the legislature probabilistically assigns an unrestrictive rule as a function of the extremity of the committee's proposal. This has two desirable effects. The committee always communicates all of its private information about the relationship between policies and outcomes, that is, the equilibrium is fully informationally efficient. Furthermore, the committee proposes the bill that yields the legislative median's ideal point, that is, the legislature suffers no distributional loss.

The "whens" of restrictive rules are consistent with the outlier and heterogeneity implications. Restrictive rules are more likely to be used on legislation from nonoutlying rather than outlying committees, heterogeneous rather than homogeneous committees, and heterogeneous nonoutliers rather than homogeneous high demanders. Again, the distributional side of informational theory contains the explanation. Nonoutlying committees will extract less of a distributional loss than outlying committees. Likewise, heterogeneous committees, through confirmatory signaling, are more likely to propose bills whose realized outcomes correspond to the chamber's median ideal point.

Commitment to Procedures

> PREDICTION 5: PROCEDURAL COMMITMENT. *Because procedural commitment undermines informational efficiency, encourages distributional losses, or both, a legislature will not—or cannot—commit to organizational forms that foster gains from trade.*

The issues of commitment and distributional-informational trade-offs are among the most subtle and difficult ones that emerge from informational theories. Their importance, however, suggests that even a relatively imprecise attempt to assess them empirically is worthwhile.

The main complication—which, in the end, is not crippling—is that apart from its comparative advantages or disadvantages, procedural commitment may not be possible in a legislature that determines the rules of its proceedings. Legislative procedures may be sufficiently fluid that commitments (by leaders, for example) to conduct legislative business in certain ways may be lacking in credibility. Multiple opportunities arise throughout the legislative process in which to change procedural course. Combined with self-interest, the Majoritarian Postulate as it pertains to procedural choice may severely undermine institutional attempts to confer disproportionate distributive benefits to committees. Certainly this was one of the implications of the cases cited at the end of chapter 2, and the issue will be brought up again in chapter 6.

The reason these complexities surrounding procedural commitment are not crippling with regard to assessing informational theory empirically is twofold. First, one theory suggests that noncommitment is advantageous to a legislative body because it enhances information transmission and precludes distributional shifts from the median voter to committees.[61] Second, the remaining and more directly testable prediction informational models are identical. Specifically, the incidence of restrictive rules should diminish with the degree to which the committee is a preference outlier.

In summary, then, informational theory predicts either the absence of procedural commitment because of its associated distributional and informational benefits, or the presence of procedural commitment but with restrictive

---

61. See Gilligan and Krehbiel 1989b. Two qualifications are in order, however. First, the model is one with a homogeneous committee. Second, unlike the similar model in which rules are endogenous (Gilligan and Krehbiel 1987), the model without commitment takes committee specialization as given.

rules used only for legislation in which informational benefits offset distributional losses, net of specialization costs. In both cases, informational predictions differ from exclusively distributive theories. Distributive theories presume commitment to procedural arrangements precisely because of the distributional benefits they confer to intense minorities at the expense of majorities, that is, because they yield distributive committee power under the guise of gains from trade. Informational theories either do not presume commitment, or presume it and yield results consistent with informational but not distributive committee power.

Discussion

The essence of legislative signaling is informational power. The essence of legislative organization is legislative control. This includes control over committee assignments and committee composition, control over rules governing the consideration of specific bills on the floor, and control over any other procedures that mediate the tensions between informational and distributional characteristics of legislative choice under uncertainty. The hallmark of a well-designed legislature is that the exercise of legislative control in the domain of procedural choice has two consequences for legislative performance. It constrains distributive committee power (which is inherently nonmajoritarian) and it facilitates informational committee power (which is inherently a common good).

The two postulates of legislative organization introduced in chapter 1 pertained to uncertainty and majoritarianism. Uncertainty about the relationship between laws and their consequences creates incentives for a legislature to organize to encourage specialization. Majoritarianism acts as a constraint on each of two domains of legislative choice: policy choice and procedural choice. Because majoritarianism pertains to procedural choice as well as policy choice, procedures—or legislative organization more broadly—are viewed as tools with which a legislature may attain collective benefits of expertise. Informational theories offer some insights into how, when, and why majoritarian procedural choice can facilitate the making of informed choices akin to the positive components of Fenno's "good public policy," Maass's "common good," and Madison's "popular government [with] popular information."

Informational theories of legislative organization are consistent with the two postulates of legislative organization for a simple reason: they were developed with the postulates in mind. However, this consistency serves only as the most preliminary check on the validity of the theories. Plausibility of assumptions may be a necessary condition for acceptability of a theory, but it surely is not sufficient. Sufficiency rests on the extraction of predictions, on distinguishing predictions from those of alternative theories, and, ultimately, on discerning how well they withstand empirical tests.

Comparison of Predictions

Table 3.1 summarizes the predictions of this chapter and juxtaposes them with empirical implications of the distributive theories reviewed in chapter 2 (numbers refer to predictions as presented in the text). Although distributive and informational theories share some axiomatic foundations (e.g., utility maximization and distributional conflict), the two classes of theory yield strikingly different empirical expectations.

Assignment and Composition of Committees
Distributive theories predict (or assume) a self-selection process that results in committees composed of preference outliers. Informational theories predict a preponderance of nonoutliers and heterogeneous committees. Only the existence of low-cost specialists may result in preference-outlying committees.

Consequences and Correlates of Restrictive Rules
Distributive theories offer mixed predictions relating the degree of particularism in bills to the choice of restrictive rules. Their common expectation is that restrictive amendment rules facilitate expeditious gains from trade. However, this benefit may be offset by distributional losses associated with restrictive rules. Informational theories predict that each of the following should be associated with the use of restrictive rules: committee specialization, nonoutliers on the committee, and heterogeneity of committee preferences.

TABLE 3.1. **Summary of Empirical Implications of Distributive and Informational Theories**

DISTRIBUTIVE THEORIES	INFORMATIONAL THEORIES
COMMITTEES: ASSIGNMENTS AND COMPOSITION	
1. Self-selection	1. Nonoutliers
Preference outliers	2. Heterogeneous
	3. Low-cost specialists
RESTRICTIVE RULES: CONSEQUENCES AND CORRELATES	
2. Particularistic policies	4. Specialist committees
Hasten agreement	Nonoutlying committees
Distributive inefficiency	Heterogeneous committees
PROCEDURAL COMMITMENT AND COMMITTEE POWER	
3. Commitment to facilitate gains from trade and distributive committee power	5. No commitment to facilitate informational efficiency and informational committee power

Procedural Commitment and Committee Power

Distributive theories either assume institutional commitment or must be interpreted in the context of commitment. They stress that the reason legislatures commit to a set of procedures or institutional arrangements is to facilitate gains from trade, especially between high-demanders of policies. Universalism sometimes results. Distributive committee power always results. Informational theories vary in terms of their assumptions about procedural commitment, but the absence of commitment has both distributional and informational advantages. Thus (assuming, perhaps heroically, that legislatures could commit to procedures), legislatures either will choose not to commit to procedures or will do so only if the informational benefits of such commitment exceed distributional costs. In other words, either distributional losses to the legislature (in favor of a committee) will not exist, or they will exist and be matched by informational gains. In this sense, committee power is not distributive: a committee can never use procedures to get the legislature to do what is not in the legislature's interest. But committee power is often informational: a committee can act to get the legislature to do what is in the legislature's and the committee's interest.

Transitional Notes

This chapter makes clear the heavy reliance of informational theories on a somewhat anthropomorphic conception of "*the* legislature" as a meaningful and majoritarian entity. Although theoretically the legislature can be thought of as the median (or pivotal) voter in a unidimensional policy space, this assumption and corresponding interpretations have nevertheless proven vulnerable to spirited attacks. Before making the transition to the empirical chapters, it is therefore useful to state and respond to the most common criticisms. Objections come in many different forms but are of three broad types:

- The assumptions and interpretation pertaining to "the legislature" are overly simple.
- They are theoretically unwarranted because, in effect, they sweep the chaos problem under the rug.
- They are empirically unwarranted because they formally ignore the important role of parties and leaders in the legislative process.

To the first objection I offer the standard response that all models employ simplifying assumptions (including, of course, distributive theories and even so-called informal theories). Whether such assumptions are "overly simple," however, ·is an empirical question.

To the second objection I assert that nothing is "theoretically unwarranted" due merely to the fact that it happens not to address or allow for a "problem" that arises from within another (class of) theory. As suggested in chapter 2 when reviewing the chaos problem, exclusively theoretical arguments about the importance or unimportance of cyclicity of the majority preference relation are not likely to lead to a convincing resolution of differing views. Thus, again, the criterion for determining whether an assumption is unwarranted should be empirical. What are the predictions of alternative models? Are they borne out?

To the third objection I affirm that the theories in question do not explicitly characterize parties and leaders, but I continue with what may now be sounding like a broken record. Whether the absence of parties and leaders in theories makes assumptions "empirically unwarranted" is not a matter for prima facie determination but rather for empirical determination.

Thus, in taking the step from formal theories to congressional data, I ask the reader to entertain a possibility, albeit one that may seem remote at this juncture. Perhaps theories that employ simplifying assumptions, sweep the chaos problem under the rug, and ignore parties and leaders, can somehow predict better than alternative theories. Whether true or not, only after empirical analysis is undertaken will we be in a position to assess convincingly the extent of damage caused by these simplifications.

Finally, the exposition of distributive and informational theories in chapters 2 and 3 may be viewed as undesirably confrontational due to its emphasis on differences rather than similarities. After all, aren't these all rational choice theories? Moreover, don't informational theories adopt many of the assumptions of distributive theories? The answers, of course, are yes. The questions, however, are misguided. First, the exposition of distributive and informational theories illustrates that rational choice theories are not all alike (not even within classes) in spite of their sharing some assumptions. Second, since the long-term value of a paradigm rests on its ability to allow theoretical controversies to arise from within and to resolve such controversies with empirical research, differences between theories should be the focus of the analysis. The real issue, then, is not the degree to which differences in existing theories represent confrontations. Rather, it concerns how best to interpret empirical results that bear directly on competing predictions. Those who feel affronted by the presence of controversy may wish to view informational theories as mere extensions of distributive theories. As such, if informational theories happen to predict well, then perhaps both classes of theory should be viewed as having been supported. Logically, however, the present situation is rarely amenable to this kind of benevolent inference. More often, the logical situation is surprisingly simple. With respect to some observable feature of legislative organization Y, theory A predicts Y, and theory B (which indeed employs some of the same assumptions as theory A) predicts not-Y. If we observe Y, should we accept theory A over theory B? Of course. If we observe not-Y, should we accept theory B over theory A? By symmetry, of course. If, in this latter case, we were instead to infer some support for theory A due to its axiomatic similarities with theory B, we not only would exceed the bounds of logical consistency but also would render theory A nonfalsifiable. In other words, given existing theories, it is no more possible to avoid confrontations logically than it is desirable to avoid them scientifically. Thus, the objective of the forthcoming analysis is not to deny or even to de-emphasize confrontations but rather to state them clearly, address them empirically, and, in the end, resolve them constructively.

CHAPTER 4

The Formation of Informative Committees

The committee should be an agent of the legislative body for the following purposes: 1. To serve as a means of investigating special fields of proposed legislation and collecting information thereon; 2. To deliberate upon (more time being available than in the chamber itself) and give careful consideration to matters referred to it; 3. To permit the application of specialized knowledge so that proposed legislation may be in such a form as to accomplish the desired end and that the chamber may benefit by more or less expert advice; 4. Finally, to recommend action.

—Clintin I. Winslow (1931, 140)

In forming an estimate of the importance of committees in legislative work, the method of appointment is a factor worthy of consideration.

—Ralph V. Harlow (1917, 105)

Why do U.S. legislatures rely so heavily upon standing committees for the formulation of policy proposals? Winslow offers a composite answer that lies solidly within the spirit of informational theory. Committees, as agents of their parent chambers, exist to investigate, deliberate, apply specialized knowledge, and recommend action. Surely these are admirable organizational functions, but the degree to which and how these objectives are attained are largely unanswered questions. To find their answers, Harlow suggests a study of how legislators are appointed to committees.

In this first of three chapters of empirical analysis, I take Harlow's understated advice by setting a modest objective. My aim is not to confirm but simply to gain a foothold for the informational perspective on legislative organization. In the process of examining theories and data on the rules and practices that determine the composition of congressional committees, five questions are addressed.

First, what can we learn about theories and practices of committees from historical research on the conception, origin, and development of the standing committee system? An initial review of historical literature supports the thesis that if committees are to play an informative and collectively useful role in the legislative process, the parent body must not only delegate some minimal resources or parliamentary rights to committees to encourage them to specialize but also retain control over committee assignments. In striking a balance between these obviously conflicting needs, U.S. legislatures have found it desirable to keep committee and chamber interests in alignment.

Second, why do these eighteenth- and nineteenth-century observations differ from so many postwar studies of the U.S. Congress, which place a much greater emphasis on self-selection to committees and the pursuit of distributive policies? After the historical review, I reassess the claim that high demanders self-select to standing committees. The findings are mixed. Some evidence can be interpreted as consistent with the self-selection hypothesis, thus keeping alive the possibility that pork barrel concerns are primary motivations for contemporary congressional organization. However, the evidence in support of this hypothesis is neither overwhelming nor fully exploitive of the available data.

Third, is the evidence for informational theories any more convincing? Results from several statistical tests suggest that the modal contemporary committee is neither homogeneous nor a preference outlier, consistent with the Outlier and Heterogeneity Predictions in chapter 3.

Fourth, are competing claims about committee composition in the distributive and informational research traditions reconcilable? With reference to the Heterogeneity and Exceptional-Outlier Predictions, an affirmative answer is sought and obtained by reinterpreting old data in terms of new theory. Two cases are then offered as illustrations.

Fifth, which, if either, theoretical perspective can be reconciled with Congress's long-standing practice of selecting committee chairmen, namely, the seniority system? An informational rationale for the seniority system is developed and culminates in three hypotheses that are special cases of the Outlier, Heterogeneity, and Commitment Predictions. Prior empirical findings and case studies of violations of the seniority criterion are assessed with these hypotheses in mind. The evidence supports the conclusion that the seniority system is difficult to reconcile with the distributive perspective on legislative organization but consistent with the informational perspective.

Much of the evidence in the chapter will not sit well with congressional scholars—neither theorists nor empiricists. To make matters worse, many of the interpretations given to previously known facts are quite different from those given in prior research on the politics of committee assignments. Thus, before presenting new evidence and interpretations, it is important to place the chapter carefully into two contexts. The broader context pertains to positive social science. The narrower context pertains to the objective of this book.

The issue with respect to positive social science is simply how to respond to evidence that does not comport with received wisdom. Consider several possible responses ranging from most unreasonable to most reasonable. First, we could casually dismiss the findings with a simple "I just don't believe it." This would be more like religion than science, however. Second, we could dispute patterns in the data with quips and counterexamples, such as, "You mean to tell me that Jesse Helms (former Chairman of the Senate Agriculture Committee) is not protobacco?" There is an important difference between regularities and residuals, however, and only analysis of systematic evidence can differentiate regularities from residuals. Third, we could accept, without qualification, the new evidence. This, in effect, ignores the accumulated evidence on which received wisdom is based. The core problem with responding to surprising findings lies in the fact that while our beliefs about the world are at stake—in this case, beliefs about the formation and composition of standing committees—we have no universally accepted standards regarding the best possible evidence and methods for creating or refining such beliefs. However, we do have a scholarly consensus on the methodological principle that beliefs about the world should somehow be responsive to evidence, even if the evidence is imperfect. Thus, a more reasonable response to this chapter is simply to update beliefs about committees in a manner consistent with admittedly imperfect evidence. Finally, the most reasonable response is to challenge the theory, methods, and data employed in this chapter by proposing an alternative theory, by collecting better data, and by implementing alternative tests.

The issue with respect to the objective of this book is whether the data and methods employed in this chapter are, by themselves, sufficient for determining whether the major principles of legislative organization are predominantly distributive or informational. They are not. Specifically, many of the empirical tests on the formation and composition of standing committees have the property that predictions of the informational theories are null hypotheses while predictions of distributive theories are alternate hypotheses. Furthermore, often we cannot reject nulls in favor of alternatives. Thus, while much of the evidence fails to corroborate predictions of the distributive perspective of legislative organization, the tests are neither direct nor strong with respect to the predictions of the informational perspective. This is exactly why the objective of the chapter is modest—only to gain a foothold for informational theory.

Figure 4.1 provides a graphic overview of the three stages of empirical analysis in the next three chapters. This figure should be kept in mind when examining this first round of systematic evidence. Since the evidence here is mixed and indirect, no definitive conclusions are warranted at this stage.

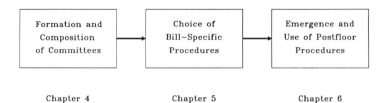

Fig. 4.1. Stages of legislative organization and sketch of empirical analysis

Rather, the imperfect data, indirect tests, and inconclusive results simply keep alive the key issues of legislative organization and put a premium on the empirical findings from the more direct tests in chapters 5 and 6.

Committees in Historical Perspective

A thesis developed with extraordinary detail by Harlow (1917) and Cooper (1970, part 1, and 1988, chap. 1) is that "Jeffersonian attitudes" formed the philosophical foundation of the standing committee system in the early U.S. House of Representatives. As individuals, Jeffersonians were intensely egalitarian and thus reluctant to delegate special privileges to any subset of legislators. As a collective body, they were intensely independent and thus wanted the Congress to become a legitimate and powerful decision-making body in its own right within the national government. Neither Jeffersonians nor historians of their era can be expected to have made a connection between the early congressional experiment with committees and the contemporary theory of legislative games with incomplete information. The connection exists, however, and can be spelled out in terms of institutional impossibilities.

Impossibilities

The Jeffersonian impossibility refers to the incompatibility of two key components of Jeffersonian thought: informed collective decision making and egalitarianism in the assignment of parliamentary rights. So significant was the conflict between these deeply held objectives that Cooper (1970), for instance, concluded that Jeffersonian theory was fundamentally flawed. Something clearly had to give. Even though Jeffersonian attitudes toward committee rights were hostile from the start, the egalitarian constraint eventually gave way to congressional desires for independent sources of information. Initially Congress began to parcel out its workload to committees. Soon thereafter it began to assign special parliamentary rights to committees to foster specialization.[1] After a century or so, the development of legislatures in terms of division of labor, specialization of labor, and unequally assigned rights came to be regarded as general and self-evident features of parliamentary development.

> Comparison of the modern history of committees in England and the United States throws a clear light on the fundamental problems involved. In each country it has been found absolutely impossible for the lawmaking body itself, acting as a whole, to do the preliminary and subsidiary work. This self-evident situation would not call for so much as a statement were it not constantly ignored by critics. They will never reach straight thinking on the subject until they recognize that much of the work must be done outside the legislative chamber, simply because the hands of the clock compel. (Luce 1922, 180–81)

The impossibilities identified in informational theories are similar, although for obvious re⁀sons less well substantiated. Historically, as the assignment of resources and parliamentary rights became asymmetric in the Congress, so did the distribution of information about the relationship between legislation and its consequences. In common parlance, specialization emerged. Theoretically, a necessary consequence of asymmetric information and conflict of interest is the opportunity for self-interested specialists to use their information strategically, that is, to attempt to reap distributional gains at the expense of the larger legislature. Legislative design problems are compounded accordingly. The relevant set of organizational issues expands to include allocation of resources and rights not only to encourage specialization (an obvious concern of Jeffersonians) but also to minimize the adverse consequences of strategic use of information (also a Jeffersonian concern, but one somewhat more difficult to detect in the writings of the era). Much as Jeffersonians learned experimentally of the fundamental tensions between informed decision making and egalitarianism, positive theorists are beginning to learn analytically of fundamental tensions between informed decision making, the distribution of benefits, and the quickness with which collective choices can be reached.[2] At the current stage of theoretical development, it is clear that without subsidizing committees in some way (e.g., through staff, special and thus nonegalitarian rights, or both)

---

1. These include jurisdictional rights of committees as specified in House rules, rights of bill referral and bill introduction, and rights to report at all times. See, for example, Alexander 1916; Cooper 1970; Cooper and Young 1989; and McConachie 1898.

2. The games reviewed in chap. 3 do not address the quickness or timeliness of agreement. See, however, Gilligan 1989 for an informational theory that does, and Baron and Ferejohn 1989a and Baron 1990 for multiperiod distributive theories.

it is impossible for a legislature to make informed collective choices that have distributional properties favorable to its median voter.

While informational theories have proven useful for identifying tensions that parallel those discovered by Jeffersonians, we have yet to see systematic empirical support for their implications. In the context of the development and composition of committees, distributive and informational theories yield different empirical expectations. The distributive perspective emphasizes the arranging of trades in particularistic policy commodities within and across high-demand committees. The informational perspective portrays the committee system as a specialization-of-labor arrangement created by the House for purposes of serving the House, with committee composition to be determined with informational goals in mind. Were issues of information or distribution (or neither, or both) predominant in the development of the congressional committee system?

Informational Origins of Committees

Most, if not all, historical studies agree that specialization—not distributive politics—was at the heart of the conception and development of the committee system.[3] This thesis is most insightfully chronicled in Cooper's monograph, *The Origins of the Standing Committees and the Development of the Modern House* (1970). Outstanding as Cooper's work is in its thoroughness, it does not stand alone in putting forth the arguments that committees were conceived as agents of the House—moreover, agents whose main purpose was to provide facts, to make recommendations, and, generally, to inform the House.[4] Nor are such arguments unique to observers of the U.S. Congress, as opposed to other legislatures. Winslow (1931, chap. 6), for example, reported extensively on the rules and practices of state legislatures, with especially detailed studies of Pennsylvania and Maryland. He showed that the evolution of states' committee systems—in particular, periodic reorganization of their jurisdictional arrangements—reflected changes in the broader and increasingly complex policy environments in which the legislatures operated (see also Harlow 1917, chap. 4). In other words, legislative institutions reflect uncertainty in the environment, uncertainty poses policy-making problems for

---

3. The only clear exception of which I am aware is Gamm and Shepsle's (1988) argument that Henry Clay, as Speaker, actively encouraged the "decentralization" of House committees for distributive purposes. As summarized by Shepsle, Clay did this "not so much to enhance the stature of the legislature in a separation-of-powers system, but rather to enhance his own stature" (Shepsle 1989, 140–41).

4. See also Alexander 1916; Galloway and Wise 1976; Harlow 1917; and MacNeil 1963. On the origins of committees in the British Parliament compatible with this discussion, see Hartwell 1950.

which legislative specialization is needed, and committee systems proved to be useful specialization-of-labor arrangements. Committees, then, were important agents of U.S. legislatures from the early years of the legislatures' existence. In all likelihood, it was because of the informational purposes committees served.

Early Committee Assignments

The existence of legislative committees immediately created a need for a procedure for assigning members to committees. How were such procedures employed, and why? More specifically, what can we discern about the compositional characteristics of early standing committees?

Procedures governing the assignment of legislators to committees were straightforward and fairly uniform throughout U.S. legislatures for at least the first century of postrevolutionary history. Much more often than not, appointment rights were granted to the Speaker or presiding officer (Winslow 1931, chap. 1). However, no evidence can be found that centralized assignment processes resulted in systematic biases in committee composition, and considerable evidence can be found that informational concerns were dominant.

A research note by Norman Risjord (1988) in effect tests some of Winslow's claims in the Congress. From the start, a small percentage of legislators held a large percentage of select committee assignments. "The House, in short, turned for leadership to men with *experience,* men with whom it was familiar" (Risjord 1988, 2). In spite of high turnover, continuity of membership was characteristic of committee assignments across Congresses, especially on the more important committees. For instance, after 1795, the Ways and Means Committee—not yet a standing committee—was annually resurrected "with about a 50 percent continuity in membership" (Risjord 1988, 5). Attempts by the Speaker to stack committees were rare, even though some Speakers were more partisan than others. Risjord focuses on party ratios and regional balance, which can be interpreted as rough measures of preferences. He shows that while party ratios varied, the minority party was rarely deprived of a near-proportionate share of committee positions. In this respect committees seem to have been heterogeneous. Similarly, distributions of seats by geographic region were also quite uniform throughout the period.[5]

---

5. Risjord cites Speaker Sedgwick's behavior in the 6th Congress as exceptional in its aim to "promote party purposes." While Sedgwick's appointments were not skewed in terms of regional balance, he nevertheless refused to give any committee assignment to the already prominent John Randolph of Roanoke. He also managed to alienate so many members that the House, at the conclusion of the Congress, fell well short of the customary unanimous vote of thanks to the Speaker. The motion passed, but only by a five-vote margin.

Unfortunately, no systematic empirical analysis comparable to Risjord's has addressed this question for recent and more fully developed committee systems in the Congress. Casual but informed observations are available, however. Luce, for example, wrote favorably (and perhaps romantically) of the motives and efforts of presiding officers in appointing committees:

> Criticisms of the system of choice of committees by presiding officers do not give credit enough for public spirit and good intentions. In spite of all that is said about the payment of political debts, about corporation and other secret influences, and about a variety of motives averred to be improper and unwise, much of which may in some States be well founded, in my judgment the great majority of presiding officers do earnestly and laboriously try to distribute the positions with regard to qualifications and experience. (Luce 1922, 111)

Similarly but more systematically, Winslow (1931, chap. 2) found a strong relationship between Maryland and Pennsylvania legislators' occupational backgrounds and their committee assignments, as well as between their prior committee service and present assignments.

Admittedly, this evidence is sketchy and somewhat difficult to interpret.[6] One generic problem is that making inferences about committee composition (howe er measured) independent of information about committees' procedural prerogatives may be misleading. Thus, Risjord's findings especially must be tempered by the fact that they pertain to a congressional era in which committees had acquired precious few parliamentary rights. Initially, almost all standing committees were select committees (Cooper 1970). First reference of bills was still to the Committee of the Whole (Harlow 1917). Precedents regarding the introduction of bills were ambiguous (Cooper and Young 1989). Committees generally were on a very short leash.

Finally, as for the broader issue of committees as agents of the House, it is noteworthy that even during what Cooper (1988) calls the peak period of committee autonomy, 1890–1910, by no means did the House relinquish its control over its committees. For one thing, the extraordinary homogeneity of the majority party during this era made chamber delegation to committees relatively safe. When a committee and a majority of the parent body agree over policy objectives, what is to be lost by conferring rights to committees? In the absence of homogeneous preference outliers dominating the committee, the prospects for distributive abuse by the committee are minimal.[7] Further-

---

6. So much so, in one instance, that the question of how to interpret evidence on committee assignments is addressed in some detail subsequently.

7. Indeed, one should entertain the hypothesis that committees were most autonomous precisely when they were distributionally superfluous due to homogeneity of preferences.

more, if by chance or design the assignment mechanism were to work in a manner inconsistent with parent-chamber preferences—for example, by permitting preference outliers to dominate an ostensibly autonomous committee—then any number of procedural fixes remained available throughout the remainder of the legislative process. Details of these are presented in chapters 5 and 6. For now, it suffices to underscore the theme of chamber control with a quotation from an (arguably) unlikely source for such a majoritarian message: the (allegedly) most powerful Speaker in the House's history, Thomas Reed.[8]

> The moment a committee is appointed which is not in accord with the wishes and desires of members, that moment the committee is such an object of suspicion that its power is utterly destroyed or lost. (quoted in McConachie 1898, 118)

Summary

In conception, the Congress was egalitarian. So were U.S. state legislatures. In evolution, however, asymmetries emerged in legislators' talents, committee resources and rights, legislative procedures, and the application of procedures. This seemingly inevitable institutional setting gave rise to the potential for abuse by committees of their resources and parliamentary rights, especially if such committees were allowed to become dominated by legislators whose preferences diverged significantly from those of the average legislator. Likewise, it put a premium on legislatively rational application of the committee assignment process. The best available evidence on committee composition—imperfect though it is—suggests that divergence in committee-chamber preferences was minimal. Committee assignments historically seem to have been strongly influenced by the legislature's common need for policy specialists who would serve the interest of the larger legislature insofar as this was possible.

Cooper's summary of three periods of committee thought—Jeffersonian, Progressive, and Reformist—brings us quickly from the eighteenth to the twentieth century.

> Thought in all three periods agreed that there was a need for a division of labor within the House both for reasons of efficiency and in order that Congress could have its own facilities for information, expertise, and bill drafting, or to put the point more broadly, in order that Congress could

---

8. The parenthetical qualifiers stem from my opinion—a minority one, I think—that Reed (and Cannon, too, for that matter) was much more majoritarian than autocratic. I will not pursue this thesis here. See, however, Cooper and Brady 1981 for a persuasive argument that relates homogeneity of preferences with ostensibly "strong" leadership.

maintain its autonomy in decision-making and formulate its own programs. On the other hand, thought in all three periods agreed that committees should be the servants not the masters of the House, that committees should be subject to the will of the House. (Cooper 1988, 298)

While all of these conclusions are roughly consistent with the informational perspective on legislative organization, at least two major gaps in the
argument remain. First, little of the discussion (and even less of the historical
evidence) has focused directly on policy preferences of committee members.
Second, contemporary Congresses may be—and, many have argued, are—
fundamentally different from those of the nineteenth century through the
1960s. The rest of the chapter attempts to fill these gaps.

Committee Assignments: The Distributive Perspective

The distributive perspective on legislative organization depicts contemporary
committee assignment processes as overwhelmingly demand driven. While a
substantial literature on committee assignments exists, in no single source is
the subject so thoroughly explored as in Kenneth Shepsle's (1978) classic
book, *The Giant Jigsaw Puzzle*. As in the distributive theories reviewed in
chapter 2, the driving theoretical principle is the reelection motive. Although
Shepsle's primary focus is on how members pursue reelection by seeking
electorally desirable committee seats, a similar secondary concern is how
collective processes have evolved to serve individual legislators. This section
explores Shepsle's predominantly individualistic themes first by summarizing
his arguments that culminate in the self-selection hypothesis, second by placing the hypothesis more firmly in the context of the distributive perspective of
legislative organization, and finally by reassessing the hypothesis empirically.

The Self-Selection Hypothesis

> HYPOTHESIS 1: SELF-SELECTION. *To facilitate gains from trade, commit-
> tee assignments will be governed by self-selection. . . .*[9]

To assess this hypothesis, Shepsle analyzes several stages of the committee
assignment process using data from the 86th through 93d Congresses. He
begins by estimating probit models in which freshmen committee requests are
predicted by a combination of personal attributes, constituency characteristics, and measures of competition for available seats. Interpreting these as
demand equations, the results become the first stage of a multistage causal

---

9. As stated in chap. 2, the prediction continues "and committees will be composed of . . .
preference outliers." The continuation clause will be tested subsequently.

argument. Since constituency characteristics are associated with requests, and requests, in turn, tend to be granted (both for freshmen and for members requesting transfers), the assignment process as a whole is characterized as an "interest-advocacy-accommodation syndrome." Interests of constituents determine requests, requesting members are natural advocates of high levels of policy benefits for their constituents, and party leaders (and ultimately the House) accommodate members' demands by adjusting committee sizes and by making individual assignments.

In its full-fledged form, the self-selection hypothesis has two parts. One part pertains to individuals' initiation of the process. To what committees do legislators seek assignments and why? The second part pertains to collective choices and their consequences. How are committees composed after the assignment process is played out? A refusal or reluctance to differentiate between these parts often causes ambiguities when interpreting the literature on committee assignments. To avoid such ambiguities, the analysis that follows uses this distinction repeatedly. Given the objectives of this study, this chapter ultimately places more weight on the consequences of committee assignment processes than the processes themselves. Specifically, the composition of standing committees is viewed as an outcome of a collective choice process that falls squarely under the rubric of legislative organization and that plays a key role in the theories to be tested.

While Shepsle's study is unique in its thoroughness and method, its main empirical claims are compatible with innumerable other observations of, and claims about, the contemporary committee assignment process and its consequences. Beliefs that committee assignments are governed by self-selection and that committees are composed of high-demanders are most definitely not held only by formal theorists. Roger Davidson, for example, offers a characterization that shares all the main components of Shepsle's "syndrome":

> Under pressure from members and factions desiring representation, party leaders not only have allowed assignments to proliferate but have tended to accede to members' preferences for assignments. Inevitably, this means that legislators gravitate to those committees with which they, or their constituents, have the greatest affinity. Thus, many congressional workgroups are not microcosms of the parent houses, but are biased in one way or another. (Davidson 1981, 111)

Ray (1980) interprets his results as supportive of the claim that the Armed Services Committee is composed of self-selected high-demanders.[10] Moe summarizes the distributive-theoretic perspective as one in which, among

---

10. See, however, Arnold 1979; Gertzog 1976; Goss 1972; and Stephens 1971 for different or mixed results.

other things, "members are assigned to committees largely on the basis of self-selection, allowing them to seek out those panels most beneficial to their concerns" (1987, 477).[11] And Hall not only adopts this view, writing that "the committee assignment process is best understood as a set of institutional arrangements that channel member interests into positions of legislative advantage" (1989, 202). He also strengthens it in a study of participation within committees, concluding that

> . . . constituency-oriented behavior at the committee level tends to *undermine* representation in the legislative system, not promote it. Shepsle and other students of committee assignments have made this point, noting that committees are deep in "interesteds" and "unrepresentative of the regional, ideological, and seniority groupings" in the parent chamber. The patterns of selective participation at the committee level, in turn, reinforce such biases. For any given issue, the membership of a committee is typically more diverse than the subset of self-selected members who dominate committee deliberations. (1989, 217)

In short, self-selection of high-demanders has come to be regarded as a robust stylized fact by theorists and empiricists alike.

The Distributive Rationale for Self-Selection

Shepsle's individualistic theoretical premise contributes to an inherently demand-side theory that does not directly confront the question of why a legislature, as a collective entity, would want to embrace self-selection as a fundamental feature of legislative organization. If its ultimate consequence is unrepresentative policy, as Shepsle suggests in his conclusion, would not a majoritarian legislative body composed of rational legislators attempt to adopt a different procedure?

Weingast and Marshall (1988) essentially answer "no" by taking a more collectivist approach to Shepsle's notion of self-selection. They depict the "industrial organization of Congress" as one in which institutions arise to enable legislators to reap "gains from trade." The following clearest and broadest statement of the distributive theory of legislative organization falls squarely in the tradition of adherents to the self-selection hypothesis:

> Each legislator gives up some influence over many areas of policy in return for much greater influence over the one that, for him, counts the

---

11. Moe does not subscribe to this view; however, he calls the perspective "familiar" (1987, 477).

most. Thus, we find that representatives from farming districts dominate agriculture committees and oversee the provision of benefits to their farm constituents. Members from urban districts dominate banking, urban, and welfare committees overseeing an array of programs that provide benefits to a host of urban constituents. And members from western states dominate interior and public lands committees that provide benefits to their constituents. (Weingast and Moran 1983, 771–72)

This view is plausible, especially with respect to the process of individual committee seeking. But how convincing is the evidence for self-selection in terms of the consequences of self-selection efforts? Certainly the strong form of the hypothesis—self-selection by high-demanders—is at odds with the conception and historical development of the committee system. It seems useful to reconsider the hypothesis in the contemporary Congress, too.

A New Test of the Self-Selection Hypothesis

Data
Empirical studies of self-selection usually have focused on constituency characteristics as measures for legislators' preferences. Cowart (1981), for example, assesses the high-demand attributes of appropriations subcommittees on Agriculture, Interior, and Labor/HEW by comparing them with the full House in terms of (respectively) mean percentage of agriculture employees, mean population density, and mean income divided by the percentage of blue-collar workers. Shepsle's approach is econometrically more advanced but conceptually similar; he includes constituency characteristics in the right-hand side of probit equations. The implicit assumption (or maintained hypothesis) with either approach is that attributes of constituencies determine legislators' preferences. Thus, for example, legislators whose districts have relatively large percentages of their work force in agriculture are presumed to be high-demanders for agriculture programs.[12]

While reasonable, this constituency focus ignores the prospect that modal preferences among geographic and reelection constituents may differ substantially.[13] An alternative approach is used in the following analysis, which focuses more directly on legislators' behavior than on their constituencies. The logic is simple. Constituency characteristics may be good predictors of legislators' potential support for various policies, but legislators' behavior more directly reflects actual support. Thus, while roll call votes may well be

---

12. See also Hall and Grofman 1990.

13. The Senate provides the clearest evidence. Compare, for example, the statements and actions of California's senators: Alan Cranston and Pete Wilson. The seminal work on concentric constituencies is Fenno 1978.

manifestations of preferences whose origins are electoral, it is not necessary for present purposes either to know the details of the electoral connection or to make assumptions about it.

Several comparative advantages of using interest group ratings of members of Congress as measures of preferences should be discussed briefly before turning to the analysis.[14] First, these ratings are based on assessments of some of the closest observers of congressional activity: organizations that have strong incentives to know the implications of votes for the legislative outcomes. Consequently, the revealed preferences in these votes are likely to differentiate legislators according to genuine policy differences rather than inconsequential or symbolic behavior.

A second advantage of using interest group ratings pertains to agenda processes. Many roll call studies are indiscriminately based on very large samples of votes that are invariably determined by endogenous agenda formation processes. Neither these processes nor the systematic biases they produce in votes are well understood. In contrast, when selecting significant votes for the computation of published ratings, interest groups incorporate information about specific and sometimes arcane strategic settings. For example, inspection of the sets of votes used in this study reveals a nontrivial fraction on what a naive observer would regard as procedural questions, such as votes on special orders or on motions to instruct conferees. For some applications, inclusion of a large number of so-called procedural votes clouds inference. However, for present purposes we can actually exploit the selection bias of informed congressional observers.

Third, and of critical importance for cross-committee studies, the proliferation of interest group ratings in recent years provides an opportunity to assess committee-chamber differences with more precision than was previously possible via general party support scores, for example, since many contemporary interest group ratings are policy-specific and, thus, jurisdiction-specific. Accordingly, in addition to assessing the evidence for self-selection from the standpoint of general-ideology measures, we are able to examine assignment patterns on issues that fall predominantly in the jurisdictions of specific committees. Table 4.1 lists the ratings and abbreviations used in the analysis.

If the distributive perspective on legislative organization is empirically viable, then we would certainly expect to see evidence of self-selection of

---

14. Data were obtained from LEGI-SLATE, a subsidiary of the *Washington Post*. These ratings differ slightly from some of those obtained directly from interest groups because, unlike some interest groups, LEGI-SLATE does not count absences as "incorrect" votes during computation. Unless noted otherwise, all data throughout the book are from the 99th Congress, and most of it is from the House. Neither LEGI-SLATE nor the *Post* bears any responsibility for the interpretations offered here.

TABLE 4.1. Ratings Used in the Analysis

ABBREVIATION	INTEREST GROUP
ACU	American Conservative Union
ADA	Americans for Democratic Action
ASC	American Security Council
BIPAC	Business-Industry PAC
CCUS	Chamber of Commerce of the United States
COPE	AFL-CIO Committee on Political Education
IBT	International Brotherhood of Teamsters
LCV	League of Conservation Voters
MNPL	Machinists' Non-Partisan Political League
NCSC	National Council of Senior Citizens
NEA	National Education Association
NFU	National Farmers Union
PCCW	Public Citizens' Congress Watch
RLEA	Railway Labor Executives' Association

high-demanders to those committees whose policy domains are particularistic, that is, committees that try to capture gains from trade with policies whose benefits are concentrated. I begin by pairing the interest group ratings from table 4.1 with committees that have substantively similar jurisdictions. National Farmers Union ratings are reasonable measures for members' support for agricultural benefits and are thus relevant for agriculture authorization and appropriations (sub)committees.[15] American Security Council ratings measure support for defense services and are thus used for the Armed Services Committee as well as the Defense and Military Subcommittees on Appropriations. National Education Association ratings gauge support for national educational programs and are therefore used to assess self-selection to the Education and Labor Committee, and so on.

Statistically, the focus is on whether committee assignments systematically favor high-demanders within the various jurisdictions. For example, are high-demanders for agriculture benefits significantly more likely than an average congressman to obtain seats on the Agriculture Committee? The method for answering such questions is straightforward. For any given rating-committee pair, I compute and compare two probabilities. P_H is the probability that a high-demander (defined as a legislator in the top decile of the distribution of the rating) is on the committee; P_L is the probability that the mean legislator is on the committee. A necessary condition for corroboration of the self-selection hypothesis is that $P_H > P_L$ by a greater margin than could

---

15. Ratings of the National Farmers Union (NFU) have proven highly controversial (even more so than others). Part of appendix B addresses this controversy.

be attributed to chance. A chi-square test assesses the null hypothesis that the probabilities are equal. The one-tailed alternative hypothesis is that $P_H > P_L$, consistent with Hypothesis 1 as stated above. Tables present p-values, that is, the smallest significance level at which the null hypothesis would be rejected. Thus, for example, $p = .01$ means that if, in fact, there were no difference, then the observed difference is a one-in-a-hundred occurrence.[16]

Results

Table 4.2 reports on the test for five authorization committees and the Select Committee on Aging. One pattern is evident from the column of P_H estimates. Being a high-demander does not guarantee a demand-compatible committee assignment. At best (Armed Services), it means a slightly better than one-in-five shot; at worst (Agriculture), the prospects are less than one-in-twenty.

The results with respect to committee-chamber comparisons in probabilities are mixed. The striking finding for the Agriculture Committee is that high-demanders have a distinct probabilistic disadvantage with respect to assignment. Members with upper decile NFU ratings—i.e., high-demanders—are less than half as likely to receive assignments to the committee than the average House member. However, in the case of Armed Services, the situation is exactly the opposite. High-demanders of defense benefits are more than twice as likely to obtain Armed Services assignments than the average member. Education and Labor results are mixed, too. On the educational side of the committee's jurisdiction, no significant differences emerge. But labor high-demanders are twice as likely to receive committee slots. This difference is statistically significant ($p = .014$), yet still only about three in twenty high-demanders actually make their way onto the committee. Finally, for Foreign Affairs and Aging, differences in the probabilities are minuscule.

Evidence on the composition of appropriations subcommittees in an earlier period is inconsistent with the outlier hypothesis. According to Mayhew (1974, 152) and Fenno (1966, 149), appropriations subcommittees were deliberately organized to exclude full committee members who would be avid program advocates. Has the postreform Congress seen a sharp reversal in this pattern? Table 4.3 suggests not. While the Agriculture differences in probabilities are positive, they fall well short of statistical significance ($p = .41$), and likewise for the Defense Subcommittee ($p = .53$) and the Military Construction Subcommittee ($p = .19$). Differences for Foreign Operations are negligible. However, the Labor, Health and Human Services, and Education Subcommittee does attract high demanders from both education (NEA) and

16. The test is based on the assumption that interest group ratings are independent draws from a hypothetical distribution of possible ratings. Thus, failure to reject the null hypothesis indicates that the observed differences could have occurred by chance when taking independent draws from the distribution.

TABLE 4.2.   Self-Selection of High Demanders onto Authorization Committees

COMMITTEE	RATING	P_H	P_L	$P_H - P_L$	p-VALUE
Agriculture	NFU	0.043	0.098	− 0.055	*
Armed Services	ASC	0.214	0.108	0.106	< 0.01
Education and Labor	NEA	0.094	0.075	0.018	0.35
Education and Labor	COPE	0.163	0.075	0.087	0.01
Foreign Affairs	ASC	0.082	0.096	− 0.013	*
Aging (Select)	NCSC	0.172	0.147	0.024	0.56

*Wrong sign.

TABLE 4.3.   Self-Selection of High Demanders onto Appropriations Subcommittees

SUBCOMMITTEE	RATING	P_H	P_L	$P_H - P_L$	p-VALUE
Agriculture, Rural Development	NFU	0.043	0.025	0.018	0.41
Defense	ASC	0.033	0.025	0.007	0.53
Military Construction	ASC	0.041	0.025	0.016	0.19
Foreign Operations	ASC	0.024	0.027	− 0.002	*
Labor, HHS, Education	NEA	0.062	0.029	0.033	0.01
Labor, HHS, Education	COPE	0.081	0.029	0.051	0.02

*Wrong sign.

labor (COPE) spectra. Statistical significance notwithstanding, the magnitude of these differences is underwhelming. For example, the value $P_H - P_L = .051$ in the bottom row of table 4.3 can be interpreted as follows. Imagine twenty randomly selected labor high demanders and twenty randomly selected House members, called group A and group B, respectively. Then the expected number of group A members on the Labor, HHS, and Education Subcommittee would exceed the expected number of group B members on the subcommittee by only one.

Analysis of individual committees or subcommittees may bias the test against self-selection in two ways. First, cross-jurisdiction demand may be correlated. Agriculture high-demanders might tend also to be defense high-demanders; education high-demanders might tend also to be labor high-demanders, and so on.[17] If so, then the P_H estimates may be deflated due to limits on the number of committees on which a legislator can serve.[18] Second, from a policy standpoint, it may be that the oversupply of services (using, say, the median voter's preference as a baseline) does not require that both autho-

---

17. In fact, only one of these conjectures is correct. The correlation between NFU and ASC ratings is − .001; the correlation between COPE and NEA ratings is .92.

18. In one respect this is a lame argument, since caps on the number of committee positions a legislator can occupy are endogenous. If legislators were sufficiently strong advocates of self-

rization and appropriations committees be havens for self-selecting high demanders. It might be sufficient, for instance, that a high demander end up on just one of these. In other words,

> the self-selection that typifies the interest-advocacy-accommodation syndrome, together with otherwise anomalous jurisdictional arrangements, permits an "interested" to gravitate to one of *many* policy pressure points in the issue area salient to him. (Shepsle 1978, 260)

To explore this possibility, table 4.4 provides results similar to tables 4.2 and 4.3, except that P_H is now computed by counting as a high-demand assignment any assignment to either the authorization committee or appropriations subcommittee.[19] Analyzed as such, the data support the self-selection hypothesis for three of the five policy domains: defense (which includes three committees—Armed Services and the Military Construction and the Defense Subcommittees), education, and labor. Necessarily, the values of P_H have increased. Nevertheless, the differences between P_H and P_L remain small.

Overall the tests confirm that assignment of high demanders occurs in some policy arenas. These findings are consistent with the empirical claims of Davidson (1974) and Shepsle (1978) as well as theoretical arguments by Niskanen (1971) and Weingast and Marshall (1988). But to conclude that homogeneous high-demand committees are firm facts of congressional life is premature, since the analysis thus far has focused on only one tail of each distribution of ratings. A more discriminating test requires assessment of committees' overall composition.

Committee Composition:
The Informational Perspective

Distributive theories paint an individualistic, conflictive, and demand-side picture of legislative politics. Informational theories extend beyond these

---

selection, they would collectively lift the cap by changing the rules that currently impose it. On the other hand, one might counter that there are individually imposed limitations on what legislators can do on committees if they are overcommitted in terms of number of assignments. This is why Hall's (1989) study of actual participation within committees is a welcome complement to the analysis reported here.

19. Since Appropriations is an "exclusive" committee, it would be exceptional to find legislators on both the appropriations subcommittee and its corresponding authorization committee. However, to reiterate a theme in the previous footnote, the exclusivity of the Appropriations Committee is itself a collective decision about legislative organization—moreover, one easily interpretable as a limitation on across-the-board self-selection. Regardless of whether this interpretation is accepted, the analysis here is lenient toward the self-selection hypothesis because only one assignment is needed to count as self-selection.

TABLE 4.4. Self-Selection of High Demanders onto Authorization Committees or Appropriations Subcommittees

Policy	Rating	P_H	P_L	$P_H - P_L$	p-value
Agriculture	NFU	0.086	0.124	− 0.037	0.42
Defense	ASC	0.280	0.151	0.129	< 0.01
Education	NEA	0.157	0.105	0.051	0.03
Labor	COPE	0.244	0.105	0.139	< 0.01
Foreign Relations	ASC	0.107	0.124	− 0.016	0.51

three features. They explicitly characterize collective objectives alongside individually rational behavior. They allow for informed decision making alongside distributional conflict. And they accommodate the supply side as well as the demand side when analyzing the choice of organizational forms. The focal question then becomes: How does a rational legislature manage individual demands for distributional benefits to ensure a reliable supply of information in policy-making?

Chapter 3 presented the informational expectations in terms of two predictions that will be reformulated into null hypotheses below.

PREDICTION 1: OUTLIERS. *Legislative committees will* not, *as a matter of practice, be composed predominantly of high demanders or preference outliers.*

PREDICTION 2: HETEROGENEITY. *Legislative committees will be composed of heterogeneous members, that is, legislators whose preferences represent both sides of the policy spectrum.*

Assessing these predictions requires an approach different from that used to assess the self-selection hypothesis. First, it is useful to establish a clear conceptual foundation regarding preference-outlying committees. Second, it is essential to expand the focus to the overall composition of committees.[20]

What Are Preference Outliers?

Three types of preference outliers can be envisioned, and the available data can be used to assess only the first two types. (The third type becomes important later when I juxtapose the present findings with earlier findings.)

First, a classical homogeneous high-demand outlier is a committee whose members have a common desire for uniquely high levels of benefits from policies within their committee's jurisdiction.

---

20. Some of the analysis and the text that follows first appeared in Krehbiel 1990.

. . . [C]ommittees for each service are dominated by representatives of the group with the highest relative demand for the service. (One might think it equally plausible that the committees would consist of those representatives who have the highest and lowest demands for a specific service. A characteristic of legislatures, however, is that advocacy is concentrated and opposition is diluted. . . .) (Niskanen 1971, 139)

Advocates of this view include most New Institutionalists and many empirical congressional scholars. The conditions for convincing empirical support of classical preference outliers are straightforward. Given estimates of the policy positions taken by legislators (here, interest group ratings), committee members' positions should be systematically different from those of the entire legislature in two ways: central tendencies (means, medians) and dispersion of policy positions (variances). In other words, the classical view has both an outlier component and a homogeneity component.

Second, a bipolar outlier is a committee that has significant factions of members on both sides of its policy spectrum. For example, the Judiciary Committee may be composed exclusively of high demanders—ostensibly à la Niskanen—but with one faction of extreme demanders of civil rights and another faction of extreme demanders of so-called law-and-order measures. The probable policy consequences of this form of outlying committee are much different from those of the classical homogeneous high-demand type. So, too, are its directly observable manifestations. For bipolar outliers, we would expect not to see systematic differences in committee-chamber means or medians. But we would observe significant differences in committee-chamber variances, since committee members' positions are substantially more dispersed than those of the parent body.[21]

Third, an intense-interest or high-salience outlier is a committee whose members share a uniquely high level of intrinsic interest in the committee, perhaps because its policy domain is highly salient to members' constituents. While this type of committee may be regarded as a preference outlier, it is for reasons quite apart from the policies espoused or level of services demanded by its members. Rather, self-selection in this context simply means following one's (constituents') innate policy interests to committees with compatible jurisdictions. This type roughly captures the notion of intensity (rather than, say, location) of preferences and obviously cannot be detected from means, medians, or variances. However, a relationship between this and other conceptions of preference outliers must be noted. If preference outliers of the first

---

21. A third variation on this mean-variance theme is a uniform-shift outlier: a committee whose members, while no more homogeneous than the parent chamber, are systematically higher demanders. In this case we should observe a difference in means or medians but not in variances. While theoretically possible, this pattern has received little attention and will not be considered.

TABLE 4.5. Types and Observability of Preference Outliers

Type of Outlier	Observation	
	Means	Variances
Classical (homogeneous high demanders)	$\bar{x}_c > \bar{x}_h$	$s_h^2 > s_c^2$
Bipolar (heterogeneous extreme demanders)	$\bar{x}_c = \bar{x}_h$	$s_c^2 > s_h^2$
Intense-interest or high-salience	*	*

*Not observable from ratings.

or second forms do not exist—that is, if the distribution of preferences within committees is essentially the same as that within the legislature—then the existence of intense-interest or high-salience outliers would be inconsequential for the ultimate distribution of policy benefits. Perhaps informational benefits are more likely to obtain when committees are composed of members who have uniquely strong interests in their committee's work and thus can specialize at relatively low cost. However, if such members share the preferences of the larger legislature, then the distributive perspective of legislative organization becomes more difficult to sustain, since any conceivable committee power that emerges under these conditions must be nondistributive.

Table 4.5 summarizes the types of preference outliers and their observational attributes. The empirical analysis that follows focuses on the classical homogeneous high-demand type and its corresponding outlier and homogeneity components. Bipolar outliers can also be detected with available data and will be noted if and when observed, although this is a lesser interest. Finally, since high-salience or intense-interest outliers cannot be detected with the data and techniques employed, no such inferences about this type will be made.

Evidence

To assess more systematically competing hypotheses regarding committee composition and to extract more from the available data than the self-selection tests did, several statistical tests are conducted. These have an advantageous feature with respect to distributive theories and a disadvantageous feature with respect to informational theories: the tests are constructed with the distributive predictions as alternative hypotheses and the informational predictions as the nulls. Inferences will be tempered accordingly.[22]

---

22. This methodological drawback could be circumvented if another substantively plausible and theoretically derived null hypothesis were available. One candidate—a majority-party or leadership hypothesis—meets the first criterion. Empirical research on committee assignments focuses overwhelmingly on the majority party and its assignment practices, taking for granted

As discussed above, the classical preference-outlier perspective has two components: an outlier component, which pertains to central tendencies of committee members as compared with noncommittee members, and a homogeneity component, which pertains to the degree to which committee members are in better agreement with themselves than are members of the larger legislature. Two types of tests will be conducted for each component.

To test whether or which committees are composed of outliers, I compute and compare median and mean ratings of committees with those of the legislature. The focus on medians is justified by formal models that typically yield variations of median voter results. Support for the distributive preference-outlier hypothesis requires that these medians be significantly different. One method of assessing significance is simply the percentage of legislators whose ratings lie between the committee and chamber medians. A second method is a standard difference-in-means test. The null hypothesis, which is broadly consistent with informational theory, is

$$H_1^o : \mu_h = \mu_c,$$

where μ_h is the average policy position of the House (excluding committee members) and μ_c is the comparable average for the committee. The alternative hypothesis, which is broadly consistent with distributive theory (Hypothesis 1), is

$$H_1^A : \mu_h < \mu_c.$$

---

that the party slate will be adopted pro forma by the House. From a perfect-information rational-choice perspective, it is easy to see why the House's vote on committee slates appears to be pro forma. A hit-the-beach-running majority party does not like to begin a Congress by stuffing its face into the sand. However, for exactly this reason, it is difficult to imagine that the parliamentary right of the full House to vote on committee assignments does not condition the majority party leaders' slate-proposal behavior. No one has fully worked out a theory in which party leaders are strategic and competitive actors in the committee assignment process. (The closest approximation to a party-based theory of committee assignments is Cox and McCubbins's [1989] majority party leader's utility function. In accord with prior empirical research, though, these authors implicitly assume that the two parties' slates will be adopted and do not account theoretically for the prospect of strategic behavior between parties.) Notwithstanding this theoretical gap, the relevant empirical hypothesis is straightforward. The null would be that $\mu_c = \mu_D$ where μ_c is the committee mean and μ_D is the Democratic party mean. Consistent with informational theory, which stresses chamber control in the committee assignment process, the sign of the inequality in the alternative hypothesis would be given by μ_h, the median voter in the House. In this manner, the information-theoretic prediction is the alternative hypothesis—a scientifically more satisfactory setup than that of this chapter. (From the results here the reader will be able to discern that if this test were conducted, this party or leadership null hypothesis would often be rejected in favor of the informational alternative hypothesis. I thank Tom Gilligan for this suggestion and regret that it does not comport better with my decision to focus on testing existing theories of legislative organization.)

Rejection of the null hypothesis constitutes support for the claim that committees are composed of outliers. A one-tailed t-test is used in which, for example, rejection of the null hypothesis at the .05 level of significance requires a t-statistic of 1.65 or greater.[23]

Analogously, to test whether committees are significantly more homogeneous than the House, a median-based approximation is obtained by ascertaining whether, for any given committee, its Democratic and Republican median members are both on the same side of the House median. When this condition holds, the committee is said to be homogeneous since majorities of committee members of both parties have ratings that exceed those of a majority of the House. Homogeneity of this sort facilitates reaching a bipartisan consensus on the committee. When this condition does not hold, the committee is said to be heterogeneous since committee members' preferences are sufficiently different from one another that a committee majority of only one party has ratings that exceed those of a majority of the House. Heterogeneity in this sense makes reaching a bipartisan consensus within committee difficult. A similar but more rigorous test of homogeneity focuses on the relative variances of the committee and the House. The null hypothesis is

$$H_2^o : \sigma_h^2 = \sigma_c^2,$$

where σ_h^2 is the variance for the House (excluding committee members) and σ_c^2 is the variance for the committee. The alternative hypothesis is

$$H_2^A : \sigma_h^2 > \sigma_c^2.$$

Rejection of the null hypothesis is necessary for support for the homogeneity component of the classical view of committee composition (Hypothesis 1). The ratio of the sample variances has an F distribution. Under a one-tailed test we reject the null only if the test statistic, s_h^2/s_c^2, is above the critical value given by F_{N_h, N_c}, where N_c is the number of members on the committee minus 1, and N_h is the number of members in the House minus N_c.[24]

The analysis is conducted in two stages. A first approximation permits

---

23. Of course, the .05 level of significance is not sacred. In the context of the article that this chapter extends, Hall and Grofman have argued that the .05 level of significance is inappropriate because it "minimizes the wrong type of statistical error" (1990, 11). The focus in Krehbiel 1990, however, was on the common claim (alternative hypothesis) that committees *are* composed of outliers, in which case Type I errors—that is, unwarranted acceptance of outlier claims—should, indeed, be minimized. In any case, I present t-statistics here (just as I did in the earlier work). Thus, the reader is free to choose his or her preferred level of significance and make inferences accordingly, from a distributive perspective, an informational perspective, or both.

24. To detect bipolar outliers, tests were also conducted with the same null hypothesis but with the alternative hypothesis $\sigma_c^2 > \sigma_h^2$. Here the test statistic is $s_c^2/s_h^2 \sim F_{N_c, N_h}$. These results will be reported in passing whenever statistically significant.

inspection of all standing committees and focuses on general-ideology ratings. More refined tests are then conducted by analyzing policy-specific ratings. Due to the more precise information available at this stage (albeit for only a subset of committees), the alternative hypotheses face a better chance of corroboration. For example, the distributive perspective suggests that committee-chamber differences will be greater with policy-specific measures than with the general-ideology measures and especially pronounced on committees where the goal of the high-demanders is acquisition of concentrated benefits, that is, distributive policies. Such committees in the House, for example, include Public Works, Interior, and Agriculture. The analysis reported in detail focuses on the House of Representatives in the 99th Congress, while the second part of appendix B summarizes comparable results for the 96th through 98th Congresses, including the Senate.

General-Ideology Results

The purpose of the first set of results is very narrow: to see whether systematic and general biases in general-ideology outliers exist or whether cross-committee variation exists. These findings are clearly not sufficient for drawing any precise conclusions about preference outliers, since our primary interest is in jurisdiction-specific preferences.

Ratings of the Americans for Democratic Action (ADA) and the American Conservative Union (ACU) were first analyzed for the House in the 99th Congress. The results were virtually identical for the two sets of ratings, so only ADA ratings are presented. Column 1 of table 4.6 summarizes the medians by listing the number of points of deviation of the committee median from the House median. A positive (negative) score designates a relatively liberal (conservative) committee. Committees that are somewhat more conservative than the House include Agriculture, Veterans' Affairs, Merchant Marine and Fisheries, Small Business, Science and Technology, and Standards of Official Conduct. The Armed Services Committee, however, is a more significant conservative outlier, with a median 27.5 points lower than the House's.

Several additional findings emerge from the remaining columns of table 4.6. Most standing committees do not have significantly different general-ideology medians or means than the House. Column 2 shows that for fifteen of the twenty-two standing committees fewer than 10 percent of the House's members lie in the gap between the House and committee medians. The paucity of general-ideology outliers is also reflected in column 3, which summarizes the hypothesis tests for differences in means. The *t*-statistics are significant at the .05 level for only five committees: Foreign Affairs, Education and Labor, Post Office and Civil Service, Armed Services, and District of Columbia. Of these, only Armed Services is currently among the five most desirable assignments as estimated by Munger (1988, table 3), and here the

TABLE 4.6. Preference Outliers Based on ADA Ratings

STANDING COMMITTEE	DIFFERENCE IN MEDIANS (1)	PERCENT IN GAP (2)	t-STATISTIC FOR H_1^o (3)	PARTY MEDIANS (4)	p-VALUE FOR H_2^o (5)
Ways and Means	2.0	0.9	0.46	Hetero	0.47
Public Works and Transportation	3.0	1.4	0.23	Hetero	0.42
Agriculture	−3.0	2.8	−0.89	Hetero	0.13
Veterans' Affairs	−3.5	3.0	−0.70	Hetero	0.14
Government Operations	4.0	1.8	0.52	Hetero	0.73
Budget	5.5	2.1	0.38	Hetero	0.73
Energy and Commerce	5.5	2.1	−0.04	Hetero	0.62
Appropriations	7.0	3.0	1.01	Hetero	0.40
Merchant Marine and Fisheries	−7.0	4.1	−0.45	Hetero	0.22
Small Business	−8.5	5.5	−0.59	Hetero	0.47
Science and Technology	−9.0	6.0	−0.91	Hetero	0.19
Interior	9.5	3.4	0.41	Hetero	0.91
Banking, Finance, and Urban Affairs	13.0	6.0	0.46	Hetero	0.52
Foreign Affairs	13.0	6.0	1.80	Hetero	0.74
Standards of Official Conduct	−14.0	9.4	−0.30	Hetero	0.63
Judiciary	18.5	10.6	1.19	Hetero	0.85
Education and Labor	21.5	12.2	2.05	Hetero	0.44
Rules	22.0	12.6	1.20	Hetero	0.70
House Administration	23.0	13.3	0.69	Hetero	0.67
Armed Services	−27.5	17.9	−3.72	Homo	0.04
Post Office and Civil Service	35.5	25.7	2.20	Hetero	0.67
District of Columbia	50.5	37.9	1.96	Hetero	0.84

Note: House median = 44.5; mean = 47.3; standard deviation = 34.4.

putative self-selection runs contrary to the majority party's preferences. In contrast to the handful of outliers, committees that appear to be microcosms of the House include Ways and Means, Budget, Appropriations, Agriculture, Public Works, and Energy and Commerce. Indeed, Davidson (1981) singles out the first three of these committees as exceptions to his generalization about outliers.

While committees exhibit substantial variation in terms of whether their means and medians are outliers and, if so, in a conservative or liberal direction, their composition is heterogeneous almost without exception. This claim is supported by the results reported in column 4: the committee's party medians lie on opposite sides of the chamber median for every committee except Armed Services. Similarly, the F-tests reported in column 5 permit confident rejection of the null hypothesis, H_2^o, only in the case of Armed Services, though the Agriculture and Veterans' Affairs Committees are somewhat more homogeneous than the House.[25]

Overall, the general-ideology results raise some preliminary doubts about the conventional wisdom on preference outliers. Cross-committee variation in outlying tendencies is evident, but the classical homogeneous high-demand committee seems, upon first glance, to be an endangered species. These results must be interpreted with extreme caution, however. The most apparent problem is that the exceptional diversity of votes on which ADA ratings are based may mask some significant jurisdiction-specific differences in committee-House preferences. This possibility is examined next.[26]

Policy-Specific Results

Table 4.7 presents results for nine standing committees and one select committee for which jurisdiction-specific ratings are available. Again, the best support for the classical outlier hypothesis is found on the Armed Services

---

25. Since critical values of the F-statistic differ both across committees (because of different degrees of freedom) and across ratings (because of different parent samples), I report the p-value for each committee. Support for the homogeneity hypothesis at the .05 level therefore requires a $p \leq .05$. For each committee, F-tests were also conducted for the bipolar outlier hypothesis, but statistically significant support was nonexistent.

Comparable data were analyzed for appropriations subcommittees. Cross-committee variation was evident, but significant outliers were confined to a few subcommittees: Defense, HUD, and Transportation. Two of these, plus the District of Columbia Subcommittee, were homogeneous according to the party median criterion. No subcommittee was homogeneous according to the F-test.

26. All of the caveats associated with general ideology ratings also accompany committee-level inferences based on Poole and Rosenthal's (1985) NOMINATE ratings, used, for example, by Kiewiet and McCubbins (1989) and Cox and McCubbins (1989). These ratings are based on a multidimensional unfolding technique and are often cited as evidence for the "unidimensional Congress" hypothesis (see various works by Poole and Rosenthal). The ratings are highly correlated with ADA ratings (.93 in the 99th Congress, for example) and thus are unlikely to reflect jurisdiction-specific preferences any more accurately than ADA or ACU ratings.

TABLE 4.7. Preference Outliers Based on Policy-Specific Ratings

COMMITTEE	RATING	DIFFERENCE IN MEDIANS (1)	PERCENT IN GAP (2)	t-STATISTIC FOR H_1^o (3)	PARTY MEDIANS (4)	p-VALUE FOR H_2^o (5)
Armed Services	ASC	50.0	21.4	4.93	Homo	0.02
Appropriations	BIPAC	−13.5	8.3	−1.95	Hetero	0.26
	CCUS	−15.0	13.3	−2.68	Hetero	0.12
Budget	BIPAC	−3.0	1.4	−0.21	Hetero	0.70
	CCUS	−2.0	0.7	−0.51	Hetero	0.65
Education and Labor	COPE	19.0	11.5	1.14	Hetero	0.61
	IBT	15.0	3.2	1.22	Hetero	0.37
	MNPL	10.5	6.7	0.97	Hetero	0.61
	RLEA	8.0	1.8	0.45	Hetero	0.48
	NEA	2.5	0.5	0.95	Hetero	0.24
Foreign Affairs	ASC	−30.0	8.0	−1.62	Hetero	0.54
Interior	CCUS	−10.5	7.1	−0.11	Hetero	0.72
	LCV	−3.0	0.0	−0.13	Hetero	0.98
	PCCW	−5.0	2.1	−0.38	Hetero	0.82
Public Works	CCUS	−4.5	2.5	−0.57	Hetero	0.55
	LCV	−3.0	0.0	−1.12	Hetero	0.16
	PCCW	−4.0	0.9	−0.13	Hetero	0.29
	RLEA	0.0	0.0	0.55	Hetero	0.47
Small Business	BIPAC	−8.0	3.0	0.42	Hetero	0.47
Agriculture	NFU	6.0	4.6	1.62	Hetero	0.01
Aging (Select)	NCSC	3.5	0.9	1.36	Hetero	0.19

Committee. American Security Council (ASC) scores, which focus exclusively on issues of foreign policy and defense, depict a committee whose members tend to be substantially more conservative than a majority of the House. Indeed, over one-fifth of the House membership has ratings between the two medians. Republicans and Democrats alike are outliers in the committee's jurisdiction, and they form a statistically significant homogeneous group, as reflected by the p-value of .02. These findings differ from at least one prior study of Armed Services, which characterized that committee as a relatively low demander that battled, often successfully, with relatively high-demand appropriations subcommittees (Stephens 1971). But it is consistent with more recent studies that claim support for high-demanders on Armed Services (Ray 1980; Weingast and Marshall 1988). Two caveats should be issued, however. First, the ASC ratings are based on only ten votes. Second, the votes for the 99th Congress sharply divided House members. The F-test presumes normality of the parent distribution and, for ASC ratings, this condition appears from the sample not to be met. Moreover, impressionistic evidence is suggestive of heterogeneity on Armed Services, contrary to the F-test. One member is Representative Ronald Dellums, a Democrat from Berkeley, whose 1986 ASC and ACU ratings are 0 and whose ADA rating is a perfect 100. Three other members also had ASC ratings of 0: Nicholas Mavroules (D.–Mass.), Dennis Hertel (D.–Mich.), and Thomas Foglietta (D.–Pa.), each of whom is very liberal on ADA and ACU ratings as well.

After Armed Services, evidence of homogeneous high-demand outliers is spotty. Candidates for support of the distributive hypotheses include Appropriations, Education and Labor, and Foreign Affairs, but in none of these instances are the findings consistent with both the homogeneity and outlier hypotheses. The Appropriations Committee is a moderately liberal and statistically significant outlier according to the Chamber of Commerce (CCUS) and Business and Industry PAC (BIPAC) ratings. These findings are consistent with Schick's (1980) postreform characterization of Appropriations members as "claimants," and they diverge from Fenno's (1966) prereform characterization of Appropriations members as "guardians."[27] But neither rating yields significant differences in variances. To the degree that the Appropriations Committee has been forced to share much of the spending spotlight in the 1980s, the results for the Budget Committee are also relevant here. From all indications (and also consistent with Schick), the Budget Committee is a microcosm of the House. Divergence in chamber-committee preferences is minimal in terms of both means and medians, and the committee is clearly heterogeneous.

27. See, however, Maass 1983, 132–35 for a convincing argument that the postreform Appropriations Committee does not operate in a fundamentally different way in terms of its "economy norm."

The Education and Labor Committee appears to be somewhat of an outlier according to the AFL-CIO's COPE score, with 11.5 percent of members lying between the committee and House medians. But this difference is not significant according to the t-test. Nor are the committee's liberal leanings strong according to other labor ratings: the International Brotherhood of Teamsters (IBT), the Machinists' Non-Partisan Political League (MNPL), and the Railway Labor Executives' Association (RLEA). On the education issues, the committee and chamber medians are virtually indistinguishable. In light of Fenno's (1973) study and the pattern of results thus far, it is not surprising that the Education and Labor Committee has party medians on the opposite sides of the House median. But variances for Education and Labor tend to be somewhat less than those for the House, which may be surprising given the high degree of partisanship in the period Fenno studied. Thus, not only does the Education and Labor Committee fail to live up to the classical outlier claim; it is not a bipolar outlier either.

The Foreign Affairs Committee has persisted in its liberal leanings in foreign policy (Fenno 1973), with the difference in means falling just short of the .05 level of significance. When compared with Armed Services, this result raises some unsolved puzzles, however. If the Armed Services and Foreign Affairs Committees have jurisdictions that the ASC ratings reflect, then why are the members on the two committees outliers on opposite sides of the spectrum—consistent with the majority party's preferences in one case but contrary to them in the other?[28] And why is one committee but not the other significantly more homogeneous than the House? In short, it is increasingly apparent that the committee assignment mechanism operates neither automatically nor uniformly and a theory is needed that explains variation in the extremity and heterogeneity of committees' preferences.

The remaining committees in table 4.7 deal most explicitly in constituency-specific benefits and thus provide what should be the best opportunity to marshal support for distributive-theoretic hypotheses. As such, the absence of strong and uniform support is striking. Regardless of the policy-specific rating employed, the quintessential pork barrel committees—Interior and Public Works—are not homogeneous high-demanders at all.[29] Nor is

---

28. One possibility is that the if clause is false: the ASC ratings might not tap policy-relevant preferences in this jurisdiction. While this possibility should be entertained, entertainment is less informative than correcting the limitation. In any event, the finding on Armed Services is a good example of refutation of the majority-party or leadership hypothesis, which is implicit in much committee assignment literature and was articulated explicitly in n. 22. The difference between the majority-party mean and the Armed Services mean is a remarkable 55.1, and the t-statistic is 12.9. The subtle but key lesson here is that believers in self-selection cannot simultaneously subscribe to the view of committees as agents of the majority party on the one hand, and self-selection of high-demanders on the other. In at least some instances, these are plainly contradictory hypotheses.

29. Only in the case of Interior and LCV ratings was a committee significantly more

there evidence of self-selection of high-demanders on the Small Business Committee. On Agriculture, ratings of the National Farmers Union provide the most jurisdiction-specific information of all ratings, yet even here the results are inconclusive. The t-statistic approaches significance at the .05 level, but only 6 percent of House members have ratings between the committee and chamber medians. And although the F-test uncovers significant homogeneity, the committee is nevertheless heterogeneous according to the party median criterion. At best, then, the Agriculture Committee is a somewhat-homogeneous medium-high demander.[30]

Finally, if classical preference outliers predominate anywhere, it should be on a committee designed to represent voters who turn out at high rates and on which, as a select committee without legislative powers, workload is low and position-taking opportunities are high. Yet the Select Committee on Aging is only slightly more predisposed to policy that is favorable to senior citizens than is the House overall.[31]

Reconciliation of Competing Claims

Two sets of data and modes of analysis seem fundamentally inconsistent with one another. On one hand, Shepsle found that geographic (interpreted as distributive) characteristics were often statistically significant predictors of requests and assignments in the 86th through 93d Congresses. From these findings he concluded that an "interest-advocacy-accommodation syndrome" systematically yields unrepresentative committees that undermine the House's institutional viability. Likewise, a diverse assortment of congressional scholars has embraced self-selection as the sine qua non of committee politics, if not distributive politics. On the other hand, I find minimal evidence of high-demand committees and even less evidence of homogeneous committees in the 96th through 99th Congresses.[32] From these findings, I am inclined to doubt the distributive perspective on legislative organization in favor of further exploration of informational theories.

As starkly contrasting as these findings and conclusions are, they are not

---

heterogeneous than the parent body, thus supporting the bipolar outlier hypothesis. The difference between s_c^2 and s_h^2 was significant at the .03 level.

30. Analysis of jurisdiction-related ratings for appropriations subcommittees revealed three subcommittees to be significant outliers: Agriculture (NFU ratings), Labor, HHS, and Education (RLEA ratings), and Transportation (RLEA ratings). But homogeneity was rare on the subcommittees, with only Agriculture and Transportation at or near the .05 significance level. Also noteworthy was the absence of significant outliers or homogeneity on the Military and Defense Subcommittees.

31. Fleck (1989) analyzes a subset of NCSC votes and finds the Aging Committee to be a more significant outlier than reported in table 4.7.

32. See appendix B for a summary of results from earlier Congresses, including the Senate.

irreconcilable. The first and simplest point is that the 99th Congress provides some evidence that the committee assignment process favors high-demanders. Thus, Shepsle's claims about the 1960s and 1970s are appropriate for at least one committee (Armed Services) in the 1980s. The second and subtler point requires a reassessment of Shepsle's findings and, in one instance, a major revision in their interpretation.

The theoretical context in which the interpretation is offered uses the Heterogeneity Prediction as a backdrop and focuses on the third prediction of informational theories:

PREDICTION 3: EXCEPTIONAL OUTLIERS. *Exceptional cases with respect to the Outlier Prediction will involve members with extreme preferences who can specialize at lower cost than moderates and therefore may be comparatively informative in spite of their preference extremity.*

To begin the revisionist interpretation, consider the fact that a typical citation to Shepsle's book mentions at least one of the following: self-selection, preference outliers, or unrepresentative committees. A two-part argument suggests that, with the possible exception of self-selection (soon to be reinterpreted), such references are unfounded. First, Shepsle's analysis does not directly support these claims. Second, many of his findings, and a sizable but underemphasized portion of his interpretation, are actually consistent with the informational rather than the distributive perspective on legislative organization.

The empirical support for the putative stylized fact of self-selection stems primarily from Shepsle's probit estimates of freshmen committee requests. As such, it focuses more on individual actions during the process of committee assignments than on the collective consequences of that process. Several other things are noteworthy but rarely noted about this analysis. The committees for which the data provide the poorest fits tend to be committees, such as Public Works and Armed Services, whose jurisdictions have a highly particularistic component.[33] Furthermore, in the eight equations reported in Shepsle's (1978) table 4.4, the only types of variables that are consistently strong and significant are not those pertaining to constituency characteristics but rather those pertaining to members' occupations. The best predictor of Agriculture requests is "farm-related occupational background." The best predictor of Banking and Currency requests is "financial or real estate occupational background." Similarly, education or labor occupational backgrounds are the only significant predictors of requests to the Education and Labor

---

33. In Agriculture, too, while the R^2 is relatively high, only one (or possibly two) right-hand variable is statistically significant. ("Possibly two" because of an error in the standard error either in Shepsle's table 4.4 or on his page 79).

Committee, and being a lawyer is the only significant predictor of requests to Judiciary. Finally, the four equations without occupational variables tend to predict requests more poorly than those with occupational variables.

Two substantively distinct interpretations can be given to this pattern of results. The one Shepsle and others have found most attractive is that "interests," by which is meant high-demand preferences, drive the entire process: requests, transfers, assignments, and, ultimately, the composition of committees.

> An important consequence of the interest-advocacy-accommodation syndrome is the unrepresentative committee composition it produces. Responding to a distinctive set of institutional interests—the so-called "interesteds"—in their assignment decisions, the CC [Committee on Committees] determines committee makeups that provide a basis for the policy subgovernments Freeman (1965) and others have described. Accommodation of revealed preferences, not representativeness, is the operating premise of the CC. And because the CC responds favorably to expressed preferences for committee assignments, it also inadvertently samples other characteristics, correlated with committee preferences, in a distorted fashion. Thus, many congressional committees are not only *deep in "interesteds"* but are also *unrepresentative* of regional, ideological, and seniority groupings of the House. (Shepsle 1978, 259; italics added)

An alternative interpretation of Shepsle's findings is readily available from an alternative, informational theory, which holds that a rational legislature is one that efficiently taps the special talents of its legislators. Such a legislature appoints to committees members who can specialize at relatively low cost due to, for example, their prior experience or intense interest in the policies that lie within a committee's jurisdiction.[34] Other things being equal, this form of interest is likely to make members work relatively hard to master the intricacies of policy-making. Given this alternative perspective, two things are noteworthy. First, Shepsle's occupation variables are very good measures—perhaps the best possible measures—of low-cost specialization. Second, while this form of interest defines preferences over committee slots, it bears no necessary relationship to preferences over policy outcomes. In other words, it is intense interest akin to that identified in table 4.5 as being unobservable using interest group ratings.

These observations cast a much different light on Shepsle's empirical findings. Indeed, this alternative interpretation lets us draw a key inference from Shepsle's results that we cannot draw from mine. As noted above, the

---

34. See Gilligan and Krehbiel 1990.

occupation variables, and only these variables, are consistently significant predictors of requests. Furthermore, when it comes to predicting assignments—which is what ultimately determines the composition of committees—occupation variables are not used and the results tend to be less convincing than those for requests. Finally, in his concluding chapter, Shepsle seems keenly aware of the specialization function of committees and the tension in legislative organizations between individual goals and collective functions. For instance, he acknowledges that one collectively desirable feature of the committee assignment process is that legislators are more likely to engage actively in policy innovation, and he approvingly quotes Professor John Bibby's testimony before the Bolling Committee:

> The most important consideration should not be representativeness of committee membership, but whether or not the Members have a real incentive to participate in the work of the committee and become specialists. I think you encourage that incentive only by allowing Members the freedom to try and get on committees where they have a special interest. (Shepsle 1978, 248, quoting Bibby)

While Bibby uses the term *special interest,* two points about the context of his argument are crucial. First, his recommendation is clearly based on the premise that a rational organizational form is one that provides members with incentives to develop committee-specific expertise. Second, consistent with informational theories, he implies that gains in expertise may entail losses in representativeness but still be worthwhile, provided that self-selection is not unrestrained. Thus, Bibby's conception of self-selection is strongly qualified: members should be given only "the freedom to try to get on committees where they have a special interest."

On balance, an alternative conception of self-selection can be found that is consistent with Shepsle's findings, my findings, and the theory of organizing informative committees. To use Shepsle's terms, an individual-level process of "self-selection" of "interesteds" may exist. However, it does not follow, theoretically or empirically, that committees as collective units are "unrepresentative" or composed predominantly of "high-demanders."[35] Why? Because legislators who have "special interests" in a specific committee may have heterogeneous preferences, and because their "special interests" may facilitate low-cost specialization. Two cases are amenable to this interpretation.

---

35. In this respect, I cannot reconcile competing claims. Specifically, Shepsle interprets his findings as consistent with Davidson's and others' claims of unrepresentative committees. I believe that these interpretations are not substantiated in his analysis, which contains only indirect measures of preference, and measures that do not predict requests particularly well at that.

Case 1: Heterogeneous Special Interests

As we have seen, much of the empirical literature on the committee assignment process is a search for independent variables with explanatory power. These include party, occupation, prior political experience, electoral marginality, and a battery of dummies for things such as state, region, and whether one's region or state was the same as the Speaker's or Majority Leader's, to mention but a few.[36] Granted, these variables get closer to nitty-gritty aspects of the process than my proxy measures for preferences, which are better characterized as consequences of the committee assignment process. It is useful, however, to see how the actual choices that bear on committee composition work through these variables in a way that is consistent with an explicit theory.

In 1979 when Jim Wright (D.–Tex.) was Majority Leader in the House, it was a good year for Texans in the committee assignment process. To many folks north of the Red River, a Texan is a Texan is a Texan, and so the widespread special interest of electorally successful Texas politicians in oil and gas issues is anything but surprising. Indeed, prior to the start of the 96th Congress, five of seven freshmen Democrats from Texas initially listed the House Energy and Commerce Committee as their first choice of committees. The Majority Leader intervened and, alas, most of the Texans received their first choice. On the face of it, this seems like the essence of self-selection of preference outliers.

However, only two of the five requestors actually received Commerce seats. The escape from this apparent contradiction is that, in intervening, Wright persuaded three of the five freshmen to have other "first choices," thus illustrating one pitfall of making inferences about self-selection tendencies on the basis of final committee requests.[37] More importantly, additional details illustrate two things: substantial heterogeneity of preferences even within the relatively cohesive Texas delegation, and how final committee assignments reflect such heterogeneity.

While folks north of the Red River may subscribe to the proposition that a Texan is a Texan is a Texan, few politicos on Capitol Hill would defend this

---

36. See, for example, Bullock 1971, 1972, and 1973; Clapp 1963, chap. 5; Deckard 1972; Masters 1961; and Shepsle 1978.

37. Some self-selection believers are aware of this pitfall but in acknowledging it fall into a different pit. In particular, they concede that when making a request, a rational congressman does not ignore the probability of receiving his true most-preferred committee and may therefore formally request a less-preferred committee for which there is less competition, thus a higher probability of assignment, thus greater expected value (see, for example, Weingast and Marshall 1988, 150, n. 23 and surrounding text). I accept this reasoning wholly, but I also believe that it distorts the meaning of the term *self-selection*. To take an extreme example, can it meaningfully be said that a man who is held up at gunpoint "self-selects" into giving a robber his wallet because to do so maximizes his expected value?

corollary: a Mickey Leland is a Jim Wright is a Phil Gramm. Yet, the two winning Texans in the assignment process in question were Phil Gramm and Mickey Leland. Why were they assigned? We cannot say definitively, of course, but we can identify clues. Gramm was an unabashed opponent of federal regulation who had written on energy issues as a former economics professor. He stated that in lobbying members of the Steering and Policy Committee, he made his case entirely on the basis of qualifications. Leland's basis for selecting Commerce stemmed from his interest and experience in health policy which he had cultivated in his six years as a state representative. Gramm and Leland received their state delegation's endorsement not because they ran together, according to Leland, but because Texans welcomed their combination of qualifications and diverse viewpoints.[38]

Two conclusions are supported. First, *self-selection* is a multifaceted and sometimes misleading term, for it refers only to the individual initiation of the committee assignment process, not to the collective choice that determines committee composition. Rather than self-selecters, a more accurate characterization of Gramm and Leland is self-promoted selectees. Second, while many or most of the customary variables in this instance would have explanatory power in an analysis of a larger sample in which these cases would be typical, and while any number of ad hoc and idiosyncratic accounts could be offered that seem intuitively to fit the facts of the case, the variables with both explanatory power and a theoretical foundation pertain to expertise and preferences. Policy-relevant experience—or, more specifically, the prospect of obtaining additional expertise at relatively low cost—helps. Heterogeneity helps, too.

Case 2: Heterogeneous Low-Cost Specialists

The House Judiciary Committee is one of the many committees for which Shepsle reports a large and significant occupation coefficient. Two simple conjectures can be explored to illustrate the exceptional-outlier and heterogeneity hypotheses from a different angle: first, that most recipients of seats on Judiciary have law-related backgrounds (what Shepsle would call "self-selection" and Gilligan and I would call "low-cost specialization"), and second, that their policy-relevant preferences will be diverse (i.e., "heterogeneous"). In the House, thirty-three of the Committee's thirty-five members have law-related backgrounds, and their ACLU and ADA ratings range from 5 to 100 and 0 to 100, respectively.[39] The ACLU and ADA ratings for Senators

---

38. *National Journal*, February 2, 1979, 183–88.

39. For a time it was a policy for House Democrats to appoint only lawyers to the Judiciary Committee. Upon first consideration, this might be regarded as a more plausible explanation for the pattern of the data. Again, though, one must view such practices (whether informal or formal) as endogenous and ask why they exist and persist. Perhaps they are attempts to institutionalize

TABLE 4.8. Heterogeneity on the Senate Judiciary Committee among Possible Occupational Self-Selecters

SENATOR	ACLU	ADA
Grassley	0	15
Thurmond*	6	0
Denton	6	0
East*	10	0
Hatch*	12	10
Heflin*	12	20
Simpson*	24	24
Byrd	52	52
Specter*	60	60
Mathias*	64	65
Biden*	66	85
DeConcini*	34	60
Simon	78	45
Leahy*	86	95
Metzenbaum*	92	100
Kennedy*	94	85
McConnell*	†	†

*Law-related background.
†Not available.

in the 99th Congress, presented in table 4.8, also are consistent with the two conjectures and thus illustrate the revisionist interpretation of Shepsle's self-selection results. Seventy-six percent (thirteen of seventeen) Judiciary members have law-related backgrounds, and their ACLU and ADA ratings span the entire spectrum.[40]

Summary

Three reconciliatory conclusions emerge. First, consistent with Bibby's "freedom to try" clause, self-selection should be seen only as a description of individuals' initiation of the committee assignment process. Second, such self-selection may occur without yielding unrepresentative committees as collective outcomes of the process, because the House retains control over the committee composition through the judicious use of intermediary organizations such as parties, state caucuses, leadership arrangements, and—not to be

---

low-cost specialization. In this vein it is noteworthy that in the 1970s, demand for Judiciary seats slacked off; Watergate had come and gone and a set of no-win issues made their way onto Judiciary's agenda (e.g., abortion, school prayer, busing). When Democrats found it difficult to fill Judiciary seats, they changed their lawyer-only practice.

40. These data were collected from Barone and Ujifusa 1986.

summarily dismissed as pro forma—the vote of approval by the full House. Third, if preference outlying committees still result, they are likely to be composed of heterogeneous members, or low-cost specialists, or both.

The Seniority System

If standing committees and their composition are crucial to the legislative process, and if an informational rationale for committee composition exists, then the emergence and durability of seniority as a robust, if not rigid, criterion for selection of committee chairmen are puzzling. Is not such a system an institutionalized instance of the House or Senate relinquishing control of its committees?[41]

Advocates of distributive theories have a ready answer to this question. "Yes," they would reply, "that's the point." The seniority system is an integral part of the committee system. As Mayhew states, "What the congressional seniority system does as a system is to convert turf into property; it assures a congressman that once he initially occupies a piece of turf, no one can ever push him off it. And the property automatically appreciates in value over time" (1974, 95–96). Combined with self-selection in the assignment process, this "property right" helps committees to become preference outliers (Weingast and Marshall 1988). So, the story concludes, logs are rolled, pork is barreled, and high-demanders happily legislate in hog heaven.

Unfortunately, the evidence we have just seen throws an empirical wrench into these theoretical works. It indicates that if self-selection occurs in Congress, it usually does not work its way through the process to the ultimate composition of committees in the manner posited by distributive theories. Thus, the seniority system is apparently not quite the distributive institution it is sometimes cracked up to be.

Can the seniority system be justified in terms of informational theories? I conclude the chapter with two arguments: that the seniority system as it exists is highly consistent with informational theories, and that indirect evidence of the informational foundations for the seniority system already exists in the literature. Contentious cases of chairman selection in the contemporary Congress and the formal status of the seniority system are explored as a check on these arguments.[42]

---

41. Polsby (1968) used the absence of seniority violations as a defining characteristic of the institutionalized House. See also Abram and Cooper 1968; Goodwin 1959; Polsby, Gallaher, and Rundquist 1969; and Price 1977.

42. By definition, the seniority system asymmetrically assigns parliamentary rights within committees and, as such, lies beyond the strictly defined scope of current informational theories in which committee members are symmetrically endowed with parliamentary rights and/or private information ("expertise"). Thus, this discussion should be viewed not as a test of informational theory but rather as an illustration of its potential for addressing more complex facets of

An Informational Perspective on Seniority

Suppose, as informational theories do, that individual legislators universally benefit from shared legislative expertise and that, likewise, specialization fulfills an institutional purpose. A central question in informational theories— as in earlier institutionalization literature—is how to organize the legislature to encourage specialization. Division of labor into a committee system is part of the answer. But division of labor by itself only saves time; it serves no immediate informational role. How can individual legislators be encouraged to engage in specialized labor?

If a legislature can be organized such that it shapes individuals' expectations that legislatively valued specialization efforts will be suitably rewarded, then committee work will be forthcoming. The seniority system is an organizational arrangement that does this in both direct and indirect ways. The direct and obvious benefit of applying the seniority criterion for chairman selection is that it ensures that chairmen have experience on the committees over which they preside. Dozens of empirical studies of dozens of legislative bodies offer support for the positive relationship between committee service and jurisdiction-specific expertise.[43] The indirect and subtle benefits of the seniority system occur beneath the level of chairman.[44] The seniority system necessitates bookkeeping of years of consecutive service down through the ranks on each committee. Committeewide incentives for specialization then arise because a legislator's ranking in the book becomes a necessary part of her decision-making calculus when she contemplates transferring to another committee. Members in the middle range of seniority on a given committee are reluctant to walk away from their irretrievable investment, particularly when they will knowingly occupy the bottom rung of the seniority ladder on the new committee. Thus, increases in the costliness of transfers attributable to the seniority system result in an increase in within-committee mean years of service.[45]

---

legislative organization. For theories in which committee members have different private information, see Austen-Smith 1990a and 1990b; and Austen-Smith and Riker 1987 and 1990.

43. See, for example, Buchanan et al. 1963, 637; Clapp 1963, 267; Huckshorn 1965, 175; Luce 1922, 121; McConachie 1898, 156; Schneier 1970, 16; and Tobin 1986, chap. 3.

44. If this were not the case, then strict adherence to the Majoritarian Postulate (or a committee corollary of it) would dictate that I omit this section. My presumption, consistent with House rules but at variance with much of the literature, is that chairman selection is invariably formally traceable to House majorities. A majority can always act to create new assignment rules or change old ones, as it did, for instance, in the revolt against Speaker Cannon. Often, as we shall see, the majoritarian means to the majority-desired end is more direct and less treacherous.

45. Though not strictly related to the seniority system, similarly salutary incentives affect the calculi of members even at the very bottom of a committee's seniority ladder. While these members give up comparatively little by transferring, they know that their ability to transfer successfully to a preferred committee is likely to be a function of their having demonstrated at

In summary, if, as numerous empirical studies suggest, committee seniority is a reasonable proxy measure for jurisdiction-specific expertise, then awarding chairmanships in accordance with committee seniority has at least two desirable properties. It facilitates specialization among committee leaders, and it has a comparable trickle-down effect. In the absence of some superior measure of expertise, the seniority system may be part of an optimal organizational arrangement from the standpoint of informative committees. By fostering expertise, it enables the legislature, potentially, to make informed decisions.[46]

Informational Expectations about Seniority

Reasoning about seniority from an informational perspective leads to two expectations that are closely related to the Commitment, Outlier, and Specialization Predictions of informational theories. Two of these have already been discussed in this chapter. The remaining one is:

> PREDICTION 5: PROCEDURAL COMMITMENT. *Because procedural commitment undermines informational efficiency, encourages distributional losses, or both, a legislature will not—or cannot—commit to organizational forms that foster gains from trade.*

The manifestation of the Commitment Prediction with respect to seniority is simply that we would expect that a legislature will not commit to a seniority rule but will follow a seniority practice. The underlying logic is straightforward. If seniority were a rule instead of a practice, incompetents or outliers would inevitably prevail on some committees in some Congresses. This flies in the face of the Majoritarian Postulate as it pertains to procedural

---

least a modicum of legislative competence and, perhaps also, party loyalty. Certainly the latter was important in earlier, more partisan eras, in which the committee assignments were centralized in the Speaker (though still subject to House approval). So too was it likely to have been important even after 1911 when the groups responsible for committee assignments were fairly homogeneous and partisan bodies. Ways and Means slots, for example, are not awarded on the basis of disillusionment with existing assignments but rather on the basis of various tests: whether the member tends to support his party, whether he has been a good public servant in the sense of other committee work, whether he holds certain views that the leadership finds conducive to the committee in question, such as support of the oil depletion allowance in the 1950s and 1960s (Manley 1970). Thus, just as discontented assistant professors have incentives to publish their way to better universities, discontented low-ranking members on undesirable committees have incentives to legislate their way to better committees.

46. "Potentially" because we have yet to test predictions about whether or how the committee of specialists may use its special policy expertise at the expense of noncommittee members and whether various rules encourage information transmission by specialist committees in predicted ways.

choice since, if the seniority criterion were a formally bestowed right rather than an informally cultivated expectation, then aggrieved majorities would be helpless to violate it. Noncommitment, in contrast, allows quick fixes for inevitable but isolated breakdowns attributable to the seniority system.

Support for this interpretation of the Commitment Prediction is readily available. Seniority is not—and never has been—a standing rule of the House. The interesting issue is why the House has not altered the seniority system's nonrule status. Two conjectures parallel the informational and distributional criteria identified in informational theories and lead to a second empirical expectation. First, informationally, seniority is an imperfect measure of jurisdiction-specific expertise. This means that the senior committee member of the majority party may not be—and indeed sometimes is not or is no longer—the expert that use of some (hypothetical) perfect measure of expertise would select. Second, distributionally, extreme preference outliers may succeed to chairmanships and cause more institutional harm than good, even if they are experts. (Of course, the worst of both worlds—an outlying incompetent—is imaginable and avoidable, too, provided seniority does not become a rule.) If these arguments are more or less correct, then it follows that the durability of the seniority system may be attributable to the very fact that it is not a rule.[47] To see if they are more or less correct, we explore the second extension of the Commitment Prediction, namely, that deviations from the practice of appointment in accordance with seniority will occur only in instances in which chairmen are preference outliers, deemed inexpert to the tasks at hand, or both.

Evidence

Four cases of seniority violations have occurred since the 95th Congress, further supporting the expectation of no commitment. Three of these occurred in 1975, the fourth in 1985. The conventional wisdom surrounding "ousting the oligarchs"[48] in 1975 following Democrats' massive gains in the 1974 election is, to make a long literature short, that it is difficult to generalize. True, all of the chairmen who lost their seats—Agriculture Chairman Bob Poage (D.-Tex.), Banking Chairman Wright Patman (D.-Tex.), and Armed Services Chairman F. Edward Hebert (D.-La.)—were southerners. But this is hardly an explanation. For one thing, ten other southerners survived the cries of the Watergate Babies and were appointed or reappointed as committee

---

47. Members are surely cognizant of its nonrule status. So, as Price (1977) claims, if prospective or actual chairmen for some reason deviate beyond prevailing notions of acceptable legislative behavior, so too might the House deviate from its pattern of reliance upon seniority as the criterion for selection of its committee chairmen.

48. The term is from Rieselbach and Unekis 1981.

chairmen.[49] For another, scores of southerners were repeatedly reinstated to their chairmanships prior and since. Beyond this already doubtful southern swipe hypothesis, accounts for the ousters turn even more ad hoc: Poage was "autocratic." Patman had a "poor record as a legislative leader." Hebert was "condescending to freshmen."[50] The task here is to find a pattern among supposed idiosyncrasies that bears on the conjecture that violations are consistent with informational theories.

Case: Poage to Foley on Agriculture
Bob "The Farmer's Friend" Poage served on the Agriculture Committee for thirty-four years and took over as chairman in 1967. At the start of the 94th Congress in 1975, the Democratic Steering and Policy Committee voted 14 to 10 to nominate him for the chairmanship again, but the Democratic Caucus overturned the decision 141 to 176.[51] Poage was a staunch defender of agriculture benefits and an even more staunch defender of sugar and cotton subsidies. High inflation had generated consumer disillusionment with food prices, and the influx of Democrats in the House increased the size of the coalition supporting food stamps. In this changing political context, Poage's anticonsumer stances and outspoken opposition to food stamps reinforced his reputation as a preference outlier. According to Bob Bergland, a committee member who later became Secretary of Agriculture, "In the past four years, whenever we reported a bill to the floor under Poage, people felt consumers were getting ripped off." Poage's standing was further eroded by his having voted against the Democratic party 63 percent of the time, and by speeches that were regarded as unsympathetic to starving Americans. For instance, he disputed claims that starvation occurred in the rural South, saying that the citizen's group that exposed hunger "was created for the purpose of developing hysteria without any regard for the facts." Committee members were especially dissatisfied with Poage's staff policies, which included keeping the total number of staff small, denying staff to subcommittees, and relying instead on outside farm groups for information.

49. Mahon (Tex.) of Appropriations, Perkins (Ky.) of Education and Labor, Brooks (Tex.) of Government Operations, Haley (Fla.) of Interior and Insular Affairs, Staggers (W.Va.) of Interstate and Foreign Commerce, Henderson (N.C.) of Post Office and Civil Service, Jones (Ala.) of Public Works and Transportation, Teague (Tex.) of Science and Technology, Evins (Tenn.) of Small Business, and Roberts (Tex.) of Veterans' Affairs.

50. See *Texas Monthly*, March, 1975, 20–26; *Congressional Quarterly*, January 18, 1975, 114.

51. Prior to 1975, Democratic nomination powers resided solely in the Committee on Committees (the Democrats on Ways and Means) with the full House then voting on the collective choices of party organizations. Subsequent to the reforms, a three-step process has been used. The Democratic Steering and Policy Committee nominates chairmen. The Democratic Caucus votes on nominees (with the option of proposing alternative candidates). Then, as in the earlier system, the full House votes on Democratic and Republican committee slates. See Davidson and Oleszek 1977 for a detailed account of the rules changes.

Thomas Foley (D.–Wash.), the Agriculture Committee's second-ranking member, was unanimously nominated by the Steering Committee the day after the Caucus turned down the Poage nomination. The Caucus then affirmed Foley with a vote of 257 to 9. The House followed suit. Foley was by no means an enemy of farmers, but he represented a partially urban district of Washington and was prolabor, proconsumer, and moderately liberal. He had also earned a reputation as an agriculture expert, a hard worker, and a consensus builder. Even Poage had great confidence in his successor: "I think he'll do a better job of it than I could possibly do. He'll have more cooperation than I could possibly have received."[52]

Case: Hebert to Price on Armed Services

F. Edward Hebert had been Chairman of Armed Services for only four years in 1975, having succeeded a classic pork barreler, L. Mendel Rivers, a South Carolina Democrat who had earned the nickname "Rivers Delivers." Hebert proved to be, if anything, more of a friend of the Pentagon than his predecessor. His American Security Council ratings were nearly perfect, and he was uniformly regarded among colleagues as a hawk. He blamed his 133 to 152 Caucus defeat on Common Cause and vowed to overturn his party's decision on the floor—a threat that proved empty. Committee colleagues regarded him as both an outlier and a suppressor of information. For example, Les Aspin (D.–Wis.) characterized Hebert's leadership as cultivating the belief that the committee's "role is to find out what the military wants and get it for them," and Michael J. Harrington (D.–Mass.) said bluntly, "I think there is much more the form of fairness than the substance of fairness. I have a feeling there is a reluctance to share information." In one instance, Hebert was alleged to have reprinted Pentagon documents almost verbatim as if they were independent judgments of the committee. Hebert's loyalty to House preferences in conference committees was also harshly questioned. Aspin once proposed a floor amendment that cut military authorizations by $950 million and that passed 242 to 163 on the floor. The Senate passed a higher figure. House conferees (Aspin having been excluded) accepted the Senate figure, with Hebert stressing that Senators had been adamant about their request. Senate conferees denied the allegation.

Melvin Price was the second-ranking member and succeeding chairman. No dove himself (ASC ratings of 80 to 90), Price was nevertheless fairly liberal on domestic issues, with an ADA score of 72 and a COPE score of 100 in 1973. Committee liberals believed that Price "would follow the wishes of the Caucus and House positions in conference more closely than Hebert did."

---

52. Quotations are from *Congressional Quarterly,* January 18, 1975, 166; and *Congressional Quarterly,* February 22, 1975, 379–80.

Moreover, he was "recognized for his knowledge of military and science problems."[53]

Case: Patman to Reuss on Banking

Wright Patman was eighty-two years old when he lost his chairmanship of the House Banking and Currency Committee. A member of the House since 1929, he had been Banking Chairman for 12 years. Patman was very liberal on banking issues, leading many scholars to regard this case as anomalous. An alternative interpretation is that he was a liberal outlier, moreover, one of dubious competence. Caucus members were generally unhappy with Patman's legislative record, and even Patman's home-state media seemed to concur. The *Houston Chronicle* quoted a committee member who called Banking the "worst run committee in the House," its legislation "an awful mess" which typically had to be "rewritten on the floor," and concluded (independently) that "quality and competence" would determine Patman's fate. A political analyst for the *Dallas Morning News* cited Patman's poor leadership and "embarrassment by adverse committee votes and complete rewritings of legislation he has had the staff draft." And the *Texas Observer* noted the committee's susceptibility to jurisdictional raids and Patman's indifference about protecting the committee's turf in spite of the contemporary importance of banking issues to Texas and the nation.

The succeeding chairman was the committee's fourth-ranking member, Henry Reuss (D.–Wis.). Accounts of Caucus members' reasoning for the Reuss choice included references to his long experience in banking (he was from a banking family), his "detailed understanding of economic matters," and his ability to lead the committee through a busy time.[54]

Case: Armed Services Revisited

In 1985, Melvin Price (Hebert's successor in the last Armed Services ouster) was eighty years old. With octogenarianism, his defense posture had stiffened (ASC rating of 100), even by Armed Services standards. Equally bothersome to many members was his leadership posture, which had slouched. Price had begun to exhibit some of the same traits as eighty-two-year-old Wright Patman had a decade earlier, and the Armed Services Committee, which had since acquired an outspoken liberal faction, voiced its dissatisfaction to Democratic leaders. The Steering and Policy Committee decided to renominate Price anyway, but the Caucus turned back the nomination. Steering and Policy countered by nominating the Committee's second-ranking member, Charles

---

53. *Congressional Quarterly,* January 18, 1975, 115; *Congressional Quarterly,* January 25, 1975, 214–15; *Congressional Quarterly,* February 8, 1975, 292.

54. *Houston Chronicle,* December 12, 1974; *Dallas Morning News,* January 8, 1975; *Texas Observer,* February 28, 1975; *Congressional Quarterly,* January 18, 1975, 114.

Bennett (D.–Fla.). The Caucus said "no" again. Finally, from the floor of the Caucus, the Committee's seventh-ranking member, Les Aspin (D.–Wis.), was nominated and elected. The House later concurred.

From the perspective of members wanting to moderate the committee, the new chairman had impeccable credentials: fourteen years of hard work on the committee, a solid reputation for expertise in defense matters, and preferences closer to the legislature's median voter than the body had seen at the head of the Armed Services Committee in decades. Aspin's behavior as chairman was not perfectly predictable, however. In the 99th Congress, he enraged many Democrats by supporting the MX missile in March, 1985, and voting for aid to the Nicaraguan Contras in June, 1986. Democratic liberals and moderates interpreted this as incriminating evidence of conservative drift, made all the worse at a time when the Reagan administration had rolled up an impressive series of defense victories. So, for the third time in a dozen years, the Armed Services chairmanship was in jeopardy.

The first hat to be tossed into the ring had been there and had been trampled on before: that of the second-ranking member, Charles Bennett. In a letter to House Democrats, he argued credibly that his challenge would be "centrist" (ASC rating of 50). Marvin Leath (D.–Tex.) had also been maneuvering for some time and eventually entered the contest formally. The fourteenth-ranking Democrat on the committee, Leath was more conservative (ASC rating of 100) than both Aspin (ASC rating of 60) and Bennett. Even though Leath had supported Contra aid, too, he had managed to earn the respect of liberal Democrats for his hard work, expertise, and defense restraint on the Budget Committee. This, plus Bennett's claim that he would not have entered the contest were it not for Leath, gave the backbencher at least some credibility. Finally, liberals on Armed Services also expressed interest in the chairmanship, including Nicholas Mavroules (D.–Mass.; ASC rating of 0), Ronald Dellums (D.–Calif.; ASC rating of 0), and Pat Schroeder (D.–Colo.; ASC rating of 10), but with the proviso that they would act only if Aspin were to be voted down in Caucus. Aspin survived the challenge but without a scintilla of autocratic flair. Rather, the consensus was that his subsequent behavior as chairman was tightly controlled. Arms control emerged as a key issue in the remainder of the 99th Congress, and Aspin's views (or at least actions) shifted noticeably to the left. The head of the Coalition for Nuclear Arms Control, for example, stated that "his choice this year is different. He's lining up with the [Democratic] Caucus crowd instead of the [Armed Services] Committee crowd."[55]

---

55. This quotation is representative of the conventional account of the Aspin case and differs somewhat from that offered here. Few observers dispute that the various ups and downs of the Armed Services chairmen have been instances of what Maass (1983), for instance, calls "external controls" on committees. But popular accounts stress the Democratic Caucus as the main agent of control whereas informational models strictly require an interpretation based on

In summary, the evidence suggests that Les Aspin took over the Armed Services chairmanship as an actual expert and expected inlier. He behaved unexpectedly as an outlier on some key issues, and his position was threatened. His subsequent behavior reflected both the credibility of the threat and the control of the House, attributable in part to its historic refusal to allow seniority to confer any form of property rights to its members.[56]

Recapitulation

These four cases should not be viewed as tests of informational theory. They are only qualitative and subjective checks on the conjecture that seniority violations have some informational underpinnings. In this respect, it is encouraging that all of these cases conform to the seniority-violations conjecture. Outgoing chairmen were either extreme outliers, past their peak of jurisdiction-specific expertise, or both. Incoming chairmen were either not outliers, highly regarded for past committee service, or both.[57] Of course, many other accounts for these events exist in the literature.[58] When considered individually, prior accounts are more comprehensive and elaborate than the interpretations offered here. But this comparison only serves to underscore the present objective: to discover general principles of legislative

---

legislative median-voter control. In this instance the qualitative predictions of the two interpretations are the same: Aspin should be "pulled" away from conservative positions on Armed Services. Few observers deny that this happened. (Liberal Democrats pout about it not happening, but what they mean is that it did not happen enough, given their preferences.) Once again, it is informative to take the party-control hypothesis seriously by asking whether the majority party, through its leaders, got what its members wanted. ASC ratings suggest not. Aspin's rating was 60, which was 10 greater than the House median and 50 greater than the Democratic Party median. At the very least, the refusal of the Caucus to nominate someone from the Dellums/Mavroules/Schroeder wing of their party suggests that either expertise was relevant, a moderate chairman was desired, they were conditioning their behavior on the chamber preferences since the chamber ultimately had to approve the Caucus's nomination, or some combination of the above.

56. *Congressional Quarterly,* August 2, 1986, 1766–67; *Congressional Quarterly,* July 12, 1986, 1564–65; *Congressional Quarterly,* July 19, 1986, 1556; *Congressional Quarterly,*October 4, 1986, 2362; *Congressional Quarterly Almanac* 1985, 5. Cox and McCubbins (1989, chap. 5, especially n. 9) also challenge the interpretation of seniority as a property right to which the Congress commits. However, their alternative interpretation of seniority differs from that offered here. In particular, they dismiss the empirical support of others for a positive correlation between seniority and specialization, calling this common claim "propaganda."

57. At approximately the same time, two other chairmen were replaced after scandals forced their retirement: Wilbur Mills (Ways and Means) and Wayne Hayes (House Administration). Informational theories cannot explain these events. However, this is not a severe limitation of the theories since the violations of these chairmen pertained to a different sort of seniority norm.

58. Hinkley, for example, attributes the three violations of the Watergate era to three factors: "(1) an undercutting of the seniority norm by an urge to reform; (2) an obvious imbalance in leadership representation, and (3) a sharp cutting-back of the age and seniority of the membership. This unique combination can postdict the unique event" (1976, 398). See also Rieselbach and Unekis 1982.

organization, not to develop comprehensive (and thus often idiosyncratic) accounts of legislative organization.

Conclusion

The modest objective of this chapter was to gain a foothold for informational theories of legislative organization. Some support for the informational perspective was found in each of the following: the historical literature on the development of standing committees, the prevalence of heterogeneous committees, the paucity of high-demand preference outliers on committees, a reinterpretation of Shepsle's empirical findings consistent with the Exceptional-Outlier Prediction (i.e., low-cost specialization), and cases consistent with an informational perspective on the seniority system.

Several caveats are in order, however. Most of the quantitative support for informational theories is indirect. The statistical tests in this chapter tend not to support hypotheses of distributive theories (e.g., that legislators self-select to committees that are therefore composed of homogeneous high-demanders), but neither do they strongly corroborate hypotheses of informational theories. Because the data cannot directly address the information-theoretic condition for rational outliers, I simply predicted that homogeneous high-demanders would be rare or, more specifically, that we would be unable to reject the (informational) null hypotheses in favor of (distributive) alternative hypotheses. It is encouraging for informational theories that homogeneous high-demanders seem to be rare and that Shepsle's influential findings can be reinterpreted plausibly in an informational light. It is also encouraging that organizational arrangements such as the seniority system can be rationalized within the contours of informational theories and that seniority violations are mostly consistent with informational theories. Still, no more than a foothold has been established. Additional research on the composition of standing committees that employs superior methods and data is surely welcome. In short, the case is not closed.

As discussed in the introduction and illustrated in figure 4.1, however, the case does not have to be closed at this stage of analysis. Just as Fenno (1973) observed generally that "committees differ," we have observed more specifically that committees differ in the degree to which they are composed of homogeneous members and high-demanders. Since both of the theoretical perspectives on legislative organization can accommodate some of these differences, no theory should be abandoned at this stage of the analysis. More direct and systematic evidence is needed about whether differences in the composition of standing committees have theoretically anticipated effects on subsequent legislative behavior pertaining to legislative organization. In search of more direct and convincing support, I next examine the processes governing consideration of committees' proposals on the floor.

CHAPTER 5

Information and the Choice of Rules

The parliamentary game is an inextricable part of the political process. You just know the timing and your particular rights, because if you don't, you're dead.

—Walter Kravitz (1989)[1]

Nothing is so boring to the layman as a litany of complaints over the more obscure provisions of House procedures. It is all "inside baseball." Even among the media, none but the brave seek to attend to the howls of dismay from Republicans over such esoterica as the kinds of rules under which we are forced to debate. But what is more important to a democracy than the method by which its laws are created?

—Robert Michel (1987)[2]

Legislative scholars, like minority leaders, have been in long-standing agreement that rules are important determinants of legislative choice. Yet, only recently have theories or even guesses about precisely how rules shape collective choices begun to emerge. A perplexing procedural puzzle can be found within the small but growing literature on legislative rules. Why do legislative majorities adopt different rules for different bills when the distributive consequences of some such rules are nonmajoritarian?

We saw in chapter 4 that although the House, in its constitutional form, is an egalitarian body, its historical development was a combination of accretion of precedents and adoption of standing rules that resulted in the emergence of hierarchies. Asymmetries in legislators' parliamentary rights vary widely in terms of their significance and duration. For instance, rules and precedents that comprise the standing committee system have proved to be robust and durable. However, other parliamentary innovations, such as special orders and suspension of the rules, are bill-specific and thus shorter lived. Often these bill-specific procedures confer special rights to members of standing committees that formulated the legislation under consideration.

---

1. Quoted in *New York Times*, June 21, 1989.
2. Quoted in Bach and Smith 1988, 91.

This chapter continues to pursue the theme of the endogenous assignment of parliamentary rights as a natural outgrowth of article 1 section 5 of the Constitution. Its distinctive focus is on committee-chamber relations as moderated by bill-specific procedures, that is, institutional devices that are adopted by the parent chamber, that are tailor-made to specific legislation, and that remain in effect only for consideration of the specified legislation. The main examples of bill-specific procedures in the U.S. Congress are unanimous consent agreements (in the Senate) and special orders (in the House). This chapter confines its attention to the House.[3]

A special order—hereafter called a rule—is technically a House Resolution that, when adopted, binds only the House. The modal sequence of decisions leading to the adoption of a rule is as follows. After completing work on a bill, a standing committee requests a rule from the Rules Committee. The Rules Committee consults with leaders of committees that have worked on the bill and schedules a public hearing. Committee and noncommittee members may testify at the hearing. In the midst of congratulatory talk about jobs well done in the standing committee, participants in the hearing make arguments about when the bill should be brought to the floor, how the bill should or should not be amended, and whether waivers on points of order should be granted (e.g., on the germaneness of various provisions or anticipated amendments, or on the compliance of the bill with the Budget Act). Upon hearing these arguments—and often with the consultation of the Speaker—the Rules Committee turns to the task of writing a rule and proposing it to the House. If and only if the House approves the rule, the rule governs floor consideration of the specified bill.[4]

---

3. For studies on unanimous consent agreements, see Ainsworth and Flathman 1990; Keith 1977; Krehbiel 1986; Smith 1989, chap. 4; and Smith and Flathman 1989.

4. A bill does not require a rule to come before the House. The House clerk automatically assigns measures reported by standing committees to one of four calendars: Union, House, Consent, or Private (Oleszek 1984, chap. 5). Almost all major legislation goes onto the Union or House Calendars in the order reported from committees where, in accordance with "the regular order," they await consideration chronologically. Due to the normally heavy House workload, only the first bills on these calendars would be considered if the regular order were always followed. Rules are, among other things, devices for getting bills off calendars out of their regular order. (The Rules Committee has the right to report at all times, meaning that its proposals do not have to wait their turn on a calendar. Nor does a rule itself need another rule.)

Suspension of the rules is another route to passage that circumvents both the regular order and the rule-choosing process discussed in this chapter (Bach 1986 and 1990). By a two-thirds vote, the House may suspend its regular procedures and pass any bill, including bills not reported by committee. Bills considered under suspension cannot be amended unless the motion to suspend itself contains an amendment. House precedents grant the Speaker strong recognition rights, but the Speaker is not unconstrained. Standing rules limit the days during which suspension is in order, and the Democratic Caucus has guidelines directing the Speaker not to schedule measures for consideration under suspension unless authorized by the Democratic Steering and

Passage in the Rules Committee is rarely a problem, as a practical matter.[5] Passage in the House is sometimes a problem.[6] As with nearly all facets of legislative organization, the use of special orders can be viewed as a majoritarian process.[7] However, as discussed in chapter 1, the degree to which procedurally majoritarian theories can explain variation in the application of these processes is presently not known.

Bach and Smith's (1988) excellent book, *Managing Uncertainty in the House: Adaptation and Innovation in Special Rules,* makes a major advance in understanding the application of bill-specific rules in recent Congresses and forms the empirical foundation for much of my analysis. The broad contours of Bach and Smith's argument are convincing due, in no small part, to the authors' (implicit) adherence to the two postulates of legislative organization developed in chapter 1 of this book. Obviously, their study is not only about legislative policy choice but also about antecedent and inextricably linked procedural choice—both of which are majoritarian processes. Equally obviously, Bach and Smith's primary argument is about uncertainty and how it affects legislative choices in the procedural and policy domains. Their thesis is that "the Rules Committee has sought to manage these uncertainties in ways that, in different respects and to different degrees, have served the interests of standing committees, majority party leaders, and representatives generally" (1988, 5).

In contrast to the book's many strengths are two limitations that also apply to other empirical research on legislative procedure. First, almost none

---

Policy Committee. The Caucus also tries to keep measures involving more than $100 million from being considered under suspension. Nevertheless, some major legislation passes via suspension. Cooper (1990), for example, reports that in the 100th Congress approximately one-fifth of the bills passed under suspension were multiple referrals, some of which are major bills. (In contrast, bills on the Consent and Private Calendars are almost invariably minor.)

Because committees that have done hard work on legislation are neither so pessimistic as to want to send their work to a probable early grave on a calendar nor so optimistic as to believe that their work will be accepted unamended by a supermajority via suspension, most major legislation is considered under rules. In this respect, procedural nomenclature takes a curious twist. "Rules" are called "special orders" because they allow the House to deviate from the "regular order" that is stipulated in its standing rules. The irony of this terminology is that the "regular order" is irregularly used due to its inflexibility or for other reasons currently not fully understood. Likewise, "special orders" are in fact common for major legislation.

5. Democrats hold a large majority on the Rules Committee: nine to four during the period under study here and up through (at least) the 101st Congress.

6. For example, in the 98th and 99th Congresses, seven rules were defeated on the floor while another thirty-four were drafted by the Rules Committee but, for a variety of reasons, were never considered on the floor. See Matsunaga and Chen 1976 for several specific cases of rules being defeated in earlier Congresses.

7. So, too, can suspension of the rules be viewed as majoritarian, since the House's act of passing its standing rules—which provide for the suspension procedure—is a majoritarian act.

of the existing empirical analysis is closely and explicitly related to a unifying body of theoretical research. Yet only if this connection is made can we begin to isolate the main determinants of bill-specific procedural choice in Congress. Second, existing empirical studies suggest that the complexity and diversity of special orders almost defy theorizing. For example, Bach and Smith make an impressive, fact-filled case when advancing their thesis that the upsurge in the use of complex and often restrictive special orders in the postreform House is due to its need to "manage uncertainty." However, the overarching form of uncertainty they identify is, under the surface, a multiplicity of different forms of uncertainty. The general problem, according to Bach and Smith, is increasing uncertainty of Democratic and committee leaders with regard to behavior of backbenchers in the Committee of the Whole. But what are the more specific sources of leaders' uncertainty? Bach and Smith's rich set of examples identifies many slightly different sources. Backbenchers may be uncertain about the consequences of legislation and amendments. Leaders, in turn, may be uncertain about how backbenchers will behave when given the opportunity to offer and vote on amendments. Alternatively, leaders may not be able to predict amendment behavior because committee members may have wrongly estimated noncommittee members' preferences and presented them with legislation that unexpectedly evokes hostile amendments. Still another possibility is that leaders, committee members, and bill managers may be uncertain about rule making itself, that is, about bill-specific procedural choice in the Rules Committee and on the floor. Certainly some of these empirically motivated arguments about the process of choosing rules are consistent with formal theories, but many details of the arguments remain to be worked out.

When Gilligan and I began our theoretical research on collective decision making under uncertainty, we were motivated by one of the same substantive concerns of Bach and Smith. Why do legislative majorities choose temporarily to relinquish their right to amend legislation? Although we took a different analytic path than Bach and Smith, we arrived at a similar destination: a hypothesis that procedural hand-tying works to decrease uncertainty, and some observations broadly consistent with the hypothesis. More specifically, our main theoretical claim was that by committing to restrictive procedures,[8] a legislature can increase its committees' incentives not only to specialize but also to share the fruits of specialization with the larger legislature. Since our conception of uncertainty concerned the unknown relationship between policies and their consequences, our thesis was compatible with at least one of Bach and Smith's notions of managing uncertainty.

---

8. In retrospect, we came to regard the commitment assumption as doubtful and thus relaxed it (see Gilligan and Krehbiel 1989b).

The empirical component of our informational argument focused on the late nineteenth century, which had been identified by others as the era in which an "institutionalized" House emerged (Polsby 1968). By studying the House's rules and precedents pertaining to restrictive procedures—namely, recognition rights, suspension of the rules, and the emergence of the Rules Committee and its use of special orders—we learned that, indeed, this was also a period marked by a sharp increase in asymmetries in the assignment of parliamentary rights. These included the delegation of rule-proposing authority to the Rules Committee; delegation of strong recognition rights to the Speaker; and increasing (and increasingly creative) use of suspension of the rules, which, in effect, became a closed rule requiring a two-thirds majority. Nearly all of the associated rules and precedents tended to confer special rights to standing committees. Gilligan and I attributed these procedural developments to rapid social and economic changes in the political environment during the Industrial Revolution, the formal representation of which was increasing legislative uncertainty about the relationship between legislation and its consequences, especially in those issue domains in which new and complex policy-making demands were forced upon the legislature.

Both Bach and Smith and Gilligan and I put forth an essentially longitudinal argument that the emergence of restrictive procedures over time was a consequence of increasing uncertainty: in Bach and Smith's work, uncertainty of several forms among leaders; in Gilligan's and mine, uncertainty about the relationship between laws and their consequences among all legislators except policy specialists. Bach and Smith identified many factors correlated with the use of restrictive rules but did not assess what would remain as a chief cause when the combined effects of these were assessed. Gilligan's and my historical argument was, if anything, even more tenuous insofar as we limited our attention to a single exogenous variable: uncertainty in the policy environment. As Smith (1988) has stated, it seems unlikely that there is any such "mono-causal" explanation since plausible alternative hypotheses for the emergence of restrictive procedures in the late nineteenth century are readily available. For instance, parties were strong and thus the majority could steamroll over the minority; leaders tended to have more assertive leadership styles then than they do now; and the Industrial Revolution coincided not only with increased policy uncertainty but also with increased activity of the national government in policy formation and, more specifically, in distributive politics.

Other hypotheses undoubtedly can be put forth, too, but the central point should be clear. Arguments that rely exclusively on simple correlations and historical arguments are of limited value in resolving competing claims. On the other hand, correlates or causes of bill-specific procedures may be assessed more convincingly via cross-sectional rather than time-series analysis.

This is because by exploiting cross-committee, cross-bill variation at a slice in time, we presumably can hold constant other intricately related institutional features and uncertainty in the policy environment. Such is the approach taken in this chapter.

Because the set of feasible special orders is bounded only by the creativity of Rules Committee members and the assent of House majorities, any systematic and quantitative treatment of bill-specific procedural choice is necessarily limited in its focus. The limited focus here is on the constraints that restrictive rules impose on legislators' amendment rights over and above those imposed by the House's standing rules. I first review arguments in the empirical literature on restrictive rules and integrate some of these into the theoretical literature while elaborating on the predictions stated in chapters 2 and 3. I then introduce data and measures for testing specific hypotheses that are derived from distributive and informational theories. The data include rules for single- and multiple-referral legislation in the 98th and 99th Congresses. The chapter concludes with two cases that illustrate, in finer detail, the systematic patterns uncovered in the quantitative analysis.

Empirical Claims about Restrictive Rules

Observation of rule making in the House has yielded at least six correlates of the use of restrictive rules. These pertain to: *urgency* or immediacy of legislation; *scope,* size, or omnibus nature of the legislation; *multiple referrals,* that is, bills that are considered by more than one standing committee; *distributive,* particularistic, or pork barrel provisions in the bill; *partisanship* or majority party support for the bill; and *personality* or style of the Speaker with respect to the Rules Committee. A point-by-point summary gives a reasonably accurate view of the empirical literature on restrictive rules.

Urgency. One of the more easily observable correlates of the use of restrictive rules is legislation that is badly needed, highly demanded, or urgent. "Most recent closed rules have been for emergency, or at least essential, money bills, especially debt ceiling and continuing appropriations measures that are highly controversial and considered under pressure of deadlines" (Bach and Smith 1988, 54).

Scope. Closely related to demand is the scope, size, or omnibus nature of the legislation.

> Restrictive rules also seem more acceptable, and their strategic effect more widely recognized, when a bill or resolution to be considered is an omnibus measure, such as the 1977 energy package and various reconciliation, tax, and continuing appropriations measures of the 1980s. Packaging many diverse proposals into a single, massive, complex and

controversial vehicle can have several advantages to committees and leaders, not the least of which is the likelihood that it will receive a restrictive rule. The sheer magnitude of these bills, combined with the time pressures under which they often are considered, is a powerful argument against considering them under open rules. (Bach and Smith 1988, 95)

Multiple Referrals. Since 1974, standing rules of the House allow some legislation to receive consideration by more than one standing committee (Collie and Cooper 1989; Davidson, Oleszek, and Kephart 1988). It has been noted that intercommittee conflict with this type of legislation is more common and overt than under rules that permit only single referrals. In turn, this conflict may create a need for restrictive rules as procedural devices for holding together cross-committee compromises (Bach and Smith 1988, 12, 18–23, 57, 59–60, 120). Broadly consistent with this view is the observation by Davidson, Oleszek, and Kephart that many multiple referrals come up under suspension of the rules (1988, 18).

Distributive Content. The prevalence of distributive or particularistic content in legislation—that is, provisions that concentrate benefits but disperse costs (Lowi 1964; Wilson 1980)—may also account for the use of restrictive rules. Arguments for this claim are common, diverse, and collectively somewhat confusing. Shapiro (1987) and Robinson (1963), for example, argue that closed rules are needed to preserve the national interest by restricting logrolling:

> Tariff and tax bills are notorious objects of bargaining among representatives of local and constituent interests, and many amendments, with no apparent relation to any conception of the "national interest," doubtless would be proposed if open rules prevailed. (Robinson 1963, 44)

Bach and Smith, in contrast, suggest that open rules are needed on the floor for logrolling to occur. Their premise is that a system of deference operates across (sub)committees (Bach and Smith 1988, 25). It culminates in an orthodox view of distributive politics in the House.

> In fact, representatives with the strongest continuing interest in the work of these committees ["constituency committees," e.g., Public Works, Interior, Agriculture] either hold seats on them or seek assistance of committee members from their state delegations, regional groups, or policy caucuses. And many local-interest amendments that noncommittee members offer to bills such as highway, public works, and water resources measures may be added on the floor without threatening the

value of these measures to committee members. In fact, floor managers sometimes accept such amendments willingly in order to attract broader support for their bills. Generally speaking, therefore, the dangers of extended amending marathons in Committee of the Whole are not as severe for constituency-oriented committees, so their need for protective special rules is quite modest in comparison with prestige and policy committees. (Bach and Smith 1988, 115)

The similarities and differences between these schools of thought can be clarified with reference to the proponents' beliefs about the effects of restrictive rules and corresponding predictions about the assignment of rules. The point of agreement is that restrictive rules constrain opportunities for logrolling. The point of disagreement concerns predictions about bill-specific procedural choice. Shapiro and Robinson implicitly incorporate normative views about the public or national interest into a positive claim: behavioral tendencies toward excessive logrolling under open rules suggest that restrictive rules will be used to avert such tendencies. Bach and Smith, in contrast, believe that individual desires to logroll will dominate the public interest at the stage of procedural choice. Thus, they would predict that unrestrictive rules will be used on distributive legislation.

Partisanship. Restrictive rules are proposed by the Rules Committee, and the postreform Rules Committee is often characterized as an "arm of the House leadership."[9] These twin facts bolster the claim, especially common among Republicans, that restrictive rules are partisan devices employed by the majority party. Charges to this effect were especially common during the 100th Congress, which opened with the consideration of two pieces of major legislation—a highway bill and a water projects bill—under closed rules.[10] Rules Committee Republican Trent Lott, for example, stated:

Now, some might argue that the American people could care less [*sic*] about restrictive rules. But, if you explain to them that the Democratic leadership has relegated their Congressman to the status of second-class citizen, they might better understand. Under restrictive rules Members are disenfranchised: They can't offer certain amendments; nor can they vote on certain amendments. It's the same as if you told John Q. Voter that he couldn't run or vote for certain offices. Oh, we're told gag rules are needed for time management and efficiency. But that's really a euphemism for political expediency. They certainly are not democratic. (*Congressional Record,* May 24, 1988, H 3578)

---

9. See Bach and Smith 1988; Oppenheimer 1977; and Price 1985.

10. These examples are also consistent with the distributive-theoretic rationales for restrictive rules.

Former Minority Whip Richard Cheney (R.–Wyo.) advanced the same thesis: "Restrictive rules of varying descriptions have been used creatively in recent years to shut off debate and produce results that Democrats favor" (1989, 42).

Bach and Smith present several types of data that are consistent with Republicans' characterization of the partisan underpinnings of restrictive rules. Minority noncommittee members tend to be shut out of the amending process (Bach and Smith 1988, 71). When they are granted the right to offer substitutes, they perceive it as "meaningless" (91). They are "less comfortable with, and less likely to share in, any emerging Democratic consensus about when restrictive rules are appropriate and what constitutes a fair restrictive rule" (94). And they are much more likely than Democrats to vote against restrictive rules (101). Bach and Smith conclude:

> Beyond question, though, the new craftsmanship that representatives have witnessed has been the product of a partnership—Republicans might characterize it as an open conspiracy—between the Speaker and his leadership associates and their fellow partisans on the Rules Committee. (120)[11]

Personality. Finally, a close cousin to the partisanship thesis is personality. Different Speakers may have different relationships with the Rules Committee, even apart from changes in the House's formal rules. Thus, "the relationship between the Speaker and the Committee remains very much a matter of personalities and personal relationships, so it was not surprising that it began to change considerably after Jim Wright was elected Speaker in 1987 to replace O'Neill" (Bach and Smith 1988, 123).

Several of these accounts are plausible and have received a mix of anecdotal and quantitative support (Bach and Smith 1988; Robinson 1963). However, these empirical analyses are limited in two respects. First, when causal claims are made, they are based only on bivariate comparisons, such as showing that the incidence of restrictive rules is greater for multiple referrals than for single referrals. Second, the claims are rarely explicitly related to a theory that specifies the precise conditions under which various rule assignment patterns should be observed. Thus, several questions remain unanswered. For example, does the scope or omnibus nature of legislation require procedural protection, controlling for other hypothesized effects? If so, what is it about omnibus bills that makes majorities choose to constrain their right to amend? Similarly, what is it about the level of demand for or

---

11. Elsewhere in their book, however, Bach and Smith are more reserved about the degree to which partisanship dictates rule selection: "But it would be a mistake to conclude that the trend toward restrictive rules arose exclusively from partisan motivations. While the increase in floor amendments was a danger to the majority leadership, it was a nuisance for all members" (69).

urgency of legislation that predisposes legislators to agree not to amend it? If such legislation is so crucial, is it not equally plausible that majorities would be more, rather than less, inclined to want to amend it? Comparable questions can be raised for any of the empirical claims. The point is that correlates may be spurious and, in any event, are not explanations. A more complete understanding of the causes of collective choices of restrictive procedures, therefore, requires greater explicitness about the conditions under which the choice of restrictive procedures occurs.

Formal Theories and Restrictive Rules

Several empirical claims can be interpreted in terms of existing formal theories of legislatures, and the discussion in this section emphasizes these interpretations. Following the structure of chapters 2 and 3, the theoretical claims regarding restrictive rules fall into distributive and informational categories.

Distributive Theories

Three predictions about procedures were extracted from the discussion of distributive theories in chapter 2 and are formulated as hypotheses below.

> PREDICTION 2A: PROCEDURAL RIGHTS GENERALLY. *To enforce gains from trade, standing committees—particularly those whose jurisdictions include highly particularistic policies—will be granted favored procedural status throughout the process.*

> PREDICTION 2B: RESTRICTIVE RULES. *To hasten agreement, closed rules will be used on highly distributive legislation.*

> PREDICTION 2C: UNRESTRICTIVE RULES. *To minimize distributive inefficiency, open rules will be used on distributive legislation.*

Gains from Trade
Distributive theories focus on political settings in which legislators' preferences are diametrically opposed. Politics is seen as a game of distributing benefits, period. Such situations are easy to characterize spatially. For n legislators, and an n-dimensional policy-benefit space, every legislator wants a policy corresponding to a move away from the origin of that space (zero benefits for everyone) and toward his or her own ideal point.[12] Likewise, every legislator opposes moves directly toward anyone else's ideal point,

---

12. See fig. 2.2, chap. 2.

since a cost (e.g., imposition of a fraction of the tax burden) is associated with the provision of benefits. The practical consequence of these purely particularistic preferences is that for any proposed allocation of benefits, there always exists a majority of $n - 1$ legislators that prefers to strip the 1 of his particularistic project. Elsewhere, I argued that this simple model suggests that restrictive rules are sufficient conditions for initiating and maintaining particularistic policies (Krehbiel 1989). The straightforwardness of the distributive rationale for restrictive rules is evident in several other works, too. In the spirit of Weingast and Marshall (1988), for instance, Weingast (1989b) elaborates:

> Restrictive rules avoid all-out floor fights and restrict the negotiation to the pre-floor stage. Because they often completely control the motions allowed on the floor, restrictive rules not only reduce uncertainty (as emphasized by Bach and Smith), they greatly enhance the enforcement of logrolls and other bargains. In particular, they limit the ability of another faction from tempting one of the parties to the original bargain to defect and support a new amendment. (Weingast 1989b, 34)[13]

Fiorina (1981) develops a similar but more sweeping thesis that culminates in the same prediction. Concerned with the growth of government and the emergence of "reciprocity" and "universalism" in legislatures, he makes a two-stage argument. First, he states that the equilibrium of a game of distributive politics is that a minimal winning coalition (MWC) will form and be composed of the $(n + 1)/2$ least expensive, particularistic projects. Second, when all committees are taken into account and this same logic is applied across committees, he suggests that the outcome will be a "superomnibus" that approximates Weingast's (1979) "norm of universalism."

Fiorina's argument is explicitly rules-based insofar as he first cites earlier results identifying the instability of logrolling arrangements in an institution-free setting and then relies upon "procedure-constrained majority rule" to induce stability.[14] He then adds to this a committee system and a "meta-theoretical" argument that is applied to multiple "high-demand committees." His concluding characterization of distributive policy-making is quintessential of the New Institutionalism models reviewed in chapter 2 and of what Fiorina calls the "Caltech-Washington University school" (1987, 338):

> Our analysis suggests that the U.S. Congress, with its career legislators, its rich, variegated and contagious distributive politics, and its highly

---

13. See also Weingast 1989c.

14. The restrictions on amendments are that a legislator may move only to add, strip, or substitute individual projects.

differentiated committee system provides a climate conducive to the development and maintenance of universalism and reciprocity practices, and by implication, a government larger in size and scope than either theory or previous practice would have led us to expect. (Fiorina 1981, 217)

Since Fiorina's argument indisputably rests on restrictions of amendment rights (see also Fiorina 1987), the corresponding prediction regarding bill-specific procedural choice is the same as in my distributive "rationale for restrictive rules" (Krehbiel 1989) and Weingast's (1989b) "fighting fire with fire." The issue is: how can gains from trade in distributive policy-making be enforced? The proposed answer is: by employing restrictive procedures when incentives to renege on implicit agreements are greatest, namely, on distributive legislation.[15] Thus, the first theoretically derived hypothesis is:

HYPOTHESIS 1: GAINS FROM TRADE. *To enforce gains from trade, restrictive rules will be used on distributive legislation.*

Hastening Agreement
Baron and Ferejohn (1989a) employ a collective choice version of non-cooperative bargaining theory to analyze a majority-rule, divide-the-dollar game. Legislators have similar preferences as in the models just discussed, with the exception that, in addition to wanting as great a share of distributive benefits as possible, they also prefer to have it in the current, rather than in a later, session. This "impatience" (also interpretable as a reelection proba-

---

15. For theoretical accuracy and completeness, one loose end in this discussion should be tightened up. Specifically, with reference to his 1981 argument, Fiorina suggests that careerism attenuates the need for restrictive rules—or that restrictive rules "can be seen as providing a layer of added protection [against stripping amendments] for the institutionalized logrolling system that contributes to the long-run well-being of most representatives" (1987, 338). This argument provides an opportunity to disown Hypothesis 1 by arguing that, if the expectation of future interactions with fellow legislators is sufficiently great, then restrictive procedures may not be needed. The argument stems from theoretical results that show how individually rational cooperation may emerge in infinitely repeated prisoners' dilemma games, of which one is the basic distributive politics model. The problem is that repeated games of this type have multiple equilibria, many of which include agents who do defect. Thus, without an equilibrium refinement in which the sole survivors are "cooperative" equilibria, the so-called alternative to the prediction stated above is really a large number of alternative predictions. For Fiorina, this is a two-edged sword. One edge does effectively cut away from what I take to be the primary distributive prediction about rules. But the other edge cuts into a morass of alternative predictions of such a diverse sort that the theory based on repeated play becomes nonfalsifiable. Few political scientists have been more consistent adherents of testability of formal models than Fiorina, so I suspect that when pressed he would be reluctant to take this escape. See Baron and Ferejohn 1989a for a collective choice theory that illustrates and proposes a solution to the problem of multiple equilibria.

bility) creates incentives for legislators to come to an agreement as quickly as possible. The set of Baron and Ferejohn's results yields a prediction about rules compatible with Fiorina's, Weingast's, and mine.[16] Under the specified assumptions, closed rules are preferred to open rules ex ante by all legislators, because under open rules, decision making may extend beyond the first session thereby effectively shrinking the quantity of benefits available to legislators. The empirical implication of this theoretical reasoning resembles Bach and Smith's observation that restrictive rules tend to be used on urgent bills. However, Bach and Smith's claim has nothing to do with distributive politics per se.

In summary, while Baron and Ferejohn's theoretical argument is unique, its empirical manifestation is very similar to Hypothesis 1.

> HYPOTHESIS 2: HASTEN AGREEMENT. *To hasten agreement regarding the distribution of particularistic benefits, restrictive rules will be used on distributive legislation.*

Distributive Efficiency

Finally, Baron 1990 extends the Baron and Ferejohn bargaining model to incorporate costs associated with distributive policies and the ratio of benefits to those costs. The positive consequence of this extension is that, under some circumstances, the legislature would like to commit to the use of unrestrictive rules because restrictive rules reduce the range of inefficient policies that a majority can adopt.[17] Although available data do not permit a direct test, the hypothesis from Baron's model is nevertheless worth stressing as a contrast to other distributive theories.

> HYPOTHESIS 0: DISTRIBUTIVE EFFICIENCY. *To prevent the passing of extremely inefficient programs,* unrestrictive *rules will be used on inefficient distributive legislation.*

Summary

The distributive theoretical rationales for restrictive rules are of two distinct forms which parallel the conflicting empirical accounts. The gains-from-trade and hasten-agreement hypotheses (Baron and Ferejohn 1989a; Fiorina 1981; Krehbiel 1989; Weingast 1989b) hold that restrictive rules are needed to secure the maximum feasible distributive benefits that individual legislators

---

16. The models differ importantly, however, in terms of their expectations regarding the size of coalitions of recipients. Weingast and Fiorina are proponents of universalism (possibly in a cross-committee way, as in the case of Fiorina 1981). Baron and Ferejohn's model predicts minimal majorities of program recipients. I was ambiguous.

17. For empirical claims and accompanying arguments consistent with this prediction, see Robinson 1963, 30.

TABLE 5.1. Distributive Perspectives on Restrictive Rules

EFFECT OF RESTRICTIVE RULES	PREDICTED RULE	
	UNRESTRICTIVE	RESTRICTIVE
Preclude Logrolling	Bach and Smith	Robinson Shapiro
Facilitate Logrolling		Fiorina Krehbiel Weingast
Hasten Agreement		Baron and Ferejohn
Reduce Distributive Inefficiency	Baron	

want but whose short time horizons preclude them from rationally obtaining within the collective choice setting. However, the distributive-efficiency hypothesis (Baron 1990) holds that open rules can be advantageous relative to closed rules in preventing the passage of highly inefficient bundles of projects.

Table 5.1 summarizes the empirical and theoretical arguments about choice of rules for distributive legislation. The rows provide four different theories or beliefs about the effects of rules on the logrolling process. That is, Bach and Smith along with Robinson and Shapiro believe that closed rules preclude logrolling, while Fiorina, Weingast, and I have proposed models in which restrictive rules facilitate logrolling. Baron and Ferejohn's model stresses quick agreement of bare majorities of project recipients rather than logrolling in the sense of forming super majority or universalistic coalitions of high demanders. And Baron's model emphasizes the distributive inefficiency of restrictive rules relative to unrestrictive rules.

The columns then further discriminate among viewpoints by stating the procedural predictions corresponding with the beliefs or theories. Some viewpoints, such as Bach and Smith's and Baron's, imply that unrestrictive rules will be used for distributive legislation. The alternative prediction, based on the viewpoints of Robinson, Shapiro, Weingast, Baron and Ferejohn, and me, is that restrictive rules will govern consideration of particularistic bills.

Informational Theories

The legislative signaling games discussed in chapter 3 center on the desire of rational legislators to adopt informationally efficient organizational forms in the presence of uncertainty about the relationship between policies and their consequences. In such legislatures, committees must be provided with incentives to specialize if the common benefits of informed decision making are to be obtained. In this theoretical context, a distinctly different informational rationale for restrictive procedures emerges. The relevant predictions were stated en masse in chapter 3:

> PREDICTION 4: RESTRICTIVE RULES. *Use of restrictive rules will be positively associated with committee specialization, nonoutlying committees, and heterogeneous committees.*

Rather than duplicate the theoretical discussion, I will simply disaggregate the Restrictive Rules Predictions into four more directly testable hypotheses, while briefly reiterating the underlying logic. (All hypotheses are of the ceteris paribus form.)

Restrictive Rules and Specialization
A rational legislature selectively chooses to use restrictive rules to stimulate committee specialization (Gilligan and Krehbiel 1987). Thus,

> HYPOTHESIS 3: SPECIALIZATION. *The greater is a committee's level of specialization, the greater will be its probability of receiving restrictive rules for its bills.*

Restrictive Rules for Nonoutliers
Informational efficiency is generally decreasing in the degree to which committees are composed of preference outliers, and the rate of this decrease is greater under unrestrictive than restrictive rules (Gilligan and Krehbiel 1987, 1988, 1989a, and 1989b). Thus,

> HYPOTHESIS 4: OUTLIERS. *The more extreme are a committee's members' preferences relative to those of the House, the lower will be the committee's probability of receiving restrictive rules for its bills.*

Restrictive Rules for Heterogeneous Committees
Informational efficiency is greater under heterogeneous than homogeneous committees, and distributive losses are nonexistent under heterogeneous committees (Gilligan and Krehbiel 1989a). Thus,

> HYPOTHESIS 5: HETEROGENEITY. *The more heterogeneous are a single committee's members' preferences, or the greater is the number of committees to which a bill is referred, the greater will be the probability of the assignment of a restrictive rule.*

Restrictive Rules and Confirmatory Signals
Gains in informational efficiency are attainable from confirmatory signaling when informed legislators have divergent preferences with respect to the legislature's median voter.[18] Thus,

> HYPOTHESIS 6: CONFIRMATORY SIGNALING. *The greater is the minority party's support for a committee's bill, the greater will be the probability that the bill receives a restrictive rule.*

From Theory to Data

The empirical analysis undertaken in the next section focuses on the two distributive and four informational hypotheses. Before turning to it, some distinctions should be stressed.

First, different distributive theories offer somewhat different predictions. Thus, the analysis provides an opportunity to discriminate within as well as between classes of theory.

Second, some of the informational hypotheses are more clearly and directly derived from existing information models than are others. The specialization and outlier hypotheses are straightforward derivations. The heterogeneity hypothesis is essentially based on a comparison of two different models rather than a single model in which the choice of rules is derived and then compared across heterogeneous and homogeneous committee types. And the confirmatory signaling hypothesis, while consistent with the spirit of the heterogeneous committees model, is obviously not derived from an n-person signaling model with majority and minority party members. Accordingly, the results will be interpreted with additional caution as the step from the theory to the hypotheses becomes longer.

Third, some empirical correlates of restrictive rules can be interpreted as consistent with theoretical explanations. For example, perhaps major revenue bills receive restrictive rules because the Ways and Means Committee has a history of hard work (policy specialization), because the committee has members with moderate yet diverse preferences (heterogeneous nonoutliers), or because the diverse members on the committee often come out united behind their bill (send confirmatory signals). Likewise, perhaps urgent legislation is considered under restrictive rules because of its high distributive content. By accentuating the potential reconciliation between empirical claims and recent theoretical developments, these possibilities help to stress the motivation of

---

18. This hypothesis rests on the interpretation of the second committee actor in the heterogeneous committees model as a minority party member and presumes that such members are informed, thus giving credibility to their signals.

the empirical analysis. It should be viewed not as a contest between empirical and theoretical accounts but rather as an attempt to identify clearly the theoretical bases for observed patterns of behavior. Nor are distributive and informational accounts for restrictive rules inherently incompatible. Both may have explanatory power. The unresolved empirical issues are whether they have independent effects that are consistent with existing theories.

Finally, this is not to deny the existence of some divergent theoretical expectations nor the fact that some empirical claims are distinctly different from theoretically derived hypotheses. The clearest example of competing empirical and theoretical claims in the context of restrictive rules is provided by the (empirical) partisanship claim and the (theoretical) confirmatory signaling hypothesis. The partisanship claim holds that rules are often, if not always, tools of the majority party that are indiscriminately deployed to trample on minority rights. We would expect, then, to see no relationship between minority support for legislation and its consideration under preferred procedures (i.e., restrictive rules). Similarly, we would expect a positive relationship between majority support for bills and the propensity of majority leaders (through the Rules Committee) to employ their instruments of asymmetric procedural rights. The confirmatory signaling hypothesis, in contrast, holds that rules are tools of chamber majorities that are deliberately deployed to elicit committees' private information. We would expect, then, to see a positive relationship between minority support for bills and the use of restrictive rules. Why? Because minority support is a credible, confirmatory signal, as in the model with heterogeneous committees.

Data and Measures

Data on bills and their associated rules were compiled from the *Final Calendars of the Committee on Rules* and from LEGI-SLATE for all bills in the 98th and 99th Congresses for which a special order was either requested or granted.[19] Of these bill-rule pairs, observations in which the rule pertained to conference reports, amendments between the chambers, or previous special

---

19. In light of the alternative paths that legislation may take in the House, this sample is obviously not a random sample of all legislation that comes to the floor. How misleading are the inferences, given this selection bias? The bad news is that relative to other bills, these are atypical. (This is borne out by a comparison of these bills with a 25 percent sample of all other bills reported from committee in the 99th Congress. The remaining bills are used in the analysis in chap. 6.) On the other hand, the sample is, in effect, the universe with respect to bills considered under rules in the 98th and 99th Congresses. To be on the safe side, the empirical analysis should be viewed as an attempt to explain variation within this class of legislation which, empirically, tends to be composed of major bills. While a more comprehensive analysis of bill-specific procedural choice that seeks to predict, for example, bills that come up under suspension as opposed to under a rule would be worthwhile, it is beyond the scope of this analysis.

orders, were omitted. Also omitted were bill-rule observations in which the rule—though proposed by the Rules Committee—was not considered, or was rejected, by the House.[20] The remaining observations were then divided into two categories: bills that received unrestrictive (open or modified-open) rules and those that received restrictive (closed or modified-closed) rules.[21] The primary source of data on the attributes of bills is LEGI-SLATE, which for any given piece of legislation gives a comprehensive listing of recorded legislative activity. LEGI-SLATE's output includes, for example, the measure number, name, cosponsor(s), committees to which it was referred and from which it was reported, Rules Committee action, calendar on which the measure was placed, all motions and amendment activity on the floor, all postfloor activity (e.g., conference committee action and/or amendments between the chambers), action on the conference report, votes on final passage, presidential action, and postveto action. LEGI-SLATE also lists "Keywords" pertaining to the content of each measure; "Laws Cited" in the bill, thereby identifying prior related legislative activity; and "Companion Measures," which are similar or identical measures introduced by other members.[22]

Measures for Empirical Claims

Of the six claimed correlates of restrictive rules, measures are available for all but personality. For the six theoretical hypotheses on which the analysis focuses, suitable variables are available for testing each one. The measures are introduced with reference to table 5.2, which lists the labels by which the variables are subsequently referred and provides some preliminary support for most hypotheses.

Urgency. The measure of urgency of legislation is a dummy variable coded 1 for measures to extend the debt ceiling, continuing resolutions, and supplemental appropriations.[23]

---

20. The majoritarian logic for this filter should be obvious. A rule that fails to receive majority support should not be treated as if it received a majority. That is, I am interested primarily in the House's procedural choice—not the Rules Committee's proposed procedures.

21. I elected not to use the *Calendar*'s labeling of rules, which is very erratic. Rather, the key determinants of a "restrictive rule" are whether it either stipulates that only amendments specified in the rule itself are in order, or provides for consideration of the legislation in the House as opposed to Committee of the Whole. (See Bach 1988 for a discussion of why amendment rights are essentially nonexistent when legislation is considered "in the House.") Consistent with the focus of this chapter, the common feature of these criteria is that they constrain members' (and typically noncommittee members') amendment rights.

22. In approximately ten instances, bill information on the House's legislation was not available, in which cases LEGI-SLATE's information for the Senate's companion version was coded.

23. Two alternative measures were also considered. A dummy variable was coded as 1 if the word *emergency* was in the title of the bill. Positive values coincided with the urgency

TABLE 5.2.   Means of Independent Variables by Type of Rule

	RESTRICTIVE RULE		
VARIABLE	YES	No	DIFFERENCE
Urgency	0.18	0.03	0.15
Scope	59.9	38.7	21.1
Referrals	1.73	1.28	0.45
Democratic cosponsors	22.7	22.5	0.23
Distributive content	0.04	0.08	−0.04
Laws cited	8.19	3.06	5.13
Committee seniority*	7.97	7.26	0.71
Preference outlier*	7.65	11.64	−3.99
Heterogeneity*	−0.54	−1.21	0.67
Republican cosponsors	6.97	4.38	2.59

*Single referrals only.

Scope. The measure of scope or complexity of a bill is simply the number of LEGI-SLATE "Keywords" listed under that bill. These cover thousands of subjects and thus are often quite specific. In the 98th and 99th Congresses, the values for the bills in the sample ranged from 1 to 447.

Number of Referrals. Referral of legislation to committees is easily discernable in most instances.[24] The variable is simply the number of standing committees to which the bill was referred.

Partisanship. The degree of partisanship or majority support for a bill is measured by its number of Democratic cosponsors. This measure is preferred to measures of partisan activity later in the process—such as roll call votes on rules, amendments, or final passage—since not all measures in the sample reach these later stages, and, even when they do, their content may have changed substantially since the choosing of the rule. In contrast, cosponsorship is indicative of support at a stage of the process more proximate to committee action and rule choice.

---

variable for only six bills, however, and the bills identified by the urgency measure were clearly those that Bach and Smith had in mind. A similarly objectionable route was to code a variable on "demand" based on the number of LEGI-SLATE "Companion Measures." Typically these include bills and resolutions pertaining to similar subjects, possibly written differently in an attempt to obtain referral to different committees. The rationale was that the greater the efforts of legislators to place an issue onto the House's agenda, the greater is the demand of legislators for legislation on that subject. The drawback is that the legislation with high values was often "hurrah" bills that indicated cheap position-taking rather than urgency or genuine and widespread demand.

24. In approximately twenty cases, LEGI-SLATE listed no referrals for measures but identified a committee as having issued a report on a measure. Most of these were appropriations or budget measures in which the standing committee simply issued an original bill thereby circumventing the normal bill introduction and referral process. These were coded as if normal referrals.

TABLE 5.3. Legislation with Greatest Distributive Content

Bill	Title
H.R. 3958	Water Resource Development Appropriations, FY 1984
H.R. 5174	Bankruptcy Amendments and Federal Judgeship Act of 1984
H.R. 5604	Military Construction Authorization Act, 1985
H.R. 1409	Military Construction Authorization Act, 1986
H.R. 3327	Military Construction Appropriations Act, 1986
H.R. 5504	Surface Transportation and Uniform Relocation Assistance Act of 1984
H.R. 5898	Military Construction Appropriations Act, 1985
H.R. 5653	Energy and Water Development Appropriations, FY 1985
H.R. 5492	Atlantic Stripebass Conservation Act
H.R. 3678	Water Resources, Conservation, Development, Infrastructure Improvement and Rehabilitation Act of 1983
H.R. 3282	Water Quality Renewal Act of 1984
H.R. 5395	Department of Energy National Security and Military Applications of Nuclear Energy Authorization Act of 1985
H.R. 2959	Energy and Water Development Appropriations, FY 1986
H.R. 1714	NASA Authorization Act of 1986
H.R. 4428	National Defense Authorization Act, FY 1987; Military Justice Amendments; Amendment to Dan Daniel Special Operations Forces Act; Military Construction Authorization Act; Department of Energy National Security and Military Applications of Nuclear Energy Authorization Act; and Strategic and Critical Materials Stock Piling Amendments.
H.R. 2587	Department of Energy Civilian Research and Development Authorization Act, FY 1984
H.R. 5167	Omnibus Defense Authorization Act, 1985; Defense Spare Parts Procurement Reform Act
H.R. 6	Water Resources Development Act of 1986
H.R. 1652	Reclamation Safety of Dams Act of 1978, Amendments

Distributive Content. The distributive content of a bill is measured by exploiting specific keywords in the LEGI-SLATE output. For most bills, one such Keyword is "States," after which is listed from 1 to 52 specific states that are specifically and directly affected by the proposed bill.[25] The measure is simply the ratio of states listed to the total number of keywords plus the number of states. Thus, the larger is this ratio, the greater is the distributive component of the bill relative to its scope. Table 5.3 verifies that bills with high values of this measure are, indeed, those associated with distributive politics. Most frequent on the list are measures pertaining to water resources, military construction, and infrastructure (formerly known as sewers, bridges, highways, etc.).

---

25. Contrary to what the upper bound suggests, annexations to the U.S. have not occurred. LEGI-SLATE's list sometimes includes the District of Columbia and Puerto Rico as states.

Measures for Theoretically Derived Hypotheses

The measure of distributive content is useful not only for verifying or refuting empirical claims but also for testing the theoretically derived predictions regarding the relationship between distributive legislation and choice of rules. Similarly, the measure of urgency—when cautiously interpreted—can shed light on the hasten-agreement hypothesis. Six additional measures are closely related to the informational hypotheses. These seek to capture legislative specialization by committees, preference-based attributes of committees, and legislative signaling.

Laws Cited. Two measures of legislative specialization are employed. The first measure is the approximate quantity of prior legislative work devoted to a bill as estimated by the number of laws that are cited in the measure. The greater is this number, the greater is the estimated amount of successful effort (in the sense of passing bills) exerted by the committee on closely related subjects. Table 5.4 lists the measures that ranked highest according to this measure of specialization. Many are omnibus bills and thus it might be suspected that the measure merely duplicates the measure of scope. However, a substantial number of omnibuses are not at the top of the specialization list, so this seems improbable. Similarly, some of the measures in table 5.4 seem to have a strong distributive component, such as a housing act, a water resources measure, and a defense authorization act. But the correlation coefficient between the laws-cited and distributive-content variables is only .12. These observations—plus the fact that most of the measures in table 5.4 indeed pertain to subjects on which legislative expertise historically has been valued (e.g., intelligence, taxation, and trade)—suggest that the measure is adequate.

Committee Seniority. The second measure of committee specialization is the average years of consecutive service (seniority) on the committee. Though more difficult to obtain than committees' mean House seniority, this measure better captures jurisdiction-specific expertise.[26] A huge literature on state and national legislatures provides strong empirical support for the relationship between committee service and policy expertise.[27] In conclusion, notice that

---

26. Sources for this variable were various volumes of the *Congressional Quarterly Almanac*.

27. See, for example, Buchanan et al. 1970, 637; Clapp 1963, 257; Huckshorn 1965, 175; Schneier 1970, 16; and McConachie 1898, 156. In spite of the weight of the empirical evidence that supports an expertise interpretation of this measure, it is clearly misleading for one committee. Members of the House Budget Committee were limited to two terms of service by the Congressional Budget and Impoundment Act of 1974. (In 1979 the restriction was relaxed to three terms.) Because prior service on any committee is associated with expertise that is transferable to Budget (e.g., many Budget Committee members have served on the major money committees: Ways and Means or Appropriations), the committee seniority measure for the Budget Committee is the average House seniority of Budget Committee members.

TABLE 5.4. Legislation with Greatest Number of Laws Cited

BILL	TITLE
H.R. 5300	Omnibus Budget Reconciliation Act of 1986; Farm Credit Act Amendments of 1986; Petroleum Overcharge Distribution and Restitution Act of 1986; Conrail Privatization Act; Program Fraud Civil Remedies Act of 1986
H.R. 3500	Budget Reconciliation, FY 1986
H.R. 2100	Food Security Act of 1985; National Agricultural Research, Extension and Teaching Policy Act Amendments of 1985; Beef Promotion and Research Act of 1985; Pork Promotion, Research, and Consumer Information Act of 1985; Watermelon Research and Promotion Act.
H.R. 4428	National Defense Authorization Act, FY 1987; Military Justice Amendments of 1986; Dan Daniel Special Operations Forces Act, Amendment; Military Construction Authorization Act, FY 1987; Department of Energy National Security and Military Applications of Nuclear Energy Authorization Act of 1987.
H.J.R. 648	Resolution Making Continuing Appropriations for FY 1985
H.R. 1718	Emergency Jobs Appropriation; Temporary Emergency Food Assistance Act of 1983
H.R. 6	Water Resources Development Act of 1986
H.J.R. 738	Resolution Making Continuing Appropriations for FY 1987; Goldwater-Nichols Department of Defense Reorganization Act of 1986; Amendment to Omnibus Drug Supplemental Appropriations Act of 1987
H.R. 1	Housing and Urban-Rural Recovery Act of 1983
H.R. 3678	Water Resources, Conservation, Development, and Infrastructure Improvement and Rehabilitation Act of 1983
H.R. 1	Housing Act of 1986
H.R. 4800	Trade and International Economic Policy Reform Act of 1986; Telecommunications Trade Act of 1986; Export Enhancement Act of 1986; International Debt, Trade, and Financial Stabilization Act of 1986; Multilateral Investment Guarantee Agency Act of 1986.
H.R. 3838	Tax Reform Act of 1986
H.R. 4170	Omnibus Deficit Reduction Act of 1984
H.R. 4151	Omnibus Diplomatic Security and Anti-Terrorism Act of 1986; Terrorism Prosecution Act of 1985; Diplomatic Security Act; Fascell Fellowship Act; Victims of Terrorism Compensation Act
H.R. 4759	Intelligence Authorization Act, FY 1987
H.R. 1210	Science Engineering and Mathematics Authorization Act of 1986

the two specialization measures capture legislative expertise in two distinct ways. The number of laws cited is bill-specific; committee seniority is committee-specific.

Preference Outliers. The degree to which a committee's preferences diverge from those of the House is measured by the absolute deviation in the committee median from the floor median ADA rating. For the reasons articulated in chapter 4, this measure is not ideal. However, alternative measures—namely, jurisdiction-specific ratings—have two major disadvantages. They are not comparable across committees, and they are available only for a subset of committees. We therefore purchase a large quantity of observations at the price of some imprecision in the measure of preferences.

Heterogeneity. The heterogeneity of committee preferences, for identical reasons, is based on the standard deviation of ADA ratings. Specifically, the measure is the committee's standard deviation minus the House's. Thus, a positive measure reflects relative heterogeneity of committee preferences while a negative measure indicates a relative homogeneity of committee preferences, using the House as a baseline.

Republican Cosponsorship. The degree of confirmatory signaling for a bill is measured by its number of Republican cosponsors. While the number of Democratic cosponsors is listed above as a measure of partisanship, the number of Republican cosponsors has a different, theoretical interpretation in the analysis. Its potential importance stems from the theory of heterogeneous committees: Republican cosponsorship reflects the strength of the confirmatory signal given by the minority party.

Findings

Using the definition of a restrictive rule discussed above, the empirical analysis consists of estimating the probability of the assignment of a restrictive rule as a function of the previously described measures.[28] Because some of the measures are committee-specific and cannot be aggregated for analysis of multiple referrals, two sets of estimates were generated: one set for single referrals and one set for all legislation in the sample. The largest sample is composed of all legislation in the 98th and 99th Congresses for which a rule was both proposed and passed, excluding rules that pertained to conference reports or amendments between the chambers. Although the latter are worthy of study in their own right, they are not directly relevant to the theories in question. Finally, unlike Bach and Smith's analysis, appropriations bills are included in this analysis. The theoretical defense is straightforward. Even though appropriations bills are different from authorizations and resolutions, no extant theory differentiates between these classes. Thus, the presumption is that the theoretical arguments reviewed apply to both classes of bills.

The primary substantive objective is to test theoretically derived hypotheses rather than simply to confirm or refute prior empirical claims. Because

---

28. The analysis presumes that all right-hand-side variables are exogenous. While strictly inconsistent with the broader theme of legislative organization in this study, this assumption is defensible in the context of bill-specific procedural choice since phenomena such as committees' levels of specialization, outliers, and heterogeneity are at least fixed in the short run. Similarly, at the stage of rule choice by the House, opportunities for cosponsorship and significant alteration of the legislation are minimal.

the set of theoretical hypotheses numbers at least six, it is essential to move beyond analysis of the simple bivariate form reported in table 5.2. The key issue is whether variables measuring the distributive content of legislation, its urgency, committee expertise, committee preferences, and signaling properties have predictable effects on rule choice while controlling for other, possibly confounding influences. Probit analysis is useful for these purposes. Appendix C presents the specific estimates on which the following tables and discussion are based and also includes a description of computations. For both single-referral analyses and analyses based on the all-bill sample, the estimates were highly significant and thus provide a good basis for inference.

Tests of Hypotheses

The initial round of analysis consists of quantifying the first-order effects of each of the exogenous variables. Using the probit estimates, all exogenous variables except one are held constant at their mean values while the remaining variable is perturbed to calculate the associated change in the probability of assignment of a restrictive rule. Table 5.5 presents the results from these calculations for single referrals and for all bills. Each cell entry answers the question: given the estimated coefficients and supposing that a bill has average attributes in terms of the exogenous variables, what is the net change in the probability that a restrictive rule is chosen for the bill if the specified exogenous variable is incremented by one standard deviation? Answers to this question provide straightforward tests of the six hypotheses.

Gains from Trade
With the exception of Baron's theory, which cannot be tested directly using

TABLE 5.5. Net Effects of Independent Variables on the Choice of a Restrictive Rule

Hypothesis and Variable	Single Referrals	All Bills
1 Distributive content	−.095*	−.110*
2 Urgency	.077	.119
3 Laws cited	.138	.131
3 Committee seniority	.029	†
4 Preference outlier	−.083	†
5 Heterogeneity	.117	†
5 Referrals	†	.043
6 Republican cosponsors	.129	.102
Democratic cosponsors	†	−.065*

*Wrong sign.
†Not in equation.

these data, distributive theories predict a positive effect of the distributive content of legislation on its probability of receiving a restrictive rule (Hypothesis 1). The greater is the concentration of benefits and dispersion of costs in a measure, the greater is the need to enforce bargains to capture gains from trade. Controlling for other influences on rule selection, however, exactly the opposite pattern is uncovered in the data. A standard deviation increase in distributive content decreases the probability of a bill receiving a restrictive rule by .095 or .110. While perhaps theoretically surprising, this result is empirically very stable. Regardless of the range of specifications for which estimates were derived, the coefficient for distributive content was always significant and negative.[29] Support for Baron's distributive efficiency hypothesis is therefore conceivable. However, these results constitute strong refutation of the standard gains-from-trade hypothesis.

Hasten Agreement
On a more positive note, the net-effect estimates in table 5.5 offer qualified support for Hypothesis 2, Baron and Ferejohn's notion of hastening agreement. The estimated coefficients for single referrals are consistent with the hypothesized positive effect, and this effect of .077 increases to .119 when multiple referrals are added to the sample. One caveat is in order, however. The coefficient and net effect of distributive content may be regarded as a more direct test of Hypothesis 2 than the coefficient and net effect of urgency, since the hypothesis clearly predicts that restrictive rules will be used on distributive legislation. Regardless of which test is considered more appropriate, the seemingly inconsistent results for distributive content and urgency need to be examined more closely. Additional analysis of the combined effects between the urgency and distributive content of legislation is taken up in the next section.

Specialization
Informational theories suggest that specialization and use of restrictive rules should be positively associated. Such rules may confer distributive benefits to committees in exchange for the informational benefits committees provide. Alternatively, on issues of great uncertainty, assigning a restrictive rule with high probability is an effective way for the House to provide incentives for a committee to reveal its private information. Support for the specialization hypothesis is found in both measures employed. A standard deviation increment in the number of laws cited in a bill (a proxy for past successful legislative effort exerted by the committee) increases the probability of a

---

29. See appendix C. In equation 4 in table C.1, the distributive-content coefficient is significant and negative through an interaction term. Once interactions were taken into account, the direct effect of distributive content was no longer significant, as reflected by its *t*-statistic of 0.16 in equation 3.

restrictive rule by more than .13—the largest effect of any independent variable.[30] Similarly, a standard deviation increase in the committee's seniority is associated with a .029 increase in the probability of a restrictive rule. While relatively small, this effect is nevertheless based on a highly significant estimate. Thus, the specialization hypothesis is strongly supported.

Outliers
The outlier hypothesis derived from informational theories suggests that the more extreme is a committee relative to the legislature, the lower is its likelihood of receiving restrictive rules. The data are consistent with this hypothesis as well. The probability effect of a standard deviation change in absolute ADA differences is −.083. Considering the crudeness of the preference-outlier measure and the stability and significance of its estimated coefficients (when interacted with laws cited, committee seniority, and distributive content) this finding is impressive. The existence of preference outliers on committees clearly seems to undermine the House's willingness to abdicate its right to amend committees' legislation.

Heterogeneity
The heterogeneity hypothesis is supported, too. For singly referred bills, an increase in heterogeneity of a committee by a standard deviation independently increases the probability of a restrictive rule by .117. For the all-bill sample, the number of committees to which a bill was referred is also regarded as a measure of heterogeneity consistent with the theory of heterogeneous committees. The effect of this variable is positive as expected, although the probability effect is small (.043). An alternative distributive interpretation of multiple referrals (Weingast 1989b) further tempers the current claim of support for this portion of the heterogeneity hypothesis. Fortunately, however, the strong and significant coefficient for the interaction term distributive-content × number-of-referrals, provides an opportunity to test a refined version of the distributive hypothesis that is consistent with Weingast's interpretation of multiple referrals. This issue, too, is taken up in the next section. Now it suffices to say that the positive and statistically significant effect of the number of referrals offers potential additional support

---

30. The bill-specific measure of specialization (given by the number of laws cited) may be questioned with respect to budget resolutions. If the Budget Committee simply staples together numerous proposals of authorizing committees whose work, in turn, cites many of the authorizing committees' prior laws, the measure for the budget resolution may overstate the Budget Committee's expertise. Probit equations were reestimated without Budget Committee bills (of which there were six). The coefficients for laws cited and committee seniority were very slightly lower but remained highly significant. Remaining coefficients were stable, and the equations overall predicted exactly as well as those reported in table C.1 in appendix C. I thank Stan Bach for raising this reservation.

for the heterogeneity hypothesis. Moreover, even in the absence of such support, the effect uncovered through the heterogeneity variable for single referrals reflects favorably on Hypothesis 5.

Confirmatory Signaling

The measure of confirmatory signaling by the minority party is the number of Republican cosponsors for the bill. Coefficients for this variable were always positive and significant. Its net effects on the probability of assignment of a restrictive rule are moderately strong, too. A standard deviation increase in the confirmatory signal, so defined, results in a probability increase of .102 or .129. This finding takes on added significance when juxtaposed with the empirical claim (especially common among Republicans) that rules are partisan steamrolling devices and when contrasted with the estimated effects of Democratic cosponsors. In a series of single-referral estimates, the coefficient for Democratic cosponsors was never significant. When multiple referrals are included in the sample, the coefficient was marginally significant ($t = -1.58$) but negative. In particular, a standard deviation increment in Democratic cosponsors reduces the probability of a restrictive rule by .065. Two conclusions are warranted that not only go against the grain of recent criticisms by minority party members about the majority party's use of rules but also challenge the received wisdom that the Rules Committee is a powerful arm of the majority party leadership. First, we should entertain the prospect that Republicans play meaningful and informational roles in the legislative process. More precisely, the endogeneity of rules enables a legislature to capitalize on the informational efficiency properties of informed minorities. Second, although anecdotes may be plentiful, there is no systematic evidence that Democrats employ rules to run roughshod over their procedurally underprivileged opponents.

Scope

Though not linked to theoretically derived hypotheses, the findings regarding the measure of scope are also revealing. While the effect of the size or omnibus nature of legislation is sometimes claimed to be positive, its effects in this analysis were essentially zero. That is, much like the partisanship hypothesis, the scope hypothesis is lacking in support once we account for other, theoretically derived effects.

Summary

As a whole, the results are consistently supportive of the informational theory as represented by Hypotheses 3–6. At a minimum, they also call into question exclusively distributive perspectives on the choice of rules. Still, not all empirical avenues have been explored with respect to distributive theories. In particular, more elaborate theoretical interpretations can be offered to dispute the negative first-order effect of distributive content. Furthermore, additional second-order effects can be quantified to further illuminate the causal processes.

Second-Order Distributive Effects

The strong negative effect of the distributive content of legislation on the choice of restrictive rules is probably the most surprising finding in the probit analyses. At first glance, the main hypothesis from distributive theories seems clearly false. In theory, restrictive procedures may be sufficient for inducing stability (Fiorina 1981), initiating and maintaining particularistic policies (Krehbiel 1989), institutionalizing committees' ability to fight fire with fire (Weingast 1989b), or mitigating shrinkage of the pork pie by hastening agreement (Baron and Ferejohn 1989a). However, in practice it seems indisputable that such restrictions are not necessary. Thus, in spite of their intuitive appeal and widespread acceptance, distributive theories continue to be lacking in predictive power. In chapter 4, distributive-theoretic predictions tended not to be borne out. Here, it seems, they are plainly refuted.

Perhaps it is not this simple, however. One can imagine—and this section explores—several reasonable and alternative interpretations of the results that keep alive the possibility of a distributive rationale for restrictive rules in particular and a distributive foundation for legislative organization more generally. The coefficient for distributive content suggests that differences exist in the procedural treatment of distributive versus nondistributive legislation. Strictly speaking, distributive theories say nothing about these cross-class differences. They only say that certain effects should be identifiable within the distributive class of bills. Thus, perhaps it is not a fair test to look only at the net change in probability based on the distributive-content measure. The effect may work through other variables in ways more consistent with distributive theories. To explore these possibilities, three additional and more refined versions of Hypothesis 1 are stated and tested.

Added Protection

Proponents of the gains-from-trade perspective on legislative organization may not be persuaded by the refutation of distributive hypotheses based on the empirical results presented thus far. For example, Weingast might reply that his "norm of universalism" (1979) does not rest explicitly upon procedural restrictions,[31] and Fiorina has been similarly cautious about offering blanket

---

31. See, however, Weingast and Marshall 1988; and Weingast 1989b and 1989c.

predictions pertaining to restrictive rules. In his 1987 comment, he elaborates on his 1981 distributive argument by stating that restrictive rules are merely "a layer of added protection" against the occasional propensity of legislators to defect from cooperative agreements (Fiorina 1987, 338). The notion of repeated play in a careerist legislature reduces the need for the added layer of procedural protection. However, instances in which high-demand, distributive committees need such protection may still exist. Therefore, the first refined version of Hypothesis 1 is:

HYPOTHESIS 1A: ADDED PROTECTION. *Restrictive rules will be used on legislation where added protection is needed most: where the shadow of the future does not loom large and where proposals from preference-outlying committees pose greater incentives for noncommittee members to defect from cooperative, gains-from-trade agreements.*

First, a theoretical note in passing. I already commented on why the repeat-play argument that underlies the first part of this hypothesis is not an alternative hypothesis but rather a multitude of conflicting alternative hypotheses. The relevant theoretical result is that any degree of so-called cooperation—including none—can be supported as an equilibrium in the appropriate n-person game. Nevertheless, we shall give the argument the benefit of the doubt, make a bold presumption that there exists some equilibrium refinement in which none of the "uncooperative" equilibria obtain, and explore the empirical implication of such an argument.[32]

In effect, the test of the first part of Hypothesis 1A has already been conducted and requires only a slightly different interpretation of one of the coefficients in table C.1 of appendix C. Given a (hypothetical) unique equilibrium in which logrolling occurs and restrictive rules are not employed, what would we expect from the data? Borrowing Axelrod's (1981) nomenclature, we first reason that for cooperation (logrolling) to emerge in the absence of restrictive procedures, reputations from past interaction and/or the shadow of the future must loom large. In other words, legislators must anticipate significant future interaction with their present trusted colleagues. As with nearly any significant congressional phenomenon, the Fenno Principle holds

---

32. Readers interested in the theoretical underpinnings of universalism are strongly advised to see the recent works of Baron and Ferejohn. In Baron and Ferejohn's (1989a) original model, for example, the assumption used to go beyond their "folk theorem" result is stationarity of strategies. This condition does not lead to universalism, however. In fact, Baron (1990) extends the Baron and Ferejohn model to study pork barrel politics and shows that universalism is essentially impossible under both open and closed rules. If the universalism versus minimum winning coalition battle is to be debated simply on theoretical grounds, Baron's result must be regarded as a severe blow to universalism and, thus, undermines the plausibility of the present exercise. Nevertheless, my preference is to pursue it and to let the data, rather than theoretical arguments, decide the dispute.

here, too. That is, "committees differ" in terms of the degree to which their members have had, and expect to have, repeated interaction. Such expectations are reasonably measured by committee seniority, so the empirical implication of the first part of Hypothesis 1A is that the greater is committee seniority (hence the longer the reputations of the past that cast the shadow of the future), the less is the need for Fiorina's added layer of protection in the form of restrictive rules.[33]

The data suggest precisely the opposite. Consistent with informational theory and contrary to this repeat-play twist on distributive theory, seniority is positively associated with the assignment of restrictive rules.[34]

The test of the second part of Hypothesis 1A is based on inspection of the interaction effects between the distributive-content and preference-outlier variables. The distributive-theoretic reasoning is that logrolling across preference-outlying committees poses the strongest incentives for reneging (Weingast and Marshall 1988). So, if legislators systematically are to capture gains from trade, procedural protection is needed most on highly distributive legislation proposed by relatively outlying committees. More concretely, within the class of highly distributive bills, the effect of increasing the preference-outlier property of committees on the probability of assignment of a restrictive rule should be positive.

A method for deciphering the interactive effects for a given pair of variables—in this case distributive content and preference outliers—is to compose a 3×3 table in which the middle cell gives the probability of a restrictive rule with all independent variables fixed at their means. Adjacent cells then give probabilities for combinations of standard deviation increments or decrements of the interacted variables, again holding all other variables constant at their means. Thus, in table 5.6, Hypothesis 1A directs our attention to the bottom row, which substantively pertains to legislation that is one standard deviation more distributive than the average bill. The hypothesis implies that as we examine the probabilities from left to right—that is, moving from distributive bills proposed by inliers, to average committees, to outliers—the probabilities should increase. Indeed they do increase, from .036 to .048 to .063. However, this evidence can hardly be regarded as strong. For one thing, the probabilities are all very small. Even in the cell most relevant to the hypothesis (the lower right cell), any given bill stands a paltry one-in-sixteen chance of being considered under a restrictive rule. For another, the outlier effect is strongly negative for legislation of average dis-

---

33. Another possibility—namely, last period effects associated with senior members—is not explored here.

34. The coefficient for preference outlier $\times$ committee seniority cannot be ignored here either. Recall from table 5.5, however, that the net effect of committee seniority is positive, even taking into account the interaction effect.

TABLE 5.6. Interaction between
Distributive-Content and Preference-Outlier
Measures (Hypothesis 1A)

DISTRIBUTIVE CONTENT	PREFERENCE OUTLIER		
	LOW	AVERAGE	HIGH
Low	.735	.318	.057
Average	.280	.143	.060
High	.036	.048	.063

tributive content (row 2), peaking at .280 for the least outlying committees. Clearly, the most likely recipient of a restrictive rule is a bill with lower than average distributive content proposed by a nonoutlying committee. In this scenario, represented by the upper left cell, chances are about three out of four (.735) that the bill will be considered under a restrictive rule. On balance, the evidence for Hypothesis 1A is insufficient for reversing the initial finding regarding the distributive rationale for restrictive rules.

Distributive Urgency

Probit analyses revealed a positive effect of the urgency of legislation on the probability of choice of a restrictive rule. Here, too, the data allow a more refined assessment of distributive theory than was given previously. Since distributive theories focus exclusively on distributive choice settings, they are strictly silent on urgency or hasten-agreement effects for nondistributive legislation. In this respect, more convincing support for Hypotheses 1 and 2 rests on a positive urgency effect for distributive bills. Specifically, the theoretical expectation is:

HYPOTHESIS 1B: DISTRIBUTIVE URGENCY. *For distributive legislation, the probability of consideration under restrictive rules will be increasing in the urgency of such legislation.*

The test is analogous to that for Hypothesis 1A. The results are in table 5.7, which shows the interactive effects between distributive content and urgency.[35] The bottom row bears most directly on the hypothesis. For highly distributive bills for which the urgency effect should be high and increasing, it is increasing but not very high. Nonurgent, highly distributive bills stand only

---

35. When distributive content × urgency was included in the equation, its coefficient was not significant. Since probit equations are nonlinear, though, interactive effects can occur and be calculated as described in appendix C.

TABLE 5.7.   Interaction between Distributive-Content and Urgency Measures (Hypothesis 1B)

DISTRIBUTIVE CONTENT	URGENCY		
	LOW	AVERAGE	HIGH
Low	.284	.405	.537
Average	.170	.266	.385
High	.090	.157	.249

a .090 chance of receiving a restrictive rule, and this probability increases to only .249 for urgent distributive legislation. The middle and top rows reveal comparable positive effects of urgency but at considerably higher levels of probability. For example, a nondistributive urgent bill (top right cell) has a better than fifty-fifty chance of getting a restrictive rule as opposed to the one-in-four chance for distributive urgent bills (bottom right cell). Thus, while these findings are narrowly somewhat supportive of Hypothesis 1B, they continue to cast doubt on the broader distributive hypothesis.

Multiple Referrals

I previously offered a distinctly informational interpretation of the coefficient and corresponding positive net-probability effect of the number of referrals. When a bill comes to the floor having received the consideration of two or more committees that bring different (heterogeneous) policy perspectives to bear on its consequences, relatively uninformed members on the floor are rationally more inclined to give up their amendment rights. A recent empirical study of multiple referrals captures much of this information-theoretic reasoning.

> While multiply-referred measures are less likely to succeed, it is also true that multiple-referrals are used as a lever to stimulate policy innovation and encourage committees to consider problems they might not other-wise do. . . . Examples of this kind of cross fertilization are not uncommon. The expertise of lawmakers and staff aides, accumulated from years of dealing with a given industry, enterprise, or federal agency, can be blended with expertise residing in other committees. . . . At its best, the procedure [of multiple referrals] allows different committees to exercise their differing expertise and express their differing viewpoints in shaping legislation. (Davidson, Oleszek, and Kephart 1988, 20–21)

The informational interpretation of the findings takes this argument one step farther. The use of restrictive procedures indeed helps the referral system to operate "at its best." Selective use of multiple referrals—along with the expectation borne out in the data that restrictive rules will accompany bills that are products of heterogeneous experts—results in the House's effectively tapping its committees' expertise, even in this arguably less committee-centered era.

Perhaps this informational interpretation is inappropriate, however. Weingast (1989b and 1989c), for example, provides an intuitive basis for an alternative, distributive interpretation of the positive effect of the number of referrals on choice of restrictive rules. In a variation on the gains-from-trade theme, he writes: "From our standpoint, one key feature of MRs [multiple referrals] is that they help members of subcommittees of different committees negotiate an agreement and then enforce it on the floor" (Weingast 1989b, 36). The same argument is placed more explicitly in the context of restrictive rules in a follow-up paper (Weingast 1989c).

Arguments about the appropriateness or inappropriateness of different interpretations given to coefficients are difficult to resolve. The best we can do is to suppose that the distributive interpretation is viable and subject its corresponding empirical claim to a test. The coefficient for the interaction effect between distributive content and the number of referrals was highly significant ($t = -2.91$). A 3 × 3 table can therefore be used as a check on the distributive interpretation of the overall effect of the number of referrals on restrictive rules. The refined distributive hypothesis in this context is:

HYPOTHESIS 1C: MULTIPLE REFERRALS. *For highly distributive legislation, the probability of use of restrictive rules will be increasing in the number of committees to which legislation is referred.*

Table 5.8 tests this hypothesis. For highly distributive bills (bottom row), an increase in the number of referrals takes an initially low probability of a

TABLE 5.8. Interaction between Distributive-Content and Referral Measures (Hypothesis 1c)

DISTRIBUTIVE CONTENT	REFERRALS		
	LOW	AVERAGE	HIGH
Low	.248	.405	.580
Average	.227	.266	.309
High	.206	.157	.116

restrictive rule (.206) and reduces it by almost half (.116). In contrast, the effect is mildly positive for moderately distributive bills (middle row), and strongly positive for nondistributive bills (top row). This finding both confirms and refines one of Bach and Smith's empirical claims, namely that there is a positive relationship between multiple referrals and restrictive rules. The confirmation is due to the mild positive net effect of the number of referrals (see table 5.5). The refinement is that the positive effect of the number of referrals is exclusively attributable to nondistributive legislation and that for distributive legislation the effect is negative (compare the first and third rows in table 5.8). In other words, Bach and Smith's observation was clearly not a distributive phenomenon of the type hypothesized by Weingast, but it may well have been an informational phenomenon of the type hypothesized by Davidson, Oleszek, and Kephart (1988) and derived from the informational theories reviewed in chapter 3. Thus, Hypothesis 1c can be confidently rejected.[36]

Additional Arguments

Robinson and Shapiro—in contrast to Baron and Ferejohn, Fiorina, Weingast, and me—argued that an alternative rationale for restrictive rules was to keep legislators from piling on particularistic provisions that ultimately would be socially disadvantageous. The implicit presumption in the argument is normative: legislators will tie their hands by consenting to constraints on their amendment rights when the situation is such that, in the absence of such constraints, their individualism will undermine the public interest. Is there support for this view?

Yes and no. On the surface, at least, the answer appears to be no. The empirical expectation is a positive relationship between distributive content and restrictive rules, and the observed coefficient is negative. But, again, let us pursue a more charitable and creative interpretation. If, by chance, what the distributive-content variable really measures is inefficiency or, even more creatively, "public badness" of legislation, then in one sense the damage already may have been done by the time these bills came to the floor. Suppose

---

36. For the two remaining interaction terms (preference outlier × laws cited and preference outlier × committee seniority) similar analysis was conducted to see whether specialization effects manifest themselves in the same way for committees with different compositional characteristics. While not relevant to the current distributive discussion, the findings were supportive of informational expectations. The preference-outlier effect was negative for all levels of specialization according to both measures. The specialization effect as measured by laws cited was positive for all levels of outliers. The specialization effect as measured by committee seniority was positive for low and medium levels of outliers but low and negative for high outliers (ranging from .080 to .060 to .045). In short, specialization effects are either robustly positive or concentrated in nonoutlying committees.

the committee had done the piling on and, thus, legislator-pigs had completed their binge at the public trough before the bill reached the floor. Satiated and having stacked the distributive deck, legislators no longer needed a restrictive rule. Although I instinctively question this interpretation, it has a grain of plausibility and certainly is compatible with the notion of distributive committee power (e.g., Shepsle and Weingast 1987a). More importantly, it is a useful vehicle in which to drive home two additional points.

First, how could we know whether this interpretation is true (or false)? Implicit in it is an assumption of a high-demand committee. As seen in chapter 4, convincing evidence for this assumption is lacking. This doesn't prove anything, but it does raise some doubt. Second, is the story theoretically complete? From the standpoint of individual rationality, the answer is unequivocally no. Suppose all of the following: the distributive deck is stacked, a high-demand committee has saturated its bill with lard, the bill is therefore blatantly inimical to the public interest, and it comes to the floor under an open rule because there is no fear of additional piling on of particularistic provisions. For one thing, this presumes that distributive desires of congressmen can be satiated, which is imaginable, but also lacking in convincing empirical support.[37] For another, the story is silent on the matter of stripping amendments. Why couldn't and wouldn't a modern day H. R. Gross patiently await the perpetuation of these outrages and at the appropriate time move to stop the robbing of the public purse? In other words, what sustains the logroll, if not rules? More fundamentally, has logrolling of universalistic proportions even occurred?

Finally, Bach and Smith would correctly interpret the set of results surrounding the distributive-content coefficients as broadly consistent with their empirical claims.[38] However, the reasoning on which their observations are based is incomplete in a manner similar to Shapiro's and Robinson's. Why are restrictive rules not needed for particularistic legislation? Bach and Smith would say: because of norms of deference to "constituency" (sub)committees. But what sustains norms of deference, and why are they presumably sustain-

---

37. I know of two exceptions and there are no doubt a handful of others. One is the Buckley case (see chap. 2). The other is a story of Representative Bob Wise, who successfully offered a stripping amendment to the Stonewall Jackson Dam in his district in 1983 (*Congressional Quarterly*, June 11, 1983).

38. So, too, would they be likely to concur in the findings with respect to the number of referrals and urgency. On the other hand, the findings on scope, Democratic cosponsors, and Republican cosponsors pose more of a problem. A potentially important reservation to the cosponsorship findings is that different bills offer different opportunities for cosponsorship. Appropriations bills, in particular, are often reported as clean bills and thus minimize these opportunities. Coding a variable for clean bills (which takes on value of 1 for several bills besides appropriations) and reestimating the equations in table C.1 does not substantially affect the estimates. I thank Steve Smith for raising this reservation.

able on some bills but not on others? Similarly, what sustains cross-committee logrolls, and, to reiterate, what is the evidence that such logrolling occurs? In short, while I do not dispute that some logrolling occurs in Congress, the empirical results lead us increasingly to question whether it occurs extensively across committees. Even the strongest advocates of the distributive perspective on legislative politics concede that members face temptations to defect from cross-committee logrolls by offering amendments under open rules on the floor.[39] Do they defect? If not, why not? While these questions exceed the scope of this chapter, the empirical results bearing on distributive theories serve to accentuate their importance.

A Hopeful Conclusion

Baron's theory stands alone in the distributive class as one that is not refuted by these results. The urgency findings as reported in table 5.7 are roughly consistent with Baron's theory, but the more important point is that the predictions of his theory are more precise than my data. The theory holds that open rules should be used when proposed projects are economically inefficient. The distributive-content variable does not capture inefficiency per se and, therefore, interpreting the coefficient as supportive of the distributive efficiency rationale for rules requires an assumption that such projects are ones in which net benefits are negative. Many observers of congressional politics in the postwar period would probably not object to such an assumption, but a firmer conclusion must await more thorough analysis. The encouraging sign is that the analysis conducted thus far leaves open the possibility of more convincing support for this distributive-efficiency rationale for unrestrictive rules. In none of the tables (5.6–5.8) that are based on the distributive-content measure is it possible to find a column in which, by moving from top to bottom (nondistributive to distributive bills), the probability of choice of restrictive rules increases markedly.

Cases

Two cases are offered as concrete illustrations of the informational rationale for restrictive rules.

Case 1: Military Construction

In May, 1985, the House Armed Services Committee officially requested a rule for the Military Construction Authorization Act of 1986 (H.R. 1409).

---

39. Such temptations or opportunities for reneging were clearly central in Weingast and Marshall 1988. See also Shepsle and Weingast 1987a, whose model is analyzed and subjected to data more thoroughly in chap. 6.

From the analysis presented in previous sections it is straightforward to predict what kind of rule the Rules Committee will propose and the House will pass. Based on the estimated coefficients, the probability of a restrictive rule is computed. Table 5.9 summarizes this computation as well as that for the second case.

The main statistical and substantive influences on the probability can be divided into positive and negative categories as determined by the calculations reported in table 5.5. The greatest negative influence in this case—statistically as well as substantively—was the high distributive content of the bill. The value of distributive content (.55) is among the highest in the sample and works both directly through $\hat{\beta}_2$ and indirectly through $\hat{\beta}_9$. The House-passed version of the bill authorized spending for hundreds of projects, totaling \$9.56 billion. While some of these funds were for overseas construction, the foreign expenditures paled in comparison with domestic expenditures, most of which would confer clearly identifiable, geographically concentrated benefits. Many of these are prominently displayed on the first pages of the committee's report (H.Rept. 99–128).

Two other negative influences relate directly to a finding of chapter 4. The Armed Services Committee was a relatively homogeneous preference outlier (and unique in that regard, according to chap. 4). On the ADA-based preference-outlier measure, the committee scored 27.5; on the heterogeneity measure it scored −6.88. In light of the signs and net effects of the related coefficients ($\hat{\beta}_5$, $\hat{\beta}_7$, $\hat{\beta}_8$, and $\hat{\beta}_9$), both of these factors reinforce the House's inclination not to consider the bill under a restrictive rule. Actual House action contains several suggestions that these preference-based forces were

TABLE 5.9. Computation of Predicted Rules for Two Cases

Variable	$\hat{\beta}*$	H.R. 1409†	H.R. 4151†
Constant	−1.54	1	1
Distributive content	−10.60	.55	0.0085
Urgency	1.015	0	0
Laws cited	‡	3	18
Committee seniority	0.251	8.66	5.76
Preference outlier	‡	27.5	13
Heterogeneity	0.166	−6.88	1.90
Republican cosponsors	0.037	1	9
Preference outlier × laws cited	0.007	82.5	234
Preference outlier × committee seniority	−0.018	238	74.9
Distributive content × preference outlier	0.586	15.3	.11
Probability of restrictive rule, $\Phi(\hat{\beta}'X_i)$		.14	.77

*See table C.1.
†Values of variables.
‡Variable enters only interactively.

working throughout the consideration of the bill. Even though the Armed Services Committee made several cuts during markups in anticipation of the House's desire to keep within budget limits, the House still adopted an amendment that stipulated that not more than $9.2 billion would be appropriated even though a larger amount ($9.56 billion) was being authorized.[40] Similarly, even though the conference delegations appointed to resolve House-Senate differences were numerically dominated by members from the high-demand authorizing committees, conferees nevertheless exercised restraint in conference.[41] For instance, in the conference report, the panel stressed its "serious concerns that at a time when the defense budget is under serious constraints, the Navy is starting a billion dollar construction program." In some instances it barred or deferred the use of money for special projects in spite of their obvious particularistic benefits (*Congressional Quarterly Almanac* 1985, 182).

In contrast to the strong negative effects of committee preferences and the distributive components of the bill, the only thing working in favor of consideration of the bill under a restrictive rule was the Armed Services Committee's moderately high degree of seniority (8.66). However, since this was not a bill that demanded a great degree of expertise to fashion (laws cited = 3) and since only a weak confirmatory signal was sent (Republican cosponsors = 1), these small positive effects were swamped in the equation.

The Rules Committee granted H.R. 1409 an open rule (H.Res. 196). Representative Hall (D.-Ohio) managed the rule on the floor and gave it a brief and straightforward description. Representative Latta (R.-Ohio), often a harsh adversarial force in rule making, offered this synopsis on behalf of the minority party:

> Mr. Speaker, there are no problems with this rule. It is a completely open rule. There are no waivers or points of order. The rule even provides two hours of general debate, which should be more than sufficient to discuss the bill. (*Congressional Record,* September 30, 1985, H 7897)

Consistent with the prediction of the equation, the rule was summarily accepted without a roll call vote.[42]

Case 2: Embassy Security

The House Foreign Affairs Committee initiated H.R. 4151, the Omnibus Diplomatic Security and Anti-Terrorism Act of 1986. This legislation autho-

---

40. Interestingly, the successful amendment was offered by one of the committee's liberal members, Ronald Dellums (D.-Calif.), indicating that a little heterogeneity goes a long way.

41. Issues such as these are explored more systematically in chap. 6.

42. See also *Congressional Quarterly Almanac* 1985, 182–86.

rized five-year expenditures of $2.4 billion to strengthen U.S. overseas diplomatic posts against attacks by terrorists. Terrorism had become a salient issue in the 1980s. In early 1984, a Staff Task Force on International Terrorism and Diplomatic Security was established to undertake an extensive review of a large number of embassies and other diplomatic facilities around the world. Over a twelve-month period beginning in March, 1985, various Foreign Affairs subcommittees and the full committee held over twenty days of detailed hearings to produce legislation (H.Rept. 99–494). Table 5.9 summarizes the computation of the predicted rule for this bill.

With the exception of provisions ensuring that U.S. contractors would be encouraged to bid for overseas construction projects and providing some funds to boost security at U.S. as well as foreign seaports, the bill was not particularistic. Quantitatively, this is reflected in the miniscule estimate of its distributive content (0.0085). While the Foreign Affairs Committee is somewhat below the House's average committee in terms of mean seniority (5.76) and about average in terms of preference outliers (13), several other factors worked to its procedural advantage. First, as noted above, it exerted considerable effort in writing the legislation (laws cited = 18). Second, the committee is more heterogeneous than the House and most other committees (heterogeneity = 1.90). Third, Republicans solidly confirmed the committee's signal that its legislation was valuable (Republican cosponsors = 9), both as it emerged from the committee and as it moved effortlessly to final passage. After turning down two amendments pertaining to reducing compensation to hostages, the House passed the bill 389 to 7 (*Congressional Quarterly Almanac* 1986, 377–79).

These positive effects were more than enough to push the estimated probability of a restrictive rule above the fifty-fifty threshold. The .77 probability suggests a high likelihood of a restrictive rule. On March 18, the House took up the modified-closed rule (H.Res. 402) proposed by the Rules Committee. The debate on the rule was more extensive than that for the military construction authorization discussed above but not much more controversial. Moreover, it clearly complements the quantitative analysis.

Representative Burton (D.–Calif.) managed the resolution on the floor, concisely explaining its provisions and their justifications.[43] Representative Lott (R.–Miss.), the Republicans' ranking member on the Rules Committee and probably its most vociferous opponent of restrictive procedures, then took the floor offering these words.[44]

> Mr. Speaker, I think I should say a few words about this expedited and closed process since it's something I usually do not think is advisable,

---

43. The rule not only restricted amendments to three relatively narrow facets of the bill but also contained a number of waivers (*Congressional Record,* March 18, 1986, H 1231–32).

44. Though not a primary focus here, Lott's speech is also a good example of a rare

and I'm even uncomfortable with it now, though I have signed off on it subject to certain conditions and understandings. As I mentioned, the majority leadership has put this antiterrorism legislation on a fast track because it is an important and urgent concern. . . . In addition, the bill was reported from both committee and subcommittee by unanimous voice vote, in fine bipartisan fashion. And other committees have cooperated on aspects of this issue which are within their jurisdiction, while waiving their jurisdictional claims to expedite matters. . . . So let's consider this a unique situation given the importance and urgency of the issue involved and the priority given to this by both the majority leadership and the administration. (*Congressional Record,* March 18, 1986, H 1233)

Other supporters of the rule reiterated Lott's justifications for the restrictiveness of the rule: its broad bipartisan support, the cooperation and consent of other committees,[45] the hard work of the Foreign Affairs Committee and its subcommittees, and the broadly perceived importance of addressing the diplomatic security problem quickly. Ultimately, the restrictive rule was adopted by a voice vote (*Congressional Record,* March 18, 1986, H 1236).

Conclusion

Why do legislative majorities adopt different rules for different bills when the distributive consequences of some such rules are nonmajoritarian? The analysis in this chapter leads to an answer that bears on each of the three bodies of literature discussed previously: empirical accounts for variation in special orders, distributive rationales for restrictive rules, and informational explanations for bill-specific procedural choice.

Results for conventional empirical accounts of restrictive rules are mixed. The urgency hypothesis was supported, but the scope of legislation had no significant effect on the assignment of restrictive rules independent of the informational and distributive effects. The multiple referral hypothesis was supported, but its effect is felt exclusively on nondistributive bills. The evidence on the relationship between distributive content of legislation and restrictive rules was consistently negative, and this naturally has different implications for differing empirical claims. Finally, the notion of rules as partisan steamrollers was resoundingly rejected.

---

instance in which an outlier (here an outlier with respect to opposition to restrictive rules) can be informative.

45. These composed an ideologically diverse group: Armed Services, Post Office and Civil Services, Judiciary, Merchant Marine and Fisheries, and Public Works and Transportation.

A caveat is in order with respect to some of these findings, though. Some empirical claims implicitly address the same themes as the informational rationale for restrictive rules. For example, "complexity of the issue" (Robinson 1963) may be construed as uncertainty about the consequences of the bill. Or, "managing uncertainty on the floor" (Bach and Smith 1988) may be construed as assigning a restrictive rule to reassure the committee that its specialization efforts will not be gutted via amendments. Accordingly, rather than discounting the empirical literature, the analysis claims only in some instances to be consistent with a more explicit theoretical foundation on which it may be placed. Thus, by no means should we disregard prior empirical literature on the choice of rules.

In contrast to the inferences in chapter 4, which were weak due primarily to the inability to reject null hypotheses, much stronger inferences are warranted here. Contemporary legislative choice is characterized by substantial variation in bill-specific choice of rules. Without exception, informational attributes are capable of explaining such variation. All null hypotheses of no effects are confidently rejected in favor of information-theoretic alternative hypotheses. Distributive theories, however, fail to explain variation in bill-specific choice of rules. Specifically, although the null hypothesis of no distributive-content effects can be rejected, the observed effect is exactly opposite that predicted by the modal distributive theory. No matter what the specified equation or sample of data from which estimates were derived, the greater is the distributive component of legislation, the less inclined is the House to grant such legislation procedural protection. Thus, while the gains-from-trade viewpoint is intuitive, it is nevertheless inadequate as an explanation for this facet of legislative organization. This is not to say that gains from trade do not occur in Congress. However it is to assert—and for the first time with systematic evidence—that restrictive rules play little or no role in enforcing bargains, if such bargains are, in fact, made. In other words, rules are not distributive devices for facilitating logrolling within or across high-demand committees. Rather, they seem to be informational devices that are chosen by the House to get the most out of its committees.

CHAPTER 6

Chamber Control and Postfloor Procedures

The Congressional Conference Committee System forms an indispens-
able part of modern Congressional procedure. Yet, with all the weight
and age and present-day importance that pertains to it, the conference
committee is still almost unknown.
                                                            —Ada C. McCown (1927)

The leverage committees gain by controlling conferences on their leg-
islation has long been recognized to be a vital source of committee
power in Congress. But the point should not be pushed too far.
                                                            —Steven S. Smith (1989)

McCown's careful research on the development of procedures for settling
bicameral disputes in the U.S. Congress did a great deal to remedy the
problem she identified in her preface, and recent works such as Smith's are
indicative of a rejuvenated interest in postfloor behavior in the legislative
process.[1] Nevertheless, rationales for and uses of postfloor procedures continue to be among the more cryptic facets of the legislative process.[2] This
chapter integrates the previous two chapters on the formation of informative
committees and the informational determinants of choice of special orders. If,
as argued above, informational considerations are central to legislative organization at the stages of committee formation and the choice of rules, then it
would be puzzling and contrary to the thesis of this book to discover that, at
the final stages of the legislative process, these informational imperatives
cease to exist while pork barrel politics returns with a vengeance. Thus, in an
additional attempt to find empirical support for distributive theories or to
bolster the informational argument, I shall weave these theoretical strands
through the final stages of the legislative process.

The empirical task is more difficult here than in chapters 4 and 5, in part

---

1. See also Longley and Oleszek 1989; Nagler 1989; Shepsle and Weingast 1987a; and
Smith 1988.

2. The term *postfloor procedures* is used rather than *conference committee procedures* to
avoid the implication that the conference committee process is the sole means for resolving
bicameral differences.

193

because of the scarcity of quantitative empirical literature on which to draw.[3] A more subtle but equally confining impediment is that the theoretical lenses through which to view data on postfloor behavior are not well-polished. The principal distributive theory of such behavior is susceptible to misinterpretation. Worse yet, incomplete information theories specifically about postfloor procedures do not exist. Nevertheless, several of the insights from distributive and informational theories can serve as bases on which to form empirical expectations about procedural choice at the end of the legislative game. This chapter develops six hypotheses and assesses them from a variety of empirical vantage points: anecdotal, historical, and quantitative.

I begin by discussing and contrasting distributive and informational perspectives on postfloor procedures. While the basic thrusts of these classes of theory should be clear from prior discussions, some new twists arise at the end of the legislative game, especially with respect to distributive theories. These are manifested at two levels: first in terms of the formal assumptions of the leading theory, and second in terms of the hypotheses that can be extracted from the theory. The chapter operates at both levels. I assess the theoretical perspectives by examining how postfloor procedures have evolved in the U.S. Congress. This stage of analysis is historical and should be viewed as a nonquantitative but direct check on assumptions. The historical evidence casts doubt on the existence of "institutional foundations of committee power" in the form of postfloor procedures.[4] Conclusions at this stage are very tentative, however, since assessments of assumptions are less compelling forms of corroboration or refutation than evidence bearing on predictions. To avoid premature rejection of the distributive theory, the remainder of the chapter focuses on testing empirical implications. Six hypotheses structure three sections of results that address the following questions. What legislation goes to conference? Who goes to conference? Does a well-worn path exist on which legislation traverses after its initial passage by the House? I conclude with two cases that illustrate many of the intervening arguments in the chapter.

The quantitative tests employ data from the 99th Congress and are motivated as follows. In light of the historically questionable basis for the assumptions of the leading distributive model, consistent support for its predictions is a necessary condition for its acceptance at this third stage of legislative organization. This is tantamount to a search for support for an "as-if" interpretation of its procedurally rigid assumptions. Barring such support, the issue is

---

3. Smith's (1989, chap. 7) recent work is a major exception. Other exceptions include the literature focusing on who wins in conference, such as Ferejohn 1975; Strom and Rundquist 1977; and Vogler 1971. The who-wins issue will not be addressed here, however.

4. The quoted phrase is the title of Shepsle and Weingast's (1987a) highly acclaimed article that presents the distributive theory on which this analysis focuses.

whether empirical expectations of informational theories are borne out any better. If so, then the distributive perspective of legislative organization must be further questioned, whereupon the evidence for informational theories should be assembled and weighed as we move into the final chapter.

Assumptions about Postfloor Procedures

Distributive and informational theories are not different from one another in every respect. For example, both classes of theory postulate that actors are goal-oriented, and both research traditions embrace the single most salient feature of congressional organization: allocation of resources and assignment of parliamentary rights to standing committees. However, the institutions for obtaining a desirable relationship between standing committees and parent bodies are quite different under the two theoretical perspectives. These differences lead to a more fundamental divergence in how legislative processes are characterized formally and, eventually, in the hypotheses derived from alternative theories. A systematic study of conference procedure is useful because, as in previous chapters, distributive and informational theories yield different predictions in spite of their common rational choice foundation. First I address the differences in institutional assumptions. These pertain to the institutions of delegation, the rationale for delegation, and the chamber's level of commitment to the delegation.

As defined in chapter 1, institutions are rules or precedents that determine the assignment of parliamentary rights to legislators. Rights are clearly at issue during every stage in the legislative process, and a diverse assortment of social scientists and legal scholars has studied rights and their assignment in one guise or another.[5] Many of their interests and concerns can be straightforwardly transported to the study of postfloor behavior. The common feature is that since legislators care deeply about who may participate in collective decision making and when, we can safely presume that assignment of parliamentary rights is important. In turn, a better understanding of these processes should yield a better understanding of the legislative product. The issue here is: How and to whom are rights assigned after legislation first passes the parent chamber? The answer obtained depends on the theory consulted, and historical evidence begins to discriminate between theories.

---

5. Up to the postfloor stage at which this chapter begins, the list includes committee assignment rights (Bullock 1972; Masters 1961; Shepsle 1978), bill introduction rights (Cooper and Young 1989), bill referral rights (Collie and Cooper 1989), proposal rights (Baron and Ferejohn 1989b; Denzau and Mackay 1983; Romer and Rosenthal 1978), recognition rights (Baron and Ferejohn 1989a), and amendment rights (Bach 1981a and 1981b; Bach and Smith 1989; Gilligan and Krehbiel 1987 and 1989; Smith 1989). A classic legal work is Calabresi and Melamed 1972.

Postfloor Rights in Distributive Theory

It should be clear from chapter 2 and subsequent summaries that in distributive theories rules of procedure are the key determinants of who gets what. Different rules yield different outcomes. More precisely, when collective choice institutions—however defined—constrain one set of agents (noncommittee members) but not another (a committee), there is no mystery in analytical results pertaining to who gets a bigger piece of the distributive pie. Asymmetric constraints on behavior work to the advantage of the relatively unconstrained.

Shepsle and Weingast (1987a) examined a special case of this more-or-less generic argument in a study of conference committees and, in so doing, give it an element of concreteness that proves useful here. They regard conference procedures generally—and, in particular, a committee's assumed right to exercise an "ex post veto" prior to the chamber's final consideration of legislation—as "the institutional foundation of committee power." The logical structure implicit in their argument sharpens the empirical analysis here when it is spelled out explicitly. The distributive-theoretic claim is of the standard if-p-then-q form, where p is a set of legislative procedures enumerated below and q is distributive committee power as defined in chapter 3. The legislative process consists of four stages: a standing committee proposes a bill; the parent chamber acts on the bill; bicameral differences are resolved; and the parent chamber reconsiders the bill in its postconference form.[6] Procedural assumptions parallel these stages as follows:

- Standing committees have the exclusive right to propose bills in their jurisdictions.
- Noncommittee members have rights to offer germane amendments on the floor. However, only the committee has a right to take the bill to conference in the form passed by its house.
- The committee has a right to kill the bill in conference, that is, to exercise an "ex post veto."
- If the bill emerges from conference, the committee has a right to constrain voting in the parent chamber to a single "up-or-down" vote where "down" (failure to receive a majority) kills the bill.

Collectively, these assumptions form the antecedent p in the logical statement. Logically, falsity of any one of them would falsify p.

Elsewhere in the literature, the second part of the second procedural assumption and all of the third and fourth procedural assumptions have been

---

6. Only one chamber is modeled in the theory.

questioned directly or indirectly.[7] For example, the two parent chambers—not their committees—formally decide which bills go to conference; attempts by committees to veto bills can be circumvented; and legislation can be considered part-by-part or sent back to the other chamber with amendments even after a conference report has been issued. Strictly speaking, these institutional facts are not criticisms of the ex post veto theoretical argument, however. They are only substantive reservations about the procedural assumptions of the theory. In other words, to the initial if-p-then-q statement, these responses are of the form: not p. As such, they do not refute the model; they merely question its relevance to the contemporary Congress.

In this vein, defenders of the ex post veto theory have countered that theirs "was a model about the Congress of the 1950s and 1960s."[8] In turn, it seems reasonable to consider exhaustively the empirical basis for this historical claim. Here we trace the development of conference procedures, not back to the 1950s and 1960s but rather forward from their origins, through the 1950s and 1960s, and to the present. If the distributive model of the postfloor process is useful for understanding any period of congressional history, then we should be able to find some period during which its procedural assumptions were at least approximated. That is, the assumptions of the model should not be so stylized as to do timeless violence to procedural facts.

Distributive theories generally, and the ex post veto model of conference behavior specifically, are valuable not only as theories but also in helping to structure empirical analysis, for they address directly the question of why we might observe rules and procedures such as those that are assumed. We might observe them because they facilitate gains from trade. But do we observe them? And more precisely, for what shall we look? The following synopsis of the assumptions of postfloor distributive theories provides a clear answer.

PROCEDURAL COMMITMENT. *Rules and precedents about postfloor decision making should reflect uniform and unchallengeable commitment to procedures that favor standing committees during the final stages of the legislative process. These include each of the following parliamentary rights enjoyed by committee members: (1) to go to conference, (2) to amend their chamber's bill in conference, (3) to veto the bill in conference, and (4) to limit the chamber's final choice to a single up-or-down vote on their conference report.*[9]

---

7. See, for example, Bach 1984; Krehbiel 1987b; and Smith 1988.

8. See Shepsle and Weingast 1987b, 941. Some readers have noted that this qualification was not made in Shepsle and Weingast 1987a.

9. This is an extension of the distributive-theoretic prediction (Prediction 3) as developed in chap. 2.

In other words, the leading distributive theory depicts postfloor procedures much as other distributive theories depict institutions at prior stages of
the legislative process: as fixed and firm parliamentary rights granted to standing committees to help secure gains from trade. Four of these rights are
considered in detail later in the historical analysis, so it is useful to spell out
the related theoretical characterizations more specifically.

A Committee's Right to Go to Conference

On one hand, the distributive theory assumes that standing committees have a
right to go to conference. On the other hand, standing committees' postfloor
rights are viewed as an empirical regularity rather than assumption. For example, the seminal work on the ex post veto theory not only employs this
assumption but also contains data on the composition of conferences that are
broadly consistent with the assumption. While these data are interpreted as
support for the model, a more precise inference is that they support one of the
assumptions of the model. In any event, the existence of such a right (or
behavioral pattern) is an essential part of institutionalizing (or implementing)
gains from trade.

Amendment Rights of Conferees

Regardless of whether the chosen method for resolving differences is a conference committee or amendments between the chambers, legislatures must determine the degree to which they, or their agents, may alter the content of
legislation. The distributive model is clear on this score. "Ex post adjustments," in the authors' vernacular, are tantamount to the exercise of amendment rights in conference. The formal characterization reflects the need in
gains-from-trade institutional arrangements to grant broad parliamentary authority to standing committees. At a minimum, conference committees have
the right to alter any provision in the bill that passed the chamber. A stronger
form of delegation also consistent with distributive theories is that conference
committees could alter any policies within their jurisdictions, regardless of
whether the legislation as it passed the parent chamber addressed all such
policies.[10] In either form, distributive theories assume that assignment of
amendment rights to conferees is substantial.

Veto Rights of Conferees

The distributive characterization of veto rights of conferees is absolutely
clear. The ex post veto—that is, the irrevocable right of conferees to enforce

---

10. Shepsle (1979) provides formal definitions of "proposal germaneness" and "jurisdictional germaneness" rules for the consideration of committee proposals on the floor. These
implicitly define noncommittee members' amendment rights. Although these were not used in
Shepsle's SIE results, they are perfect parallels of these two forms of delegation. The only
difference is that the rules determine conferees' amendment rights in this context.

the status quo unilaterally—is *the* institutional foundation of committee power. To confer jurisdiction-by-jurisdiction distributive policy benefits to standing committees—that is, to capture gains from trade—committees necessarily must be delegated the right to kill legislation in the final stages of the process.

Rights to Amend Conference Reports

The formal characterization of amendment rights on the floor in the ex post veto model is also clear. When a conference committee chooses not to exercise its veto right, it has a similarly inviolable right to an up-or-down vote on its report. This parliamentary prerogative, too, is central to the institutionalization of gains from trade. Were the right not to be guaranteed, a distributive shift in policy away from the committee's preferred position would always be possible at this stage, and all prior procedural restrictions (in this and other distributive models) will have been for naught.

Postfloor Rights in Informational Theory

Informational theories contrast exclusively distributive views of the ex post veto model and similar gains-from-trade theories. The following synopsis of informational approaches parallels that offered above for distributive models.

> NONCOMMITMENT. *Rules and precedents about postfloor decision making should be characterized by selective and carefully monitored delegation of parliamentary rights to relatively expert members of standing committees. These may include—but will never guarantee—the following parliamentary rights: to go to conference, to amend or veto their chamber's bill in conference, and to have a single up-or-down vote on the conference report.[11]*

Generally, the informational theories depict legislative organization as a process of selective delegation of parliamentary rights in which the rationale for such delegation has much more to do with efficient use of policy expertise than with capturing gains from trade. The main substantive issues of postfloor legislative organization then naturally follow, yet they sharply contrast the distributive premises articulated above. First, how can a legislative majority exploit procedural endogeneity to capture the informational benefits from policy specialists? Second, how can a legislative majority minimize distributive committee power?

Majoritarianism in the domain of procedural choice along with the multi-

---

11. This is an extension of the information-theoretic prediction (Prediction 5) as developed in chap. 3.

stage nature of legislative choice essentially dictates that legislatures cannot commit to a set of procedures and, therefore, will employ restrictive procedures selectively.[12] Uncertainty and asymmetry indicate that, notwithstanding the legislature's inability to commit to restrictive procedures, it will nevertheless want to use its policy experts effectively. Integral assumptions of the informational perspective can also be spelled out in terms of the four types of postfloor parliamentary rights discussed above.

A Committee's Right to Go to Conference

Informational theories tend to minimize assumptions about asymmetric allocation of parliamentary authority.[13] The Majoritarian Postulate of legislative organization holds that parent-chamber majorities have control over postfloor as well as other procedures. The Uncertainty Postulate implies that chamber majorities will delegate to minorities, such as committees, only if a compelling informational rationale exists. Never will such delegation occur without strings attached, however. To ensure that its delegates are faithful, the legislature would presumably adopt rules or establish precedents that ensure monitored appointment of conferees and permit the issuing of instructions to conferees.

Amendment Rights of Conferees

Informational theories embody institutions of control and thus would characterize the issuing of instructions to conferees as signals of chamber preferences. If delegation of amendment rights to conferees occurred, it would have either an informational rationale (e.g., conferees are specialists . . .), a distributive rationale (. . . who can bargain better with the other chamber), or both.

Veto Rights of Conferees

To confer veto rights to conferees is to hand conferees distributive benefits on a silver platter. This is blatantly inconsistent with the assumptions of informational theories. Thus, if parliamentary rights were to be granted to conferees, they would arise from some compensating advantages such as informational benefits, distributive benefits vis-à-vis the other chamber, or expediency. In the latter case, we would expect postfloor procedures to bias the process to completion rather than stalemate, provided that conferees can be induced to act as faithful delegates of the legislature.

---

12. Moreover, at least some analysis suggests that if procedural commitment were feasible, the legislature might not want it (Gilligan and Krehbiel 1989b). See also Gilligan 1989.

13. The chief exception is that they postulate the existence of a committee system and thus an opportunity for the committee to specialize and a right to offer the first proposal.

Rights to Amend Conference Reports

Since the conference-floor sequence closely parallels the committee-floor sequence, we can transport some of the implications from informational models of committee-floor decision making to conference-floor decision making. A majoritarian, information-conscious legislature may give up its right to amend conference reports, but it would also preserve the right to revert to an alternative procedure in which such amendments can be made by the parent chamber. Thus, for example, if the conferees' "ex post adjustments" are contrary to chamber majorities' wishes, amendments of the conference report will be possible in one way or another. Several institutions can be envisioned that, consistent with informational theory, would achieve this form of chamber control, too. It should be possible for the conference to issue a report in partial agreement, for the chamber to amend portions of the bill on which conferees could not agree, to call a new conference, to issue instructions, or to revert to direct amendments between the chambers. Furthermore, rules or precedents regarding the privilege of motions would bias the process to completion rather than stalemate. If an up-or-down vote is taken, down would not mean out. That is, the process can, and in all likelihood would, go on.

Summary

The institutions for the assignment of parliamentary rights are concrete and thus afford unambiguous opportunities to bring historical evidence to bear on the plausibility of formal assumptions. Distributive theories fundamentally rest upon the existence of *procedural commitment* which trickles down the list of possible parliamentary rights in postfloor stages of legislative decision making. In contrast, the postulates of legislative organization underlying informational theory forego procedural commitment in favor of *chamber control*.

Historical Evidence on Postfloor Procedures

The nearer is legislation to the end of its journey through the Capitol, the greater is the level of awareness about its objectives and content, the greater is the probability that the majority approved changes in its content will become permanent, and, thus, the more valued are legislators' rights to block, change, or pass the legislation. Yet, in spite of the large amount of modern research on institutionalization and numerous separate studies on contemporary conference committee behavior, little attention has been given to the historical origins and subsequent practices, precedents, and rules associated with resolving bicameral differences.[14] As we shall see, the evolution and development

---

14. Bach 1984 is a major exception.

of what McCown calls "The Congressional Conference Committee System" is a superbly informative saga of legislative organization.

To assess postfloor procedures in terms of the distributive and informational theories, two types of historical evidence can be used. How did the procedures evolve? And, once in place, how are they employed? The potential for different answers to these questions deserves emphasis. It is quite possible, for instance, that institutions arose for one set of reasons (say, informational) but that at a much later time they are employed for an entirely different set of reasons (say, distributive). I will, therefore, attempt to be exhaustive of empirical focuses and approaches before reaching a final assessment.

Predecessors to Congressional Conference Procedures

The origins of modern conference procedures are found in the British Parliament during the twelfth through fifteenth centuries. McCown (1927, chap. 2) makes it clear that the main issues surrounding the development of these procedures had little if anything to do with committee-chamber tensions. The Parliament, unlike the Congress since its formative years, did not rely upon standing committees. Early British conference committees were composed of all members of the House of Commons and House of Lords. Later conference committees, while smaller, were composed of delegates with very limited authority. The stages involved in these "simple conferences" were strikingly rigid and cumbersome. First, a committee was appointed for drawing up "reasons" for the House of Commons' position, to be presented to the House of Lords. The committee then reported to the House, which would amend its reasons prior to the conference. Next, a different committee was selected to present the position to the Lords. At the conference itself, papers were exchanged but no real conferring or negotiating occurred. Finally, conferees reported back to their houses.

"Free conferences" were soon to emerge, however. At these, rights of conferees were extended so that managers could make their own arguments. Still, amendment rights were at issue in this development phase only to the extent that the most frequent arguments pertained to whether the House of Lords had any right to amend the House of Commons' legislation. In short, virtually all conflict seems to have been between houses, not between committees and their chambers. Even as late as 1851, conference procedures of this sort remained feasible in the Parliament. However, the preferred method was simply to transmit the arguments between chambers via messengers.[15]

When congressional scholars engage in discussions of a comparative

---

15. Thus, the process of amendments between the chambers (or houses) is sometimes called "messaging."

nature—which, to true comparativists, seems a pitifully rare occurrence (Rogowski 1989)—one of the first things they note about the U.S. Congress relative to many parliamentary legislatures is its extraordinary reliance upon standing committees. Perhaps, then, the British experience is misleading insofar as committees have played a major role in the Parliament only sporadically (Hibbing 1988). What of the U.S. colonial experiences?

McCown presents several examples that suggest the development of conference procedures in colonial legislatures was not much different from that in the Parliament. In Maryland, New Jersey, North Carolina, and Virginia, as in the Parliament, the major disputes were again between the upper and lower houses—not between committees and chambers. Likewise, the New York experience suggested an initial, strong, and institutionalized form of control of conferees for the purposes of securing bicameral advantage and to thwart shenanigans by the historical equivalent of high demanders. New York's 1777 Constitution provided for conferences to be held in the presence of both houses and managed by committees chosen by ballot. In McCown's words, "There was to be no secret agreement between powerful groups in the two houses if the constitution makers could help it" (1927, 36).

In summary, the historical roots of postfloor practices reveal little direct evidence consistent with the procedural assumptions of distributive theories. Of the few procedural innovations that occurred, fewer, if any, seem to have been instances of delegation motivated by conferring distributive benefits to preference outliers.

Postfloor Procedures in the First Congress

As we move to congressional practices in resolving bicameral differences, we see no general differences between Parliamentary and colonial experiences. Furthermore, many specifics speak directly to the issues of institutions of control, the level of commitment to those institutions, and their underlying rationales. The early history can be told quickly. The system, once in place, requires a more detailed treatment.

The U.S. Congress wasted no time deciding upon its basic procedures for resolving differences between its houses. On the first day of the 1st Congress a conference was appointed to decide on such rules. One of the rules decided upon was for a "free conference," that is, one in which conferees would exercise at least some discretion.[16] Many more conferences were held in the 1st Congress, with the same men serving as "managers" repeatedly. But their reports were always subject to amendment. Chamber control of conferees was apparently on the minds of nonconferees from the start. As early as

---

16. Additional details are provided in section 46 of *Jefferson's Manual*, which is the U.S. version of "general parliamentary law."

the second session of the 1st Congress, managers were charged with exceeding their authority. A hint of an informational rationale for deciding on whether conferees exceeded their authority can be extracted from the case. The conference committee in question defended its action with reference to new information from the president regarding salaries of foreign ministers. Finding these arguments persuasive, the House and Senate accepted the conference committee's amendments even though they clearly exceeded the scope of the original House-Senate differences (McCown 1927, 46–47).

Additional evidence that touches on informational and distributive characterizations includes the ostensible inability of a conference to agree on a post office bill (a candidate for an ex post veto on a bill with substantial distributive consequences) and a refusal on the part of the House to use the conference procedure at all late in the session, opting instead for amendments between the chambers (an example of a chamber preferring not to delegate) (McCown 1927, 46–47). Of course, these cases cannot be regarded as definitive evidence. But they do serve to illustrate that, once the basic structural apparatus was in place, questions of chamber control immediately emerged. Overall, early congressional practices remained flexible. Sometimes conference committees were used, sometimes not. There were no presumptions about the composition of conference committees when used. While legislators undoubtedly had some common expectations about managers' authority once in conference, the degree of such authority was not well-defined. Finally, although amendment rights on conference reports were presumed to reside in the chamber, such amendments were rare as a matter of practice. All things considered, institutionalization of postfloor procedures had not yet begun. However, it was just around the corner.

The Institutionalization of Postfloor Procedures

The full story of the emergence of the modern body of rules and precedents for resolving House-Senate differences is an intriguing case study in legislative organization of the following sort. First, behavioral practices emerge within the collective choice organization. Next, when challenged and upheld, the practices are codified in the precedents of the organization. While this codification may not give regular practices the force of a rule, at a minimum it increases legislators' expectation that the practice will continue to be regular. Finally, sometimes but not always, a chamber consciously opts to write its precedents into its standing rules, thus figuratively stepping to a higher rung of a ladder of institutionalization. An assumption in the analysis that follows is that differences in institutional status (ranging from practices, to precedents, to rules, to constitutions) are theoretically significant, even though practically they are often difficult to delineate. Often they are the very issues over which legislators battle: Who has what rights and at what stages of the process? Likewise, they are at the heart of the question that students of political institutions are asking with increasing regularity: Why?

Volume 5 of *Hinds' Precedents* contains seven chapters (208 large pages, 426 sections) on conference procedures and amendments between the houses. Volume 8 of *Cannon's Precedents* contains an equal number of chapters and approximately equal number of pages and sections. Deschler organized his precedents differently, but Deschler and Brown's *Procedure in the House of Representatives* contains two chapters that are analogous to Hinds' and Cannon's earlier works. To organize and synthesize these is a nontrivial task, but the various parliamentary rights discussed earlier provide useful focal points and permit concise comparisons of distributive and informational theories in terms of their fundamental assumptions.

Rights of Standing Committees to Go to Conference
Never in the history of the U.S. Congress have members of standing committees possessed an uncontested right to represent their chamber in conference proceedings. First, the chamber may choose not to appoint a conference committee at all, opting instead for either amendments between the chambers or outright acceptance of the other house's bill. Second, if the House chooses the conference procedure, precedents stipulate that the Speaker shall appoint conferees (Hinds 1,383).[17] As a matter of practice, conferees in early Congresses were not from related standing or ad hoc committees (McCown 1927, 62). By the late nineteenth century this pattern had changed. "It is almost the invariable practice to select managers from the members of the committee which considered the bill" (Hinds 1,383). Even so, the regularity of the practice is hardly evidence of a right. Indeed, Hinds continues, "But sometimes, in order to give representation to a strong or prevailing sentiment in the House, the Speaker goes outside the ranks of the committee" (Hinds 1,383). He then provides several specific examples.

The basic procedure regarding appointment of conferees is essentially the same today as it was in the late nineteenth century. One exception, which is nevertheless consistent with chamber control of its conferees, is that the House amended its rule 10, clause 6(e) in the 93d Congress to require the Speaker to appoint "a majority of members who generally supported the House position" (Deschler and Brown 33.5.1) While the objective of representative confer-

---

17. Citation conventions for precedents are as follows. References to Hinds without dates are to his 1899 edition, *Parliamentary Precedents in the House of Representatives of the United States*. The number given is the precedent number—not a page number. Likewise, references to Cannon are to his (1936) *Precedents of the House of Representatives*, and references to Deschler and Brown are to their (1982) *Procedure in the U.S. House of Representatives*. In these references, too, precedent numbers, rather than page numbers, are given.

ence delegations had been elevated to the status of a formal rule, this is somewhat misleading insofar as "the exercise of the Speaker's discretionary authority under the rule to (1) determine whether a majority of the conferees generally supported the House position, and (2) to appoint 'to the maximum extent feasible' the principal proponents of major provisions of the House-passed bill, is not subject to a point of order" (Deschler and Brown 33.5.1). The Speaker, then, may be relied upon as an enforcer of cross-committee deals, systematically biasing the composition of conference committees consistent with distributive theories. But at least two caveats accompany such an argument. First, additional evidence is needed to bolster such a claim. Second, for distributive theory to be both logically sound and empirically plausible, the assignment of rights has to be consistent with its assumptions at each of the postfloor stages. The institutional evidence thus far suggests only a modicum of support at the first stage: going to conference.

Another institutional indication of doubt about distributive-theoretic assumptions regarding postfloor processes is the existence of monitoring mechanisms during the conference committee selection process. The motion to go to conference always is subject, at least, to majority approval. Again, the practice deviates from the formal requirement in that unanimous consent has come to be a common method. But what inference can be drawn from this practice? That the chamber unanimously agrees to send outliers to committee so that they can make "ex post adjustments" contrary to the chamber's wishes? Or that it unanimously agrees to send committee members (not necessarily outliers, as we saw in chap. 4 and explore further below) because it either trusts that they will be faithful delegates or knows that, if not, it has procedural recourse at a later stage? The latter seems more defensible, prima facie. But this, too, is an issue that requires and is amenable to more systematic quantitative analysis.

In the event that the Speaker is more a cross-committee wheeler-dealer than a dimension-by-dimension majoritarian, the chamber has yet another control mechanism prior to conference: the issuing of instructions to conferees. The recorded precedent for instructions is dated 1884 (Hinds 1,376). However, Speaker Carlisle's ruling in the cited case occurred in 1864 and made it clear that it was not a new practice even then.

> The chair thinks that the original parliamentary practice was not to instruct committees of conference, but to leave them entirely free. However, a practice has grown up in this House, and has prevailed for several years, under which the House has very frequently passed resolutions instructing its managers as to the sense of the House with respect to certain amendments. There have been frequent occasions when it has been done. . . . The Chair remembers several such cases in the House during the last eight or ten years. (*Congressional Globe,* March 1, 1864, 892)

Instructions can be and are used today as well: "A motion to instruct the House managers at a conference is in order after the House has agreed to a conference and before the appointment of conferees" (Deschler and Brown 33.7.1). Instructions are not binding on conferees (Hinds 1,382; Deschler and Brown 33.10.1); however, they help to inform the Speaker of the chamber's wishes and thereby influence his appointments. Furthermore, it is not unusual for conferees actively to seek or come back to their parent chamber for instructions (Cannon 3,312). Thus, it seems all but certain that instructions help shape the beliefs of the managers themselves regarding what sorts of behavior will and will not be acceptable to the chamber. More succinctly, instructions play an informational role.

In summary, the rights of standing committee members to serve on conference committees are tenuous. The preponderance of historical evidence suggests that when conference committees are the chosen institutions for reconciling bicameral differences, the array of related procedural mechanisms at the chamber's disposal works more to guide or constrain conferees than to empower them.

Amendment Rights of Conferees

Of the four types of postfloor rights that are determined by congressional rules and precedents, those pertaining to the "authority of managers" have exhibited the most variation over the two centuries of the institution. The general point that emerges from the numerous precedents and occasional rules on the subject, however, is that informational rationales underlie Congress's institutional tinkering on matters of conference authority.

As early as 1812, it had been ruled in the House that "Conferees may not include in their report matters not committed to them by either House" (Hinds 1,414). Early rulings of this sort were none too precise, but clarification came at least by 1871. Then an appropriations bill was in conference during which the conference added provisions for the Sutro Tunnel and for the Agriculture Department, neither of which had been included in the legislation that was submitted to conference. Speaker Blaine ruled on Representative Holman's point of order. The Speaker said the issue was not one of whether the provisions were new matter—they were—but rather whether they were germane to the original bills. After further debate it was revealed that the tunnel appropriation was added to mollify the Senate for stripping an appropriation for the Carson Mint. The Speaker held this to be nongermane but submitted the question to the House. The House sustained his ruling,[18] thereby establishing the standard that, with minor exceptions, has remained unchanged until the present: the authority of conferees is constrained by germaneness, and the

18. Then, since the Senate had not yet acted on the report, the report was recommitted to conference—a possibility discussed in further detail below.

narrower of two forms of germaneness at that. Specifically, proposed changes must be germane to the houses' bills. Germaneness in the broader context of committees' jurisdictions is irrelevant.[19]

Two general patterns stand out in rulings of this sort. First, the bases for the rulings are almost invariably chamber control of conferees. Second, the precedents cited in Hinds seem disproportionately to be instances in which conferees attempted to add distributive provisions to the legislation in question. In the above-cited instance, the controversial provision was an appropriation for a tunnel. The subsequent precedents on authority of conferees in Hinds arose over the following issues: inclusion of powers of the Department of Interior over swamp-land claims into a bill on settlement rights (1,416), inclusion of a fishery provision into a bill extending homestead laws and providing a right of way for railroads in Alaska (1,417), and inclusion of a provision for establishing a war claims commission into an Army appropriations bill.[20] Hinds may or may not have presented a representative sample of disputes pertaining to authority of conferees. But it appears that control of conferees, as embodied in the precedents that clarify their authority, is inconsistent with the assumptions of distributive theory. On the contrary, the evidence is mounting that postfloor procedures were motivated by parent chambers' willingness and ability to curb distributive excesses.

Veto Rights of Conferees
The strongest factual statement in support of the distributive-theoretic assumption regarding veto rights of conferees is that they have a right to *attempt* a veto. There is almost no evidence in the congressional experience, however, that such attempts are common,[21] valued by the committee, or credible threats to the House or Senate. Rather, almost all rules and precedents point in the opposite direction: once bills have obtained initial passage in both houses, the process is deliberately biased toward completion, not toward veto.

Procedural biases against veto rights and in favor of reaching agreement come in numerous forms, beginning with precedents on the precedence of motions. The relevant barrage of parliamentary precedents falls short of what most sane people would regard as riveting reading, but only a few examples

19. A procedural issue of equal importance under the rubric of amendment rights of conferees is the scope of disagreements. See Bach 1982 for an excellent account of germaneness rules in the context of bicameral conflict and Bach 1984 for a more extensive study of conference procedures.

20. This was ruled germane. However, most other precedents arise from cases in which distributive issues invoked institutions of control (Hinds 1,373, 1,376, 1,382, and 1,415).

21. Shepsle and Weingast (1987b) argue that the actual exercise of ex post vetoes is not the appropriate test for their theory since, in equilibrium, the veto would not be exercised. I later assess whether the paths of actual legislation conform to the theoretical conception of an equilibrium path.

are needed to make the general point. When the houses have reached a stage of disagreement, the motion to recede (agree to the other house's amendments) has precedence over the motion to insist (continue the stalemate) and request a conference (Hinds 1,364).[22] Conference reports are highly privileged (Hinds 1,394),[23] cannot be tabled (1,407), and do not have to be reported back to the Committee of the Whole (1,410) or to standing committees (1,413). While these precedents speak generally to the issue of completion as opposed to stalling or veto, an additional set of precedents speaks specifically to the inability of the conference committee to veto legislation. Rules and precedents permit discharging a conference committee (1,373), calling a new conference (Deschler and Brown 33.11.2), changing from the conference procedure to amendments between the chambers (Hinds 1898, chap. 23), and various combinations of these (Hinds 1,384–88). For instance, in 1894 a conference on H.R. 4864, a tariff bill, was in progress when the Rules Committee reported a special order that called for discharging the conference and agreeing to the Senate amendments (1,373). A point of order was raised by Thomas Reed. In overruling the point of order, Speaker Crisp cited a previous instance of discharge in 1872 by the Senate and underscored the purpose of the related procedures: "Now, the object of all conferences between the two Houses is to get the minds of the Houses together and pass the bill" (1,373). To reiterate, rules and precedents not only stop short of conferring a veto right to conference committees; they contain numerous institutions to prevent attempted and unwanted vetoes.[24]

Amendment Rights on the Floor after Conference
In early Congresses, conference reports were amended frequently (McCown 1927, 15). Since at least the mid-nineteenth century, however, the normal practice has been not to amend conference reports.[25] However, to embrace the conclusion that the chambers therefore have no rights to alter the content of legislation after the conference committee acts would be imprudent. The chambers' commitment to a single up-or-down vote is mild at best. It is not a rule in either the House or Senate, and the Senate has, on occasions, explicitly refused to allow the practice to become a rule. Furthermore, in each house a

---

22. See Bach 1984 for more details, other similar precedents, and an interpretation consistent with the one offered here. See Cannon 1936, vol. 8 for a much longer list.

23. This became part of the standing rules of the House in 1880 (McCown 1927, 76).

24. All of these parliamentary mechanisms, and more, are alive and well today, too (Krehbiel 1987b).

25. In chap. 5, McCown spells out some of the more arcane details of this claim. These relate to the fact that the conference report is distinct from the bill. Sometimes in the early Congresses the report was amended, but the bill was not. As time passed, action on the report became implicitly coupled with action on the bill; thus the terms *bill* and *report* can be used interchangeably without doing great violence to the facts.

variety of circumstances can arise whereby provisions of legislation can be considered separately after conference. For example, a conference committee may issue a report in partial agreement and allow the chambers to resolve remaining disagreements via messaging (Hinds 1,392).

One response to this chamber-control interpretation of procedural possibilities is that the decision that creates these opportunities for chamber control—namely, the decision of reporting in disagreement (or partial agreement)—is made by conferees, not by the parent chambers. If so, the relevant issue becomes whether the body of rules and precedents is such that the parent chamber, against its will, can be forced by conferees into a single up-or-down vote. It cannot. Strictly speaking, the chambers' commitment to a single vote is nonexistent. As we have seen above, the process of amendments between the chambers is a viable alternative before or after conference. In fact, when a conference report is defeated the automatic default procedure is to revert to amendments between the chambers. Still another option is for the first-acting chamber to recommit the report, possibly with instructions. A revealing example is the House's action on the conference report on the Fordney-McCumber Tariff bill in 1922. Conferees exceeded their authority by reinstating a dye embargo provision that each parent chamber had stricken from the bill via amendment. When the report from the impudent conference committee came to the floor, the House voted 177 to 130 to recommit it to conference with instructions to strike the dye embargo provision. While the case would seem to be a natural one for an ex post veto, the new conference complied with the House's instructions, and the bill became law.[26]

Another response to the chamber-control interpretation of postfloor procedures is that while there is no strict institutional basis for vetoes by conference committees, conferees may circumvent the chamber's wishes in eleventh-hour rushes at the end of a session. The claim is that these timing ploys create a strategic advantage when institutions fail to capture gains from trade.[27] Clearly, this argument is more behavioral than institutional. Moreover, its implicit behavioral assumption is that conferees are timing-smart while nonconferees are timing-stupid. Yet, congressional history indicates that nonconferees not only can foresee but also can address these potential abuses of conference authority. Early Congresses, for example, forbade conferences entirely in the last days of the session (McCown 1927, 57). In the contemporary Congress, the relevant questions are essentially the same. Can nonconferees anticipate abuses contemplated by conferees? Yes.[28] To answer "no" would be to contradict blatantly the rationality postulate on which the distributive theory is based (and informational theories, too, of course). Are

---

26. *Congressional Record,* September 15, 1922, 12709–18.
27. See, for example, Shepsle and Weingast 1987b; and Smith 1989, chap. 7.
28. See Longley and Oleszek 1989; and Smith 1989 for many examples.

institutions available so that, upon suspicion or recognition, nonconferees can thwart abuses contemplated by conferees? Unquestionably. These include amendments between the chambers (before or after conference) and, in some instances, discharge of conferees.[29]

Summary

While the sheer quantity of facts surrounding postfloor procedures can be overwhelming, the central messages can be reduced to three concise points.

First, postfloor procedures enable parent chambers to delegate parliamentary rights to conference committees just as other features of legislative organization enable the delegation of parliamentary rights to standing committees. However, the use of such procedures is selective and cautious. At no postfloor stage can a body of procedures be found that amounts to a strong and irrevocable commitment by the chamber to members of committees.

Second, the body of rules and precedents in which this selective delegation occurs, appears to be the product of expectations or instances of abuses by conference committees in the realm of distributive politics. While this evidence is impressionistic, we can confidently reject the opposite view—that postfloor procedures are commitments to restrictive procedures for the purpose of enforcing gains from trade.

Third, the overall lack of commitment to procommittee postfloor procedures, as well as bits and pieces of precedents and rulings, is consistent with at least one of the postulates underlying informational models. Postfloor procedures are majoritarian institutions.

To reiterate, however, nothing is intended to be definitive thus far. To supplement historical and qualitative analysis, we also need to examine contemporary and quantitative evidence that moves beyond assumptions and addresses more directly the empirical implications of distributive and informational theories. This section has provided some insights regarding the development and evolution of postfloor procedures, but it has been largely silent about how these procedures are employed today. In the remainder of the chapter we seek to learn whether the legislative organization of postfloor procedures—which appears to be majoritarian and informational in conception—is majoritarian and informational in practice.

Hypotheses

Distributive and informational predictions about legislative activity follow fairly directly from the respective research traditions. In no small part this is due to Shepsle and Weingast's brave statement of what, for present purposes,

---

29. Discharge is procedurally more difficult in the Senate than in the House according to Bach.

serves as a maintained hypothesis for empirical analysis. Specifically, while they agreed that institutions exist for some chamber control of conferees, they asserted that choice of postfloor procedures "is largely (though not exclusively) a *committee* matter" (Shepsle and Weingast 1987b, 940). This, in turn, supports the conclusion that the strict procedural assumptions of the ex post veto theory are adequate as a "stylized" description of postfloor processes. In terms of the if-*p*-then-*q* logical construction, the ex post veto rejoinder is tantamount to an admission that *p* is strictly false. However, the claim is that the model has not really been refuted since congressional procedure is nevertheless as if *p* were true.[30] Fortunately, this argument is amenable to empirical analysis. Three hypotheses follow from the ex post veto model and the subsequent claim that choice of postfloor procedures "is largely . . . a *committee* matter." They pertain to three empirical questions. What legislation goes to conference? Who goes to conference? What is the postfloor sequence of events?

HYPOTHESIS 1: DISTRIBUTIVE LEGISLATION. *Bills that go to conference will tend to be highly distributive, since opportunities for gains from trade are greatest on such bills.*

HYPOTHESIS 2: HOMOGENEOUS HIGH DEMANDERS. *Homogeneous high-demand legislators will be advantaged in the choice of who goes to conference.*

HYPOTHESIS 3: POSTFLOOR EQUILIBRIUM PATH. *Postfloor events will consist of perfunctory appointment of conferees, minimal monitoring by the parent chamber, a conference report that confers distributive benefits to committees, and a single affirmative vote on conference reports.*

Although informational theories are less explicit in their implications for postfloor behavior than distributive theories, three informational hypotheses parallel Hypotheses 1–3 above and are consistent with the informational theories reviewed in chapter 3 and the Majoritarian and Uncertainty Postulates developed in chapter 1.

---

30. This argument elicits a different response. If the "institutional foundation" (condition *p*) is really only an "as if" condition—that is, if members only behave as if there exists an ex post veto, etc.—then in what sense is it "institutional"? In other words, the distributive-theoretic response to questions about assumptions does not answer the initially posed puzzle about deference to committees; it merely redefines it from a form of substantive deference (e.g., not rolling the committee via amendments) to a form of procedural deference (e.g., consenting to restrictive procedures). While self-proclaimed institutionalists often retreat to behavioralism in this manner, it is almost surely more productive to move the debate to the empirical arena than to chase vague (if not moving) concepts.

HYPOTHESIS 4: INFORMATIONAL LEGISLATION. *Bills that go to conference will tend to be those about whose consequences legislators are
uncertain and thus in need of the services of expert agents from whom the
parent chamber stands to benefit.*

HYPOTHESIS 5: SPECIALISTS AND NONOUTLIERS. *Policy experts will be
advantaged in going to conference. Controlling for "expertise effects,"
"preference effects" will be negative. That is, outlying or high-demand
preferences will reduce the likelihood of a legislator's selection as
conferee.*

HYPOTHESIS 6: NONCOMMITMENT. *Postfloor decision making will be
characterized by noncommitment to a procedural route or routine. Appointment of conferees, behavior of conferees, and the conference report
will all be subject to monitoring and alteration by the House.*

I now test these hypotheses using data from the 99th Congress, focusing
again on the House.

What Legislation Goes to Conference?

The standard how-a-bill-becomes-a-law story almost invariably contains a
conference committee stage prior to final passage in the House and Senate.
This is misleading insofar as the percentage of public laws for which a
conference committee is appointed and convened is very low. For instance, in
the 99th Congress only 10.7 percent (71 of 640) of public laws received
conference consideration, and the comparable figure for the 98th Congress is
13.6 percent (85 of 625).

Defenders of the claim that conference procedures form the institutional
foundations of committee power are quick to point out, however, that most
"major" bills pass through conference.[31] As a rough estimate of whether this
is true, as well as to assess Hypotheses 1 and 4, bill-specific data were
assembled from the 99th Congress. The three parts of the sample are summarized in figure 6.1. Part *A* consists of all measures for which a special order
was requested of, or granted by, the Rules Committee. Part *B* consists of all
bills passed by both the House and Senate and for which both houses requested and appointed conferences. (Of these 71 bills, approximately half
also belong to part *A*, thus the overlap in fig. 6.1.) Part *C* is a simple random
sample of 25 percent of all remaining bills that were reported from a standing
committee in the House.

Do most major bills go to conference? When a *major bill* is defined as

---

31. See, for example, Longley and Oleszek 1989; and Shepsle and Weingast 1987b, 940.

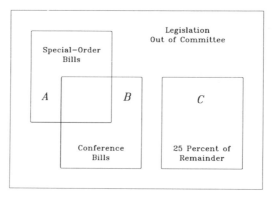

Fig. 6.1. Sample of legislation from the 99th Congress

one that is mentioned in the *Congressional Quarterly Almanac's* "Legislative Summary," the answer appears to be yes. As summarized in table 6.1, of the 43 bills so mentioned, 28 (65.1 percent) went to conference. In contrast, only 41 of 314 (13.1 percent) of nonmajor bills that passed both the House and Senate went the conference route.[32]

What inference is warranted from such a finding: that standing committees "dominate" the final stages of the process on most measures of "importance,"[33] or that parent chambers selectively choose among the range of postfloor procedures, opting for conference if and when there is an informational rationale, such as to enhance bicameral bargaining strength? Obviously, the answer must lie in additional analysis. As a first step, we can search for and assess independent effects on conference use where the predictor vari-

TABLE 6.1. Major Bills and Use of Conference Committees

| TYPE OF BILL | USE OF CONFERENCE | | TOTAL |
	No	YES	
Major	15	28	43
	(34.9)*	(65.1)	(12.0)†
Nonmajor	273	41	314
	(86.9)	(13.1)	(88.0)

*Row percentages.
†Column percentages.

32. Due to the sample properties described above, the N in table 6.1 includes all type A and B bills passed by both houses, plus four times the type C bills that passed both houses.

33. Such were the interpretations and words in Shepsle and Weingast 1987b.

TABLE 6.2. Predictors of the Use of
Conference (Probit Estimates for Single
Referrals, N = 143)

	Equation 1	Equation 2
Constant	−2.49	−2.58
	(−4.24)	(−4.67)
Laws cited	0.14	0.14
	(3.52)	(3.50)
Committee seniority	0.25	0.26
	(3.55)	(3.66)
Preference outlier	−0.10	
	(−0.69)	
Distributive content	0.95	
	(0.88)	
Major bill	0.68	0.65
	(2.27)	(2.20)
Log likelihood	−74.91	−75.54
Percentage correct	77.60	76.90

Note: Asymptotic *t*-statistics in parentheses.

ables are embodiments of formal theories and casual claims about the process. Hypothesis 1 holds that distributive bills are likely to go to conference. Hypothesis 4 holds that conference will be used when the parent chamber can benefit from bicameral negotiations by experts.

Table 6.2 presents two sets of estimates of the probability of use of the conference procedure. Most of the independent variables are familiar from chapter 5. The number of *laws cited* in a bill and average *committee seniority* are measures of specialization. The bill's *distributive content* is measured using LEGI-SLATE's keywords as described in chapter 5. The *preference-outlier* measure is the absolute difference between the committee and chamber median ADA ratings.

The specialization coefficients are positive and significant, consistent with Hypothesis 4. Committee composition seems not to have a significant effect on whether conference is the adopted postfloor procedure, nor does the distributive content of the legislation. The latter of these findings fails to support Hypothesis 1.[34] Conferences therefore seem not to be procedural devices whose primary purpose is to institutionalize gains from trade by giving committees final cracks at distinctly distributive legislation. Finally, in spite of the predicted specialization effects, the dummy variable for a major bill still has a positive

---

34. The null hypothesis of zero joint effects of the preference-outlier and distributive-content variables cannot be rejected (p = .53).

and significant bearing on use of conference committees.[35] In other words, the bivariate relationship identified in table 6.1 is not spurious.

Thus, the question raised above persists: What inference is warranted from such a finding? A partial answer is that the insignificant distributive-content coefficient casts doubt on distributive theories and that the specialization effects provide some additional corroboration for informational theories. A more complete answer, however, requires an expanded focus on conferees themselves.

Who Goes to Conference?

Although much of the historical analysis identified institutions of potential chamber control in the postfloor stages of the legislative process, perhaps it is ludicrous to entertain the hypothesis that conferee selection is a majoritarian process. After all, who appoints conferees? A majority of the House? No. In fact, an individual—the Speaker—selects conferees, usually with the consultation of other leaders of his party, most notable of whom is the chairman of the committee or subcommittee that had jurisdiction over the legislation. Furthermore, the Speaker's slate cannot directly be challenged by the House. Viewed as such, the process on which we are about to focus is as oligarchic and partisan as any key stage of the legislative process.

Viewed another way, however, majoritarianism lurks (perhaps deeply) beneath the surface of these alleged institutions of oligarchy. Granted, the Speaker chooses conferees; but who chooses the Speaker? Some would say, "the majority party." Others, including advocates of the informational perspective of legislative organization, would quickly add and stress, "subject to the approval of a House majority." Granted, the Speaker consults committee chairmen when choosing conferees; but who chooses committee chairmen? Some would say, "the Democratic Caucus." Others would again quickly add and stress, "subject to approval by a House majority."

The difficult issue here is not whether processes such as conferee selection can be traced to chamber majorities in principle. They can be. Indeed, every aspect of legislative organization in the U.S. Congress is at least indirectly majoritarian due to the majoritarianism of general parliamentary law

---

35. Although table 6.2 is confined to single referrals, comparable analysis for multiple referrals yields parallel conclusions: the laws-cited variable is positive and significant; distributive content is positive but insignificant; and the variable denoting a major bill has an independent, positive, and significant effect. Regarding the latter, a concluding caveat is probably in order. The measure can be questioned on endogeneity grounds as follows. Just as I have used the *Congressional Quarterly Almanac*'s summaries as indicators of major bills, the writers or editors of *Congressional Quarterly* may use conference activity as indicators of the newsworthiness ("majorness") of bills.

plus article 1 section 5 of the Constitution. Rather, the difficult issue is whether the postfloor institutions of chamber control identified above somehow comprise a legislative organization that enables this (perhaps deep) majoritarianism to surface in practice.

To answer the question of who goes to conference in a comprehensive but manageable fashion requires several steps. First, the distributive hypothesis on conferee selection is developed. Second, some preliminary evidence is presented that raises doubts about this specific variation of the general gains-from-trade theme. Third, the alternative, informational hypothesis is reintroduced along with a specific test that discriminates between Hypotheses 2 and 5. Finally and most significantly, results from issue-specific multivariate analyses of the determinants of conferee selection are presented.

Elaboration on Hypothesis 2: Homogeneous High-Demanders

The homogeneous high-demand hypothesis can be developed in the form of a composite sketch of distributive theories.[36] The raison d'être of legislative organization is to facilitate gains from trade. Thus, conference procedures, including the appointment of conferees, are designed so that when they are optimally employed the legislature effectively commits to or "enforces" trades. A system of "property rights" has evolved wherein conferences are "dominated" by members of standing committees that are composed of "high demanders" or "preference outliers." The "seniority rule" is an example of a property right that facilitates trades among high demanders and can therefore be expected to operate throughout many stages of the legislative game: in determining committee assignments; in selecting committee chairmen; and in designating conferees with exclusive authority to resolve bicameral differences, typically with like-minded Senate conferees. Thus, the combination of procedural restrictions and rights of homogeneous high demanders to serve on conference committees achieves the primary, gains-from-trade objective.

Aggregate Characteristics of Conferees

Of the seventy-one bills that went to conference in the 99th Congress, all but nine were for singly referred bills. For these sixty-two bills, 1,031 conferees were appointed. Table 6.3 breaks these down in terms of committee status (whether the conferee was a member of the standing committee that had jurisdiction over the bill) and authority of the conferee (whether the conferee

---

36. Quoted phrases are taken from Shepsle 1977; Shepsle and Weingast 1987a and 1987b; Weingast 1989a, 1989b, and 1989c; Weingast and Marshall 1988; and Weingast and Moran 1983.

TABLE 6.3. Committee Status and Authority of House Conferees in the 99th Congress

COMMITTEE STATUS	AUTHORITY		TOTAL
	PARTIAL	FULL	
Nonmember	181	41	222
	(81.5)*	(18.5)	(21.5)†
Member	181	628	809
	(22.4)	(77.6)	(78.5)
Total	362	669	1,031
	(35.1)	(64.9)	(100.0)

*Row percentages.
†Column percentages.

was authorized to participate over some or all portions of the bill).[37] The marginals show that more than one-fifth of the conferees (21.5 percent) were not members of the standing committee that had jurisdiction over the measure, and over one-third of the conferees (35.1 percent) did not have full authority. This may be somewhat misleading insofar as some conferees without full authority were not on committees with original jurisdiction but were from committees whose jurisdictions were touched by Senate-added provisions. Even with this caveat in mind, however, it is striking that committee members with full authority comprise only 60.9 percent (628 of 1,031) of conferees.

Table 6.4 breaks down these findings by committee and provides additional data on the number of bills from various committees that were sent to conference and the average size of the conference delegations. Cross-committee variation is evident in most columns. The only possible evidence consistent with the presumption that standing committee members "dominate" conference committees is in column 5, which gives the percentage of full authority conferees who were from the standing committee with jurisdiction. This percentage is almost always large, but it is based on a subsample of conferees and its denominator varies greatly across committees (see col. 4). Thus, overall, the claim of committee dominance of conferences awaits more convincing support.

In light of the percentage of conferees who do not have both full authority and originating-committee status, it is perhaps not surprising that seniority is not a rigidly used criterion for conferee appointments. If committee seniority confers any form of "property right" to members, it is not apparent in these

---

37. See Smith 1989, chap. 7 for a lucid discussion of "complex" conference arrangements pertaining to the authority of conferees.

TABLE 6.4. Characteristics of Conference Delegations by Committee

Standing Committee	N of Bills (1)	Average Size (2)	Percentage of Conferees from Standing Committee (3)	Percentage of Conferees with Full Authority (4)	Percentage of Full Authority Conferees from Standing Committee (5)
Agriculture	1	22.0	64	36	100
Appropriations	22	15.7	99	83	99
Armed Services	5	29.8	62	34	100
Banking	1	19.0	84	53	100
Budget	2	18.5	100	100	100
Education and Labor	8	17.4	78	43	98
Energy and Commerce	6	6.7	95	88	100
Foreign Affairs	5	17.4	63	62	100
Interior	1	7.0	100	100	100
Judiciary	1	1.0	100	100	100
Post Office	1	18.0	28	0	*
Public Works	1	14.0	100	86	100
Science and Technology	3	6.0	94	0	*
Ways and Means	5	25.2	42	63	53

*Not applicable.

data. A strict interpretation of such a right would hold that all nonmembers selected as conferees are violations of seniority, since seniority is determined at the committee level. Moreover, even within the set of committee members, fewer than 40 percent of conferees were appointed consistent with seniority. Some caveats necessarily accompany this finding, though. First, seniority is defined strictly and at the committee rather than subcommittee level.[38] Second, in spite of the rampant violations, conferees are anything but rookies. Their average committee seniority was 9.0 years, and their average house seniority was 13.8 years.[39] Notwithstanding these caveats and ambiguities, it should be clear that conferee selection is not a perfunctory, committee-dictated process. The remaining task is to find out more precisely how legislators' preferences—a necessary feature of a policy-relevant conception of "committee dominance"—fit into the conferee-selection calculus.

Preferences of Conferees

In the absence of information about the preferences of conferees, it is very difficult to assess the effects of processes—a point persuasively argued by Smith (1989, chap. 7). Perhaps standing committees are not composed of homogeneous high-demanders, as argued in chapter 4. However, if conference procedures are employed in a manner consistent with the ex post veto model, and if conference committees are composed of homogeneous high-demanders, then distributive committee power might arise at the end of the legislative game. This claim ultimately requires systematic treatment that holds constant other (informational) considerations pertaining to conferences. Before turning to such analysis, it is instructive to examine measures of preferences in the aggregate.

Paralleling the analysis in chapter 4, an easy assessment of systematic biases in conferee selection is attainable from general-ideology ratings. A simple comparison of House versus conferee mean ADA ratings reveals that, on average, conferees are only 0.16 standard deviations more liberal than the House, and they are more homogeneous by a minuscule amount.[40] The limitation of this kind of evidence, of course, is that general-ideology ratings may mask policy-relevant preferences because they lack issue-specific content. What is the "liberal" position on Commodity Futures Trading? What are "conservative" preferences on the Older Americans Act Amendments? And

---

38. An appointment is coded as a violation of seniority if any member of the committee with higher seniority was excluded from the conference committee.

39. Average seniority across all committees is 6.6 years. Average house seniority is 9.3 years.

40. Based on z-scores in which the standard deviation for the House is 1.00, the standard deviation for conferees is 0.98.

so on. To tap these bill-specific preferences, special-interest ratings were selected for each of the sixty-two single-referral bills that went to conference.[41] From all indications, conferees in the aggregate seem to share the policy predispositions of the parent chamber. The normalized conferee mean special-interest rating is −0.031, somewhat but not significantly on the low-demand side of the House mean.[42] And the normalized conferee standard deviation is 0.96, somewhat but not significantly more homogeneous than that for the House.

While these findings begin to suggest that the distributive theory is empirically untenable with respect to the choice of conferees, conclusions are still premature. It is always preferable to corroborate an alternative hypothesis rather than fail to refute a null hypothesis, and we have yet to assess directly the main informational hypothesis in this chapter.

Elaboration on Hypothesis 5: Specialists and Nonoutliers

The informational hypothesis regarding conferee selection is reducible to expertise effects and preference effects.

Expertise Effects

We have already seen that conferees tend to be committee members, and senior ones at that. To the degree that committee membership and seniority are proxy measures for specialization,[43] the first portion of Hypothesis 5 has already been corroborated with a simple bivariate analysis (table 6.3). Proponents of distributive theories would probably give a different interpretation to this relationship, however, beginning with the premise that members self-select onto committees of interest to their constituencies so they can employ procedural prerogatives to bring home the bacon. To flesh out the argument, let us ignore, for the time being, the findings in chapter 4 on the composition of standing committees and the questions surrounding committee members' rights to go to conference. Then the alternative interpretation of what I shall

---

41. Because of the substantive focus on standing committees and associated problems with measuring multiple committee attributes simultaneously, the remainder of this chapter focuses on single referrals.

42. This presumes that liberals are high-demanders, a presumption that is more tenable in the domestic than defense policy arena.

43. See n. 27 in chap. 5 for citations on the positive correlation between committee seniority and expertise generally. Steiner (1951, 174) gives a compatible, conference-specific argument: "Presumably the rationale for the appointment of senior committee members [to conference] was that a greater degree of *expertise* might be reached than would occur if appointments were made on some other basis. Moreover, the use of seniority took the question of appointment out of the speculative and favor-seeking areas."

call expertise effects goes something like this. Distributive tendencies, too, ought to be manifested in positive influences of committee membership and committee seniority on conferee selection. Membership confers a "right." Adherence to a "seniority rule" is the device for securing it (see, for example, Weingast and Marshall 1988). Thus, once again we confront a situation in which viewing the same data through different theoretical lenses causes us to see different things. And once again, we need a method by which empirical evidence, rather than theoretical argumentation, discriminates between different views.

Preference Effects

A discriminatory test is possible by focusing on the effects of preferences, independent of expertise effects (or, under the distributive interpretation, what might be called "rights effects"). Here the classes of theory offer unambiguously divergent predictions. The distributive hypothesis is that self-selection of homogeneous high demanders will characterize conference delegations, just as in many empirical accounts of assignments to standing committees. The informational hypothesis is that, controlling for expertise effects, the House will not appoint preference outliers. Accordingly, we should observe an independent negative relation between extreme policy-specific preferences and the probability of being appointed to represent the House in conference.

Data and Measures

As noted above, for the seventy-one pieces of legislation for which the 99th House and Senate appointed conferees, sixty-two (87 percent) were single referrals. The statistical objective is to discern which factors facilitate or hinder selection of a legislator as a conferee for these bills. Thus, the unit of observation is a legislator. For a variety of obvious reasons it does not suffice to confine attention to a data set composed of 434 observations.[44] To keep the analysis manageable, we consider separately four classes of legislation: education, agriculture, labor, and defense and foreign policy. For each of the n bills within any one of these classes, the data set consists figuratively of a stack of n legislatures—that is, one set of 434 legislators for each bill—yielding a total of $n \times 434$ observations.[45] The dependent variable is a dummy variable whose value is 1 if the member is a *conferee* for the given bill, and 0 otherwise. The estimation technique, as in chapter 5, is probit analysis.

---

44. The number of bills exceeds the number of standing committees. Any given member may serve on more than one committee. He or she may also serve on more than one conference committee, and so on.

45. The Speaker is excluded because he rarely votes and thus does not receive ratings by interest groups.

Expertise effects are estimated using three predictor variables: a dummy variable, *committee,* that equals 1 if the member serves on the committee that had jurisdiction over the bill and 0 otherwise; *committee seniority,* defined as the member's number of years of consecutive service on the committee with jurisdiction and 0 otherwise; and *House seniority,* defined as the member's number of years served in the House. The coefficient for House seniority can be thought of as an estimate of the effect of general legislative expertise, that is, legislative experience independent of the committee's jurisdiction. The coefficients for the committee dummy variable and committee seniority are estimates of the effect of jurisdiction-specific expertise. The coefficient for committee membership may be regarded as the fixed committee effect, while the coefficient for committee seniority gives the marginal effect of a year of committee service. These three variables are highly collinear and thus can be expected to yield somewhat unstable coefficients. Nevertheless, Hypothesis 5 requires at minimum that their joint effects should be positive and significant.

Preference effects are estimated using from two to four variables, depending upon the policy domain under consideration. Some policy areas, such as agriculture and national defense, have readily identifiable high-demand positions, in which case the direction of preference outliers is relevant. For these issues, special-interest ratings, such as those of the National Farmers' Union (NFU) and American Security Council (ASC), respectively, are normalized and employed. The measure of *high demand* is the z-score of the special-interest rating: legislator i with rating x_i has a normalized rating $z_i = (x_i - \bar{x})/s_x$. For other issues, such as labor, it is more sensible to assess whether preference outliers at both ends of the spectrum are treated systematically differently than moderates. Thus, equations also include a variable, *preference outlier,* that is the absolute value of the normalized special-interest rating.

Finally, to discern whether different preference effects occur for legislators off and on the committee, we also estimate the independent impact of committee preferences with the interactive variables *committee $\times$ high demand* and *committee $\times$ preference outlier.*[46]

To reiterate, the preference effects are crucial for empirically differentiating between Hypotheses 2 and 5 or, more broadly, between the distributive and informational theories. Distributive theories imply positive coefficients on these variables: at the margin, high-demanders and/or bipolar preference outliers should be favored in the appointment of conference delegations.

---

46. To assess the robustness of the estimates obtained, supplementary analysis included variables such as party and electoral margin. Due to their theoretical insignificance (with respect to the theories under consideration, that is) and statistical insignificance, however, these results are not presented. Still, advocates of the conference committee analog of the procedures-as-partisan-steamrollers hypothesis should know that, controlling for expertise and preference effects, Democrats are not advantaged in going to conference. See appendix D.

Informational theories, in contrast, hold that these effects should be negative: apart from the House's desire to have experts to conduct bicameral negotiations, conferees' preferences should more closely reflect those of the House's median voter.

Results

Specific probit results are presented in appendix D, and the text and tables that follow are based on, and frequently refer to, findings in the appendix. Overall, the analysis is similar to that for restrictive rules in chapter 5. For a given class of legislation, cell entries in the tables that follow give the estimated probability that a hypothetical legislator with the given attributes will be chosen to represent his or her chamber in conference. Three variables are of substantive interest. First, is the member on the committee that proposed the bill? This determines whether the left or right half of a given table is relevant. Second, is the member a junior or senior legislator? For noncommittee members, a junior member is one whose House seniority is one standard deviation below average, and a senior member is one whose House seniority is one standard deviation above average. For committee members, the definitions are analogous with respect to committee seniority. Third, are the member's preferences moderate or extreme with respect to the House average? An outlier (or high demander) is defined as one whose preference-outlier (or high-demand) value is a standard deviation above average, while a nonoutlier (low demander) is one whose rating is one standard deviation less than the mean.[47]

The eight estimated probabilities in each of the tables bear directly on Hypotheses 2 and 5 as follows. First, we should observe committee effects regardless of the hypothesis. That is, the probability in a given committee cell should always be greater than the probability in the corresponding noncommittee cell. Second, the within-group comparisons begin to discriminate between hypotheses. Expertise effects, consistent with Hypothesis 5, are manifested by "senior" probabilities that are greater than "junior" probabilities, holding committee status and preferences constant. Both hypotheses predict these effects among committee members, albeit for different reasons—informational theories because experience is associated with expertise; distributive theories because seniority is seen as conferring rights. However, since the scope of rights in distributive theories is explicitly confined to committee members, these effects are not anticipated off the committee. The informational perspective, in contrast, holds that expertise is valued and thus

---

47. Because the high-demand and preference-outlier variables had different effects for different classes of legislation—sometimes significant and sometimes not—the variable used in the computation of probabilities reported in the tables below differs across types of bills. See appendix D for details.

TABLE 6.5.   Expertise and Preference Effects on
Education Bills

| | EXPERTISE | | | |
| | OFF COMMITTEE | | ON COMMITTEE | |
PREFERENCE	JUNIOR	SENIOR	JUNIOR	SENIOR
Nonoutlier	.004	.016	.354	.653
Outlier	.002	.008	.308	.605

will be tapped even if the expertise happens to be of an extrajurisdictional sort. Finally and most discriminately, preference effects should be observed in the columns of the tables. The distributive hypothesis implies that probabilities for outliers (or high demanders) will be greater than that for nonoutliers (or low demanders), while the informational hypothesis implies the opposite.

Education Conferences
Three education bills went to conference during the 99th Congress: one on school lunch and child nutrition, one on protection of handicapped children, and one amending the Higher Education Act. For each of these, the Education and Labor Committee had jurisdiction. The committee was the source of about 65 percent of conferees—somewhat below the House average. In this respect, these data provide a good opportunity to identify preference effects both on and off the committee. Measures of preferences are based on ratings of the National Education Association (NEA).

Expertise effects were always positive and jointly significant in the probit equations, and the magnitude of these effects is evident in table 6.5. Although probabilities are small, a senior noncommittee member has a four times greater likelihood of being selected conferee than does a junior noncommittee member. For comparable committee members the difference is substantial, too, and at higher probabilities. For nonoutliers, the probability goes from .354 for junior members to .653 for senior members. The corresponding probabilities for outliers are .308 and .605.

Preference effects on selection of education conferees are weaker than expertise effects but are still noticeably negative. Several details are noteworthy. First, the preference effect is not a high-demand effect but rather an outlier effect. That is, pro- or anti-education positions per se do not matter, but the bipolar extremity of such positions does matter.[48] Second, the statis-

---

48. Appendix D describes the likelihood ratio tests and presents the estimates that support this claim.

TABLE 6.6.   Expertise and Preference Effects on
Agriculture Bills

| | EXPERTISE | | | |
| | OFF COMMITTEE | | ON COMMITTEE | |
PREFERENCE	JUNIOR	SENIOR	JUNIOR	SENIOR
Nonoutlier	.002	.008	.144	.304
Outlier	.001	.005	.088	.211

tically significant coefficient in the equation was that for all members (the preference-outlier variable), not just committee members (committee × preference outlier). The substantive implication of this finding is that when the House chooses to go beyond the standing committee for conferees—as happened for over one-third of the education conferees—it goes neither for high demanders nor preference outliers but rather for moderates. Thus, education bills provide support for the informational hypothesis.[49]

Agriculture Conferences
Four agriculture bills originating from three different committees went to conference in the 99th Congress: a regular and a supplemental appropriations bill (from Appropriations), a futures trading and grain quality improvement act (from Agriculture), and a family farmer bankruptcy act (from Judiciary). The agriculture bills were considered in conference by a total of fifty-eight members, fifty (86 percent) of whom were members of the originating committee.

As with the education estimates, the agriculture estimates uncovered the predicted positive expertise effects. These are clearly manifested in row comparisons in table 6.6.

The preference effects for agriculture conferee selection are best interpreted in the context of prior substantive literature. Agriculture policy is often regarded as the quintessential case of logrolling. If any class of federal programs is aptly characterized as one in which intense minorities use (or abuse) the committee system to reap concentrated and disproportionate benefits while dispersing costs to the broader collectivity, this is it. Accordingly, these bills provide an ideal opportunity to identify high-demand effects. Yet, it proved impossible to reject the null hypothesis of zero joint effects of the variables committee × high demand and high demand. In other words, high demanders

---

49. The findings strongly refute a bipolar-outlier hypothesis. However, Hypothesis 2 was stated in terms of homogeneous (or one-sided) outliers. Thus, the findings simply fail to corroborate the distributive hypothesis.

for agriculture benefits do not have a net comparative advantage in going to conference.

On the other hand an identical statistical test for outlier effects—namely, a test of the null hypothesis that the coefficients for committee × preference outlier and preference outlier are zero—yielded a positive result. These two coefficients were jointly significant. Of greater substantive interest is their negative sign. That is, holding expertise effects constant, the greater is the deviation (in either direction) of a legislator's agricultural preferences from the House mean, the less likely he or she is to go to conference. This is exactly what the column comparisons in table 6.6 show. For example, in the case of senior committee members, nonoutliers stand a .304 chance of conferee selection. For outliers, however, the probability drops to .221.

In summary, as with the education findings, these too fail to support the homogeneous high-demand hypothesis yet are consistent with the specialization-nonoutlier hypothesis. Net of expertise considerations, the system works against high-demanders and preference outliers in the resolution of bicameral disputes in this classical logrolling policy domain.

Labor Conferences

Seven labor bills reached conference in the 99th Congress. Two were appropriations bills reported by the Appropriations Committee. One was a federal employee retirement and foreign service pension act proposed by the Post Office and Civil Service Committee. Four originated from the Education and Labor Committee: Rehabilitation Act amendments, a domestic volunteer service act, a human services and child development reauthorization, and a fair labor standards and employee compensation act. Members of the originating committees comprised 76 percent of conferees, but only about half of the conferees had full authority over their bills. Expertise effects are measured and calculated in the usual way. Preference effects are based on ratings from the AFL-CIO's Committee on Political Education (COPE).

Expertise effects were again strong, positive, and statistically significant. They are also obvious in table 6.7.

TABLE 6.7. Expertise and Preference Effects on Labor Bills

| | EXPERTISE | | | |
| | OFF COMMITTEE | | ON COMMITTEE | |
PREFERENCE	JUNIOR	SENIOR	JUNIOR	SENIOR
Nonoutlier	.006	.015	.164	.419
Outlier	.006	.015	.263	.556

Labor, like agriculture, is a policy domain in which high-demanders may attempt to exploit various aspects of the committee system and legislative procedure to secure high levels of policy benefits. Also like Agriculture, the preference effects of the demand measures—committee × high demand and high demand—were not significantly different from zero. That is, high demanders for prolabor legislation have no special advantage in going to conference. This finding, too, supports Hypothesis 5 and fails to support Hypothesis 2.

In contrast to previous findings, however, outlier effects on labor bills are significant and positive at the committee level and nonexistent off the committee. A proper substantive interpretation of this result requires simultaneous consideration of the absence of high-demand effects and presence of strong expertise effects. Bipolar preference outliers have a marginal advantage in conferee selection on labor issues, but since high demanders possess no such advantage, the basis for the outliers' advantage must be that outliers are balanced from opposite ends of the labor spectrum. In other words, conferee selection on labor legislation appears to be a process of tolerance on the part of the House of offsetting outliers among its conferees. Combined with the strong expertise effects of committee seniority and the insignificance of the outlier effect off the committee (the weak and insignificant coefficient of the preference-outlier variable), this is further supportive of the interpretation that the House permits outlying tendencies only among heterogeneous labor specialists.

No existing theory of conferee selection—informational or otherwise—predicts that conferees will be heterogeneous outlier specialists. However, the results on labor legislation can be viewed as doing three things: providing further refutation of the homogeneous portion of Hypothesis 2, providing further corroboration of the specialization portion of Hypothesis 5, and identifying a previously undetected empirical regularity worth pursuing—a pattern of heterogeneous outliers among conferees for labor legislation.

Defense and Foreign Policy Conferences

The final class of legislation includes the largest number and most diverse set of bills. Thirteen defense and foreign policy bills reached conference, having originated in either the Armed Services Committee (five bills), the Appropriations Committee (three bills), or the Foreign Affairs Committee (five bills). These range from Department of Defense reorganization and reauthorization bills, to foreign relations authorizations, military construction bills, and Overseas Private Investment Corporation amendments. Roughly 28 percent of the 318 conferees for these bills were not members of the originating committee, but of these noncommittee conferees none were granted full authority over the bill in conference. The estimation procedure paralleled that for education,

TABLE 6.8.   Expertise and Preference Effects on Defense and Foreign Policy Bills

	EXPERTISE			
	OFF COMMITTEE		ON COMMITTEE	
PREFERENCE	JUNIOR	SENIOR	JUNIOR	SENIOR
Low Demander	.011	.023	.221	.499
High Demander	.008	.017	.253	.541

agriculture, and labor legislation, except that preference measures are based on ratings of the American Security Council (ASC).

As always, expertise effects are strong and positive. In this instance each of the three variables—the committee dummy, committee seniority, and House seniority—was individually significant as well. Thus, table 6.8 shows sharp increases in probability associated with committee membership and seniority.

Unlike the results for the three previous types of bills, defense and foreign policy analysis failed to identify significant outlier effects but did uncover what, upon first reflection, seems to be significant high-demand effects. The coefficients for the relevant variables—committee × high demand and high demand—were significant but of opposite signs, the former positive and the latter negative. Thus, probability computations in this instance are especially important in sorting out net preference effects.[50] Table 6.8 shows a negative preference effect among noncommittee members and essentially no preference effect among committee members. In other words, for committee members the two opposite-signed and roughly equal-sized coefficients cancel out.

Since these findings are based on a diverse set of bills and are unique in their inability to confirm all portions of the informational hypothesis, it may be worthwhile to question whether something is peculiarly particularistic about defense policy. Can the ex post veto theory be rescued by gun-barrel politics? To see, we disaggregate this class of bills and perform comparable committee-by-committee analyses.

Defense Appropriations. Separate analysis of the three defense appropriations bills shows that almost all of the explained variation was attributable to the committee dummy variable and the preference-outlier variable. However, even in the presence of numerical dominance by a standing committee, there is an independent and significant preference effect. Moreover, as shown in

---

50. In the case of committee members, the positive coefficient for committee × high demand and the negative coefficient for high demand enter into the estimated probabilities.

TABLE 6.9. Expertise and Preference Effects
on Defense Appropriations Bills

| | EXPERTISE | |
PREFERENCE	OFF COMMITTEE	ON COMMITTEE
Nonoutlier	.001	.535
Outlier	.0003	.390

table 6.9, the effect is negative. The more extreme are legislators' preferences (again, on either side of the defense spectrum), the less likely they are to go to conference. The probability calculations indicate that a nonoutlying committee member has a .535 chance of assignment; in contrast, an outlying committee member's chance drops to .390. Thus, defense appropriations bills are consistent with Hypothesis 5.[51]

Armed Services. The specific results for Armed Services legislation that went to conference are revealing in several respects. First, from the distributive perspective, recall that this was the *sole* standing committee that lived up to the stylized depiction of congressional committees as homogeneous high demanders. It is therefore a good prospect for discovering a heretofore undiscovered positive high-demand effect in keeping with Hypothesis 2. Second, from an informational perspective, it is also a plausible committee in which to search for the conference committee analog to the Exceptional-Outlier Prediction. The House may rationally permit homogeneous outliers to occupy privileged positions (such as on standing committees or in conference) if such members have extraordinary talents (such as the ability to specialize at relatively low cost or the ability to negotiate more effectively due to their acquired expertise). Can the data speak to these possibilities?

The expertise effects for Armed Services bills are highly significant and evident in table 6.10. The committee seniority coefficient, in particular, is greater and more significant than any discovered thus far, and the positive but somewhat less than significant coefficient for House seniority indicates that the preponderance of expertise effects are committee specific. The expertise effects yielded by the probability computations are strong especially on the committee where a move from a junior to senior member more than doubles the probability of conferee assignment. Indisputably, experience on Armed Services counts when it comes to appointing House delegates to conference.

The preference effects for Armed Services are also quite clear. Recall that defense and foreign policy results are unique in their absence of outlier effects. Indeed, Armed Services bills are the subset within the subset that

---

51. In keeping with the pattern above, the coefficient for the high-demand variable was insignificant. Hypothesis 2, accordingly, is not supported.

account for this anomaly. Outlier effects are insignificant, while high-demand effects are significant with opposite sign coefficients for high-demand and committee × high-demand. When quantified via probability calculations, however, the preference effects are either negative (in the case of noncommittee members) or essentially zero (in the case of committee members). In other words, the potential support for a positive high-demand effect for Armed Services bills is not realized. The two opposite-sign coefficients cancel out.

Inferences drawn with respect to Hypothesis 2 are therefore straightforward: the results fail to confirm it. In the case of Hypothesis 5, however, unqualified corroboration is not possible since the predicted negative preference effects are manifested only at the noncommittee level (where the probabilities are very small). The best that can be said is that juxtaposing the exceptionally strong expertise effects with the negative-to-zero preference effects lends some credence to the notion of specialization as an occasional justification for outliers in the spirit of the Exceptional-Outlier Prediction. This prediction has not been the focus of this analysis, however, and the conjecture therefore requires additional analysis before firm conclusions can be drawn.

Foreign Affairs. Estimates for the Foreign Affairs bills bring this stage of the analysis to a confirmatory conclusion. The expertise effects are apparent in all respects. Table 6.4 showed that Foreign Affairs conference delegations are, on average, composed of 37 percent noncommittee members. The strength and significance of House seniority in the probit estimates suggest when outsiders are called in, they tend to be senior members of the House. High-demand effects, which appeared potentially positive for defense and foreign policy bills overall, are nonexistent on Foreign Affairs bills. The outlier effect, in contrast, proved significant on the committee but no different from zero overall. The corresponding probability estimates are given in table 6.11. The expertise effects are very strong. The preference effects are negligible for noncommittee members and mildly negative for committee members. So once again, the homogeneous high-demand hypothesis is not supported, while the specialization-nonoutlier hypothesis is supported.

TABLE 6.10. Expertise and Preference Effects on Armed Services Bills

	EXPERTISE			
	OFF COMMITTEE		ON COMMITTEE	
PREFERENCE	JUNIOR	SENIOR	JUNIOR	SENIOR
Low-Demander	.022	.031	.209	.566
High-Demander	.014	.020	.220	.581

TABLE 6.11. Expertise and Preference Effects on
Foreign Affairs Bills

| | EXPERTISE | | | |
| | OFF COMMITTEE | | ON COMMITTEE | |
PREFERENCE	JUNIOR	SENIOR	JUNIOR	SENIOR
Nonoutlier	.006	.025	.125	.453
Outlier	.007	.027	.086	.370

In conclusion, Hypothesis 5—not Hypothesis 2—answers the question. Who goes to conference? Specialists and nonoutliers.

What Paths Does the Legislation Take?

The final pair of hypotheses—Hypotheses 3 and 6—differentiate between distributive and informational theories in terms of the existence of something approximating an equilibrium path (implicit in distributive theories) or the reluctance or inability of the parent chamber to commit to procommittee procedures (explicit in informational theories). The test of these hypotheses consists of tracing conference bills through their final stages to see whether the path that bills take through conference can somehow resurrect the as-if-p portion of the distributive argument. In other words, does it seem as if the choice of postfloor procedures "is largely . . . a *committee* matter"?[52] This exercise is motivated by a common dialogue between antagonists and defenders of formal theories.

> Antagonist: If committees are powerful and the ex post veto is the foundation of committee power, then why do we rarely observe ex post vetoes?

> Defender: Because in equilibrium we expect not to see them. Ex post vetoes occur only *off* the equilibrium path. Thus, absence of the use of the veto is not evidence against its effectiveness.

> Antagonist: Then what *is* evidence against its effectiveness?

This section is based on the following logic. If the absence of exercises of the ex post veto is either not regarded as evidence or, more boldly still, regarded as confirmatory evidence according to defenders' equilibrium-path reasoning, then at minimum there should be evidence of the existence of a well-traveled equilibrium path. If conference bills complete their journey to

---

52. Shepsle and Weingast 1987b, 940; italics in original.

passage in a manner consistent with the assumptions of the distributive model and Hypothesis 3, then perhaps we should continue to entertain the validity of the model. Do bills that go to conference go straight to conference without attempts to use other procedures and without snags in terms of appointing conferees? Do conferees have free rein once the conference is convened? Do bicameral committee-dominated coconspirators in conference typically succeed in coming to agreement? If not, is their ostensible inability to reach an agreement indicative of an ex post veto? Finally, are their reports always voted up-or-down as a whole and without reconsideration? It is easy to answer these questions but difficult to say definitively what the answers mean. We begin with answers and move on to interpretations.

Answers

How easily do bills begin the conference trip? The aggregate legislative history of conference legislation is presented in figure 6.2. The main road goes down the middle of the figure; detours are graphed on the right side of the road; and stop signs denote terminal points prior to enactment into law. A simple glance at the figure shows that a journey through conference can be a long haul. The preponderance of public laws (640) never went to conference. Moreover, of the 71 bills on which most of the quantitative analysis focused, 25 began their postfloor journey not by going directly to conference but rather by being "messaged" back across the rotunda in the process of amendments between the chambers.[53] These all returned to the main path.[54] More detours followed, however. Nineteen of the bills were temporarily bumped off the road prior to the convening of conference. These include conference appointments via special orders or roll calls (2 bills), instructions issued by the House prior to conference (6), and adjustments in the conference slate after its initial appointment (11). Thus, many bills that go to conference do not go straight and effortlessly to conference.

How free are conferences? The legislative histories from the 99th Congress show that instructions can be issued during conference (1 bill), additional conferees can be added while a conference is in progress (3), entirely new conferences can be appointed (4), bills can die in conference (3), or they

---

53. I expected that most of these were appropriations or taxation bills in which the first and sole stage of amendments between the chambers was merely a courtesy of the Senate in allowing the House, as originator of money bills, to ask for a conference. I was wrong. Only one of the twenty-five was an appropriations bill, and only three were tax bills. The remaining bills were distributed fairly evenly across committees.

54. This may suggest that amendments between the chambers are a temporary diversion, but they are not. Many of the 978 bills used amendments between the chambers as the sole postfloor procedure.

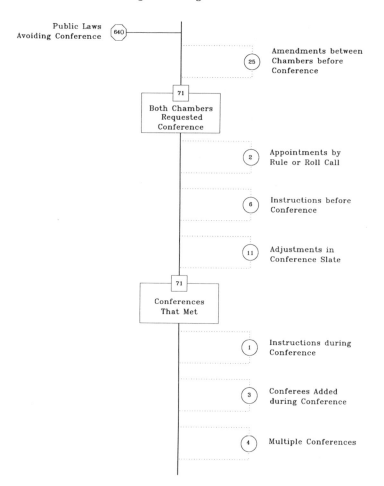

Fig. 6.2. Paths of legislation through conference in the 99th Congress

can be stalled and subsequently incorporated into other measures (2). Thus, once a conference convenes, it seems unlikely that the House ignores the performance of its conferees.

What is the nature of conference reports? Occasionally there are reports in disagreement (3 bills);[55] often there are extenuating circumstances that make it desirable for a special order to govern consideration of the report (18); often the legislation ends up being amended or recommitted (18); and occa-

---

55. LEGI-SLATE does not identify reports in *technical* disagreement, so if anything these results overstate the ability of conferees to agree as well as the indivisibility of conference reports. See Bach 1984 for details on reporting in true versus technical disagreement.

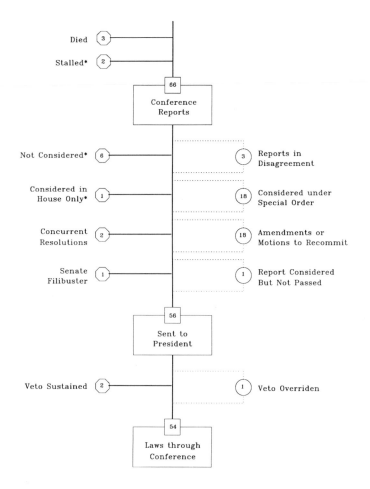

Died ③
Stalled* ②

66
Conference
Reports

Not Considered* ⑥ ── ③ Reports in Disagreement

Considered in House Only* ① ── ⑱ Considered under Special Order

Concurrent Resolutions ② ── ⑱ Amendments or Motions to Recommit

Senate Filibuster ① ── ① Report Considered But Not Passed

56
Sent to President

Veto Sustained ② ── ① Veto Overriden

54
Laws through Conference

* Subsequently incorporated into continuing resolution

sionally a conference report is defeated on the floor (1). Also, a handful do not make it to the president, albeit for idiosyncratic reasons. In some cases reports were not directly considered by both houses (7). The reason, however, is that they were bundled into a continuing resolution that did attain final passage. Concurrent (budget) resolutions are exclusively congressional documents and therefore do not require presidential action (2). Bills may also die in the other chamber, for example, from a filibuster in the Senate (1). Finally, (and outside existing congressional models), the president can and does put some kinks into the process through vetoes that are sustained (2) or overridden (1).

Interpretations

Some of these diversions from the equilibrium path are surely more significant than others, but unfortunately we have no straightforward methods for measuring their significance. What, then, do these findings mean?

A very strong view is that this legislative history illustrates the absurdity of perfect-information models. Strictly, any such model implies that deviations from the equilibrium path ought not to occur: no vetoes, no deadly filibusters, no defeated conference reports, and no detours either. Yet, of the 54 bills (of 978 total) that took the conference route in becoming law, only 8 (14.8 percent of 54, 0.8 percent of 978) never strayed from the path.

The strong view is too strong, though, because it takes the ex post veto theory in particular, and perfect-information theories in general, too literally. A moderate view is that the findings question the notion of a distributive-theoretic equilibrium path (Hypothesis 3) and support the hypothesis that the parent chamber does not commit systematically to procommittee postfloor procedures (Hypothesis 6). Having given the moderate view, however, I hasten to add that reasonable people will have reasonable and different responses to these empirical idiosyncrasies. Consider two likely ones: stacking assumptions, and conducting alternative tests that focus on explaining the variation.

Stacking Assumptions
We have already seen how theoretical disputes about the empirical plausibility of formal assumptions in models give rise to exchanges in which proponents of a model extend their argument by adding conditions to it. In the present discussion, the issue has been: Are congressional procedures and practices formulated as if committees had a credible ex post veto? One argument is that they are not, because alternative procedures exist. A counterargument is that if alternative procedures are costly to employ (call this condition o), then it is as if committees had an ex post veto (condition as-if p), in which case they are powerful (consequent q). Thus,

$$o \rightarrow \text{as-if } p \rightarrow q.$$

Next it is asserted that alternative procedures are costly, and the debate iterates. First, the empirical plausibility of the new "stacked" condition is questioned. Alternative procedures are not costly to employ; thus condition o is empirically false, too. Next, another as-if resurrecting condition is advanced. If committees substantially determine who goes to conference (condition n), then it is as if alternative procedures are costly, then it is as if committees had an ex post veto, in which case they are powerful. Symbolically:

$$n \rightarrow \text{as-if } o \rightarrow \text{as-if } p \rightarrow q.$$

The persistence of defenders of the ex post veto model is most impressive in this dialogue. However, the dialogue seems destined to become an instance of reductio ad absurdum rather than to lead to truths about postfloor processes. Surely better responses exist.

Conducting Alternative Tests
One better response is to elevate the argument from a relatively subjective dispute about empirical plausibility of (stacked) formal assumptions to a level of empirical analysis that focuses on predictions. This is precisely what most of this chapter has done. However, while the preceding analysis serves as a foundation for the relatively confident conclusions in the next section, it has not yet resolved the issue in the present section: What do we infer from idiosyncrasies in the use of conference procedures? An answer must lie in new theories and additional data analysis that seek to explain variation in the use of postfloor procedures. Other than to identify in figure 6.2 that there is plenty to explain, this approach has not been taken by advocates of either distributive or informational theories. Thus, we lack knowledge not only about general patterns of postfloor paths of legislation but also about specific instances of postfloor decision making.[56] Some specifics follow.

A Tale of Two Agriculture Bills

Uncertainties and ambiguities about postfloor paths of legislation seem to pose problems whose solutions require a mixed, inductive-deductive approach. That is, rather than rushing into the production of new theories, it seems preferable to supplement systematic quantitative findings with case studies conducted with the broad theoretical issues and empirical findings in mind.[57] Before concluding the chapter, I offer two cases that clarify and underscore some of the points made in the quantitative analysis.

---

56. Longley and Oleszek 1989 is a major exception. See especially their chap. 11.

57. This, for example, was the approach in an early response to the ex post veto model (Krehbiel 1987b), albeit without the benefit of either information models or empirical results such as those reported above. Interestingly, Shepsle and Weingast included in their rejoinder a section entitled "Imperfect and Incomplete Information," in which they "warn the reader, however, that models of asymmetric or imperfect information existing in the literature are extremely delicate, fragile and specialized" (1987b, 938–39). While clairvoyant, the section was orthogonal to the

Close and keen observers of bicameral politics have documented dozens of detailed instances of postfloor legislative decision making. Longley and Oleszek (1989), for instance, give accounts of such a vast array of legislative histories that one is inclined to conclude that generalization about postfloor politics is difficult if not impossible. The objective of this section is to suggest that even in the face of behavioral and procedural diversity, generalization is possible. The general theme is (not coincidentally) the title of this chapter: chamber control and postfloor procedures.

Case 1: CCC Supplemental

The Commodity Credit Corporation (CCC) is an agency in the Agriculture Department that distributes price- and income-support benefits to farmers. In 1986, it ran out of money. H.J.Res. 534 was the second supplemental appropriation for the CCC that was passed during the fiscal year in addition to the $13.3 billion included in the fiscal 1986 continuing resolution. The House passed its version on February 26, by a 321 to 86 vote. The Senate followed suit with a voice vote on March 5. Before its final vote, however, the Senate stripped the House's provision stipulating that crop insurance and conservation reserve programs be funded separately from the general CCC account.

Conferences were appointed by both houses to resolve bicameral differences. The House conference delegation was anomalous with respect to the patterns of appointees discovered and reported above. All thirteen conferees were members of the Appropriations Committee, and eleven of the thirteen formed the entire Appropriations Subcommittee on Agriculture. Thus, this is exactly the sort of case that composed the sample from which advocates of the ex post veto model inferred that committees "dominate" conferences and from which support for the ex post veto model was claimed. Moreover, the analysis in chapter 4 takes the claim beyond mere numerical notions of dominance by demonstrating that this particular subcommittee was a rare, statistically significant preference outlier. In light of these facts, this case should be easy to reconcile with the distributive committee-power thesis and difficult to reconcile with the chamber-control thesis. The issue is whether committees can be dominant over substantive outcomes in addition to being dominant numerically on conference delegations.

On March 12, the House filed its conference report (H.Rept. 99–493). House conferees had conceded to Senate demands to drop their provision on soil conservation programs. In return, the House conferees insisted on adding a new provision increasing spending levels for Farmers Home Administration

---

original critique, which neither mentioned nor relied upon incomplete information models. In any event, at present we are much better situated to evaluate the merit of their warning.

(FmHA) loans. On March 13, by a vote of 272 to 141, the House disposed of the conference committee's amendment in disagreement, thereby clearing the way for House approval of the report. Some additional facts caution against jumping to a committee-power conclusion, however. First, while bicameral differences were resolved in conference, conferees exceeded the scope of disagreements and therefore issued a report in technical disagreement. This provided an opportunity for parent chambers to consider certain portions of the bill individually rather than casting a single up-or-down vote. Indeed, the Senate deleted the conference-added and House-demanded FmHA funds.[58] Second, a new conference was called that proposed that FmHA loans would not exceed the amount appropriated in prior legislation for the fiscal year. The Senate and House then both accepted this pared back version of the bill.[59]

The case suggests that contrary to most of the above quantitative results, conferences may be numerically dominated by committee members who are high-demanders. The average NFU rating for House conferees was 73.3; for the full House it was 58.5. However, while such dominance may be a necessary condition for committee power, it is not sufficient. Here, chamber control happened to be exercised principally by "the other chamber," that is, the Senate. But in many other instances, the relevant chamber is that from which the committee is drawn.[60] Moreover, the institutions of chamber control include the inability (or unwillingness) of chamber majorities to commit to restrictive postfloor procedures.

Case 2: CFTC Authorization

The Commodity Futures Trading Commission (CFTC) received a three-year authorization in 1986 with the passage of H.R. 4613. In addition to the main provisions of this complex bill that pertained to the CFTC, other portions pitted the president versus Congress, House versus Senate, and members versus members over various particularistic provisions. One key issue was "leverage contracts," which are long-term installment contracts for the purchase of precious metals and other nonagriculture commodities. Unlike futures contracts, leverage contracts were traded privately at the time by only two authorized dealers: one located in Newport Beach, California, and the

---

58. The procedural richness of the case is not fully exposed here. Of several instances of parliamentary maneuvering, one of the most interesting was a motion by Senator Phil Gramm (R.–Tex.) to waive a provision of the Gramm-Rudman-Hollings Act. Gramm was opposed to his motion but made it so that a vote of sixty rather than of a simple majority would be required to accept the amendment in disagreement. See *Congressional Record,* March 13, 1986, S 2640–56.

59. *Congressional Quarterly Almanac* 1986, 161–62.

60. Several examples exist. The case of supplemental appropriations in chap. 2 is one. The case of gun control legislation in the 98th Congress is another (Krehbiel 1987b). Longley and Oleszek (1989) present still others, as do McCown (1927) and Smith (1989).

other in Fort Lauderdale, Florida. The House-passed bill limited leverage contracts to platinum, gold, and silver and—of special importance to certain sunbelt legislators—allowed other companies to enter the business after a two-year period. The Senate went one step farther by banning all leveraged transactions in two years, but final action on its bill was stalled when Senator Pete Wilson (R.–Calif.) threatened to filibuster. Eventually, he agreed to let the measure proceed after he was assured a spot on the Senate's conference delegation.

The Senate had also incorporated two additional particularistic provisions. One was an amendment sponsored by Agriculture Committee Chairman Jesse Helms (R.–N.C.) pertaining to sugar quotas. The other was a provision that would have transferred National Forest System lands to the state of Nebraska. Its main supporter was Edward Zorinsky (D.–Nebr.), ranking minority member of the Senate Agriculture Committee.

In contrast to the first case but consistent with the preponderance of empirical findings in this chapter, the House conference delegation exhibited positive expertise effects and negative preference-outlier effects. These are summarized in table 6.12. Among senior committee members, for example, a nonoutlier stood about a fifty-fifty chance of conferee selection while an outlier stood only a one-in-three chance. The preference effects are similarly negative for junior committee members and for noncommittee members.

Table 6.13 underscores some other facts that were implicit in much of the preceding quantitative analysis. In the case of a somewhat outlying committee such as Agriculture, nonoutliers from the committee tend to be sent to conference, as reflected by the drop in means in the right column. (This difference is very small, but recall that the probit estimates focused on preference effects independent of expertise effects in which case preference effects are more significant than these averages indicate.) Furthermore, when noncommittee conferees are appointed, two additional tendencies emerge. First, those members are less high-demanding than committee members overall (which, of course, is the distinguishing feature of a high-demand committee). Second, the noncommittee conferees are relatively low-demanders among the already

TABLE 6.12. Expertise and Preference Effects on the Futures Trading Bills

| | EXPERTISE | | | |
| | OFF COMMITTEE | | ON COMMITTEE | |
PREFERENCE	JUNIOR	SENIOR	JUNIOR	SENIOR
Nonoutlier	.006	.030	.112	.498
Outlier	.004	.021	.051	.336

**TABLE 6.13. Average NFU Ratings
on the Futures Trading Bill**

	OFF COMMITTEE	ON COMMITTEE
Nonconferee	57.8	66.1
Conferee	53.6	64.5

relatively low-demand noncommittee members. Thus, moving generally from
the northeast to the southwest in table 6.13—by rows, columns, or both—the
average of the measure of demand for agriculture benefits decreases.

In conference, House conferees held fast to the House's leveraged contracts provision, while Senate conferees (among whom was Senator Wilson)
were split. After only token opposition, the divided Senate delegation caved
into the unified House delegation and accepted the House's version. The
conference also dropped the Helms amendment on sugar quotas. Zorinsky, on
the other hand, fared better for the time being. Although his parkland amendment drew objections from the House side, it survived the conference and
stayed in the bill.

The conference report went before the House on October 15, and the
lengthy debate that ensued is informative in several regards. A special order
(H.Res. 590) was used to make consideration of the complex bill proceed
more smoothly. In particular, it provided that

> . . . all points of order against the conference report and against its
> consideration are hereby waived, except against any matter in the confer-
> ence report originally contained in sections 406, 504 and title VI of the
> Senate amendment to the bill, under clause 4 of rule 28. (*Congressional
> Record,* October 15, 1986, H 10104)

Clause 4 of rule 28 prohibits conferees from agreeing to include Senate
amendments in a conference report which, if offered in the House, would have
violated its standing rule on germaneness (clause 7 of rule 16). The provisions
in question were: (1) a change that would permit wheat farmers to receive
deficiency payments sooner than other grain farmers, (2) Zorinsky's Nebraska
land provision, and (3) some relatively innocuous amendments to the Federal
Meat Inspection Act. By expressly not waiving points of order on these Senate
amendments, the rule essentially invited points of order which, if offered and
upheld, would guarantee separate consideration of nongermane provisions.

The rule was passed without controversy. Immediately thereafter,
Charles Whitley (D.–N.C.) raised a point of order against, and then spoke
bitterly toward, the Zorinsky provision. Conferees are often alleged not only
to be outliers with respect to their respective chambers but also bicameral

coconspirators when it comes to ironing out their chambers' differences. The interesting facts in this case are that Whitley was Chairman of the House Agriculture Subcommittee on Forests and that his point of order had the explicit endorsement of the Chairman of the full Agriculture Committee, Kika de la Garza (*Congressional Record,* October 15, 1986, H 10105). Furthermore, an ex post veto of sorts was clearly threatened. During debate, Whitley stated, "We were unmistakably led to understand in the conference that if we did not give away this 173-acre tract of land without consideration, there would be no CFTC bill" (H 10105–6). During the crucial stages, no one spoke in favor of the provision, and Whitley's motion "to delete section 207 from the conference report" was agreed to without a roll call vote (H 10105–6).[61]

Next, the ranking Republican on the House Agriculture Committee, Representative Madigan (R.–Ill.), raised a point of order against the wheat provision. Again the initiators and chief participants were Agriculture Committee members, but now they were doing battle with each other rather than with the other chamber. Specifically, corn-state members such as Madigan opposed the wheat provision not because it was nongermane but rather because efforts in conference to incorporate corn deficiency payments in the bill failed. When members such as Representative Neal Smith (D.–Iowa) stated, "So what we are doing . . . is separating out wheat for 1986 and then leaving for another time the feed grains part which they [the administration] will oppose then, too" (*Congressional Record,* October 15, 1986, H 10107), they may as well have said, "Please let's not let this logrolling opportunity get away." In the end, however, it did get away. The motion to strike the provision was voted down 162 to 239.[62]

No point of order was offered on the meat inspection provision,[63] and House consideration of the report came to an anticlimactic conclusion. The report—minus the Zorinsky provision—was adopted without a roll call vote. Amendments between the chambers then perfunctorily ensued.

---

61. Section 207 of the conference report corresponded to section 406 of H.R. 4613 (the reference in the rule). Although no roll call vote was taken at first, pages later in the *Record* proceedings on Whitley's motion were vacated by unanimous consent as a courtesy to Representative Virginia Smith (R.–Nebr.), who wished to speak on the motion. Then a roll call vote was taken and the House affirmed its earlier decision by stripping the provision by a vote of 274 to 130.

62. Explanations for the survival of the wheat provision deserve more scrutiny than will be given here, but a fact and a conjecture can be offered. First, much of the debate centered on the budget neutrality of the wheat provision and the fact that corn deficiency payments would have vastly exceeded budget limits. Second, the wheat provision's relatively low budgetary impact plus the relatively large geographic spread of wheat farmers made the provision less particularistic than it might seem upon first consideration.

63. Speeches, all but one of which was inserted into the *Record* rather than delivered on the floor, indicated that it was not controversial.

Eventually, Zorinsky took his case to the Agriculture Secretary, from whom he extracted a promise that the land would eventually be turned over to the state in a thirty-year lease arrangement. Upon receiving the promise from the Secretary (the credibility of which is unclear), Zorinsky withdrew his threat (the credibility of which, in hindsight at least, seems small) to kill the stripped-down conference report. The Senate then passed H.R. 4613 by a voice vote. Soon thereafter the bill became law.

Implications

It bears repeating that these cases are not offered as tests or as systematic evidence in and of themselves. They are merely examples intended to make concrete the broader arguments of the chapter. Was conference used? Yes. Bills were sufficiently complex manifestations of committee work that the House evidently valued having experts represent it in bicameral negotiations. Who went to conference? Experts always; outliers sometimes (case 1) but not always (case 2). What paths did the legislation take? Winding ones, characterized by chamber monitoring and by the absence of procedural commitment in order to enhance such monitoring.

Strong incentives for logrolling undoubtedly existed. However, conference procedures seem not to have been effective vehicles for securing gains from trade, neither by ex post veto threats nor restrictive procedures for considering conference reports. Rather, postfloor procedures as a whole seem to come into play quite naturally as constraints on—not opportunities for—distributive excesses by conferees. Finally, the cases also illustrate that, even within relatively outlying conference delegations composed of members from relatively outlying committees, a little heterogeneity goes a long way. More often than not, resistance to what parent chambers agreed were excessive distributive demands came from within the committee.

Discussion

The relatively undeveloped state of formal theories of postfloor procedures and lack of a body of prior systematic empirical research have made the analysis in this chapter somewhat more laborious than that in chapters 4 and 5. A range of approaches was taken in an attempt to answer the question of whether the existence and use of postfloor procedures are principally explicable in terms of distributive considerations, or whether they have a better substantiated informational foundation. Table 6.14 summarizes the more specific issues, the methods by which answers were sought, the empirical results as they broadly pertain to informational and distributive theories, and finally whether the evidence was relatively direct or indirect in its support or refutation of informational and distributive theories.

TABLE 6.14. Summary of Focuses and Findings

	EVIDENCE		FINDINGS	
SUBSTANTIVE FOCUS	TYPE	DIRECTNESS	DISTRIBUTIVE THEORY	INFORMATIONAL THEORY
Historical development	Qualitative	Indirect	−	+
What goes to conference	Quantitative	Direct	H1: 0	H4: +
Who goes to conference	Quantitative	Direct	H2: 0	H5: +
What paths	Quantitative	Indirect	H3: −	H6: +
Chamber control	Case	Direct	−	+

Note: − = theory is refuted; 0 = neutral finding; and + = theory is supported.

The first issue was whether qualitative historical evidence (beginning with the fifteenth century Parliament and ending with the twentieth century Congress) could be brought to bear on the prevalent formal characterizations of postfloor procedures and their underlying distributive or informational rationales. Viewed historically, the rationales for, and concrete manifestations of, conference procedures seem never to have been consistent with the unique assumptions of the distributive theories. However, they do embody at least one of the fundamental postulates of informational theories: majoritarianism. Its key by-products include chamber control of conferees and the absence of commitment to restrictive postfloor procedures. This is indirect evidence with regard to both classes of theory, since the purpose was only to provide a qualitative check on formal assumptions—not to test empirical implications per se.

Guided by six hypotheses, the empirical tests began by addressing the question: What bills go to conference? Multivariate quantitative analysis showed that the small subset of measures that went to conference in the 99th Congress were not significantly more likely to be distributive bills but were significantly more likely to be bills that were products of specialization by committees. This evidence is directly supportive of the informational hypothesis and, owing to the lack of statistical significance, neutral with regard to the distributive hypothesis.

The most comprehensive and direct quantitative analysis in the chapter focused on the question: Who goes to conference? Controlling for expertise effects (which have interpretations consistent with both classes of theory), preference effects in conferee selection were never consistent with the distributive, homogeneous high-demander hypothesis but almost always consistent with the informational, specialist-nonoutlier hypothesis. Controlling for expertise, conferees are neither homogeneous nor high demanders and, when appointing them, the Speaker appears to exercise discretion to keep conferees' preferences aligned with those of the parent chamber.

Next I examined the paths taken by bills for which conference committees are the chosen postfloor procedure. The method was quantitative, and the findings were indirect. The frequency of deviations from the equilibrium path of the ex post veto model is at least weak evidence against the distributive hypothesis insofar as it casts further doubt on the "as-if" variation of the procedural assumptions on which the theory builds. Conversely, the chamber's willingness to employ a wide array of postfloor procedures is evidence of noncommitment.

Finally, the cases were somewhat more direct in their positive and negative implications for informational and distributive theories, respectively. However, rather than generalizing from an N of 2, these are better viewed as concrete illustrations of the previous, more convincing support for Hypotheses 4, 5, and 6. Each step of the analysis has limitations, of course. Nevertheless, a strong pattern is detectable in table 6.14. With a reiteration of the caveat that these findings cannot support an informational theory that does not yet exist, the conclusion is modest. It appears worthwhile to continue joint work—empirical and theoretical—aimed at bringing such a theory into existence. Little if anything in the chapter suggests that the informational foundations of legislative organization crumble during the final stages of the legislative game.

CHAPTER 7

Legislative Organization, Policy, and Performance

It is not too much to say that if all members did nothing but pursue their electoral goals, Congress would decay or collapse.

                    —David Mayhew (1974, 141)

Congress has not collapsed. Its members—most of them, anyway—have other goals besides reelection. Holding office may be essential to the achievement of these other ends, but it is only worth the effort because it allows their pursuit. Richard Fenno has identified making good public policy and earning influence and respect in Washington as the most important of these goals; Congress' institutional performance is crucial to both. Members have therefore developed and supported institutional structures and processes designed to harness the individual energies of its members to collectively important ends.

                    —Gary Jacobson (1983, 158)

The publication of seminal works in the 1970s by Mayhew, Ferejohn, Fiorina, and others marked the blossoming of a scholarly consensus whose seed had been planted decades earlier. The increasingly orthodox view has been that the U.S. Congress is organized according to distributive principles because the resulting committee-based form of legislative organization helps substantially to fulfill individual legislator's reelection goals. Whether embroidered into formal theories or woven through informal descriptions of legislative politics, this view is invariably intuitive. Indeed, the major works of distributive theory have been so persuasive that attempts to test systematically their most immediate implications—that is, their implications for legislative organization as opposed to legislative policy—have been uncommon. Why verify the obvious? Similarly, attempts to supplement or supplant the leading theory have been even less common. Why try to refute, revise, or replace theories that have achieved widespread acceptance through the labors of dozens of esteemed scholars?

As a former subscriber to the orthodox distributive view of legislatures but an increasing skeptic regarding its fit with a similarly impressive body of empirical research, I regarded it as important in this book to confront distributive-theoretic predictions pertaining to legislative organization head-on. Intuitiveness may be a nice property of theories, and surely it deters challenges from skeptics. However, positive social science is not primarily about the intuitiveness of theoretical arguments; it is about the derivation and assessment of refutable hypotheses. The appropriate standards in this context are standards of evidence rather than intuitiveness, and while distributive theories are strong on intuitiveness, they have proven here to be rather weak in terms of evidence. Theory says: committees are composed of homogeneous high-demanders. Evidence says: probably not true. Theory says: special rules are adopted mainly to facilitate gains from trade. Evidence says: false. Theory says: legislatures commit to restrictive postfloor procedures to enhance distributive committee power and cross-committee logrolling. Evidence says: false again.

Juxtaposition of theory and evidence as such is not inaccurate, but it is incomplete and thus misleading in its negativism. The more important aim of this book has been to advance an alternative, informational theory of legislative organization. To do this it was useful and ultimately constructive to refute the predictions of distributive theories. By suggesting that committees are not generally composed of homogeneous high-demanders, that the choice of rules is not a process used to capture distributive gains from trade, and that postfloor procedures are among the best available examples of the absence of procedural commitment, we not only learn of the limitations of prevalent theories but also clear the way for new and potentially better theories. The issue then becomes, can the new generation of theory predict better than the old?

As presented here, informational theory focuses on legislative organization—that is, a legislature's rules and precedents that bear directly on the allocation of resources and assignment of parliamentary rights to individual legislators or to groups of legislators. Legislatures in their primitive states are egalitarian collective choice bodies. However, over time (and usually very quickly) abstract egalitarian principles give way to concrete policy-making needs. In the research tradition of organization theory, this process is described as the evolution of a legislature as a response to ever changing and never ending "external stresses" and "internal demands" (Cooper 1977). In another compatible research tradition, it is called "institutionalization" (Polsby 1968; Hibbing 1988). In yet another but shorter line of research—namely, that employed here—it is characterized as the emergence of "asymmetries." Asymmetries in incoming legislators' talents give rise to asymmetries in their information and, ultimately, in their endogenously assigned parliamentary rights. Procedurally favored individuals may include speakers, leaders, chairmen, or bill managers. Procedurally favored groups may include ad hoc, standing, or conference committees. Regardless of one's preferred research tradition and jargon, the contemporary state of knowledge about legislatures and their development can be summarized in commonly understood terms. Considerably more is known about what assignment of parliamentary rights occurs than why. Furthermore, the inability to identify precisely the conditions under which organizational forms are adopted severely inhibits reaching a clear understanding of broader issues pertaining to legislative policies and legislative performance. What types of policy will we observe? Why? How well does the legislature perform? According to what criteria? The objective of this chapter is to address these broader issues of legislative policy and performance with the assistance of our expanding knowledge about legislative organization.

Legislative Organization

In the spirit of McConachie (1898), we began with a search for a parsimonious set of principles of legislative organization. Two postulates were offered that subsequently became the foundation for the informational perspective on legislative organization. The Majoritarian Postulate holds that objects of legislative choice in both the procedural and policy domains must be chosen by a majority of the legislature. The Uncertainty Postulate holds that legislators are often uncertain about the relationship between policies and their outcomes. The theoretical issue was whether incorporating these into formal theories of legislative choice makes a difference (relative to theories that do not embody the postulates) in terms of predictions about legislative organization. The empirical issue was whether predictions of theories based on these postulates are borne out. At both theoretical and empirical levels, the postulates were shown to be significant. Five unique predictions were identified. In each of three stages of the legislative process—the formation and composition of standing committees, the choice of bill-specific rules on the floor, and the development and use of postfloor procedures—informational theories predicted substantially better than their distributive forerunners. Table 7.1 summarizes the evidence.

The Outlier Prediction was supported in all three chapters. Although there is some evidence of self-selection on some committees, the overall composition of committees seems rarely to be significantly biased relative to the parent chamber. To the degree that committees vary in their preference-outlying attributes, the House's choice of rules used for consideration of committees' bills reflects informational principles: extreme committees are significantly less likely than moderate ones to have their bills considered under restrictive procedures. Postfloor procedures also operate against committee biases once expertise effects are controlled.

The Heterogeneity Prediction was supported in two of three chapters.[1] Almost no committees are significantly more homogeneous than their parent

---

1. It was not tested in chap. 6. Generally, blank cells in table 7.1 mean that the prediction was not relevant—not that it was not supported.

chamber, and the more heterogeneous is a committee, the greater is its likelihood of receiving restrictive rules for its bills.

The Exceptional-Outlier Prediction—though not tested directly—was supported in chapter 4 by an informational interpretation of Shepsle's (1978) seminal study on committee assignments. Similar interpretations can be given to the probit estimates in chapter 6 on the choice of conferees. Preference outliers may go to conference, but when they do, they almost invariably are senior specialists. Moreover, if they employ their expertise in a manner substantially contrary to chamber interests, the chamber has ample procedural devices to express and redress its grievances.

The Restrictive Rules Predictions received solid, across-the-board support in chapter 5. Specialization and heterogeneity are positively associated with restrictive rules, while outliers are negatively associated with restrictive rules. For this prediction, too, compatible interpretations of the results in chapter 6 can be offered. Restrictive postfloor procedures are employed often, but the level of commitment to such procedures is tenuous at best. Moreover, informational principles—and, most notably, the Majoritarian Postulate as it pertains to procedural choice—seem to dominate their use.

Finally, the Commitment Prediction was supported in the interpretation offered of the seniority system and in a more comprehensive study of postfloor procedures. Informationally efficient legislative organizations seem to be ones

TABLE 7.1. Summary of Findings

	EMPIRICAL FINDINGS		
INFORMATIONAL PREDICTION	FORMATION OF COMMITTEES	CHOICE OF RESTRICTIVE RULES	POSTFLOOR PROCEDURES
1. Preference outliers	Some self-selection Few outliers	See 4	No outliers, controlling for specialization
2. Heterogeneity of preferences	Few homogeneous committees	See 4	
3. Exceptional outliers	Reinterpretation of Shepsle's findings in terms of informational theory		See 1
4. Restrictive rules		Support for specialization, outlier, and heterogeneity hypotheses	See 5
5. Commitment	No commitment to seniority system		No commitment to postfloor procedures

in which stable expectations are fostered regarding rewards provided for legislatively useful behavior, but not ones in which the legislature commits to such rewards independent of the behavior of their recipients.

Having seen and summarized the evidence on information and legislative organization, we can now begin to interpret it in terms of legislative policy and legislative performance.

Legislative Policy

Legislative organization has both causes and consequences, and, for reasons presented in chapter 1, this study has been mainly interested in causes. Ultimately, however, the importance of legislative organization rests on its consequences. Stated more bluntly, who cares about why we observe systematic patterns in committee assignments, in complex rules governing committees' bills, and in arcane procedures for reconciling bicameral differences? What difference do these attributes of legislative organization make with regard to legislative policy? That they make some difference is implicit in the literatures on organization theory and institutionalization. However, prior to the New Institutionalism movement in legislative studies, exactly what difference they make had been a subject of continuing ambiguity. Needed were explicit theories of policy choice that could in turn form the basis for comparable analyses of procedural (or institutional) choice. Two classes of such theories have formed the foundation on which this study builds. Aided now by evidence as well as theory, we can elaborate on the relationship between legislative organization and legislative policy to reach some more precise conclusions about the latter.

A fully convincing theory of legislatures ideally should be directly corroborated at both of two levels of observation—institutions and policy. According to this high standard, this book is at best half-convincing with respect to informational theory. Consider, however, the negation of the standard. Specifically, an unconvincing theory of legislatures can be identified by refuting its predictions at either of two levels: institutions or policy. Nearly all of the predictions of distributive theories were either lacking in support or refuted at the level of institutions, and the policy implications of distributive theories are clear. Their core concepts are *particularism, universalism,* and *distributive committee power.* To reassess these in light of the current findings and to invite additional research, I state several claims that are broadly consistent with the findings of this study. The claims are deliberately strong and provocative. The hope is that if they are convincingly refuted in future research, such research will have improved our understanding of legislative policy in a manner that parallels the improved understanding of legislative organization that has come from refutation of distributive-theoretic claims here.

Particularism

Few students of American legislative politics would deny that particularism has played prominently in legislative studies. Its role has been twofold. Often it is regarded as a behavioral axiom, that is, a postulated motivation for legislative behavior. Often it is regarded as a primary policy consequence of legislative behavior, that is, an outcome of the legislative process.

> CLAIM 1. *While particularism surely plays a role in motivating legislators, it does not play a primary role. While particularism is one consequence of legislative choice, it is not the quintessential feature of legislative policy.*

Direct, systematic evidence for this claim has not been provided here. However, direct, unsystematic evidence as well as indirect, systematic evidence has been provided.

The indirect, systematic evidence is in chapters 4–6 which refute or fail to support the predictions of distributive theories about legislative organization. Many of these theories presume, directly or indirectly, that legislators maximize net district benefits and that, to do so, they bargain over particularistic policies, that is, those in which benefits are concentrated and costs are dispersed. If the most immediate empirical implications (regarding legislative organization) of such theories are not borne out or are refuted, then their more distant implications (regarding legislative policy) must be doubted as well. At the very best, if particularism is the quintessential feature of legislative policy, it would seem to be for reasons other than those provided by extant distributive theories.

The direct, unsystematic evidence is simply the roster of legislation that emerges from committee. Randomly selected from the 99th Congress are the following ten bills:

- H.R. 1239   Emergency Famine Relief and Recovery in Africa
- H.R. 1452   Refugee Assistance Extension Act
- H.R. 7   School Lunch and Child Nutrition Amendments
- H.R. 1617   National Bureau of Standards Authorization Act
- H.R. 2889   Computer Security Act
- H.R. 1460   Anti-Apartheid Act
- H.R. 512   Vietnam Veterans of America, Inc., Charter
- H.R. 2484   Judiciary and Judicial Procedure, Title 28 U.S.C., Amendment
- H.R. 3132   Law Enforcement Officers Protection Act
- H.R. 2455   Hate Crime Statistics Act

Surely most or all such bills have some distributional consequences—even those whose titles suggest the noblest of intentions. However, the claim that most or even many of them are predominantly distributive stretches the imagination. So does the prospect that such bills are somehow all parts of a grand, comprehensive, multidimensional, cross-committee logroll, held together by restrictive procedures.

Universalism

A sweeping congressional generalization that is often linked to distributive theories of legislative organization is that congressional politics is "universalistic." The institutional mechanics of the argument have been covered exhaustively above and will not be repeated here. I focus instead on the hypothesized policy product of the legislative machine: "something for everyone."

> CLAIM 2. *Depending on how universalism is defined, its existence in Congress is either devoid of policy content, trivial, or unsubstantiated.*

The literature on universalism is large and often perplexing. As Collie (1988a) notes in her recent review, much of the confusion stems from the widespread reluctance to specify what is meant by universalism. Drawing on Collie's essay, I offer and elaborate on three definitions that clarify claim 2.

DEFINITION 1. Universalism might refer to (near) unanimous roll call votes.[2] If so, then what is to be inferred from observing universalism? That everyone receives concentrated benefits from the legislation on which a unanimous vote is cast? Or that only a few high-demand legislators receive concentrated benefits, while all others are merely exercising deference? It is fundamentally impossible to tell without an explicit maintained model to guide inference. Barring such a model, this form of universalism is devoid of policy content.[3]

DEFINITION 2. Universalism might refer to the set of net beneficiaries across all bills. Because it identifies an attribute of policy, this definition is more germane to the present discussion than definition 1. But what does it rule out? Suppose that a legislator is not in this set. That is, she (or her constituents) are net losers when the consequences of all legislation are realized and tallied up. The very essence of voluntary organizations—whether political, economic, social, religious, or some combination of these—is that their individual mem-

---

2. For example, one common operational definition of universalism is any roll call vote on which greater than 90 percent of legislators voted the same way (Collie 1988b and 1989).

3. Furthermore, "For evidence of the universalistic coalition [consistent with this definition], the literature on congressional voting is, unfortunately, not the place to look" (Collie 1988a, 466).

bers reap benefits above and beyond what they could reap by acting alone. If this is not the case, then in the long term individuals will cease to join, work, or stay in the organization. Likewise, this form of universalism is, if anything, an implicit and common assumption in collective choice theories—not a refutable hypothesis that lends itself to tests that discriminate between theories. To be sure, the phenomenon exists. Defined as such, however, its existence is trivial.

DEFINITION 3. Finally, universalism might refer to the set of net beneficiaries of a single bill. This definition is neither devoid of policy content nor trivial. However, systematic empirical support for this form of universalism is either nonexistent or else corrupts the prevalent definition of distributive policies. The best candidates for existence of this form of universalism are programs that use formula allocation schemes, which, indeed, are increasingly common (Arnold 1979 and 1981). But these are hardly particularistic or distributive in the classical sense of the term. Their costs are dispersed, but so too are their benefits when the allocation includes something for everyone (or everyone's district), which usually is the case. Thus, quoting Collie again, even given this most reasonable and empirically tractable definition of universalism, "empirical support for the prevalence of universalism is awfully hard to come by" (1988a, 446).[4]

Committee Power

Two unequivocal necessary conditions for distributive committee power are pervasive in the literature: first, that committees are composed of members whose preferences diverge systematically and significantly from those of the larger legislature (i.e., committees are preference outliers), and second, that the legislature commits to restrictive procedures that assign committees unique parliamentary rights when their legislation is considered by the parent chamber (e.g., gatekeeping power, restrictive rules, an ex post veto, a single up-or-down vote on conference reports).[5] Relevant empirical findings are scattered through-

---

4. A deeper theoretical problem arises here, too. Suppose someone were to provide systematic empirical support for this form of universalism. Even so, we have no distributive theory that accounts for its existence in the classical pork barrel sense of inefficient programs, that is, programs whose social benefits are exceeded by their social costs. In fact, in the only theoretical research in which the programs may be classically inefficient, Baron (1990) proves the impossibility of universalism under specified conditions.

5. Baron and Ferejohn's models do not fall quite so neatly into this framework but nevertheless are consistent with the claim about necessary conditions. Two interpretations of their models and results can be offered. First, while the player who is recognized (and whom it is natural to interpret as a committee) receives larger payoffs than other players in equilibrium even under an open rule, ex ante payoffs are equal across all players due to random recognition. Second, if a member is designated with the "power to propose" (Baron and Ferejohn 1989b), then such a power (or right) is, in effect, a procedural restriction. The committee has an exclusive right to offer the initial proposal; in that sense, all other members' parliamentary right of recognition is denied at the first stage.

out chapters 4–6. Few standing committees seem to be composed of preference outliers. By all indications, the Congress seems unwilling, if not unable, to commit to restrictive procedures either at the first floor stage or at the postconference stage. And the probability of the House selectively employing restrictive procedures is inversely related to the degree to which legislation is distributive. Thus, if distributive committee power is widespread in Congress, it must be for reasons not specified in leading distributive theories.

CLAIM 3. *Most committee power in Congress is informational, not distributive.*

Several paths of future research might be taken at this juncture. One is to cling to the notion of distributive committee power as something real and important in the legislative process, and to seek new and better theoretical explanations for it.[6] This is not only an increasingly arduous task but also an increasingly risky investment as evidence mounts. For one thing, rigorous and complete theories in which minorities benefit at the direct expense of majorities are likely either to be difficult to develop, to rest on extremely ad hoc assumptions, or both. Almost surely they would violate the Majoritarian Postulate at the level of procedural choice[7]—a postulate that has served us well here. More important, political scientists who have studied committee power with systematic data (as opposed to case studies) seem increasingly to be persuaded that, in its distributive embodiment, distributive committee power is a misnomer if not a myth. Smith's (1989) comprehensive study surely casts doubt on the hypothesis during the postreform period.[8] Cox and McCubbins (1989) criticize the hypothesis of committee autonomy even more harshly and for the entire postwar period. Rivers and I (1988) found that the Senate Labor and Human Resources Committee gave in to the Senate's (median voter's) wishes on minimum wage legislation in 1977. Wilkerson (1989) refined this analysis and reached a comparable substantive conclusion. And finally, even the classic case studies suggest less committee power than is commonly acknowledged. For instance, the studies of agriculture reviewed in chapter 1 are replete with examples of the difficulty of the Agriculture Committee's attempts to extract levels of commodity supports above and beyond those desired by the House. Taken together, these findings caution against investing more effort in explaining distributive committee power. Such an enterprise may well turn out to be the legislative studies equivalent of *Waiting for Godot.*

Admittedly, this discussion of committee power is rather nihilistic thus far. In the absence of an alternative theory, we are at a loss to explain the fact that

6. See, for example, Campos 1990; Smith 1988; and Weingast 1989a.

7. All of the aforementioned "committee power" theories do, for example.

8. He further subdivides that period and identifies some differences between the 1970s and 1980s, but these need not concern us here.

committees are important in the legislative process—even in the so-called postreform era that some have characterized as a bad one in terms of norms such as apprenticeship and specialization (Rohde, Ornstein, and Peabody 1985). Today's legislators are stretched very thinly in terms of their committee work (Hall 1989), but they nevertheless do a great deal of committee work. Consistent with Woodrow Wilson's century-old thesis, Congress at work is still, largely, "Congress in its committee rooms" (1885, 69). As such, it seems that legislators must somehow reap nondistributive benefits from committee service.

Extrapolating from the supporting evidence for informational theory at the level of organization, the current claim is that congressmen reap significant informational benefits from committee service. If the attempt in chapter 3 to relate informational theory to various strands of empirical literature was successful, then this should not seem farfetched. All of the following are roughly consistent with claim 3: Fenno's premise that some legislators seek "good public policy," Maass's conception of the "common good," and, perhaps more conspicuously instrumental, Mayhew's discussion of "credit claiming."[9] Mayhew uses credit claiming in two ways. Surely the one that has received most frequent casual mention is distributive: voters reelect their member of Congress because she brings home the bacon. However, even Mayhew concedes that such claims are lacking in credibility when a congressman is one in 535. In contrast, when a congressman exerts enormous effort in shepherding major legislation through the Congress—including hours spent in informal negotiations, in committee hearings, defending the bill on the floor against often ill-informed (and sometimes ill-behaved) opponents, and bargaining in conference—the credibility of credit claiming is appreciably bolstered. In many respects, Fenno's (1989) biography on Senator Dan Quayle's efforts on the jobs training legislation and Quayle's subsequent electoral success provides further evidence consistent with the informational committee power hypothesis.

In summary, committee power is not a myth. It is only broadly misunderstood or misinterpreted. The essence of committee power is no different from the essence of presidential power according to Neustadt (1960). Successful committee members influence others not by wielding formal authority or by engaging in command-and-control tactics. Rather, they persuade. More specifically, committees earn the compliance of their parent chamber by convincing the chamber that what the committee wants is in the chamber's interest. In this respect, committee power is not only inherently informational but also inherently majoritarian.

---

9. Recall from chap. 3 that I am referring to the nonideological and non-normative components of Fenno's "good public policy" and Maass's "common good."

Generality

In light of a voluminous literature on the Congress following the reforms of the early 1970s, the fourth and final claim may prove to be the most controversial.[10]

> CLAIM 4. *Claims 1–3 are not unique to the postreform U.S. Congress, even though the supportive quantitative data were drawn primarily from the 1980s.*

While systematic evidence supporting claim 4 is lacking here, others have been assembling it.[11] Rather than attempt to summarize the excellent longitudinal studies of others—some of which are still in progress—I will simply emphasize that intertemporal variation in legislative organization can occur without contradicting the postulates of legislative organization or the attributes of legislative policy. For example, a given committee may wax and wane in the degree to which it is composed of preference outliers or in terms of the heterogeneity of its members' preferences. But the existence of a homogeneous outlying committee in an earlier era does not automatically disprove the informational theory; it only raises an additional opportunity to test it. For example, was this hypothetical prereform committee composed of low-cost specialists? Was its policy domain one of extreme uncertainty? Was the committee granted fewer resources than would otherwise be expected? Was its legislation less distributive than in subsequent years or less likely than other committees' bills to be considered under restrictive procedures?[12]

In this vein it is useful to establish some more precise guidelines for a study that would challenge claim 4. Suppose (as is true in many congressional studies in the 1970s and 1980s) that one observes major changes in various facets of legislative behavior and notices that they correspond with changes in legislative procedures. The strong temptation is to argue that rules changes caused the behavioral changes. Such an argument is very tricky, however. Obviously, any proper research design and empirical analysis must work around the fallacy of post hoc ergo propter hoc. In so doing, it must explicitly

---

10. See Ornstein 1975a for an early and excellent sample of this postreform Congress literature. See Shepsle 1989 for a review of the literature and an argument counter to claim 4.

11. See especially Cox and McCubbins 1989; Smith 1989; and Stewart 1990.

12. Bach and Smith (1988) and others have noted that the emergence of modified-closed, complex, or restrictive rules are primarily postreform phenomena. It should not be inferred, however, that all procedures in the prereform era were unrestrictive. An appropriate procedural focus for the prereform era would be on the use of suspension of the rules. Some qualitative evidence of the relationship between restrictive procedures generally (recognition rights, suspension of the rules, special orders) and uncertainty in the policy environment is presented in Gilligan and Krehbiel 1987.

acknowledge that changes in the rules are not exogenous but rather are conscious collective choices of legislators, most of whom expect soon to be working under the new rules. Finally, a design that properly takes institutional endogeneity into account must also pay attention not just to narrow slices of rules but rather to the entire corpus of rules. Appendix E provides a more detailed example focusing on 1970s rules changes pertaining to postfloor procedures.

Cross-sectional evidence from contemporary Congresses clearly cannot say anything definitive about the claimed artificiality of pre- and postreform differences in legislative organization and legislative policy. At a minimum, however, it seems sufficient to transfer the empirical challenge to skeptics. For the time being, then, we should entertain the proposition that the postulates of legislative organization identified in chapter 1 not only predate 1970 in the U.S. Congress but also extend to other legislatures.

Summary

To the degree that claims 1–4 survive future challenges, a dramatic midcourse correction is needed with regard to contemporary characterizations of legislative policy. The correction should abandon the view of legislatures as institutions that are overwhelmingly preoccupied with distributive politics. It should instead adopt the view of legislatures as institutions of issue-by-issue majoritarian policy-making under uncertainty. In this new, informational view, both the objectives and the achievements of legislative decision making extend well beyond the classical pork barrel.

Legislative Performance

To take the informational argument one last step—from legislative policy to legislative performance—I offer an intentionally inadequate synopsis of this study that spans assumptions, predictions, and implications. The synopsis culminates in three statements that are subsequently dissected and corrected.

The assumptions from which the informational theory was developed were that individual legislators can reap benefits from reducing uncertainty about the relationship between policies and their consequences, and that policies can be ordered on a unidimensional issue space. The set of assumptions did not include any formal characterization of political parties or leaders.

The predictions of the informational theory included several attributes of legislative organization including, most notably, committee composition and choice of procedures. Analogous, but often opposite, predictions were extracted from theories whose axiomatic base is exclusively distributive, that is, theories that focus on multidimensional pork barrel politics, capturing gains from trade, or solving the chaos problem. Predictions of the informational theory received considerable support, while analogous predictions of distributive theories were either refuted or not supported.

The implications of the informational theory may then be extracted as follows. Suppose that empirical support for a theory at the level of legislative organization constitutes implicit support for the theory at the level of legislative policy and, ultimately, at the level of legislative performance. Suppose further that reaching informed legislative-median outcomes is a valued attribute of legislative performance.[13] Then this combination of assumptions, predictions, and findings might be construed as implying the following:

- Legislators do not care about distributive benefits. They just want to serve the "common good," make "good public policy," etc.
- Congress is unidimensional. Parties and leaders are unimportant in the legislative process.
- In spite of caustic claims by critics from all walks of life—including citizens, journalists, politicians, and political scientists—Congress performs well.

The first implication is unwarranted and dead wrong. The second implication is unwarranted. The third implication is sufficiently warranted to receive additional attention. A more detailed discussion of these implications yields accurate conclusions about information, legislative organization, and legislative performance.

Perspective on Distributive Politics

The inference that legislators do not care about distributive benefits is unquestionably flawed. Granted, the findings are generally negative with regard to distributive theories, but it simply does not follow that legislators do not care about distributive benefits or that they care only about being good "students" of public policy-making in the "school" of Congress.[14] On the contrary, and as emphasized in chapter 3, the axiomatic foundation of informational theory has both informational and distributional components. If the distributional component—specifically, divergent preferences over outcomes—were to have

---

13. The normative defense for this generalized median criterion might be regarded as policy-disaggregated majoritarianism. If one disaggregates the domain of legislative choice into individual (unidimensional) policies, and each policy choice corresponds with the median voter's most preferred policy in the given policy domain (given available information), then there exist no single-policy changes that a majority prefers.

14. See Muir 1982 for an excellent study of the California legislature that employs the metaphor of a school and that, in many respects, is compatible with the findings of this study.

been excluded, the predictions of the resulting theory would have been much different, exceedingly boring, and almost surely lacking in empirical support.[15]

The proper inference from the findings is that legislators care about distributional *and* informational benefits. However, due to preeminent positions of uncertainty in the policy environment and majoritarianism in procedural choice, legislators are more severely constrained in obtaining distributional benefits than is suggested in most theoretical research.

In contrast to the rather dismal prospects for massive distributional gains, legislators both care a great deal about, and in some cases can achieve, reductions in policy uncertainty. This is a clear plus for legislative performance if a valued attribute of collective decision making is the passage of policies whose likely consequences are known. Put another way, legislators want pork, they want to logroll, and they may even want to create institutional arrangements in which cross-committee multidimensional logrolling is easy. Anecdotes and intuition aside, however, systematic evidence suggests that legislators not only cannot always get what they want in terms of pork barrel policies; they cannot even usually get what they want. It should therefore come as no surprise that many legislators channel their energies elsewhere. In the context of informational theory, they perform "informational" services. In the context of earlier works, they perform "institutional maintenance" functions.[16]

Unidimensionality, Parties, and Leaders

Several intriguing controversies have arisen in recent decades regarding the implications of Arrow's Theorem,[17] the dimensionality of the congressional issue space,[18] the waxing and waning of parties in the legislative process,[19] and the trials and tribulations of legislative leaders.[20] Informational theories

15. Without the distributional component in informational theories, all legislators' preferences would be identical. Without conflicting interests, the rationale for a committee system would be much different, as would be the means to encourage specialization. Without specialization, there would be no informational asymmetries. With specialization, there would be no incentives for strategic use of information. It is similarly difficult to imagine procedural diversity arising in this context.

16. Pursuit of distributional benefits and institutional maintenance is, of course, not exhaustive of legislators' activities. Constituency service might be added to the list, although this is, in some respects, the ultimate distributive activity since benefits are extremely concentrated and (opportunity) costs are diffuse but real (see Mayhew 1974, 54–55). Leisure is occasionally valued by legislators, too (see, for example, Fenno 1989 on Dan Quayle in the House).

17. See, for example, Buchanan 1954; McKelvey 1976; and Riker 1961 and 1982.

18. See, for example, Clausen 1973; Poole and Rosenthal 1987; and Schneider 1979.

19. See, for example, Brady 1988; Brady, Brody, and Epstein 1989; Collie 1988c; Collie and Brady 1985; Cox and McCubbins 1989; and Hurley and Wilson 1989.

20. See, for example, Davidson 1985 and 1989; Dodd and Oppenheimer 1989; Peabody 1985; and Sinclair 1983.

omit or assume away these concerns and thereby invite reactions ranging from carping to apoplexy. The assumption of unidimensionality is variously regarded as overly simple, as locking the Arrow problem in the closet, or as rigging the theory against the standard multidimensional logrolling view. The omission of parties and leaders receives similar reactions: parties might not be what they once were, but neither should they be ignored; likewise for leaders.

These objections were addressed briefly in chapter 3 with a standard response: whether simplifying assumptions are overly simple is an empirical question. Now, with the assistance of empirical findings, I would argue more strongly that the assumptions are not overly simple. Why? Because the results suggest that a unidimensional model that is without leaders and parties, that is grounded in majoritarianism in the domains of both procedure and policy, that posits a mix of distributional and informational individual goals, and that places simple but clearly articulated constraints on individual behavior, is sufficient for explaining a significant portion of heretofore unexplained variation. If unidimensionality of the legislative choice space is an egregious simplification in informational theory, and if multidimensionality plays the same role in the world as it is does in distributive theories, then the distributive theory should have explained more variation in the data examined here than did informational theory. Likewise, if parties and leaders are egregious omissions in extant informational theory, then forthcoming theories that accommodate parties and leaders will be able to explain more variation than was explained here. In the process of developing and testing such theories, we will continue to learn more about the genuine importance of multidimensionality of conflict, parties, and leaders in legislative processes.

Congressional Performance

Topics such as legislators' willingness and ability to pass distributive policies and the importance and role of leaders and parties in legislative policy-making almost surely have a bearing on legislative performance. However, thus far most of the discussion suffers from the same ambiguities that surround earlier works on legislative institutions. To assess legislative performance adequately, we need at least three things: explicit performance criteria, a theory that links legislative organization with legislative performance, and empirical support for such a theory. These include both positive and normative components. The first prerequisite is inherently normative. What should a legislature do? The second and third prerequisites are inherently positive. How do legislators behave, and with what observable consequences? A major portion of this book has been concerned with the positive issues. However, with the assistance of recent work by Gilligan (1989)—and aided further by the empirical results here—I can justifiably speak to some normative issues.

Within the context of a two-period, committee-floor model with incomplete information, Gilligan defines three quantifiable performance criteria: "informativeness," a "distributive property," and "timeliness." Each of these is defined from the parent chamber's perspective, though they would not have to be.[21] The informativeness criterion refers to the extent of information transmission in equilibrium (which in our previous works we called "informational efficiency" and here can be interpreted as "good public policy" in the precise sense of reduction of uncertainty). The distributive criterion refers to the degree to which the realized policy outcome is consistent with the legislature's pivotal voter's ideal point (here, the median voter's desire to minimize "distributive losses"). The timeliness criterion refers to the ability of the legislature to reach a decision in the first period (which has no analog in the information models tested here but is consistent with Baron and Ferejohn's notion of hastening agreement). Gilligan finds and identifies several irreconcilable tensions between these performance criteria. The tensions between informational and distributive performance are essentially the same as those identified in previous information models.

The rather vague initial implication that "Congress performs well" can now be assessed with greater precision. To the degree that empirical findings have been consistent with the predictions of theories that identify optimal institutional designs, the inference is not far from the mark. Of course, Congress is not absolutely informationally efficient. The policies it addresses are too complex. Its organizational form is not perfect. And informational efficiency is not worth achieving at all costs but rather has to be traded off against other objectives, some of which lie outside the present theoretical framework. Similarly, distributive shifts in policy away from legislative medians undoubtedly occur, and at least some information models suggest that they should occur (albeit to provide incentives for acquiring and divulging information). Qualifications aside, however, when an evaluator of legislative performance has a proper understanding of what is possible in an institution that may "determine the rules of its proceedings," these shortcomings are almost surely less severe than is typically alleged.

Gauging more precisely the severity of the shortcomings of existing legislative organization vis-à-vis what is possible will require additional empirical research. Hoping that such research will not lose sight of theoretical foundations, I offer for continued empirical assessment a legislative hypothesis derived from one of the simplest and best-known theories in political science—Black's (1958) median-voter theory.

---

21. For example, if one's normative orientation were that gains from trade were good (e.g., through an intense-preference or Benthamite-utilitarian argument), then Gilligan's distributive performance measure could simply be negated. The positive analysis would remain the same; only the normative interpretation would change.

THE MEDIAN LEGISLATOR HYPOTHESIS. *Legislative choices in salient policy domains are median choices.*

Though perhaps radical with respect to what many congressional scholars believe, this hypothesis is nevertheless consistent with most of the findings of this study. Two related issues are noteworthy. First, readers who believe that the hypothesis is preposterous should take heart that their belief suggests that the hypothesis should be easy to refute. I would only add that refutation, if convincing, will be systematic rather than anecdotal, for anecdotal instances of pork barrel politics are, if not a dime a dozen, at least cheap.[22] Second, it is quite easy to envision future research that finds a middle ground between median (and majoritarian) policies and purely distributive, committee-power, (and nonmajoritarian) outcomes. For example, Gilligan's addition of multi-period play in an asymmetric information game results in equilibria in which the committee (as informed actor) may, under specified conditions, reap distributive benefits at the expense of the pivotal (median) voter of the legislature, even when the pivotal voter does not commit to a restrictive rule. Gilligan's theoretical legislature is consistent with the Majoritarian Postulate as introduced here and thus sharply constrains the degree to which the legislature's median voter incurs distributional losses. Indeed, so sharp are these constraints that an apt substantive characterization of the prediction is that some legislators receive pork only at the margin.

The more concrete implications of results such as these pertain to who are the likely recipients of disproportionate distributive benefits. The conjecture here is not unique. The hard workers in the legislature or, in Mayhew's terms, the "institutional maintainers" are the likely prime beneficiaries of pork at the margin. Anecdotal evidence, as suggested above, is readily available. Former Senate Majority Leader Robert Byrd recently relinquished his leadership post to become Senate Appropriations Committee Chairman, which he claims is the position he always wanted. Although he seems to have taken a beating in the 1989 supplemental appropriations bill discussed at the end of chapter 2, he seems not to be faring badly overall. In the 101st Congress he has won pork prizes in each of the following areas: energy and water, transportation, interior, military construction, defense, agriculture, veterans' affairs/NASA/HUD, treasury/postal service, and commerce, state, and justice.[23] Perhaps this is to be expected in light of his years spent as the Senate's chief institutional maintainer.

---

22. With the price of *Congressional Quarterly* about $100.00 per year, the price of a pork barrel anecdote is more like $2.00. Still, this is sufficiently low that one must wonder why distributive enthusiasts have relied so heavily upon the Reeves/Mayhew account of the Buckley case (see chap. 2).

23. See *Congressional Quarterly*, December 9, 1989, 3354–59.

I hasten to add, however, that the conjecture about pork at the margin for institutional maintainers is just that: a conjecture, not a theory. Additional work remains to be done before we can identify, with greater precision, the recipients of disproportionate distributive benefits and before we can state with precision the extent to which legislative policy-making is nonmajoritarian and prodistributive, dimension-by-dimension. The claim here is only that legislative policy is considerably more majoritarian than is widely believed—so much so that the null hypothesis of median (majoritarian) outcomes needs to be refuted in favor of alternative hypotheses that follow from well-specified theories. As long as the median-legislator hypothesis is not refuted, we should not abandon it. Nor should we abandon the assessment that Congress in particular—and legislatures in general—strike more-or-less optimal balances between informational and distributional performance criteria.

Conclusion: Institutions and Incentives

In his classic treatise, *The Wealth of Nations,* Adam Smith advanced the argument that the reason people produce efficiently has little or nothing to do with efficiency being a desirable societal goal. Rather, they produce efficiently because, given the constraints they face in the marketplace, efficient production is the best way to achieve their individual economic goals (typically, to make a buck). Likewise, the key to creation and maintenance of economies that perform well lies in harnessing self-interest. This first entails reaching a clear understanding of economic actors' goals, the constraints they face, and how they interact with one another. It then requires aligning, as best as possible, individual incentives with collective goals.

Much of this study suggests that the fundamental principles of legislative politics are no different from those of capitalistic economics. The reason legislators acquire and share policy expertise has little or nothing to do with specialization being a legislative common good. Rather, they specialize because, given the constraints they face in the legislature, specialization is the best way to achieve their political goals (typically, to get reelected). Likewise, the key to the creation and maintenance of legislatures that perform well lies in harnessing self-interest. This first entails reaching a clear understanding of legislators' goals, the constraints they face, and how they interact with one another. It then requires aligning, as best as possible, individual incentives with collective goals.

While straightforward as a conceptual device, this comparison is bounded in its practical legislative uses by article 1 section 5 of the Constitution. In the U.S. Congress, as in most legislatures across the world, the task of creating and maintaining well-designed legislatures (or any other political entity, for that matter) is not delegated to a single, neutral, collective-welfare-maximizing agent. The creation and maintenance of political institutions is endogenous and, as such, is a product of a set of complex individual actions. It therefore should not be surprising that political institutions do not perform perfectly either by informational or distributional criteria. As an empirical matter, purely collective goals simply cannot be expected to be predominant in the design phase of democratic political institutions. It should also be increasingly clear that understanding how to make institutions perform better requires an approach in which the line between normative and positive theories is clearly drawn, and in which normative prescriptions are based not necessarily on the most intuitive positive theories but rather on the theories whose predictions are most consistent with evidence.

Guided by positive theories but based on evidence, the thesis of this study pertains to the relative merits of two ways of theorizing about legislative politics within the same paradigm. I have argued that while distributive concerns are undeniably a part of legislative politics, current distributive theories mischaracterize the key components of legislative politics in empirically significant ways. In contrast, informational concerns—in the sense of how politicians can be provided with incentives to study public problems and formulate public policy—are at the heart of legislative organization. In all likelihood, the same informational concerns are central to legislative policy and legislative performance, too. By implication, the uncertainties confronted by members of a majoritarian collective choice body cannot be ignored when seeking a deeper and more accurate understanding of legislative politics.

This thesis can be read in two ways. The first and easier way is as-is: simply adopt it as truth in light of the evidence presented. The second and more difficult way is with skepticism: entertain the central arguments of this book and their broader implications, but try actively to disprove them. Instinctive antagonists of exclusively distributive theories may be content to opt for the first reading. However, active researchers in the fields of U.S. politics or legislative studies should opt for the second reading. The skeptical response is the scientific response insofar as a good theory is one that withstands repeated tests. To say "enough is enough" with respect to informational theory after this one round of analysis, therefore, would be inappropriate.

Furthermore and finally, this prescribed best response—namely, to read skeptically and to respond critically with additional research—conveniently illustrates several information-theoretic insights regarding institutions and incentives. Relative to the median reader, I am favorably predisposed toward informational theories of legislative politics. My predisposition has made it relatively easy to acquire some expertise in this area. At the completion of this paragraph, my move will have been made and my signal will have been sent. Other players in the game, however, will not have moved. Academic disciplines—like legislatures—do not, cannot, and should not commit to highly restrictive procedures such as, in this instance, acceptance or rejection of a thesis as-is. Accordingly, amendments to the theory espoused here can and should be offered. Indeed, if the incentives between the collective discipline and its individual members are properly aligned, heterogeneous specialists will emerge, the clarity of scholarly signals will improve, and so too will our collective understanding about the relationship between political organizations, public policy, and institutional performance.

Appendixes

APPENDIX A

Summary of Terms in Legislative Signaling Games

Legislators choose *policies* (means) but have utility defined over the *outcomes* (ends) yielded by policies after their implementation. *Incomplete information* refers to the inability of legislators to predict perfectly the outcomes associated with policies.

Some legislators may have more precise knowledge than others about the relationship between policies and outcomes. This *asymmetric information* results, for example, from a committee devoting resources to acquire *specialization* or *expertise* about policies that lie in its jurisdiction.

When a committee specialist proposes a bill, the action may implicitly contain information about his or her expertise. This implicit transmission of information is called *signaling*. When the legislature observes a specialized committee's bill, it attempts to discern what the committee knows about the relationship between policies and outcomes. As receiver of the committee's signal, the legislature makes an *inference,* and reaches a new or updated set of *beliefs* about the relationship between policies and outcomes.

A *legislative equilibrium* is a bill choice by a committee, a set of beliefs by the legislature, and a policy choice by the legislature, such that actions of the players are expected utility maximizing, and the beliefs of the legislature are realized in equilibrium.

Informational efficiency refers to the precision of the inference the legislature draws from the committee's equilibrium behavior, that is, the clarity of the received signal. Maximal informational efficiency is obtained when the legislature can infer precisely the committee's private information. Minimal informational efficiency is obtained when the committee's action contains no information whatsoever and thus fails to change the legislature's beliefs. A committee is *informative* to the degree that the equilibrium is informationally efficient, that is, to the degree that the committee's private information becomes public throughout the play of the game.

The distributional effect of an equilibrium is given by the deviation of the expected outcome from the legislature's median voter's ideal point. A *distributional loss* is incurred when the expected outcomes deviate from this point.

Distributive committee power refers to behavior that results in committee gains at the expense of a majority. In instances of distributive committee power, a committee exercises its parliamentary rights to get a majority to do what is not in the majority's interest. *Informational committee power* refers to behavior that results in gains to committee and noncommittee members alike. In instances of informational committee power, a committee transmits private information to get a majority to do what is in the majority's and the committee's interest.

APPENDIX B

Additional Analysis of Committee Composition

This appendix assesses some common criticisms of interest group ratings by focusing on one such set of ratings. It then presents some additional findings regarding the composition of standing committees in the Senate as well as the House in the 96th through 99th Congresses.

The ratings of the National Farmers Union (NFU) have proven to be most controversial thus far. Four chief criticisms are as follows: (1) The NFU is a union and therefore its ratings do not properly reflect agrarian sentiments. (2) Other agriculture ratings, such as those of the National Farm Bureau or National Farmers Organization, would be significantly different and better. (3) No such ratings can capture agricultural demand because so much of agriculture policy is commodity-specific. (4) It would have been better for me to select roll call votes myself and calculate my own index, employing only contested roll call votes. Responses to these criticisms follow.

First, the National Farmers Union is not a labor union but rather uses the word "union" in its generic sense. In its brochure entitled "Questions and Answers," the NFU stresses that ". . . it is an organization of independent farmers . . . [and] has used the term 'union,' meaning 'united effort,' since 1902—long before labor organizations became widely identified with the term."

Second, the National Farm Bureau has a policy of identifying votes of special importance to its members and listing legislators' votes in occasional issues of *Farm Bureau News*. However, it is expressly opposed to calculating indexes and does not produce them. The National Farmers Organization (NFO), however, does produce and distribute ratings comparable to the NFU's. Though not available from LEGI-SLATE, I collected these separately as a check on the NFU ratings used here. The correlation coefficient between the ratings for the 99th Congress is .85.

Third, it is true that these ratings do not capture commodity-specific demand. (It is also true that none of the "jurisdiction-specific" ratings are as fine-grained or specific to the jurisdiction as we would like.) As figure B.1 suggests, however, the ratings can be interpreted plausibly as measures of overall agriculture support or, perhaps, as willingness to trade across commodities. Imagine an n-dimensional space ($n = 2$ in fig. B.1) with commodity-specific dimensions and a set of ideal points in that space. NFU or NFO ratings then can be thought of as the projection of these ideal points onto a unidimensional proagriculture dimension as shown. In this projection, commodity-specific information is indeed lost, but information on overall agricultural support is not.

Fourth, it is true that I could have selected roll call votes and calculated my own agriculture index. Whether this would have resulted in better measures seems to depend on the answers to several questions. Who has more of a stake in agriculture policy: agricultural interest groups or me? Who has more expertise in agriculture policy: agricultural interest groups or me? Who is better able to understand and account for complex parliamentary strategies in an attempt to distinguish trivial from nontrivial roll call votes: agricultural interest groups or me? I leave it to the reader to answer these questions.

More generally, the limitations of ratings based on roll calls are fully acknowledged, and the development of superior measures is heartily endorsed. Meanwhile, however, it seems reasonable to proceed under the mild presumption that ratings of the NFO and other interest groups are meaningful approximations of legislators' preferences from which we can gain some insights. This was the aim of chapter 4.

Empirical analysis in chapter 4 on the composition of standing committees was based primarily on the House of Representatives in the 99th Congress. Are committees in the 99th House atypical? Do Senate committees conform to claims regarding preference outliers better than House committees do? Comparable data from the 96th through 98th Congresses (and 99th for the Senate) suggest not.

According to general-ideology measures, the 99th Congress is much like the 96th through 98th Congresses. Armed Services is consistently more conservative than the House. Veterans' Affairs and Public Works join the conser-

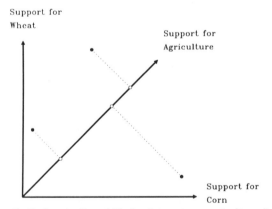

Fig. B.1. Hypothetical projection of ideal points onto an agriculture dimension

vative list for late 1970s Congresses but become moderate thereafter. In contrast, the Education and Labor, Foreign Affairs, and District of Columbia committees are occasionally significantly more liberal than the House.

Jurisdiction-specific special-interest ratings exhibit only a few minor deviations from the pattern discovered in the 99th Congress. While Armed Services was always high on the ASC scale, it was clearly not homogeneous in the 96th and 97th Congresses. Agriculture was a barely significant outlier in the 96th Congress according to the NFU ratings, but this finding has not proven robust. Similarly, Education and Labor exhibited some outlying tendencies on labor ratings in the 96th Congress but was less prolabor during the 97th and not significantly different from the House in the 98th and 99th Congresses. Moreover, it was clearly heterogeneous throughout the period. Public Works was significantly antienvironment according to the LCV ratings in the 96th Congress, but in each succeeding Congress, the results from the 99th are typical of this nonoutlying pork barrel committee. Finally, the Select Committee on Aging was (barely) significantly predisposed to senior citizens in the 97th and 98th Congresses; but here, too, heterogeneity of preferences was characteristic of the committee in each Congress. Thus, for the eight-year period beginning in 1979, there are almost no instances of homogeneity of committee preferences in the House and only occasional instances of significant outliers.

For the Senate, the data reveal more of the same. In the 99th Congress, for example, not a single standing committee in the Senate was a general ideology outlier. Special-interest ratings also reveal a robust pattern of moderation in Senate committee preferences. Even the somewhat conservative Senate Armed Services Committee fell short of the .05 significance level on the ASC scale. Instead, the closest thing to an outlier in the Senate seems to be the Environment and Public Works Committee, which is somewhat more proenvironment than the Senate according to LCV ratings (cf. the House Public Works Committee in table 4.7). Finally, the Senate Agriculture Committee is not significantly more proagriculture than the Senate according to (controversial) NFU ratings.

Probit Estimates and Calculations for Restrictive Rules

This appendix provides an overview of probit analysis as used in chapter 5. It also presents probit estimates for the analysis of choice of restrictive rules and describes the calculation of the probabilities in tables 5.5–5.9.

Overview and Estimates

The probit analyses in chapter 5 consisted of estimating equations of the following form:

$$Pr(RR = 1) = \Phi(X'_i\beta),$$

where

$$RR = \begin{cases} 0 & \text{if the rule is open or modified-open, and} \\ 1 & \text{if the rule is closed or modified-closed,} \end{cases}$$

X_i = a vector of exogenous variables,

β = a vector of coefficients to be estimated, and

$\Phi(\cdot)$ = the standard normal cumulative distribution function.

Table C.1 presents two pairs of findings. The first pair includes only observations in which the legislation was referred to a single committee. These observations were first analyzed separately from multiple-referral legislation to capitalize on the availability of committee-level measures: *committee seniority,* and the degree to which committees are composed of *preference outliers* and characterized by *heterogeneity* of preferences. The second pair excludes committee-level variables and includes a variable for the *number of referrals.* For each pair, the first set of results—equation 1 for single referrals, equation 3 for all bills—includes all variables and theoretically plausible interaction terms. The second set of results—equations 2 and 4 respectively— represents the culmination of several steps of estimation in which likelihood ratio tests were used to test for statistical significance of (sets of) coefficients.

TABLE C.1.   Probit Estimates of Choice of Restrictive Rules

VARIABLE	SINGLE REFERRALS		ALL BILLS	
	EQUATION 1	EQUATION 2	EQUATION 3	EQUATION 4
Constant	−2.32	−1.54	−0.995	−1.04
	(−1.81)	(−2.62)	(−5.12)	(−6.11)
Distributive content	−12.31	−10.60	0.382	*
	(−3.24)	(−3.39)	(0.16)	
Urgency	0.803	1.015	1.32	1.29
	(1.70)	(2.59)	(3.15)	(3.88)
Laws cited	0.038	*	0.049	0.037
	(0.85)		(3.16)	(3.14)
Committee seniority	0.352	0.251	*	*
	(1.92)	(2.96)		
Preference outlier	0.086	*	*	*
	(0.68)			
Heterogeneity	0.164	0.166	*	*
	(3.06)	(3.23)		
Referrals	*	*	0.276	0.259
			(2.52)	(2.73)
Republican cosponsors	0.038	0.037	0.021	0.022
	(1.82)	(2.22)	(1.96)	(1.99)
Democratic cosponsors	−0.002	*	−0.005	−0.005
	(−0.43)		(−1.44)	(−1.45)
Scope	−0.001	*	−0.003	*
	(−0.27)		(−1.21)	
Preference outlier × laws cited	0.004	0.007	*	*
	(1.20)	(3.41)		
Preference outlier × committee seniority	−0.028	−0.018	*	*
	(−1.47)	(−4.60)		
Distributive content × preference outlier	0.677	0.586	*	*
	(3.51)	(3.65)		
Distributive content × urgency	4.518	*	4.96	*
	(0.51)		(0.59)	
Distributive content × referrals	*	*	−2.35	−2.15
			(−1.16)	(−2.80)
Log likelihood	−79.1	−80.1	−134.3	−135.1
N	208	208	267	267
Percent correct	82.7	82.2	77.2	77.2

Note: Asymptotic *t*-statistics in parentheses.
*Not in equation

These refined equations form the basis for the calculations reported in tables 5.5–5.9 and the corresponding substantive interpretations in chapter 5.

The *t*-statistics (in parentheses) show that interaction effects are often significant. Two interaction terms are included to clarify the relationship between preference outliers and specialization. Three interaction terms entail the distributive-content variable and its possible indirect effects through the preference-outlier, urgency, and number-of-referrals variables. In some instances the effects of variables are captured only through these interaction terms (e.g., laws cited and preference outliers for single referrals and distributive content in the all-bill sample). Although the inclusion of interaction terms confounds direct inferences from single coefficient estimates, additional computations based on all coefficients correctly isolate the independent effects of any given exogenous variable.

Overall, the estimates in table C.1 are highly significant. Equation 2 for single referrals has significant parameter estimates for each of its variables and predicts correctly over four out of five rule choices. Equation 4 predicts only somewhat less well overall, which is encouraging when considered in context. First, multiple referrals are fairly new procedural innovations and are not yet well understood. Even experts on the subject are amazed by how much they differ and are thus reluctant to generalize about their nature and uses.[1] Second, although the percentage of rules predicted correctly diminishes as multiple referrals are added to the sample, the available measures are fewer in number and less tailor-made for this analysis, so we would expect some attenuation in the percentage of successful predictions. Finally, the individual parameter estimates and their associated net-probability effects (calculated below) are stable both across and within the single-referral and all-bill data sets. Therefore, we can be reasonably confident of substantive interpretations based on these estimates.

Calculation of Probabilities

In addition to statistical significance, we are interested in the magnitude of changes in the probability of a restrictive rule associated with changes in the exogenous variables. In a standard linear regression equation, this poses no problem: a unit change in any given exogenous variable x_i yields an expected change of $\hat{\beta}_i$ units in the dependent variable. Interpretation of probit coefficients in this manner is inappropriate though, since the cumulative normal distribution function, $\Phi(\cdot)$, is not linear. Thus, the change in the probability of a restrictive rule (the dependent variable) associated with a unit change in an

---

1. See, for example, Collie and Cooper 1989; and Davidson, Oleszek, and Kephart 1988.

exogenous variable is not constant but rather depends on the values of the remaining exogenous variables.

To address this problem in a manner that allows for cross-variable comparisons of the magnitude of effects, the following calculations were performed for the first column of table 5.5. These are based on the estimates reported for equation 2 of table C.1.[2] The equation is:

$$Pr(RR = 1) = \Phi(\beta_0 + \beta_1 x_1 + \beta_2 x_2 + \beta_3 x_3 + \beta_4 x_4 + \beta_5 x_5$$

$$+ \beta_6 x_6 x_7 + \beta_7 x_6 x_3 + \beta_8 x_1 x_6),$$

where

x_1 = distributive content,
x_2 = urgency,
x_3 = committee seniority,
x_4 = heterogeneity,
x_5 = Republican cosponsors,
x_6 = preference outlier, and
x_7 = laws cited.

Also let $\bar{x}_i$ equal the mean of x_i and s_i equal the standard deviation of x_i, $i = 1, \ldots, 7$.

For each of the seven exogenous variables, x_i, we want an estimate of the increment or decrement in $Pr(RR = 1)$ associated with a standard deviation increase in x_i, holding all other exogenous variables constant at their mean values. Obtaining these estimates is straightforward with the minor exception that some exogenous variables enter into the equation more than once— possibly directly and possibly as part of an interaction term. Thus, for example, in the case of estimating the marginal effect of the distributive content of a bill on $Pr(RR = 1)$, we take the following steps. First let

$$\bar{R} = \Phi(\hat{\beta}_0 + \hat{\beta}_1 \bar{x}_1 + \hat{\beta}_2 \bar{x}_2 + \hat{\beta}_3 \bar{x}_3 + \hat{\beta}_4 \bar{x}_4$$

$$+ \hat{\beta}_5 \bar{x}_5 + \hat{\beta}_6 \bar{x}_6 \bar{x}_7 + \hat{\beta}_7 \bar{x}_6 \bar{x}_3 + \hat{\beta}_8 \bar{x}_1 \bar{x}_6).$$

---

2. This discussion focuses on the estimates for single referrals. The multiple referral calculations in the second column of table 5.5 are conducted similarly but based on equation 4 of table C.1.

This is the estimated probability of a restrictive rule with every exogenous variable fixed at its mean, that is, $\bar{R} = \Pr(RR = 1|\bar{X})$. This number (.143) serves as the baseline from which we subtract the comparable estimate with one exogenous variable perturbed by one standard deviation, s_i. Thus, in the case in which the distributive-content variable (x_1) is perturbed, the first entry in table 5.5 $(-.095)$ was computed as follows:

$$\Phi(\hat{\beta}_0 + \hat{\beta}_1 (\bar{x}_1 + s_1) + \hat{\beta}_2\bar{x}_2 + \hat{\beta}_3\bar{x}_3 + \hat{\beta}_4\bar{x}_4$$

$$+ \hat{\beta}_5\bar{x}_5 + \hat{\beta}_6\bar{x}_6\bar{x}_7 + \hat{\beta}_7 \bar{x}_6\bar{x}_3 + \hat{\beta}_8(\bar{x}_1 + s_1)\bar{x}_6) - \bar{R}.$$

Notice that the proper estimate requires that the standard deviation be added within the interaction term that includes the distributive-content variable, too. As described in the text, the resulting number is the expected change in the probability of a restrictive rule associated with a standard deviation increase in the distributive content of a bill. The remaining cell entries in table 5.5 are calculated in a perfectly analogous manner.

Calculation of the probabilities in tables 5.6–5.8 is a variation on the same theme. The differences are as follows. This analysis focuses on two exogenous variables rather than one. All possible combinations of holding a variable fixed at its mean, subtracting a standard deviation, and adding a standard deviation are examined. Unlike the figures reported in table 5.5, these probabilities are not netted out by subtracting the mean. (The mean, given as $\bar{R}$ above, is necessarily the middle entry of table 5.6, which is based on single-referral estimates.)

Nine probabilities are computed for each table. Consider the first 3×3 table that inspects interactions between distributive content and preference outliers, or x_1 and x_6, respectively, given the notation used above. The probability for the upper left cell (low distributive content, low preference outlier) is given by:

$$\Phi(\hat{\beta}_0 + \hat{\beta}_1(\bar{x}_1 - s_1) + \hat{\beta}_2\bar{x}_2 + \hat{\beta}_3\bar{x}_3 + \hat{\beta}_4\bar{x}_4$$

$$+ \hat{\beta}_5\bar{x}_5 + \hat{\beta}_6(\bar{x}_6 - s_6)\bar{x}_7 + \hat{\beta}_7(\bar{x}_6 - s_6)\bar{x}_3$$

$$+ \hat{\beta}_8(\bar{x}_1 - s_1)(\bar{x}_6 - s_6));$$

the probability for the upper right cell (low distributive content, high preference outlier) is given by

$$\Phi(\hat{\beta}_0 + \hat{\beta}_1(\bar{x}_1 - s_1) + \hat{\beta}_2\bar{x}_2 + \hat{\beta}_3\bar{x}_3 + \hat{\beta}_4\bar{x}_4$$

$$+ \hat{\beta}_5\bar{x}_5 + \hat{\beta}_6(\bar{x}_6 + s_6)\bar{x}_7 + \hat{\beta}_7(\bar{x}_6 + s_6)\bar{x}_3$$

$$+ \hat{\beta}_8(\bar{x}_1 - s_1)(\bar{x}_6 + s_6));$$

and so on. Again, standard deviations are necessarily added or subtracted everywhere in which the given variable enters the equation—not just where the variable enters in noninteracted form.

Analysis of Conferee Selection

This appendix describes three things: the probit analysis of conferee selection, the probability calculations reported in chapter 6, and some additional tests not discussed in chapter 6 but of potential interest to skeptics of its content. The discussion presumes a basic familiarity with probit estimation such as that given in appendix C.

Probit Estimations on Conferee Selection

Several probit equations were estimated, focusing initially on four types of bills (education, agriculture, labor, and defense and foreign policy issues) and subsequently on committee-specific analysis of defense and foreign policy bills. The first set of estimates was always based on the following unrestricted equation:

$$\Pr(\text{Conferee} = 1) = \Phi(\beta_0 + \beta_1 x_1 + \beta_2 x_2 + \beta_3 x_3$$

$$+ \beta_4 x_1 x_4 + \beta_5 x_4 + \beta_6 x_1 x_5 + \beta_7 x_5).$$

The exogenous variables are as defined in chapter 6:

x_1 = committee,
x_2 = committee seniority,
x_3 = House seniority,
x_4 = high demand, and
x_5 = preference outlier.

Coefficients for the expertise variables (committee, committee seniority, and House seniority) were always jointly significant, usually individually significant, and never negative. With only one exception, these variables were always kept in the equation in subsequent estimations.[1] Coefficients for the preference variables (high demand, preference outlier, and the committee

---

1. The exception was appropriations bills on defense policy, in which case eighty-one of eighty-two conferees were committee members, thus causing severe multicollinearity for which it was impossible to estimate the coefficients for equation 1.

TABLE D.1.   Expertise and Preference Effects for Four Agriculture
Bills (N = 1,736)

VARIABLE	EQUATION 1	EQUATION 2*	EQUATION 3
Constant	−2.72	−2.73	−2.98
	(−9.02)	(−9.06)	(−12.97)
Committee	2.13	2.16	1.94
	(5.73)	(5.81)	(7.53)
Committee seniority	−0.021	0.038	−0.004
	(−0.12)	(0.22)	(−0.25)
House seniority	0.036	0.032	0.035
	(2.65)	(2.50)	(2.64)
Committee ×	0.27	†	0.24
high demand	(1.35)		(1.37)
High demand	−0.19	†	−0.12
	(−1.16)		(−0.90)
Committee ×	−0.25	−0.36	†
preference outlier	(−0.67)	(−0.96)	
Preference outlier	−0.35	−0.26	†
	(−1.21)	(−0.91)	
Log likelihood	−149.10	−150.06	−152.9
Percent correct	96.72	96.72	96.78

*Specification on which probability computations are based.
†Not in equation

interactions with these) were idiosyncratic across issues. The analysis therefore consisted of using likelihood ratio statistics to test whether particular sets
of variables could be excluded from the equations. This process always led to
a specification whose estimates were then used in the computation of
probabilities.

Rather than describe this process in its entirety for each issue area, we
focus here on agriculture, which was a typical case. Table D.1 presents three
equations using individual-level data for agriculture bills. The estimates in the
first column are those for equation 1 above. Equations 2 and 3 are nested (or
restricted) versions of equation 1, and thus the log likelihoods reported at the
bottom of the table can be used to test hypotheses about joint effects of
coefficients. Three such tests led to the choice of equation 2 for the probability
calculations for agriculture conferees.

First, the null hypothesis that $\beta_4 = \beta_5 = 0$ in equation 1—substantively,
that high-demand effects are nonexistent—could not be rejected. Its p-
value was .38.[2]

---

2. If H_0 is obtained by placing r restrictions on H_1, then the statistic is $LR = -2[\log L(H_0)$
$- \log L(H_1)] \sim \chi_r^2$. The p-value is $p = 1 - F(LR)$, where $F(\cdot)$ is the cumulative distribution
function of a central χ^2 random variable with r degrees of freedom. The p-value is the smallest
significance level at which the null hypothesis would be rejected.

Second, the null hypothesis that $\beta_6 = \beta_7 = 0$ in equation 1—substantively, that outlier effects are nonexistent—could be rejected. Its p-value was .02, thus indicating that these two outlier coefficients are jointly significant.

Third, before choosing equation 2 as the estimate on which the probability calculations would be based, the null hypothesis that $\beta_6 = \beta_7 = 0$ in equation 2 was tested. This entailed a comparison of the log likelihood for equation 2 with that from an identical equation in which β_6 and β_7 were constrained to equal zero. The log likelihood for this equation (not presented in table D.1) was -153.99, and the corresponding p-value for the hypothesis was .02. Thus, the joint outlier effects in equation 2 were significant, so equation 2 was used for the probabilities in table 6.6.

Likelihood ratio tests such as these were always sufficient to identify a jointly significant pair of preference coefficients. As reported in table D.2, the outlier coefficients were jointly significant for education bills and labor bills, while the high-demand coefficients were jointly significant for defense and foreign policy bills. For reasons described in chapter 6, table D.3 breaks down the analysis of defense and foreign policy bills to the level of committees. Here the preference effects are outlier effects for Appropriations and For-

TABLE D.2.   Expertise and Preference Effects for Remaining Bills

VARIABLE	EQUATION 1	EQUATION 2	EQUATION 3
Constant	−2.22	−2.56	−2.33
	(−8.12)	(−12.95)	(−33.12)
Committee	2.05	0.75	1.53
	(4.87)	(2.21)	(15.21)
Committee seniority	0.020	0.029	0.029
	(0.80)	(2.21)	(3.47)
House seniority	0.036	0.022	0.020
	(3.41)	(3.01)	(4.22)
Committee × high demand	*	*	0.23
			(3.21)
High demand	*	*	−0.12
			(−2.65)
Committee × preference outlier	0.28	0.86	*
	(0.64)	(2.80)	
Preference outlier	−0.58	−0.003	*
	(−1.92)	(−0.01)	
Log likelihood	−138.33	−307.16	−816.35
N	1,302	3,038	5,642
Percent correct	95.62	96.51	94.84

Note: Equations are for education, labor, and defense and foreign policy bills, respectively.
*Not in equation

TABLE D.3. Expertise and Preference Effects for Defense and Foreign Policy Bills, by Committee

VARIABLE	EQUATION 1	EQUATION 2	EQUATION 3
Constant	−2.55	−2.03	−2.71
	(−5.75)	(−21.09)	(−10.20)
Committee	3.00	1.20	2.13
	(7.92)	(6.74)	(5.04)
Committee seniority	0.052	0.049	0.038
	(0.59)	(3.78)	(2.09)
House seniority	−0.019	0.010	0.036
	(−0.50)	(1.35)	(5.00)
Committee × high demand	*	0.221	*
		(1.72)	
High demand	*	−0.184	*
		(−2.95)	
Committee × preference outlier	*	*	−0.788
			(−2.09)
Preference outlier	−0.57	*	0.143
	(−2.10)		(0.63)
Log likelihood	−125.80	−391.92	−256.00
N	1,302	2,170	2,170
Percent correct	93.86	94.24	96.27

Note: Equations are for Appropriations, Armed Services, and Foreign Affairs Committees, respectively.
*Not in equation

eign Affairs legislation and high-demand effects for Armed Services legislation.

Probability Calculations

Given a set of estimates such as those in tables D.1–D.3, estimated probabilities of conferee selection were calculated for eight types of legislators. This analysis parallels that in chapter 5 for restrictive rules and thus will not be explained in as much detail here as in appendix C. An illustration with respect to Armed Services conferees, based on equation 2 in table D.3, suffices.

Let $\bar{x}_i$ ($i = 1, \ldots, 4$) equal the mean values of the exogenous variables in equation 2, namely, committee, committee seniority, House seniority, and high demand. Likewise, let s_i ($i = 1, \ldots, 4$) be the standard deviations of $x_1, \ldots, x_4$. Suppose we want to know the estimated probability of going to conference for a legislator who is on the Armed Services Committee, has a high degree of seniority, and is a high demander. (This example corresponds to the lower rightmost entry for Armed Services bills in table 6.10.) That probability is given by:

$$\Phi[\hat{\beta}_0 + \hat{\beta}_1 + \hat{\beta}_2(\bar{x}_2 + s_2) + \hat{\beta}_3(\bar{x}_3 + s_3) + \hat{\beta}_4(\bar{x}_4 + s_4)$$

$$+ \hat{\beta}_5(\bar{x}_4 + s_4)].$$

Other probabilities in tables 6.5–6.12 are calculated by simply adding or subtracting standard deviations depending on whether the focal legislator is high or low in terms of specialization (measured by House or committee seniority) or demand for defense (measured by ASC ratings). Most of the expressions are simpler than this example since one or more terms cancel to zero. For instance, if the legislator is not on the committee, only the constant ($\hat{\beta}_0$), the House seniority variable (times $\hat{\beta}_3$), and the high-demand variable (times $\hat{\beta}_5$) enter into the calculation.

Additional Tests for Distributive Effects

The probit analyses summarized in chapter 6 and described above included all legislation in the 99th Congress for which relatively jurisdiction-specific measures of preferences were available. Two additional techniques were employed to search more exhaustively for effects predicted by distributive theories.

First, for each of the fourteen committees for which at least one bill went to conference, equation 1 above was estimated separately. In no instance other than Armed Services (as discussed in detail in chap. 6) was there a positive and significant high-demand effect.

Second, separate analyses on the selection of noncommittee conferees were conducted. For each of the eight committees,[3] the following two equations were estimated:

$$\Pr(\text{Conferee} = 1) = \Phi(\alpha + \beta_1 \text{ preference outlier})$$
$$\Pr(\text{Conferee} = 1) = \Phi(\alpha + \beta_1 \text{ high-demand})$$

Here, too, preference effects were never both positive and significant.

Partisanship or Majoritarianism?

Finally, to verify that hard-core majoritarian interpretations of postfloor processes are not blatantly inappropriate, the following hypothesis was tested:

---

3. In six instances, all or all but one of the conferees were from the committee.

TABLE D.4.   Party Effects in Appointment of Conferees

	$\hat{\beta}_{party}$	t-STATISTIC
Type of legislation		
Agriculture	$-.12$	-0.74
Labor	.001	0.12
Education	$-.10$	-0.46
Defense or foreign policy	$-.05$	-0.48
Committee-specific bills		
Appropriations	.06	0.34
Armed Services	$-.25$	-1.71
Foreign Affairs	$-.07$	-0.60

PARTISAN APPOINTMENTS. *Other things being equal, the Speaker—as a faithful agent of the majority party (rather than, say, the House)—will favor members of his party when appointing conferees.*

To make this a ceteris paribus test, the specifications given in tables D.1–D.3 were simply augmented with a dummy variable for party (1 if Democrat, 0 otherwise). Support for the partisan-appointments hypothesis would be obtained from positive and significant coefficient estimates of β_{party}.

Table D.4 presents the results, first for the four types of legislation, and then for the three committee-specific sets of defense and foreign policy bills. (For parsimony it omits the specialization and preference coefficients, close approximations of which are given in tables D.1–D.3.) Five times out of seven, the party effect is negative, including the only instance in which it approaches statistical significance (for Armed Services conferees). In other words, there is no support for the hypothesis of partisan appointments. Those who believe the Speaker to be an agent of his party first and foremost and of the House only secondarily must therefore seek empirical support for their beliefs elsewhere. The bulk of evidence in chapter 6 and this appendix is clearly more consistent with the Majoritarian Postulate of chapter 1 than with a partisan postulate implicit in other works.

On Rules Changes: The Case of Conference Committees

In chapter 7 of his excellent book (1989), Steve Smith argues that inferences about committee power from observable features of postfloor behavior are difficult. I agree wholeheartedly. However, a closely related part of Smith's argument has a more direct bearing on this work. Generally, the issue is whether changes in legislative rules (a.k.a. "reforms") made the Congress sufficiently different in the "prereform" and "postreform" eras that the arguments advanced about legislative organization are time-bound. This appendix uses Smith's arguments about reforms surrounding conference committees as a specific vehicle for exposing whether, when, and why rules changes are significant with respect to the thesis of this book.[1]

Smith's discussion of rules changes pertaining to conference committees overstates the significance of those rules changes in my opinion. He writes:

> Several developments in formal procedure since the early 1970s have provided additional means for challenging committee autonomy at the postpassage stage. These developments reflect the changes in attitudes described in previous chapters. The consequences of weakened norms of apprenticeship and committee deference were not limited to floor amending activity, nor could they be; rather, they extended to the exercise of power by senior committee members in all aspects of the legislative process, including the postpassage stages. . . . Developments in four areas of formal rules are worth special notice: appointment of conferees, conference procedure, conference authority, and floor procedures for responding to conference reports. (1989, 199)

Smith identifies and later discusses four areas of changes in formal rules that were presumably "consequences of weakened norms." Although I am in-

---

1. This appendix is not intended to undermine Smith's broader concerns with levels of activity on the floor of the House and Senate (as opposed to, for example, in standing committees and conference committees), since the focus here is distinctly different (on whether legislative organization is governed primarily by distributive or informational or both forces).

stinctively skeptical of causal arguments whose exogenous variables are "norms" (which I regard as fundamentally and unequivocally endogenous), the causal argument is not of concern here. Rather, I am more interested in the consequences, if any, of the rules changes. Specifically, if the rules changes were significant in terms of fundamentally changing the nature of congressional outcomes, then the arguments advanced in chapter 6 are susceptible to the criticism that they pertain only to the "postreform Congress." On the other hand, if the essence (as opposed to every specific feature) of postfloor procedures has remained constant, then the informational thesis is more likely to be generally valid.

In a similar vein, we should address the following issue in light of Smith's argument. If indeed the formal procedural changes that Smith identifies "have provided additional means for challenging committee autonomy," then a critical concern is whether additional procedures for challenging committee autonomy were formally needed. If the answer is yes, then the rules changes were significant. This is as if a previously formally binding constraint on noncommittee members were relaxed via rules changes, and therefore a new and different equilibrium should result.[2] If, however, the answer is no, then the rules changes are undoubtedly of lesser substantive significance in terms of how the Congress addresses committee-floor tensions in postfloor stages of collective decision making. The remainder of this appendix makes an argument that the answer is no.

Narrow assessments of rules changes place emphasis on isolated parts of postfloor procedures and may add up to a misleading picture of the whole. The real issue is not whether some rules changed. Of course, they did. Rather, it is whether the formal ability of chamber majorities to preempt or correct expected or actual abuse of conferees changed. I will argue that it did not for each of Smith's "four areas of formal rules . . . worth special notice" (1989, 199).

Appointment of Conferees. Smith notes that appointment powers traditionally reside in the Speaker in the House and presiding officer in the Senate. He dates these rights at 1946, and identifies House rules changes in 1975 and 1977 that strengthened these powers. I would argue that these changes were minor. First, the rules changes are more aptly characterized as codifications of

---

2. Smith does not propose a formal theory or an equilibrium argument. However, his conception of "committee power" is unquestionably distributive. "Committee power in Congress usually is addressed in terms of committee autonomy, the ability of committees to obtain legislative outcomes that reflect their own policy preferences, whether or not those outcomes are consistent with the preferences of their parent chamber" (1989, 198). In the previous chapter entitled "Floor Power, Committee Power" he adopts a similarly distributive definition (1989, 169).

long-standing precedents—precedents that, in fact, predate 1946. This is not to imply that such codification is always unimportant. But in this case I believe it was. First, even Smith notes that loopholes or ambiguities remain. Second and more important, the narrow focus on appointment criteria misses the broader issue: if a chamber majority suspects that a leader will stack the conference deck, it has multiple forms of recourse as described in chapter 6.

Conference Procedure. In 1974 and 1977, the House experimented with and passed a rule regarding open conference committees. Conceivably, the openness of the conference might have a bearing on what outlying conferees may get away with. I believe this at the margin. However, the argument has only marginal significance. Both before and after this rules change, other rules were in place that enabled parent-chamber majorities to preempt (and punish) conferees who were expected to (tried to) get away with too much.

Conference Authority. In 1971 and 1972, the House clarified its precedents regarding the authority of conferees when House-Senate differences pertained to amendments in the nature of substitute or nongermane Senate provisions. Bach's (1982) superb discussion of these changes suggests that they were precipitated primarily by House-versus-Senate concerns, not committee-versus-chamber concerns. Be that as it may, the broader point is the same here as with other so-called reforms: these did not remove a binding constraint on chamber majorities. They could vote down a conference report (possibly in pieces rather than all at once) after 1971–72; they could vote down a conference report and then consider Senate amendments in pieces via amendments between the chambers before 1971–72.

Floor Procedures for Responding to Conference Reports. In 1970, the House adopted a layover requirement for conference reports and clarified rights of dissenting members to speak during floor debate on reports. Some 1985 rules changes had similar effects on speech rights. Smith argues that such changes improve the prospects for mobilization of opposition to conference reports. Again, he may well be right. But again, the issue for present concerns is whether majority rights came to exist as a consequence of these rules changes that did not exist prior to them. Again, the answer is no.

I repeat that this discussion is not meant to trivialize rules changes of the sort Smith reports. Many members fought hard to achieve these specific rules changes and presumably had nontrivial reasons for fighting. But the issue of importance—not only here but also more broadly in the growing literature on rules and conference committees—is whether postfloor procedures as a whole have had fundamentally different consequences for the rights of majorities to make collective choices before or after such rules changes. To me the answer seems unequivocal. To others it might not. The challenge for dissenters with respect to my judgment, therefore, is twofold. First, select a time in congressional history—any time in congressional history—and study the complete set of postfloor procedures. Second, demonstrate that within those procedures it was not possible for a House and Senate majority to pass a bill that each majority prefers to the absence of a bill. Until a challenge such as this one is met, claim 4 in chapter 7 should be entertained.

References

Abram, Michael, and Joseph Cooper. 1968. The Rise of Seniority in the House of Representatives. *Polity* 1:52–85.

Ainsworth, Scott, and Marcus Flathman. 1990. Leadership in a Sparse Environment: A Formal Model of UCAs in the U.S. Senate. Presented at the annual meeting of the Midwest Political Science Association, Chicago.

Akerlof, George. 1970. The Market for Lemons: Qualitative Uncertainty and the Market Mechanism. *Quarterly Journal of Economics* 84:488–500.

Aldrich, John. 1988. Modeling the Party-in-the-Legislature. Presented at the annual meeting of the American Political Science Association, Washington, DC.

Alexander, DeAlva Stanwood. 1916. *History and Procedure of the House of Representatives.* Boston: Houghton-Mifflin.

Arnold, R. Douglas. 1979. *Congress and the Bureaucracy.* New Haven, CT: Yale University Press.

Arnold, R. Douglas. 1981. The Local Roots of Domestic Policy. In *The New Congress,* ed. Thomas E. Mann and Norman J. Ornstein. Washington, DC: American Enterprise Institute.

Arnold, R. Douglas. 1990. *The Logic of Congressional Action.* New Haven, CT: Yale University Press.

Arrow, Kenneth J. 1951. *Social Choice and Individual Values.* New York: Wiley.

Asbell, Bernard. 1978. *The Senate Nobody Knows.* Garden City, NY: Norton.

Asher, Herbert B. 1974. Committees and the Norm of Specialization. *Annals of the American Academy of Political and Social Science* 67:63–74.

Austen-Smith, David. 1990a. Credible Debate Equilibria. *Social Choice and Welfare* 7:75–93.

Austen-Smith, David. 1990b. Information Transmission in Debate. *American Journal of Political Science* 34:124–52.

Austen-Smith, David, and William H. Riker. 1987. Asymmetric Information and the Coherence of Legislation. *American Political Science Review* 81:897–918.

Austen-Smith, David, and William H. Riker. 1990. Asymmetric Information and the Coherence of Legislation: A Correction. *American Political Science Review* 84:243–45.

Axelrod, Robert. 1981. The Emergence of Cooperation among Egoists. *American Political Science Review* 75:306–18.

Bach, Stanley. 1981a. Special Rules in the House of Representatives: Themes and Contemporary Variations. *Congressional Studies* 8:37–58.

Bach, Stanley. 1981b. The Structure of Choice in the House of Representatives: The Impact of Complex Special Rules. *Harvard Journal on Legislation* 18:553–602.

Bach, Stanley. 1982. Germaneness Rules and Bicameral Relations in the U.S. Congress. *Legislative Studies Quarterly* 7:341–58.

Bach, Stanley. 1984. Resolving Legislative Differences in Congress: Conference Committees and Amendments between the Chambers. Congressional Research Service. Manuscript.

Bach, Stanley. 1986. Suspension of the Rules in the House of Representatives. Congressional Research Service. Manuscript.

Bach, Stanley. 1987. The Nature of Congressional Rules. Presented at the annual meeting of the American Political Science Association, Chicago.

Bach, Stanley. 1988. Patterns of Floor Consideration in the House of Representatives. Congressional Research Service. Manuscript.

Bach, Stanley. 1990. Suspension of the Rules, the Order of Business, and the Development of Congressional Procedure. *Legislative Studies Quarterly* 15:49–64.

Bach, Stanley, and Steven S. Smith. 1988. *Managing Uncertainty in the House of Representatives: Adaptation and Innovation in Special Rules.* Washington, DC: The Brookings Institution.

Bailey, Stephen K. 1950. *Congress Makes a Law: The Story behind the Employment Act of 1946.* New York: Columbia University Press.

Balutis, Alan. 1977. Legislative Staffing: Does It Make a Difference? In *Legislative Reform and Public Policy,* ed. Susan Welch and John Peters. New York: Praeger.

Banks, Jeffrey S. 1989. Agency Budgets, Cost Information, and Auditing. *American Journal of Political Science* 33:670–99.

Banks, Jeffrey S. 1990. Monopoly Agenda Control and Asymmetric Information. *Quarterly Journal of Economics* 105:445–64.

Banks, Jeffrey S. 1991. *Signaling Games in Political Science.* Chur, Switzerland: Harwood Academic Publishers.

Baron, David P. 1990. Majoritarian Incentives, Pork Barrel Programs, and Procedural Control. *American Journal of Political Science,* forthcoming.

Baron, David P., and John A. Ferejohn. 1988. Legislative Bargaining under Incomplete Information. Presented at the annual meeting of the American Political Science Association, Washington, DC.

Baron, David P., and John A. Ferejohn. 1989a. Bargaining in Legislatures. *American Political Science Review* 89:1181–1206.

Baron, David P., and John A. Ferejohn. 1989b. The Power to Propose. In *Models of Strategic Choice in Politics,* ed. Peter C. Ordeshook. Ann Arbor: University of Michigan Press.

Barone, Michael, and Grant Ujifusa. 1986. *The Almanac of American Politics.* Washington, DC: National Journal.

Bartels, Larry M. 1990. Constituency Opinion and Congressional Policy-Making: The Reagan Defense Buildup. University of Rochester. Manuscript.

Bauer, R., I. Pool, and L. A. Dexter. 1963. *American Business and Public Policy.* New York: Atherton Press.

Bendiner, Robert. 1964. *Obstacle Course on Capitol Hill.* New York: McGraw-Hill.

Benson, Bruce L. 1981. Why Are Congressional Committees Dominated by "High-Demand" Legislators? *Southern Economic Journal* 48:68–77.

Benson, Bruce L. 1983. Logrolling and High Demand Committee Review. *Public Choice* 39:427–34.

Black, Duncan. 1958. *The Theory of Committees and Elections.* London: Cambridge University Press.

Brady, David. 1988. *Critical Elections and Congressional Policy Making.* Stanford, CA: Stanford University Press.

Brady, David, Richard Brody, and David Epstein. 1989. Heterogeneous Parties and Political Organization: The U.S. Senate, 1880–1920. *Legislative Studies Quarterly* 14:205–24.

Bryce, James. 1905. *The American Commonwealth.* New York: Macmillan.

Buchanan, James. 1954. Social Choice, Democracy, and Free Markets. *Journal of Political Economy* 62:114–23.

Buchanan, William, Heinz Eulau, LeRoy C. Ferguson, and John C. Wahlke. 1970. The Legislator as Specialist. *Western Political Quarterly* 13:636–51.

Bullock, Charles S. 1971. The Influence of State Party Delegations on House Committee Assignments. *Midwest Journal of Political Science* 15:525–46.

Bullock, Charles S. 1972. Freshman Committee Assignments and Re-election in the United States House of Representatives. *American Political Science Review* 66:996–1007.

Bullock, Charles S. 1973. Committee Transfers in the United States House of Representatives. *Journal of Politics* 35:85–120.

Burns, James MacGregor. 1949. *Congress on Trial: The Legislative Process and the Administrative State.* New York: Harper.

Calabresi, Guido, and Douglas A. Melamed. 1972. Property Rules, Liability Rules and Inalienability: One View from the Cathedral. *Harvard Law Review* 85:1089–1128.

Campos, Jose Edgardo L. 1990. Instrument Choice and the Robustness of the Median Voter with Implications for Lobbying Activity. The Wharton School, University of Pennsylvania. Manuscript.

Cannon, Clarence. 1936. *Precedents of the House of Representatives.* Washington, DC: Government Printing Office.

Cheney, Richard B. 1989. An UnRuly House: A Republican View. *Public Opinion,* January-February, 41–44.

Cherryholmes, Cleo H., and Michael J. Shapiro. 1969. *Representatives and Roll Calls: A Computer Simulation of Voting in the Eighty-eighth Congress.* Indianapolis: Bobbs-Merrill.

Clapp, Charles L. 1963. *The Congressman: His Work as He Sees It.* Washington, DC: Brookings Institution.

Clausen, Aage R., and C. E. Van Horn. 1977. The Congressional Response to a Decade of Change, 1963–1972. *Journal of Politics* 39:624–66.

Collie, Melissa P. 1988a. The Legislature and Distributive Policymaking in Formal Perspective. *Legislative Studies Quarterly* 32:427–58.

Collie, Melissa P. 1988b. The Rise of Coalition Politics: Voting in the U.S. House, 1933–1980. *Legislative Studies Quarterly* 13:311–42.

Collie, Melissa P. 1988c. Universalism and the Parties in the U.S. House of Representatives, 1921–80. *American Journal of Political Science* 32:865–83.

Collie, Melissa P. 1989. Electoral Patterns and Voting Alignments in the U.S. House, 1886–1986. *Legislative Studies Quarterly* 14:107–28.

Collie, Melissa P., and David W. Brady. 1985. The Decline of Partisan Voting Coali-
tions in the House of Representatives. In *Congress Reconsidered*, ed. Lawrence
C. Dodd and Bruce I. Oppenheimer. Washington, DC: Congressional Quarterly
Press.

Collie, Melissa P., and Joseph Cooper. 1989. Multiple Referral and the "New" Com-
mittee System in the House of Representatives. In *Congress Reconsidered*, ed.
Lawrence C. Dodd and Bruce I. Oppenheimer. Washington, DC: Congressional
Quarterly Press.

Cooper, Joseph. 1970. *The Origins of the Standing Committees and the Development
of the Modern House*. Houston, TX: Rice University Studies.

Cooper, Joseph. 1977. Congress in Organizational Perspective. In *Congress Reconsidered*, ed. Lawrence C. Dodd and Bruce I. Oppenheimer. Washington, DC:
Congressional Quarterly Press.

Cooper, Joseph. 1988. *Congress and Its Committees: A Historical Approach to the
Role of Committees in the Legislative Process*. New York: Garland Publishing.

Cooper, Joseph, and David W. Brady. 1981. Institutional Context and Leadership
Style: The House from Cannon to Rayburn. *American Political Science Review*
75:411–25.

Cooper, Joseph, and Cheryl D. Young. 1989. Bill Introduction in the Nineteenth
Century: A Study of Institutional Change. *Legislative Studies Quarterly* 14:67–
106.

Cooper, Samuel. 1990. Suspension of the Rules in the House. Honors thesis. Harvard
University.

Cowart, Susan C. 1981. Representation of High-Demand Constituencies on Review
Committees. *Public Choice* 37:337–42.

Cox, Gary, and Mathew McCubbins. 1989. Parties and Committees in the U.S. House
of Representatives. University of California, San Diego. Manuscript.

Cummings, Milton C., and Robert L. Peabody. 1969. The Decision to Enlarge the
Committee on Rules: An Analysis of the 1961 Vote. In *New Perspectives on the
House of Representatives*, ed. Robert L. Peabody and Nelson W. Polsby.
Chicago: Rand McNally.

Dahl, Robert A. 1950. *Congress and Foreign Policy*. New York: Harcourt, Brace.

Davidson, Roger H. 1974. Representation and Congressional Committees. *Annals of
the American Academy of Political and Social Science* 441:48–62.

Davidson, Roger H. 1981. Subcommittee Government: New Channels for Policy
Making. In *The New Congress*, ed. Thomas E. Mann and Norman J. Ornstein.
Washington, DC: American Enterprise Institute.

Davidson, Roger H. 1985. Senate Leaders: Janitors for an Untidy Chamber? In *Congress Reconsidered*, ed. Lawrence C. Dodd and Bruce I. Oppenheimer. Washington, DC: Congressional Quarterly Press.

Davidson, Roger H. 1989. The Senate: If Everybody Leads, Who Follows? In *Congress Reconsidered*, ed. Lawrence C. Dodd and Bruce I. Oppenheimer. Washington, DC: Congressional Quarterly Press.

Davidson, Roger H., Walter J. Oleszek, and Thomas Kephart. 1988. One Bill, Many
Committees: Multiple Referrals in the U.S. House of Representatives. *Legislative
Studies Quarterly* 13:3–28.

Davis, Raymond. 1975. The Evolution of California Legislative Staff. In *Legislative Staffing: A Comparative Perspective*, ed. James Heaphey and Alan Balutis. New York: Halstead.

Deckard, Barbara. 1972. State Party Delegations in the U.S. House of Representatives: A Comparative Study of Group Cohesion. *Journal of Politics* 34:199–222.

Denzau, Arthur T., and Robert J. Mackay. 1983. Gatekeeping and Monopoly Power of Committees: An Analysis of Sincere and Sophisticated Behavior. *American Journal of Political Science* 27:740–61.

Deschler, Lewis, and William Holmes Brown. 1982. *Procedure in the U.S. House of Representatives*. Washington, DC: Government Printing Office.

Deutsch, Karl W. 1963. *The Nerves of Government: Models of Political Communication and Control*. New York: The Free Press of Glencoe.

Dobra, John L. 1983. An Approach to Empirical Studies of Voting Paradoxes: An Update and an Extension. *Public Choice* 41:241–50.

Dodd, Lawrence C., and Bruce I. Oppenheimer. 1989. Consolidating Power in the House. In *Congress Reconsidered*, ed. Lawrence C. Dodd and Bruce I. Oppenheimer. Washington, DC: Congressional Quarterly Press.

Enelow, James M. 1986. The Stability of Logrolling: An Expectations Approach. *Public Choice* 51:285–94.

Eulau, Heinz. 1985. Committee Selection. In *Handbook of Legislative Research*, ed. Gerhard Loewenberg, Samuel Patterson, and Malcolm Jewell. Cambridge, MA: Harvard University Press.

Feller, I., M. King, and D. Menzel. 1975. *Sources and Uses of Scientific and Technological Information in State Legislatures*. State College, PA: Pennsylvania State University Press.

Fenno, Richard F. 1966. *The Power of the Purse: Appropriations Politics in Congress*. Boston: Little, Brown.

Fenno, Richard F. 1973. *Congressmen in Committees*. Boston: Little, Brown.

Fenno, Richard F. 1975. If, as Ralph Nader Says, Congress Is "The Broken Branch," How Come We Love Our Congressmen So Much? In *Congress in Change*, ed. Norman Ornstein. New York: Praeger.

Fenno, Richard F. 1978. *Home Style: Representatives in Their Districts*. Boston: Little, Brown.

Fenno, Richard F. 1989. *Dan Quayle: The Making of a U.S. Senator*. Washington, DC: Congressional Quarterly Press.

Ferejohn, John A. 1975. Who Wins in Conference Committee? *Journal of Politics* 37:1033–46.

Ferejohn, John A. 1986. Logrolling in an Institutional Context: A Case Study of Food Stamp Legislation. In *Congress and Policy Change*, ed. Gerald C. Wright, Leroy N. Rieselbach, and Lawrence C. Dodd. New York: Agathon Press.

Fiorina, Morris P. 1974. *Representatives, Roll Calls, and Constituencies*. Lexington, MA: Lexington Books.

Fiorina, Morris P. 1977. *Congress: Keystone of the Washington Establishment*. New Haven, CT: Yale University Press.

Fiorina, Morris P. 1981. Universalism, Reciprocity, and Distributive Policy-Making in

Majority Rule Institutions. In *Research in Public Policy Analysis and Management*, ed. John Crecine. Greenwich, CT: Jai Press, Inc.

Fiorina, Morris P. 1987. Alternative Rationales for Restrictive Procedures. *Journal of Law, Economics, and Organization* 3:337–43.

Fleck, Rob. 1989. Using Spatial Models to Estimate Political Preferences. Stanford University. Manuscript.

Freeman, J. Leiper. 1965. *The Political Process: Executive Bureau–Legislative Committee Relations.* New York: Random House.

Galloway, George, and Sidney Wise. 1976. *History of the House of Representatives.* New York: Thomas Y. Crowell.

Gamm, Gerald, and Kenneth Shepsle. 1988. The Evolution of Legislative Institutions: Standing Committees in the House and the Senate. Presented at the annual meeting of the American Political Science Association, Washington, DC.

Gertzog, Irwin N. 1976. The Routinization of Committee Assignments in the U.S. House of Representatives. *American Journal of Political Science* 20:693–712.

Gilligan, Thomas W. 1989. Performance of an Institutionalized Legislature. Hoover Institution. Manuscript.

Gilligan, Thomas W., and Keith Krehbiel. 1987. Collective Decision-Making and Standing Committees: An Informational Rationale for Restrictive Amendment Procedures. *Journal of Law, Economics, and Organization* 3:287–335.

Gilligan, Thomas W., and Keith Krehbiel. 1988. Complex Rules and Congressional Outcomes: An Event Study of Energy Tax Legislation. *Journal of Politics* 50:625–54.

Gilligan, Thomas W., and Keith Krehbiel. 1989a. Asymmetric Information and Legislative Rules with a Heterogeneous Committee. *American Journal of Political Science* 33:459–90.

Gilligan, Thomas W., and Keith Krehbiel. 1989b. Collective Choice without Procedural Commitment. In *Models of Strategic Choice in Politics,* ed. Peter C. Ordeshook. Ann Arbor: University of Michigan Press.

Gilligan, Thomas W., and Keith Krehbiel. 1990. Organization of Informative Committees by a Rational Legislature. *American Journal of Political Science* 34:531–64.

Goodwin, George. 1959. The Seniority System in Congress. *American Political Science Review* 53:412–36.

Goodwin, George. 1970. *The Little Legislatures: Committees of Congress.* Amherst, MA: University of Massachusetts Press.

Grofman, Bernard. 1989. Will the Real "New Institutionalism" Please Stand Up and Take a Bow? University of California, Irvine. Manuscript.

Hall, Richard L. 1989. Committee Decision Making in the Postreform Congress. In *Congress Reconsidered,* ed. Lawrence C. Dodd and Bruce I. Oppenheimer. Washington, DC: Congressional Quarterly Press.

Hall, Richard L., and Bernard Grofman. 1990. The Committee Assignment Process and the Conditional Nature of Committee Bias. *American Political Science Review,* forthcoming.

Hammond, Susan. 1984. Legislative Staffs. *Legislative Studies Quarterly* 9:271–317.

Harlow, Ralph V. 1917. *The History of Legislative Methods in the Period before 1825.* New Haven, CT: Yale University Press.

Hartwell, Max. 1950. Committees of the House of Commons: 1800–1850. Hoover Institution. Manuscript.

Hatfield, Mark O. 1967. Vietnam: Charted on a Distorted Map. *Saturday Review,* July 1.

Hibbing, John R. 1988. Legislative Institutionalization with Illustrations from the British House of Commons. *American Journal of Political Science* 32:681–712.

Hill, Jeffrey S. 1985. Why So Much Stability?: The Input of Agency Determined Stability. *Public Choice* 46:275–87.

Hinds, Asher C. 1899. *Precedents of the House of Representatives.* Washington, DC: Government Printing Office.

Hinds, Asher C. 1907. *Precedents of the House of Representatives.* Washington, DC: Government Printing Office.

Hinkley, Barbara. 1976. Seniority 1975: Old Theories Confront New Facts. *British Journal of Political Science* 39:283–99.

Hoenack, Stephen A. 1983. On the Stability of Legislative Outcomes. *Public Choice* 41:251–60.

Huckshorn, Robert. 1965. Decision-making Stimuli in the State Legislative Process. *Western Political Quarterly* 18:164–85.

Huntington, Samuel P. 1969. *Political Order in a Changing Society.* New Haven, CT: Yale University Press.

Hurley, Patricia A., and Rick K. Wilson. 1989. Partisan Voting Patterns in the U.S. Senate, 1977–86. *Legislative Studies Quarterly* 14:225–50.

Jacobson, Gary C. 1983. *The Politics of Congressional Elections.* Boston: Little, Brown.

Jones, Charles O. 1961. Representation in Congress: The Case of the House Agriculture Committee. *American Political Science Review* 55:358–67.

Jones, Charles O. 1962. The Role of the Congressional Subcommittee. *Midwest Journal of Political Science,* 6:327–44.

Jones, Charles O. 1968. Joseph G. Cannon and Howard W. Smith: An Essay on the Limits of Leadership in the House of Representatives. *Journal of Politics* 30:617–46.

Jones, Charles O. 1969. The Agriculture Committee and the Problem of Representation. In *New Perspectives on the House of Representatives,* ed. Robert L. Peabody and Nelson W. Polsby. Chicago: Rand McNally.

Jones, Charles O. 1975. *Clean Air: The Policies and Politics of Pollution Control.* Pittsburgh: University of Pittsburgh Press.

Keith, Robert. 1977. The Use of Unanimous Consent in the Senate. *Committees and Senate Procedures.* 94th Cong., 2d sess. Committee Print.

Kiewiet, D. Roderick, and Mathew McCubbins. 1989. The Spending Power: Congress, the President, and Appropriations. California Institute of Technology. Manuscript.

Kingdon, John. 1973. *Congressmen's Voting Decisions.* New York: Harper and Row.

Koford, Kenneth. 1982. Centralized Vote Trading. *Public Choice* 39:245–68.

Kramer, Gerald H. 1977. A Dynamical Model of Political Equilibrium. *Journal of Economic Theory* 16:310–34.

Krehbiel, Keith. 1985. Obstruction and Representativeness in Legislatures. *American Journal of Political Science* 29:643–59.

Krehbiel, Keith. 1986. Unanimous Consent Agreements: Going Along in the Senate. *Journal of Politics* 48:306–29.

Krehbiel, Keith. 1987a. Sophisticated Committees and Structure-Induced Equilibria in Congress. In *Congress: Structure and Policy,* ed. Mathew McCubbins and Terry Sullivan. New York: Cambridge University Press.

Krehbiel, Keith. 1987b. Why Are Congressional Committees Powerful? *American Political Science Review* 81:929–35.

Krehbiel, Keith. 1988. Spatial Models of Legislative Choice. *Legislative Studies Quarterly* 8:259–319.

Krehbiel, Keith. 1989. A Rationale for Restrictive Rules. In *Home Style and Washington Work,* ed. Morris P. Fiorina and David W. Rohde. Ann Arbor: University of Michigan Press.

Krehbiel, Keith. 1990. Are Congressional Committees Composed of Preference Outliers? *American Political Science Review* 84:149–63.

Krehbiel, Keith, and Douglas Rivers. 1988. The Analysis of Committee Power: An Application to Senate Voting on the Minimum Wage. *American Journal of Political Science* 32:1151–74.

Kreps, David, and Robert Wilson. 1982a. Reputation and Imperfect Information. *Journal of Economic Theory* 27:253–79.

Kreps, David, and Robert Wilson. 1982b. Sequential Equilibria. *Econometrica* 50:863–94.

Lasswell, Harold D. 1936. *Politics: Who Gets What, When, How?* New York: McGraw-Hill.

Longley, Lawrence D., and Walter J. Oleszek. 1989. *Bicameral Politics: Conference Committees in Congress.* New Haven, CT: Yale University Press.

Lowi, Theodore J. 1964. American Business, Public Policy, Case-Studies, and Political Theory. *World Politics* 16:676–715.

Lowi, Theodore. 1979. *The End of Liberalism.* New York: Norton.

Luce, Robert. 1922. *Legislative Procedure: Parliamentary Practices and the Course of Business in the Framing of Statutes.* Boston: Houghton Mifflin.

Maass, Arthur. 1983. *Congress and the Common Good.* New York: Basic Books.

McConachie, Lauros G. 1898. *Congressional Committees.* New York: Thomas Y. Crowell.

McConnell, Grant. 1966. *Private Power and American Democracy.* New York: Vintage Books.

McCown, Ada C. 1927. *The Congressional Conference Committee.* New York: Columbia University Press.

McCubbins, Mathew, and Thomas Schwartz. 1985. The Politics of Flatland. *Public Choice* 46:45–60.

Mackay, Robert, and Carolyn Weaver. 1979. On the Mutuality of Interests between Bureaus and High Demand Review Committees: A Perverse Result. *Public Choice* 34:481–91.

Mackay, Robert J., and Carolyn L. Weaver. 1983. Commodity Bundling and Agenda Control in the Public Sector. *Quarterly Journal of Economics* 98:611–35.

McKelvey, Richard D. 1976. Intransitivities in Multidimensional Voting Models and

Some Implications for Agenda Control. *Journal of Economic Theory* 12:472–82.

MacNeil, Neil. 1963. *Forge of Democracy: The House of Representatives*. New York: David McKay.

Malbin, Michael J. 1980. *Unelected Representatives*. New York: Basic Books.

Manley, John F. 1968. Congressional Staff and Public Policymaking: The Joint Committee on Internal Revenue Taxation. *Journal of Politics* 30:1046–67.

Manley, John F. 1970. *The Politics of Finance: The House Committee on Ways and Means*. Boston: Little, Brown.

Masters, Nicholas. 1961. Committee Assignments. *American Political Science Review* 55:345–57.

Matsunaga, Spark M., and Ping Chen. 1976. *Rulemakers of the House*. Urbana, IL: University of Illinois Press.

Mayhew, David. 1974. *Congress: The Electoral Connection*. New Haven, CT: Yale University Press.

Milgrom, Paul, and John Roberts. 1982a. Limit Pricing and Entry under Incomplete Information: An Equilibrium Analysis. *Econometrica* 50:443–59.

Milgrom, Paul, and John Roberts. 1982b. Predation, Reputation, and Entry Deterrence. *Journal of Economic Theory* 27:280–312.

Moe, Terry M. 1987. An Assessment of the Positive Theory of "Congressional Dominance." *Legislative Studies Quarterly* 7:475–520.

Morrow, William L. 1969. *Congressional Committees*. New York: Scribner's.

Muir, William K. 1982. *Legislature: California's School for Politics*. Chicago: University of Chicago Press.

Munger, Michael C. 1988. Allocation of Desirable Committee Assignments: Extended Queues versus Committee Expansion. *American Journal of Political Science* 32:317–44.

Nagler, Jonathan. 1989. Strategic Implications of Conference Selection in the House of Representatives. *American Politics Quarterly* 17:54–79.

Neustadt, Richard E. 1960. *Presidential Power*. New York: Wiley.

Niemi, Richard G. 1983. Why So Much Stability?: Another Opinion. *Public Choice* 41:261–70.

Niskanen, William A. 1971. *Bureaucracy and Representative Government*. Chicago: Aldine-Atherton.

Oleszek, Walter J. 1984. *Congressional Procedures and the Policy Process*. Washington, DC: Congressional Quarterly Press.

Oppenheimer, Bruce I. 1977. The Rules Committee: New Arm of Leadership in a Decentralized House. In *Congress Reconsidered*, ed. Lawrence C. Dodd and Bruce I. Oppenheimer. Washington, DC: Congressional Quarterly Press.

Ordeshook, Peter C., and Thomas Schwartz. 1987. Agendas and the Control of Political Outcomes. *American Political Science Review* 81:179–200.

Ornstein, Norman J. 1975a. *Congress in Change*. New York: Praeger.

Ornstein, Norman J. 1975b. Legislative Behavior and Legislative Structures: A Comparative Look at House and Senate Resource Utilization. In *Legislative Staffing: A Comparative Perspective*, ed. James Heaphey and Alan Balutis. New York: Halstead.

Ostrom, Elinor. 1986. An Agenda for the Study of Institutions. *Public Choice* 48:3–25.

Patterson, Samuel C. 1970. The Professional Staffs of Congressional Committees. *Administrative Science Quarterly* 15:22–37.

Peabody, Robert L. 1985. House Party Leadership: Stability and Change. In *Congress Reconsidered*, ed. Lawrence C. Dodd and Bruce I. Oppenheimer. Washington, DC: Congressional Quarterly Press.

Plott, Charles. 1967. A Notion of Equilibrium and Its Possibility under Majority Rule. *American Economic Review* 57:787–806.

Polsby, Nelson W. 1968. The Institutionalization of the U.S. House of Representatives. *American Political Science Review* 62:148–68.

Polsby, Nelson W., Miriam Gallaher, and Barry S. Rundquist. 1969. The Growth of the Seniority System in the House of Representatives. *American Political Science Review* 63:787–807.

Poole, Keith T., and Howard Rosenthal. 1985. A Spatial Model for Legislative Roll Call Analysis. *American Journal of Political Science* 29:357–84.

Poole, Keith T., and Howard Rosenthal. 1987. Analysis of Congressional Coalition Patterns: A Unidimensional Spatial Model. *Legislative Studies Quarterly* 12:55–76.

Porter, H. Owen. 1974. Legislative Experts and Outsiders: The Two Step Flow of Communications. *Journal of Politics* 36:703–30.

Price, David E. 1972. *Who Makes the Laws? Creativity and Power in Senate Committees*. Cambridge, MA: Schenkman.

Price, David E. 1985. Congressional Committees in the Policy Process. In *Congress Reconsidered*, ed. Lawrence C. Dodd and Bruce I. Oppenheimer. Washington, DC: Congressional Quarterly Press.

Price, H. Douglas. 1977. Careers and Committees in the American Congress: The Problem of Structural Change. In *The History of Parliamentary Behavior*, ed. William O. Aydelotte. Princeton, NJ: Princeton University Press.

Ray, Bruce A. 1980. The Responsiveness of the U.S. Congressional Armed Services Committees to their Parent Bodies. *Legislative Studies Quarterly* 5:501–15.

Redford, Emmette S. 1966. *American Government and the Economy*. New York: Macmillan.

Reeves, Richard. 1974. Isn't It Time We Had a Senator? *New York*, February 25.

Reid, T. R. 1980. *Congressional Odyssey: The Saga of a Senate Bill*. San Francisco: Freeman.

Rieselbach, Leroy N., and Joseph K. Unekis. 1982. Ousting the Oligarchs: Assessing the Consequences of Reform and Change on Four House Committees. *Congress and the Presidency* 9:83–117.

Riker, William H. 1961. Voting and the Summation of Preferences. *American Political Science Review* 55:900–912.

Riker, William H. 1980. Implications from the Disequilibrium of Majority Rule for the Study of Institutions. *American Political Science Review* 74:432–46.

Riker, William H. 1982. *Liberalism against Populism*. San Francisco: Freeman.

Ripley, Randall B. 1969. Legislative Bargaining and the Food Stamp Act, 1964. In *Congress and Urban Problems*, ed. Frederic Cleaveland. Washington, DC: Brookings Institution.

Risjord, Norman K. 1988. The Evolution of Congressional Committees: House of Representatives. University of Wisconsin, Madison. Manuscript.

Robinson, James. 1963. *The House Rules Committee*. Indianapolis: Bobbs-Merrill.

Rogowski, Ronald. 1989. Agenda Control, Committee Structure, and the Comparative Analysis of Political Institutions. Presented at the John M. Olin conference on political institutions and behavior, Graduate School of Business, Stanford.

Rohde, David W., Norman Ornstein, and Robert L. Peabody. 1985. Political Change and Legislative Norms in the U.S. Senate, 1957–74. In *Studies of Congress,* ed. Glen R. Parker. Washington, DC: Congressional Quarterly Press.

Romer, Thomas, and Howard Rosenthal. 1978. Political Resource Allocation, Controlled Agendas, and the Status Quo. *Public Choice* 33:27–43.

Rosenthal, Howard. 1989. The Setter Model. In *Readings in the Spatial Theory of Elections,* ed. James Enelow and Melvin Hinich. New York: Cambridge University Press.

Sabatier, Paul, and David Whiteman. 1985. Legislative Decision-making and Substantive Policy Information: Models of Information Flow. *Legislative Studies Quarterly* 10:395–421.

Salisbury, Robert H., John P. Heinz, Edward O. Laumann, and Robert L. Nelson. 1987. Who Works with Whom: Interest Group Alliances and Opposition. *American Political Science Review* 81:1217–34.

Schick, Allen. 1976. The Supply and Demand for Analysis on Capitol Hill. *Policy Analysis* 2:72–85.

Schick, Allen. 1980. *Congress and Money.* Washington, DC: Urban Institute.

Schick, Allen. 1981. *Reconciliation and the Congressional Budget Process.* Washington, DC: American Enterprise Institute.

Schneider, Jerrold E. 1979. *Ideological Coalitions in Congress.* Westport, CT: Greenwood Press.

Schneier, Edward. 1970. The Intelligence of Congress: Information and Public Policy Patterns. *Annals of the American Academy of Political and Social Science* 388:14–24.

Schofield, Norman. 1978. Instability of Simple Dynamic Games. *Review of Economic Studies* 45:575–94.

Scicchitano, Michael J. 1981. Legislative Goals and Information Use. *American Politics Quarterly* 9:103–10.

Shapiro, Martin. 1987. The Concept of Information: A Comment on Gilligan and Krehbiel's "Collective Decisionmaking and Standing Committees." *Journal of Law, Economics, and Organization* 3:345–50.

Shepsle, Kenneth A. 1978. *The Giant Jigsaw Puzzle.* Chicago: University of Chicago Press.

Shepsle, Kenneth A. 1986a. Institutional Equilibrium and Equilibrium Institutions. In *Political Science: The Science of Politics,* ed. Herbert Weisberg. New York: Agathon.

Shepsle, Kenneth A. 1986b. The Positive Theory of Legislative Institutions: An Enrichment of Social Choice and Spatial Models. *Public Choice* 50:135–78.

Shepsle, Kenneth A., and Barry R. Weingast. 1984a. Political Solutions to Market Problems. *American Political Science Review* 78:417–34.

Shepsle, Kenneth A., and Barry R. Weingast. 1984b. Legislative Politics and Budget Outcomes. In *Federal Budget Policy in the 1980s,* ed. Gregory B. Mills and John L. Palmer. Washington, DC: Urban Institute.

Shepsle, Kenneth A., and Barry R. Weingast. 1987a. The Institutional Foundations of Committee Power. *American Political Science Review* 81:85–104.

Shepsle, Kenneth A., and Barry R. Weingast. 1987b. Why Are Congressional Committees Powerful? *American Political Science Review* 81:935–45.

Sinclair, Barbara. 1983. *Majority Leadership in the U.S. House.* Baltimore: Johns Hopkins Press.

Smith, Steven S. 1988. An Essay on Sequence, Position, Goals, and Committee Power. *Legislative Studies Quarterly* 8:151–77.

Smith, Steven S. 1989. *Call to Order: Floor Politics in the House and Senate.* Washington, DC: Brookings.

Smith, Steven S., and Christopher J. Deering. 1984. *Committees in Congress.* Washington, DC: Congressional Quarterly Press.

Smith, Steven S., and Marcus Flathman. 1989. Managing the Senate Floor: Complex Unanimous Consent Agreements since the 1950s. Presented at the annual meeting of the Midwest Political Science Association, Chicago.

Spence, A. Michael. 1974. *Market Signaling: Information Transfer in Hiring and Related Screening Processes.* Cambridge, MA: Harvard University Press.

Steiner, Gilbert Y. 1951. *The Congressional Conference Committee.* Urbana: University of Illinois Press.

Stephens, Herbert W. 1971. The Role of the Legislative Committees in the Appropriations Process: A Study Focused on the Armed Services Committees. *Western Political Quarterly* 26:142–62.

Stevens, Arthur G. 1971. Informal Groups and Decision-making in the U.S. House of Representatives. Ph.D. diss. University of Michigan.

Stewart, Charles H. 1990. Committees from Randall to Clark: Some Preliminary Evidence about Committee Assignments in the House of Representatives. Presented at the Carl Albert Center conference on Congress in the twenty-first century, Norman, OK.

Strom, Gerald S., and Barry S. Rundquist. 1977. A Revised Theory of Winning in House-Senate Conferences. *American Political Science Review* 71:448–53.

Sundquist, James L. 1981. *The Decline and Resurgence of Congress.* Washington, DC: Brookings.

Tobin, Maurice B. 1986. *Hidden Power: The Seniority System and Other Customs of Congress.* New York: Greenwood Press.

Truman, David B. 1957. *The Governmental Process.* New York: Alfred A. Knopf.

Tullock, Gordon. 1981. Why So Much Stability? *Public Choice* 37:189–202.

Uslaner, Eric, and Ronald Weber. 1977. Partisan Cues and Decision Loci in U.S. State Legislatures. *Legislative Studies Quarterly* 2:423–44.

Vogler, David J. 1971. *The Third House: Conference Committees in the United States Congress.* Evanston, IL: Northwestern University Press.

Webber, David J. 1984. Political Conditions Motivating Legislators' Use of Policy Information. *Policy Studies Review* 4:110–18.

Weber, Robert P. 1989. Home Style and Committee Behavior. The Case of Richard Nolan. In *Home Style and Washington Work,* ed. Morris P. Fiorina and David W. Rohde. Ann Arbor: University of Michigan Press.

Weingast, Barry R. 1979. A Rational Choice Perspective on Congressional Norms. *American Journal of Political Science* 23:245–62.

Weingast, Barry R. 1989a. Floor Behavior in the U.S. Congress: Committee Power under the Open Rule. *American Political Science Review* 83:795–816.

Weingast, Barry R. 1989b. Fighting Fire with Fire: Amending Activity and Institutional Change in the Post-Reform Congress. Hoover Institution. Manuscript.

Weingast, Barry R. 1989c. Writing Scripts for the Floor: Restrictive Rules in the Post-Reform House. Hoover Institution. Manuscript.

Weingast, Barry R., and William Marshall. 1988. The Industrial Organization of Congress. *Journal of Political Economy* 96:132–63.

Weingast, Barry R., and Mark J. Moran. 1983. Bureaucratic Discretion or Congressional Control? Regulatory Policymaking by the Federal Trade Commission. *Journal of Political Economy* 91:765–800.

Weingast, Barry R., Kenneth A. Shepsle, and Christopher Johnsen. 1981. The Political Economy of Benefits and Costs: A Neoclassical Approach to Distributive Politics. *Journal of Political Economy* 89:642–64.

Whalen, Charles, and Barbara Whalen. 1985. *The Longest Debate: A Legislative History of the 1964 Civil Rights Act.* Washington, DC: Seven Locks Press.

Wilkerson, John. 1989. Analyzing Committee Power: A Critique. University of Rochester. Manuscript.

Wilson, James Q. 1980. *The Politics of Regulation.* New York: Basic Books.

Wilson, Woodrow. 1885. *Congressional Government.* New York: Houghton Mifflin.

Winslow, Clintin I. 1931. *State Legislative Committees: A Study in Procedure.* Baltimore: Johns Hopkins Press.

Wissel, Peter, Robert O'Connor, and Michael King. 1976. The Hunting of the Legislative Shark: Information Searches and Reforms in the U.S. State Legislatures. *Legislative Studies Quarterly* 1:251–67.

Name Index

Subject Index